Women Who Taught
Perspectives on the History of Women and Teaching

In an era when women are moving into so many areas of the labour force, we all remember some of the first working women we ever encountered: 'women teachers,' as they were too often known. The impact of women on education has been enormous throughout the English-speaking world. It has also been ignored, for the most part, by mainstream historians of education. Alison Prentice and Marjorie R. Theobald have addressed this omission by bringing together a wide range of essays by feminist historians on the role of women in education at all levels, in Canada, Australia, Britain, and the United States.

All the essays were ground-breaking when first published. Among the subjects they explore are the experience of women in private, or domestic, schooling and the rigours of teaching as single women in remote areas. Other essays discuss the impact on women's working lives of various developments in education: the establishment of state schools in the nineteenth century; the growth of professional teachers' organizations; and the blurring of public and private in the lives of twentieth-century teachers.

The editors provide an introduction that traces the growth of the emerging field of the history of women in teaching and identifies new directions currently developing. A bibliography offers further resources.

ALISON PRENTICE is a professor in the Department of History and Philosophy of Education at the Ontario Institute for Studies in Education. She is co-author, with Susan Houston, of *Schooling and Scholars in Nineteenth-Century Ontario*.

MARJORIE R. THEOBALD is a lecturer in the Institute of Education, University of Melbourne, and co-editor of *History of Education Review*.

Women Who Taught

Perspectives on the History of Women and Teaching

Edited by

ALISON PRENTICE and
MARJORIE R. THEOBALD

UNIVERSITY OF TORONTO PRESS
Toronto Buffalo London

© University of Toronto Press 1991
Toronto Buffalo London
Printed in Canada

ISBN 0-8020-2745-8 (cloth)
ISBN 0-8020-6785-9 (paper)

Printed on acid-free paper

Canadian Cataloguing in Publication Data

Main entry under title:

Women who taught

Includes bibliographical references.
ISBN 0-8020-2745-8 (bound). — ISBN 0-8020-6785-9 (pbk.)

1. Women teachers — History. I. Prentice, Alison,
1934–   . II. Theobald, Marjorie R.

LB2837.W65 1991   371.1′0082   C90-095572-4

Cover illustration: *Church Street School #9, circa 1915*. Photograph, 10.5 × 8 cm. Photographer unknown. Gift of Derwyn Foley. Records, Archives, and Museum, Toronto Board of Education.

This book has been published with assistance from the Canada Council and the Ontario Arts Council under their block grant programs.

Contents

Women Teaching in Higher Education

Preface

This book has been a long time in the making. Previous to our discussions with each other, both of us talked about the possibility of such a book, and the need for it, with colleagues in several countries. Their interest in this volume and their discussion of our research on the history of teachers generally have been of enormous benefit. We would like to thank, in particular, Marion Amies, Joan Burstyn, Bruce Curtis, Inga Elgqvist-Saltzman, Nadia Fahmy-Eid, Christina Florin, Jane Gaskell, Noeline Kyle, Bob Gidney, Martin Lawn, Alison Mackinnon, Wyn Millar, Pavla Miller, Jennifer Monaghan, Margaret Nelson, Harry Smaller, Andy Spaull, David Tyack, and Wayne Urban for their thoughtful interest in our work. Needless to say, the contributors to the book have also been important contributors to our analysis of the history of gender and teaching. We wish particularly to thank Geraldine Clifford, Dick Selleck, Don Wilson, and Ailsa Zainu'ddin for the insights they have fed into our thinking on the subject.

Several further, special acknowledgments are in order. Firstly, the late Marta Danylewycz contributed not only to the article which bears her name in this volume, but also to an article entitled 'Revising the History of Teachers: A Canadian Perspective' (*Interchange*, December 1986), which provided some of the inspiration for the introductory historiographical essay. We are grateful for her ideas, which have continued to enrich our own. Secondly, we wish to thank Susan Gelman, for her painstaking work on the bibliography, and Marian Press, for her assistance with it. Their interest in the project and conscientious attention to detail have resulted in a fine research tool. Finally, we thank the dedicated people who have helped us to put this book together. The talents of Jill Given-King, Laura Macleod, and Gerry

Hallowell have combined to make our task a lighter one and to enhance our enjoyment of the project at all stages of it. Working with them has been a delight, and we are very appreciative of their efforts on behalf of *Women Who Taught*.

Of patient husbands, family members, students, and other friends we almost hesitate to speak. Their support has been constant and we are grateful. Many of them are, or have been, teachers too. To them we dedicate this book.

Alison Prentice
Ontario Institute for Studies in Education

Marjorie R. Theobald
University of Melbourne

Contributors

GERALDINE JONÇICH CLIFFORD is the author of a number of books dealing with the progressive period in American educational history as well as of articles on the history of teachers. A professor of education at the University of California at Berkeley, she has recently indulged her talent for biography by editing and contributing to a collection of essays on women who taught at North American universities.

MARTA DANYLEWYCZ was a member of the History Department of Atkinson College, York University, at the time of her tragic death in 1985. Her interest in the history of religious women who taught and did charitable work in French Canada resulted in a path-breaking monograph on two important female religious orders in nineteenth- and early twentieth-century Quebec, in addition to her work on the history of teachers.

SARAH KING has made a major contribution to the history of British teachers and the history of feminism in the twentieth century through her research on the organizational activities of women teachers in the interwar years. She lives and continues to pursue her interests in Great Britain.

PATRICIA A. PALMIERI is the author of several studies on women and education in American history, and is especially well known for her important doctoral dissertation on the history of the women who taught at Wellesley College in the late nineteenth and early twentieth centuries. She has taught at Dartmouth College and is now a lecturer in history and literature at Harvard University.

JOYCE SENDERS PEDERSEN is the author of several highly regarded articles on the history of women and British education. Her dissertation on the history of nineteenth-century education for women in England has recently been published and she is currently teaching at Odense University in Denmark.

ALISON PRENTICE is a professor at the Ontario Institute for Studies in Education in Toronto, where her work focuses on the history of teachers and the history of women in higher education. She has written about the ideology of school reform in the nineteenth century and is the co-editor and co-author of books and documentary studies dealing with schooling in nineteenth-century Ontario and the history of women in Canada.

R.J.W. SELLECK is the author of major studies dealing with the new education movement among other topics in the nineteenth- and twentieth-century educational history of Great Britain and Australia. Also a noted educational biographer and the co-editor of a volume devoted to the biographies of lesser known Australian educators, he is professor of education at Monash University in Melbourne.

MARJORIE R. THEOBALD is a lecturer at the Institute of Education at the University of Melbourne. She has published widely on the history of girls' and ladies' colleges as well as on the history of public schools and their teachers in Australia, and is the co-editor, with R.J.W. Selleck, of a collection of essays dealing with the family, the school, and the state in Australian history.

J. DONALD WILSON has written on a great variety of subjects in the history of Canadian education and in Finnish-Canadian history as well as on the history of teachers. The editor of a number of important collections and texts in educational history, and the author of a series of historiographical articles on the field, he is a professor in the Faculty of Education at the University of British Columbia.

AILSA G. THOMSON ZAINU'DDIN is a senior lecturer in the Education Faculty at Monash University. The author of a number of studies dealing with the history of women and education and co-compiler of an important bibliography on the same topic, she is especially known for her study of one of Australia's major ladies' colleges as well as for her new work on the history of education for women in Indonesia.

WOMEN WHO TAUGHT

The Historiography of Women Teachers:

A Retrospect

Alison Prentice and
Marjorie R. Theobald

'Woman teacher' is a phrase that still has evocative power. In an era when the spotlight has been focused on the position of women in the labour force generally, we have had cause to ponder the case of the woman teacher. Who are the women who teach and what is their status in the profession? Students of contemporary education have come to recognize that sexual stereotyping and gendered occupational struc- tures have profoundly affected and continue to affect the position of women teachers at all levels.[1] At the same time, historians interested in the status of women in education have been searching for the roots of women's roles in the schools and universities of the past. Where did the stereotypes and the gendered occupational structures, which seem so familiar and so deeply entrenched in educational systems today, come from?

In common with other feminist scholars, those of us who, fifteen or twenty years ago, began to look for the history of women teachers discovered that women who taught in the past had suffered the same fate as most women in history. The schoolmistress was largely absent from mainstream historical work on education. To the extent that traditional histories of schooling considered teachers at all, we learned, they tended to focus on the quest for professionalism in the occupation and their concern was chiefly the male educator. Indeed, although we did not articulate this perception very clearly, we began to realize that historical writing itself perpetuated stereotypes, as far as teachers were concerned.[2] Poorly educated, itinerant schoolmasters peopled older works in educational history, along with poverty-stricken dame school teachers and unserious mistresses of schools for young ladies – as they had often peopled nineteenth-century reformers' gloomier visions of education as they knew it.

Equally stereotyped, strangely enough, were the images of the 'new' men and women who were drawn into teaching as nineteenth-century school reform progressed. In England and Australia, where the children of elite groups are still largely educated outside state school systems, the focus was on the heroic men who ran famous boys' schools. Historical studies concerned themselves with the relative merits of leading head-masters, such as Arnold of Rugby or Thring of Uppingham. In the context of the developing state school systems of North America, mature and energetic males – educational leaders and professionalizing teachers alike – captured the attention of historians. These men stood in sharp contrast to women teachers who, if they were discussed at all, were frequently portrayed as young, naive, and malleable; it was their acceptance of low wages and poor working conditions, some histor-ian implied, that undermined men teachers' more important profes-sional quest.[3]

It soon became apparent that the concentration on professional sta-tus, as well as the concern with ideal types, derived from the narrow focus of most traditional educational history. The context for teachers' work in such historical writing was rarely the larger world. Attention to broader social contexts and systems was thus a hallmark of the first wave of revisionist historical work that dealt with teachers. It was an American study in the revisionist mode that first alerted North American historians to the importance of exploring the roles of women in the emerging state school systems of the nineteenth century. Michael Katz was more interested in the formation and character of bureaucra-cies in education than in women's subordination in the workplace when he wrote in the late 1960s about the creation of hierarchy in the Boston school system.[4] But it was impossible for him not to notice that the hierarchies he discovered were gendered. The superintendents and principals who governed these systems, who inspected the lower ranks and wrote secret reports about them, were men; most of the teachers in the lower ranks – the people who were inspected and reported upon – were women.

As far as teachers were concerned, revisionist educational history soon began to draw on two major sources of inspiration. Feminism taught us to explore the history of teachers from the point of view of the women who taught school and to look for the structures that subordinated and exploited women in education. From Marxism, we learned to look for the material conditions of teachers' lives: their class backgrounds and economic status, the ways in which their work was structured, and how it changed over time. Some of us (especially in North America) began with a concern to understand what we called, for want of a better term, the 'feminization' of teaching – that is, the gradual increase in the numbers and proportions of women teaching in most state school systems, along with their low status and pay within those systems. Most of us gradually moved to broader concerns. Our goal was, increasingly, to understand the history of all kinds of women teachers in whatever social and political settings they were to be found. This meant comparing women teachers' lives and work with those of the men who taught in the past. It also meant looking at the history of women teachers in two broad contexts: the history of women more generally, and of the changing family and community structures in which their lives were embedded; and the history of work, and of the shifting economic and social structures that encompassed, in particular, women's work in educational institutions. What we were increasingly engaged in, whether we were fully conscious of it or not, was the study of gender in the history of a profession which had been implicated in the articulation and perpetuation of gender inequality in Western society.

Following the example of Michael Katz, the early North American work on the feminization of teaching tended to set this phenomenon in the urban context, identifying connections between feminization and the development of bureaucratic school structures in cities. In the urban school systems that emerged in the mid-nineteenth century, women were shown to be typically segregated into lower paying positions as the instructors of junior grades, while men monopolized the better paying jobs as senior teachers, principals, and inspectors. Wherever such urban hierarchies came into existence, the percentage of female teachers tended to be higher than the average for the region or period in question – and a growing gap between male and female average salaries could be shown. Alison Prentice's early work demonstrated this to be true for the mid-nineteenth-century Canadian provinces of Ontario, Quebec, Nova Scotia, and New Brunswick, where she noted that the major justification that school boards used for hiring women teachers was a financial one. Women teachers saved their employers money, for they could often be paid as little as half the male teacher's wage. In 1980, Myra Strober and David Tyack's provocatively entitled article 'Why Do Women Teach and Men Manage?' took up the same themes. Strober and A.G. Langford later demonstrated how measures of formalization, such as rules dictating a longer school year or a larger number of pupils per school, correlated with growing proportions of women teachers, even in the countryside. Metropolitan models of schooling, transferred to rural environments, were thus put forward as essential keys to the emergence of predominantly female teaching forces everywhere in North America.[5]

Studies of the feminization of teaching in North America also pointed to the voluminous nineteenth-century literature in which school reformers explored the question of female involvement in public education, for the advent of the woman teacher was accompanied by much rhetoric idealizing women's role in the schoolroom. The supposedly superior ability of the woman teacher to nurture the young, especially when it came to children in the lower grades, along with the supposedly 'natural' role of women teachers as assistants to men, clearly preoccupied many nineteenth-century school promoters. It was also apparent that much of the rhetoric surrounding women's own education in the nineteenth century was directed to the preparation of women to play a highly idealized and romanticized role as teachers of their own and, more often, other people's children.[6]

Historians soon discovered difficulties with an undue focus on ideology, however. As the Canadian case demonstrated, leading promoters of school reform accepted the doctrines idealizing the schoolmistress very reluctantly, and only when the numerical dominance of women teachers in the state elementary schools was already a reality.[7] A second difficulty was the tendency to equate rhetoric with experience. In some studies, women teachers emerged as all too accepting of their portrayal as ideal, natural educators of the young or as docile transients easily dominated by their employers. Although some historians used such stereotypes as only partial explanations for the feminization of teaching, others used them more pejoratively to explain the ills they diagnosed in modern education. One distinctly non-feminist analysis blamed the watered-down, anti-intellectual schooling believed to be characteristic of the twentieth century on the image and reality of the nurturing 'motherteacher.' Approaching the question from an entirely different and feminist perspective, another analysis faulted women teachers, not for their negative impact on the overt curriculum, but for their acceptance of the hidden curriculum: the reproduction of patriarchy. Embedded in a hierarchically structured and gendered school system, women teachers were seen both as its victims and unwitting perpetuators.[8] The problematic of women teachers' nurturing role in the classroom has been further elaborated by Carolyn Steedman and Madeleine Grumet both historically and in the present.[9]

Moreover, the various explanations we had been putting forward for the feminization of teaching, while powerful, did not fully account for a phenomenon that was subject to much regional variation and ideological complexity. In much of North America historians could document a developing focus on the ideal of woman as mother and as teacher of young children, arguing that the advancement of both ideologies paralleled – or at the very least followed – the growing proportion of women teachers in state schools. Yet elsewhere the story was different. Noeline Kyle's study of one Australian state, New South Wales, revealed that feminization of public school teaching was not as pronounced there as it was in North America and Britain, and that the process was actively resisted at the political, bureaucratic, and ideological levels. It is possible that resistance to the feminization of elementary schooling was an Australia-wide phenomenon that deserves more detailed analysis.[10] One likely explanation of this phenomenon is the early entrenchment of public service tenure and a defined career structure for teachers in Australia's state schools, a feature that may have particularly attracted men to elementary school teaching. Another explanation calls attention to the relative dearth of analytical studies, so far, on women and men teaching in state secondary schools. It could be that the late establishment of publicly funded high schools in Australia (as late as 1905 in the state of Victoria) denied male teachers the opportunity to colonize the secondary school as a superior, masculine domain, forcing them into more defensive positions in elementary school systems. Clearly, the history of secondary school teaching and gender in state school systems is a topic that deserves attention not only for its own sake but, as Barry Bergen argues, because secondary and primary school systems were contexts *for each other*, as were all levels of educational systems as they developed.[11]

At the same time as historians of state schooling were attempting to come to grips with the complexities of shifting gender ratios in public teaching forces, another group of historians focused on private teaching. Historians of women had tended to concentrate first on women's paid work in public labour markets. But we quickly realized that this focus ignored a huge area of women's labour: the work that women did – both paid and unpaid – in the home. And, as far as teaching was concerned, it was important to recognize that women had always taught. As Marion Amies has shown for late eighteenth-century Britain, their domestic and private teaching was often far from haphazard and deserves study.[12]

In Britain, interest in rehabilitating the reputation of the lowly dame school teacher emphasized the important role these women had played. Two studies of such teachers conducted in the mid-1970s pointed out that the teaching of the dame schoolmistress amounted to something more than inadequate childcare and should be taken seriously. Later, Philip Gardner developed this theme in a larger study, showing that private teaching extended well beyond the borders of the middle class and played an important role in nineteenth-century British working-class life.[13] In the United States, E. Jennifer Monaghan has examined the work of the American colonial schoolmistress. She argues that in New England before the Revolution women, teaching in their homes, were primarily responsible for the basic instruction of young children of both sexes in reading. The teaching of writing and arithmetic, for the most part, was not woman's province and belonged quite clearly to the schoolmaster. Some of the women were even paid out of the public purse for the teaching of reading; others provided a more advanced schooling in reading and other arts, particularly sewing, for older girls.[14]

Feminist historians have paid increasing attention to such higher status teachers of young ladies, especially in Great Britain and Australia where they played a particularly important role. A study by M. Jeanne Peterson, published in the mid-1970s, examined the position of the governess in British education; during the same period, Joyce Senders Pedersen published her examination of the changing situation and attitudes of schoolmistresses in elite girls' schools, as these schools sought academic status for their students and professional status for their teachers.[15] In Australia, interest in domestic or private female teachers has resulted in research on the women who taught in and managed nineteenth-century girls' private schools, both small and large. Marjorie Theobald's work, in particular, has shown that, far from frivolous or ephemeral, the schools created by these private schoolmistresses were essential resources in their communities – not least for the many, in some cases highly educated, women who made their living by running them.[16] Private teaching clearly had many dimensions, its extent and importance varying in complex ways across time and space.

The complexity is related, in part, to the problem of definitions. The term 'private' may refer to any education not under the jurisdiction of the state: education in domestic settings and private venture schools as well as larger corporate and church-sponsored institutions. Women teaching in domestic settings and those who owned their own schools have been the least visible in the historiography of education. Such women were also overlooked by the first wave of revisionist historians, especially in Britain and Australia, who sought the origins of *worthwhile* education for women in the nineteenth-century reform movement known then and now as 'the movement for the higher education of women.'[17] There is now a growing body of literature on teaching which begins from this larger perception of women teaching: as mothers and female relatives in the home; as governesses (the term was used synonymously with female teacher in the nineteenth century); in a variety of dame schools; in Catholic convent schools; in the middle-class ladies' academies that sprang up in great numbers from the end of the eighteenth century in Britain, America, Canada, and, slightly later, in Australia. The recruitment of women as teachers by the state signalled a shift of location, a transformation of their teaching labour, a loss of autonomy, but not a radical new departure in the history of women's work.

The recovery and interpretation of this hidden, private world of female teachers presents formidable methodological and theoretical problems. As the traditions they created and sustained acknowledged no direct prescription from church or state, sources are scarce and widely scattered. Such women can seldom marshall the impressive feminist credentials of women like Dorothea Beale and Frances Buss who sought to displace them in the second half of the nineteenth century. To write their history is to confront a central theoretical problem in understanding women in the past: how to evoke the oppressive structures that maintained a patriarchal order while at the same time affirming that women were not the passive victims of that oppression. The lady-principal of a fashionable academy in Bath, Toronto, New York, or Melbourne was at one and the same time defending the boundaries of class privilege, colluding in her own and her pupils' oppression as women, and carving out for herself an area of autonomy that she did not have in the church and state bureaucracies which began to threaten her livelihood in the latter part of the nineteenth century.

Even the definition of 'school' presents difficulties. The customary male-focused definitions, which place considerable emphasis on size, continuity, longevity, corporate existence, and the accumulation of real estate and distinguished alumnae are of little use. The nineteenth-century female school, like the Cheshire cat, has the ability to fade into the landscape depending on the preconceptions of the observer. Some schools had a handful of pupils in the proprietor's front parlour, others had enrolments of over one hundred housed in elegant mansions. Some lasted less than a year; others evolved into prestigious institutions which have survived to the present time. The same ambiguities surround the definitions of secondary and tertiary education in the nineteenth century. Like colleges and academies for boys, many ladies' academies welcomed all ages but regarded themselves as in the business of providing 'higher education.'[18] Yet they constituted the workplaces of countless women teachers whose stories we are only just beginning to tell.

Increasingly, complex interpretations also marked the work on teachers in state schools. In the case of one American state, sophisticated quantitative methodology made it possible to demonstrate how widespread teaching was for young women in the first half of the nineteenth century. In Massachusetts before the American Civil War it was estimated that one in four white women must have been teachers during at least a few years of their lives.[19] Did other jurisdictions have similarly high figures?

By the early 1980s regional differences in the rates of public teaching force feminization were coming to light in Canada. In Quebec, it had long been recognized that the history of teaching did not seem to follow the 'standard' Canadian pattern. The statistics for this predominantly French Catholic province showed that over 50 per cent of government school teachers were women as early as 1851. A study by Marta Danlye-wycz, Beth Light, and Alison Prentice brought to the feminization debate a more complex interpretation of the changing place of women teachers in schools.[20] Their study of nine counties in Ontario and Quebec, drawing on the manuscript census returns and annual school reports available for the period between 1851 and 1881, revealed that such factors as the lengthening of the school year or increasing numbers of pupils in schools could not explain the early predominance of female teachers in either rural Quebec or in several eastern Ontario counties. The more likely reasons were shown to be poverty and the presence of a resource frontier which offered important alternative employment to young men. Reinforcing the effect of such factors in Quebec was a strong tradition of female teaching promoted by the existence of women's religious communities devoted to education, although by no means did nuns account for the majority of female teachers. Furthermore, in those parts of rural Ontario which did not feminize their teaching forces early, the high proportion of immigrants among male teachers suggests that school boards in those localities had an alternative labour pool not available to school commissioners in Quebec or in much of eastern Ontario. In most regions that feminized early, men who might have taught school were probably typically native to Canada: they either did not want to supplement farm incomes through other employment or preferred working in resource industries, like lumbering and fishing, to teaching school.

At the same time, Quebec's largest metropolitan centre, the city of Montreal, failed to develop a monolithic public school system governed by a few men at the top and staffed by large numbers of women in the lower ranks. The city produced two school systems, one French Catholic and the other English Protestant. The system created by French Catholics in Montreal was divided along gender lines, favouring boys' schools and male teachers; as a result, the lay teachers who worked in state-supported French Catholic schools in that city continued to be predominantly male up to the end of the nineteenth century. It was clearly essential to look beyond the basic question of gender and to explore social and economic as well as religious factors affecting the changing structure of teaching on a comparative basis. Such studies were possible where the manuscript census was available. Research using the census for late nineteenth-century Montreal and Toronto also revealed something of the class origins of the women who staffed urban state schools. At least half of the women teachers, it appeared, came from lower-middle-class or working-class backgrounds.[21]

Explorations of the social structure of the occupation have reinforced material explanations for the feminization of teaching in the nineteenth century. If school boards wanted to hire women teachers in order to save money – and they were explicit on the subject, in some cases emphasizing the connection between age grading and economy – women themselves increasingly were in need of and welcomed paid employment outside the home. The Australian work on private schoolmistresses by Marjorie Theobald, and the early work on governesses, demonstrated the same point. Whether it was a widow with children to feed and educate, a wife whose husband had failed in the goldfields, or a young woman making her way in the world alone or assisting her family, women who taught in domestic or private situations also did so chiefly because they needed the income.[22] This viewpoint has also been confirmed by recent studies of teaching in New England and in London: Jo Anne Preston's examination of nineteenth-century common school teachers' correspondence reveals a diverse group of American women who nevertheless focused very strongly on the material reasons for their involvement in the profession; Dina Copelman has documented the economic motivation of London's married women teachers at the turn of the century.[23]

It is becoming apparent that, as women moved into state-financed school teaching, the character of teachers' work in elementary schools underwent subtle but important changes. By the turn of the century in Ontario and Quebec, new subjects had been added to the elementary school curriculum. At the same time, daily classroom teaching became increasingly structured by outside authority. The amount of paperwork grew, as schools and school systems became the targets of state intervention and as the competitive examination of pupils and teachers alike increased.[24] Through his analysis of a British teacher's diary kept during the Second World War, Martin Lawn has shown how the workload of one woman teacher could increase during a period of crisis. Extra responsibilities also brought a measure of additional power to the teacher in question, as she and her community responded to national priorities and demands. But local authorities were quick to reduce that power when it was no longer backed up by a national agenda at the war's end.[25]

Evidence of ever-increasing workloads, together with the politicizing effect that school teaching appears to have had on many schoolmistresses, accounts for the growing interest of nineteenth- and especially twentieth-century women teachers in organizing protective associations. In Australia, pioneering studies by Andrew Spaull and Bernard Hyams in the 1970s traced the origins of female teacher unionism;[26] research elsewhere is beginning to fill in the story. Historians have demonstrated both the existence of organized resistance by teachers by the turn of the century and the variety of forms it could take. We have also begun the task of placing the history of organized teachers in the context of the developing labour movement and of late nineteenth-century and twentieth-century feminism.[27]

The character of associational work varied enormously according to the politics and possibilities of given localities: women teachers organizing in Chicago, for example, tended to be more radical than their counterparts in Atlanta, New York, or Toronto.[28] In Australia, women teachers organized specifically around the classification of teachers.[29]

A characteristic that all shared in varying degrees, however, was ambivalence about the place of teachers in the labour force. It is clear that most elementary teachers were not accepted by their communities as genuine professionals. Yet female and male teachers alike found it difficult to see themselves as 'workers' or to form alliances with the trade unions whose members shared similar problems. Teachers perceived themselves as poorly paid and not in control of the workplace but, for the most part, continued to identify themselves as mental rather than manual labourers. For women teachers in Australia's non-government schools successful salary negotiations were delayed until after the Second World War precisely because these women were mystified by such categories and they could not reconcile their own perceived gentility with the tactics of a trades union.[30] There is every evidence that similar inhibitions affected women teachers in many Western jurisdictions. Indeed, the categories devised by historians and social scientists, dividing the world into mental and manual (or blue and white collar) workers, or into professionals and non-professionals, seem increasingly inappropriate to describe their case.[31]

The fact that the majority of elementary school teachers were women was certainly at the core of the confusion about the social position and identity of the occupation. Just as they occupied a middle ground between professional and industrial workers, women teachers were torn between the image of true womanhood and their position as paid members of the labour force. The feminist context of women teachers' associational activity in central Canada was a pervasive maternal feminism. Equal rights feminism existed in Quebec and Ontario, but maternal imagery and the cult of feminine domesticity must have remained overpowering for many teachers. At the same time, middle-class feminists did not fully understand the plight of working women. In Toronto, for example, women teachers were forced on several occasions to remind the Local Council of Women that they could not attend its meetings if they were held in working hours. Supportive as the feminist movement was to the women teachers who organized in Canada, it does not appear to have provided a genuinely alternative vision of the woman teacher's role in society or in the labour force.[32]

In turn-of-the-century Chicago and interwar Britain the picture was quite different, however. At least some women teachers were more militant and some were explicitly feminist in their quest for decent working conditions and equality with men. Cherry Collins' study of the Chicago Teachers' Federation (which included women and men) and its leaders, Catherine Goggin and Margaret Haley, is about women's analysis of the public realm and of their determination to change it. In pursuit of salary justice they successfully lobbied through the Illinois state legislature a one per cent increase in the school tax. When the promised salary increases did not eventuate, the Chicago Teachers' Federation investigated municipal taxation in Chicago, found it to be utterly corrupt, then pursued the offenders through the courts. Goggin and Haley also successfully led the federation in a battle against 'administrative Progressivism,' encapsulated in the notorious Harper Bill which effectively disenfranchised grade school teachers from decision-making. Their commitment to non-hierarchical, democratic decision-making processes led them to set up, across the United States, a grass-roots professional movement of classroom teachers. As Collins argues, the Chicago Teachers' Federation in the days of Catherine Goggin and Margaret Haley holds out to women teachers today an alternative model, ideologically and organizationally, to male-dominated unions, which women in the classroom still tend to reject as irrelevant to them. In Britain between the wars, the National Union of Women Teachers also sought radical change: the recognition of the right of married women to teach and the elimination of gender bias in textbooks were only two of the feminist goals for which they waged unceasing battles on several fronts.[33]

Recognizing that ideology provides only a partial explanation of behaviour, and that economic and social structures too are not the whole story, historians have recently begun to examine teachers' history through the eyes of its female subjects. This new work demonstrates the influence of recent feminist historiography, with its increasing insistence on understanding historical women on their own terms rather than from the vantage point of men who as fathers, husbands, employers, or political representatives sought to define or influence women's lives.[34] Drawing on the writings of women who taught in schools, and on a variety of biographical and autobiographical sources, historians espousing this approach have been able to illustrate the variety of women's experience in teaching. They have also begun to define resistance other than in terms of unionism by focusing on the ways in which some women circumvented the prescriptions and strictures that underpinned their social and economic inferiority. The work of women teachers in the past is thus seen as having both negative and positive dimensions. That subordination and oppression were endemic and systemic, there can be no doubt. Nevertheless, historians have been able to document the liberating impact of teaching on some of the women who travelled to the American South or to the North American prairies, not to mention the continent of Australia.[35] They also point to individual teachers who resisted control of their work by the state or community. Like male teachers, many used teaching as a stepping stone to more powerful professional or political roles. Geraldine Jonçich Clifford has argued for the importance of teaching in the background of many American feminists, while biographies and autobiographies of leading Canadian feminists suggest that the same may be true for Canada.[36]

On a more humble level, research on the most obscure and ordinary schoolmistresses is beginning to document a strand of resistance that predates late nineteenth- and early twentieth-century feminism and goes back at least to the middle of the nineteenth century. Feisty, even angry women teachers made their grievances known. One mid-nineteenth-century teacher confronted the male superintendent who 'tantalized,' 'insulted,' and 'provoked' her by simply leaving the school-room. When the superintendent withheld her certificate she complained to higher authorities and won her certificate back. In 1909, another wrote to the male inspector who had dared to criticize her work (and who had also cancelled her certificate) that she nevertheless remained 'as independent as the sun that shines' and that 'overbearing and deceptive' men in positions of authority had a lesson to learn from her.[37] Such women fought their subordination and there is clear evidence that, over the years, individual battles were sometimes won, as were those fought collectively through their organizations.[38] Studies of women teachers in Australia, the United States, and Britain suggest that family relationships and intimate friendships were probably more important in sustaining the majority of women than union activity, however.[39] Through their work and their resistance, women teachers were involved in the construction of meaning. Indeed, both the idea and the reality of the 'woman teacher' in history is proving evocative in ways far more complex than most of us first imagined could be the case.

The articles gathered in this book by no means cover all of the geographical areas or topics of concern to historians of women teachers today. To begin with, the focus is on four largely English-speaking countries: Australia, Britain, Canada, and the United States. We have selected articles that we consider moved in important new directions at the time of their publication. The organization of the volume is thematic: the first section focuses on women teaching in the 'private' sphere, while the second section deals with teachers in state schools; the third and final section turns to the women who taught in institutions devoted to higher learning.

Women Teaching in the Private Sphere
The articles here are diverse in their approaches but all three illuminate the fact that the so-called feminization of teaching in the nineteenth-century Western democracies is a misnomer, a product of the tunnel-vision of historians who looked only at the rise of state-sponsored systems of schooling.

The first article, Joyce Senders Pedersen's 'Schoolmistresses and Headmistresses: Elites and Education in Nineteenth-Century England,' represented an important conceptual advance in the field at the time it was written. Published in 1975, Pedersen's study is concerned to rescue the private school teacher from the scorn of posterity and place her on the terrain of respectable academic debate. Women who ran ladies' academies, with the exception of a handful of American women whose institutions have survived to the present day, have suffered the common fate of economic women in the past; they have been reduced by the attrition of time and neglect to an unflattering caricature – unmarriageable, ill-educated, money-grubbing, and pretentious. This stereotype passed into Australian popular mythology with the publication of Joan Lindsay's novel, *Picnic at Hanging Rock*, and was disseminated abroad by the film of the same name.[40] Pedersen acknowledges the existence of this stereotype, but she is not concerned to test its veracity. Instead she employs sociological concepts to compare the values and roles of the traditional lady-principal and her academy with the new headmistress and her corporate high school. She concludes that while both teachers aspired to elite status, they defined the roles and values of a lady differently: the private schoolmistress stressed good birth and the leisured lifestyle of a tradition stretching back to the pre-industrial era; the new headmistress subscribed to the meritocratic, impersonal institutional values of the rising middle classes against whom the lady-principal was inclined to close her doors. Although she may have overdrawn the contrast between the personal intimacy of the earlier schools and the cool professionalism supposedly characteristic of the later ones, Pedersen's study was among several which pointed the way for future scholars to place the history of women teachers within the wider structures of class and gender. Joan Burstyn's portrait of Catharine Beecher, followed by Kathryne Kish Sklar's more comprehensive study of Beecher, began a similar revisionist project for the United States. Although subsequent works did not always focus on the teachers or lady principals of schools like Emma Willard's Troy Female Seminary or Mary Lyon's Mount Holyoke College, an extremely stimulating body of literature has continued to illuminate the careers of such women.[41]

Nearly ten years separate the publication of the second and third articles from the appearance of Pedersen's pioneering study. The decade of feminist endeavour in women's history is apparent. Marjorie Theobald's article, ' "Mere Accomplishments"? Melbourne's Early Ladies' Schools Reconsidered,' carries on the theme of the schoolmistress for young ladies. She begins with a critique of orthodox interpretations of the reform of women's education, a process she redefines as 'the masculinization of female education,' then calls for a reappraisal of the women who taught in the private sphere, and sets out to 'disinter ... a tradition of female education which has fallen victim to male/bureaucratic definitions of education and professionalism.' In contrast to Pedersen's, Theobald's approach is through detailed biographical reconstruction of individual women who ran female schools in mid-nineteenth-century Melbourne. She argues that women created and sustained a tradition of female 'accomplishments' education which could be excellent and allowed women to push at the boundaries of female professionalism and learning. The case studies she presents are eloquent testimony that many women were committed professionals within their own sphere of excellence and that the accomplishments were, in fact, eminently practical professional preparation for many women in the nineteenth century.

Ailsa Zainu'ddin's article, ' "The poor widow, the ignoramus and the humbug": An Examination of Rhetoric and Reality in Victoria's 1905 Act for the Registration of Teachers and Schools,' establishes that in the Australian context women teachers in the ladies' academy tradition had successfully defended their territory until the beginning of the twentieth century. In an innovative study of legislation in the state of Victoria to bring private schooling under state control, Zainu'ddin traces the process by which such women were cast as 'the enemy' by legislators and male educationists – 'the poor widow, the ignoramus and the humbug' – to facilitate legislation that forced women out of entrepreneurial roles and into waged teaching labour in the employ of church and state. Zainu'ddin's study, based on some four hundred applications for school registration and over seven thousand applications for teacher registration, confirms in a concrete historical situation what Joan Burstyn has characterized as a 'disturbing analogy ... between the "industrialization" of teaching and the industrialization of other occupations, where small-scale workshops, initiated and maintained by women, were replaced by large-scale operations organized by men.'[42]

Women Teaching in the Public Sphere

The five studies included in this section were chosen for their different approaches and for their diverse geographical settings: the broad sweep of the nineteenth-century United States; Melbourne, Australia, in the 1880s; turn-of-the-century central Canada; England between the two world wars; and the Canadian province of British Columbia in the 1930s.

The section begins with Geraldine Jonçich Clifford's wide-ranging analysis of the process of feminization, ' "Daughters into Teachers": Educational and Demographic Influences on the Transformation of Teaching into "Women's Work" in America.' Her study synthesizes the statistical and speculative literature, from the late eighteenth century to the modern phenomenon of the married female teacher – by 1975 nearly 80 per cent of all American women teachers were or had been married. Clifford's work on feminization acknowledges the reality that women had been teachers before they became waged workers for the state. She also draws attention to questions of religious affiliation and ethnicity. In New York, for example, young Irish Catholic, Jewish, and German women had all established their bailiwicks in teaching by the turn of the century. In the South by 1920 teachers ranked seventh among all waged black women workers. Clifford also brings to this study the wealth of her research into women teachers' letters, diaries, and autobiographies. The words of a one-time pupil in the New York City schools encapsulates Clifford's (unstated) verdict on the place of the lady-teacher in American history: 'I have forgotten everything the schools ever taught me. But the glamour of the lady teachers, shining on the East Side world, I shall never forget.'

Fascinated with questions of who taught school and why, historians of teachers tended to neglect the question of teachers' daily work. Yet the dimensions of their labour were surely intrinsic to the other questions; work patterns clearly had much to do with the ways in which women teachers were regarded and how they thought about themselves. 'Teachers' Work: Changing Patterns and Perceptions in the Emerging School Systems of Nineteenth- and Early Twentieth-Century Central Canada' probes the daily work and changing working conditions of teachers in the two Canadian provinces that Marta Danylewycz and Alison Prentice studied, Quebec and Ontario. Demonstrating that teachers' workloads were both increasing – and *seen to be increasing* – at the turn of the century, their article also questioned the dichotomous labels that historians and others used to categorize work under industrial capitalism. Teaching, like secretarial work, did not fit the labels that had been devised to describe men's work. While their study did not spell out the details, it underscored the predicament that women teachers faced when they attempted to analyse their subordination and overwork: the words and concepts typically used for analysis did not work for them.

R.J.W. Selleck's contextual and narrative study of teacher politics in Australia, 'Mary Helena Stark: The Troubles of a Nineteenth-Century State School Teacher,' encapsulates in the person of Mary Helena Stark the social, economic, and labour conditions of women teachers in the 1880s. Stark was not among the lady teachers 'shining bright' in colonial Melbourne: she lived in shabby, middle-class poverty, partially supporting her widowed mother and sister; she was in poor health, frequently absent, a reluctant servant of the state, much given to querying the orders of her fastidious headmaster. In 1885, with hundreds of other women, Stark was dispatched to the lowest possible rung of the newly created classified roll for Victoria's teachers. The dispute which ensued led directly to the establishment of the Victorian Lady Teachers' Association. Selleck argues that the lowly classification of teachers like Stark was a punishment meted out to young women who would not go to the 'bush' to teach, and that departmental control over teachers, rather than simply dollars and cents, was at stake. Selleck tells a sorry tale of official bullying and duplicity, but Stark, backed by the Lady Teachers' Association and the burgeoning suffragist network of Melbourne, stood firm – right to the Privy Council in London, which in May 1890 found in her favour. The story of Mary Helena Stark challenges the stereotype of the nineteenth-century lady teacher as timid in the presence of male authority, and reminds us that some of them quickly learned to use the structures that were seldom, in the first instance, of their own making.

How did women teachers' dissatisfaction with their status and working conditions translate into collective action? American historian of teacher unionism, Wayne Urban, recently took feminist historians to task for their relative neglect of female teacher unions.[43] By and large the charge is true, reflecting perhaps the determination of women in the 1980s to break free of that compensatory imperative to notice the activities of their sisters in the past only when those activities mirrored the preoccupations of men. To concentrate narrowly on women's participation in teacher unions, especially in the nineteenth century, is to overlook the localized and personal struggles they undertook in order to shape the conditions and culture of their work. It is also to overlook other ways in which women teachers demonstrate commitment to teaching. Then as now, there were structural and ideological reasons why women did not support unions.

There is now a growing body of literature on female teacher unionism. Sarah King's study, 'Feminists in Teaching: The National Union of Women Teachers, 1920–1945,' confronts the orthodoxy that English feminism was fragmented and divided in the interwar years. King argues that a vibrant network existed which, although operating in a hostile social and political climate, remained theoretically strong and very active. The women of the National Union of Women Teachers saw clearly the importance to women of economic independence and therefore of the right to work. They articulated as basic to patriarchal oppression that 'men claim the right to approve or disapprove any enlargement of women's sphere.' Affirming J.S. Mill's famous analysis of women's condition, they saw that inequality between the sexes has its roots in the traditional marriage relationship of domination and subordination through the power of the purse. Their activities were eclectic and prodigious, but they saw themselves as 'pre-eminently an educational body.' In an era when official policy re-emphasized the need to differentiate between the educational experiences of boys and girls the women teachers were convinced that education was women's strongest weapon and that their sex must control the provision made for girls. Their critique of the curriculum, both overt and covert, in the co-educational secondary school has a decidedly modern ring. Yet as King points out, knowledge of their critique of gender and schooling, and of their courage in swimming against the tide, did not survive to empower feminist teachers in the 1980s.

J. Donald Wilson's study of British Columbia's unique welfare officer for women teachers, ' "I am ready to be of assistance when I can": Lottie Bowron and Rural Women Teachers in British Columbia,' reminds us that, for all the ways in which women teachers struggled to improve their working lives, many continued to live and work in worlds that were isolated and even threatening. Lottie Bowron, as the Rural Teachers' Welfare Officer of her province, was briefly in a position to try to help such women. Through her correspondence with the rural teachers of this western Canadian province, we catch a glimpse of isolated rural women teachers' difficulties – and of their occasional triumphs. As Wilson's narrative reveals, the position Bowron held eventually fell victim to the power politics of men, and she was forced to move on to other work. Her story reminds us, once more, of both the fragile power and the resourcefulness of the women who attempted to make careers in education.

Women Teaching in Higher Education
'Scholarly passion,' remarked the Canadian academic Mossie May Kirkwood, 'is caught by persons from persons.'[44] If this is true, it should give us food for thought, for not until the 1970s did feminist academics begin to ask the question: 'Who were our foremothers?' In her study of the personal lives of the first generation of college women in England, Martha Vicinus suggests that by the Edwardian era an intergenerational rift had occurred, as in the eyes of female students colleges such as Girton, Cambridge, and Westfield, London, had already moved from being dangerously innovative institutions to being conservative bastions.[45] Vicinus suggests that young women chafing under the moral supervision of reserved and high-minded spinsters were supported by a conservative backlash in the Edwardian era, when oppositional rhetoric swung from whether women *could* succeed in the male intellectual domain to whether women *should* succeed. Under the circumstances, scholarly passion, at least between women, may have been the first victim. And, in any case, scholarly passion must still be translated into places for graduate students and secure employment.

Patricia Palmieri's study, 'Here Was Fellowship: A Social Portrait of Academic Women at Wellesley College, 1895–1920,' presents a collective picture of a remarkable group of women who shaped 'a triumphant reality' at one of the leading colleges for women in the United States. A socially homogeneous group, most had also enjoyed special familial sponsorship and support: many continued to live with mothers and sisters who followed them to the Wellesley campus and relieved them of domestic duties. All of them were single. Unlike Martha Vicinus's emotionally tortured Constance Maynard and her colleagues, the

Wellesley faculty were also astonishingly good friends. Palmieri argues that for these reasons the women were able to create a cohesive intellectual and social community outside the research universities that were often assumed to be the only sites of genuine intellectual creativity.

Palmieri, who begins her study with the controversial observation that such outstanding academic women are relatively unknown today, is not centrally concerned with the problem of intergenerational renewal. Nevertheless, some facts emerge to cloud this idyllic portrait of women and the scholarly life. Junior faculty were kept firmly in their place. It was not until the late 1940s, when most of the charmed circle had either retired or died, that younger women faculty found a voice. Perhaps most tellingly, these earlier academic women fashioned their world within the institutional paradigm of the older, liberal arts college; sisterhood and the community of intellect, at least among the chosen few, took precedence over the vertical mobility, individualism, and social science 'objectivity' characteristic of the modern research university. Did the younger generation perceive that the rewards, as defined by the dominant academic culture, lay elsewhere?

Individual biographies can often reveal much about the marginal position of women teaching in institutions of higher learning. Alison Prentice's article, 'Scholarly Passion: Two Persons Who Caught It,' sets out to reclaim two Canadian women scholars. One of them, Mary Electa Adams, was a nineteenth-century lady-principal and founder of ladies' academies. Prentice argues that women like Adams have been overlooked as pioneer female teachers at the tertiary level because the nineteenth-century female academy did not fit the subsequently created categories of 'secondary' and 'tertiary.' It is only when we challenge the categories rather than the women that new insights are generated. All her teaching life Adams was associated with ladies' schools which had tertiary ambitions. Her struggles to be involved in higher education for women were not satisfactorily resolved in her view; yet, with feminist hindsight, we can recognize her significance in the history of women's quest for higher learning.

Mossie May Kirkwood, the second of Prentice's subjects, used her position as dean of women to achieve her goals in university life. Juggling marriage and motherhood with her work in higher education, Kirkwood made a distinctive career for herself and was no doubt a model for others in her period. Yet, what she and her contemporaries failed to do, Prentice suggests, was to empower a new generation of women scholars to take their place. Patricia Albjerg Graham is among the historians of women university teachers who have attempted to explain why.[46] Graham sees the twentieth-century co-educational university as a frequently alienating and unsupportive environment for the women who attempted to make scholarly careers in them. Indeed, the mid-twentieth-century university was in some ways less welcoming to women teachers than earlier institutions of higher education had been. The university continues, like most educational institutions, to be an important site of feminist struggle.

This collection on the history of women teachers suggests several important avenues for future research. A thorough understanding of feminization, it is now clear, requires further analysis of the sexual division of labour in teaching *before* the rise of state school systems and a more refined breakdown of the stages in the transition to predominantly female teaching forces in public schools. Indeed the concept of feminization itself may be inappropriate. One problem with the concept, certainly, is that it ignores the presence of large numbers of women teachers in colonial and pre-industrial communities, thus reinforcing women's invisibility in the more distant past. It may also mask profound differences between early Protestant and Catholic forms of education by placing too much emphasis on the mid-nineteenth-century transition to public schools. Female involvement and lifetime careers in formal schooling had long been an established fact in female religious communities devoted to the instruction of girls. These teachers need to be rescued from the hagiographic historical tradition in which they are customarily presented.[47] In areas where Roman Catholic convent schools existed, the feminization of state school teaching must be studied in the context of church/state relations and women's acceptance or rejection of religious vocations. In such societies, the relations between lay and religious teachers are an important part of the history of the occupation.[48] Finally, we must pay attention to the work of social historians who have focused on the ways in which traditional attitudes and patterns of work tended to persist in new settings in both Europe and North America. It is possible that what historians of education have assumed was 'modern' and essentially new about women's developing role in public school teaching was, in fact, the continuation of traditional patterns in greatly altered environments.[49]

Of course, even if this is the case, the gradual predominance of women teachers in public elementary schools remains an important phenomenon and one which continues to be worthy of further analysis.

In Britain and Australia the field is certainly under-researched. The complex regional patterns that have emerged in the study of the occupation in Quebec and Ontario suggest the importance of looking at regional economies and how they may have influenced the composition of local teaching forces. Future regional studies may reveal new factors and configurations.[50] Regional studies may also provide further insight into the relative significance of the different variables associated not only with feminization but also with other ways in which the occupation has been socially structured. The relationships between such factors as age, gender, and work experience in schools, and how these changed over time, need further exploration if we are to establish more precisely how they affected the status and salaries of teachers and the conditions of their work. Important also are the variables of family status and domestic circumstances. We need to know more about how teachers lived and with whom; and about how both the ideologies and realities of their sexuality affected their lives.[51]

Equally interesting are the questions of class and ethnicity. There is clearly more to learn about the changing social, cultural, and educational background of teachers. Did the expansion of teaching forces in the nineteenth and twentieth centuries result in shifts in their social class and ethnic composition? The significant participation of working-class women and women of colour in teaching raises the question of how their presence influenced not only the sexual division of labour in the occupation but also school boards' treatment of their female employees.[52] An important aspect of this discussion is the new work that is beginning on the history of Normal Schools and teacher training, clearly a major, and neglected, site of tertiary education for women in the past.[53] In addition, we need to know much more about the women who taught, increasingly, in secondary schools and tertiary educational institutions.

While an analysis of the class, ethnic, and educational backgrounds of teachers will shed further light on who taught school, it is also important to further our understanding of what teachers actually did in the classroom. In other words, it is essential to treat teaching as work and the history of teaching as labour history. This means examining the tasks that were assigned to teachers and their responses to those assignments. Such an approach not only places the worker at the centre of the inquiry but also underscores the need to examine very closely the whole question of occupational categories when speaking of teachers and their history.

Finally, there is a need for much more work on teachers' resistance. How did individuals and groups of women who taught construct their lives? To what extent were they involved in a feminist quest for autonomy, not only economically but in their familial and sexual self-definitions? How did they battle against the various structures and ideologies that constrained them? The agenda for the historiography of female teachers is a very exciting one indeed and we hope this book will inspire a new generation of feminist historians to engage in it.

NOTES

1 See, for example, Michael W. Apple, *Teachers and Texts: A Political Economy of Class and Gender Relations in Education* (New York: Routledge and Kegan Paul 1986); R.W. Connell, *Teachers' Work* (Sydney: Allen & Unwin 1985), and *Gender and Power: Society, the Person and Sexual Politics* (Cambridge: Polity in Association with Blackwell 1987); Jane Gaskell and Arlene Tigar McLaren, *Women and Education: A Canadian Perspective* (Calgary: Detselig Enterprises 1987); Jenny Ozga, ed., *Schoolwork: Approaches to the Labour Process of Teaching* (Milton Keynes: Open University Press 1988); Patricia Schmuck, ed., *Women Educators: Employees of Schools in Western Countries* (Albany: State University of New York Press 1987).
2 For a complex and stimulating discussion of the ways in which the discipline of history itself must be taken to task for perpetuating an imperfect understanding of gender, and gender stereotypes and inequalities, see Joan Wallach Scott, *Gender and the Politics of History* (New York: Columbia University Press 1989), esp. pp 9–10 and chapters 1 and 2.
3 See, for example, J.G. Althouse, *The Ontario Teacher: A Historical Account of Progress, 1800–1910*, D.Paed. diss., University of Toronto, 1929 (published by University of Toronto Press 1967); W.S. Elsbree, *The American Teacher: Evolution of a Profession in a Democracy* (New York: American Book Company 1939); A. Tropp, *The School Teachers: The Growth of the Teaching Profession in England and Wales from 1800 to the Present Day* (London: Heinemann 1957).
4 Michael B. Katz, 'The Emergence of Bureaucracy in Urban Education: The Boston Case, 1850–1884,' *History of Education Quarterly*, 8, 2 and 3 (summer and fall 1968)
5 Alison Prentice, 'The Feminization of Teaching in British North

America and Canada, 1845–1875,' *Histoire sociale/Social History*, 8 (May 1975); Myra H. Strober and David Tyack, 'Why Do Women Teach and Men Manage? A Report on Research on Schools,' *Signs*, 5, 3 (1980), and David B. Tyack and Myra H. Strober, 'Jobs and Gender: A History of the Structuring of Educational Employment by Sex,' in P. Schmuck and W.W. Charles, eds., *Educational Policy and Management: Sex Differentials* (San Diego: Academic Press 1981); Myra H. Strober and Audri Gordon Langford, 'The Feminization of Teaching: A Cross-Sectional Analysis, 1850–1880,' *Signs*, 11, 2 (winter 1986). For a recent overview of the social characteristics of American teachers, see John L. Rury, 'Who Became Teachers? The Social Characteristics of Teachers in American History,' in Donald Warren, ed., *American Teachers: Histories of a Profession At Work* (New York: Macmillan 1989).

6 See Keith Melder, 'Women's High Calling: The Teaching Profession in America, 1830–1860,' *American Studies*, 13 (fall 1972); Joan N. Burstyn, 'Catharine Beecher and the Education of American Women,' *New England Quarterly*, 47 (summer 1974); and Glenda Riley, 'Origins of the Argument for Improved Female Education,' *History of Education Quarterly*, 9, 4 (winter 1969).

7 Prentice, 'The Feminization of Teaching'

8 Redding S. Sugg, *Motherteacher: The Feminization of American Education* (Charlottesville: University of Virginia Press 1978) takes the most pejorative view of women teachers' impact on schooling, while Madeleine Grumet, 'Pedagogy for Patriarchy: The Feminization of Teaching,' *Interchange*, 12, 2–3 (1981), puts forward a picture of women teachers as victims of a hidden process that is beyond their control. An excellent critique of Sugg's book, along with a discussion of other recent American studies, may be found in Geraldine Clifford, 'Eve: Redeemed by Education and Teaching School,' *History of Education Quarterly*, 21, 4 (winter 1981).

9 Carolyn Steedman, ' "The Mother Made Conscious": The Historical Development of a Primary School Pedagogy,' *History Workshop*, 20 (autumn 1985); 'Prisonhouses,' in Martin Lawn and Gerald Grace, eds., *Teachers: The Culture and Politics of Work* (London: Falmer Press 1987); and *Landscape for a Good Woman: A Story of Two Lives* (London: Virago 1986); Madeleine R. Grumet, *Bitter Milk: Women and Teaching* (Amherst: University of Massachusetts Press 1988)

10 Noeline Kyle, 'Woman's "Natural Mission" But Man's Real Domain: The Masculinization of the State Elementary Teaching Service in New South Wales,' in Miriam Henry and Sandra Taylor, eds., *Battlers and*

Bluestockings: Women's Place in Australian Education (Canberra; Australian College of Education 1989)

11 Barry H. Bergen, 'Only a Schoolmaster: Gender, Class, and the Effort to Professionalize Elementary Teaching in England, 1870–1910,' *History of Education Quarterly*, 22, 1 (spring 1982). On the history of gender and secondary teaching, see also Gwyneth Dow and Leslie Scholes, 'Christina Montgomery,' in R.J.W. Selleck and Martin Sullivan, eds., *Not So Eminent Victorians* (Melbourne: Melbourne University Press 1984), and the special issue, 'Teachers: Class, Gender and Professionalism,' *Historical Studies in Education/Revue d'histoire de l'éducation*, 2, 1 (spring 1990), esp. Anne Drummond, 'Gender, Profession, and Principals: The Teachers of Quebec Protestant Academies, 1875–1900' and Susan Gelman, 'The "Feminization" of the High Schools? Women Secondary Teachers in Toronto, 1871–1930'; and David F. Labaree, 'Career Ladders and the Early Public High-School Teacher: A Study of Inequality and Opportunity,' in Warren, *American Teachers*.

12 Marion Amies, 'Amusing and Instructive Conversations: The Literary Genre and Its Relevance to Home Education,' *History of Education*, 14, 2 (1985)

13 J.H. Higginson, 'Dame Schools,' *British Journal of Educational Studies*, 22, 2, (1974); D.P. Leinster-Mackay, 'Dame Schools: A Need for Review,' *ibid.*, 24, 1, (1976); Philip Gardner, *The Lost Elementary Schools of Victorian England* (London: Croom Helm 1984)

14 E. Jennifer Monaghan, 'Noted and Unnoted School Dames: Women as Reading Teachers in Colonial New England,' paper presented to the International Standing Conference for the History of Education, Oslo, Norway, 1989; see also her 'Literacy Instruction and Gender in Colonial New England,' *American Quarterly*, 40, 1 (1988).

15 M. Jeanne Peterson, 'The Victorian Governess: Status Incongruence in Family and Society,' in Martha Vicinus, ed., *Suffer and Be Still: Women in the Victorian Age* (Bloomington, Indiana: University of Indiana Press 1973), and Joyce Senders Pedersen, 'Schoolmistresses and Headmistresses: Elites and Education in Nineteenth-Century England,' reprinted in this volume. See also Josephine Kamm, *How Different from Us: A Biography of Miss Buss and Miss Beale* (London: Bodley Head 1958) and the revisionist essay by Carol Dyhouse, 'Miss Buss and Miss Beale: Gender and Authority in the History of Education,' in Felicity Hunt, ed., *Lessons for Life: The Schooling of Girls and Women, 1850–1950* (Oxford: Basil Blackwood 1987); Nonita Glen-

day and Mary Price, *Reluctant Revolutionaries: A Century of Headmistresses, 1874–1974* (London: Pitman 1975).

16 Marjorie R. Theobald, 'Women and Schools in Colonial Victoria, 1840–1910,' Ph.D. thesis, Monash University, Melbourne, 1985; ' "Mere Accomplishments"? Melbourne's Early Ladies' Schools Reconsidered,' reprinted in this volume, and 'Julie Vieusseux: The Lady Principal and Her School,' in Marilyn Lake and Farley Kelly, eds., *Double Time: Women in Victoria – 150 Years* (Melbourne: Penguin 1985)

17 See, for example, Margaret Bryant, *The Unexpected Revolution: A Study in the History of the Education of Women and Girls in the Nineteenth Century* (London: University of London Institute of Education 1978).

18 For an enlightening discussion of the ambiguities surrounding definitions of secondary and tertiary education, see R.D. Gidney and W.P.J. Millar, *Inventing Secondary Education: The Rise of the High School in Nineteenth-Century Ontario* (Montreal: McGill-Queen's University Press 1990).

19 Richard M. Bernard and Maris A. Vinovskis, 'The Female School Teacher in Ante-Bellum Massachusetts,' *Journal of Social History*, 10, 3 (spring 1977)

20 Marta Danylewycz, Beth Light, and Alison Prentice, 'The Evolution of the Sexual Division of Labour in Teaching: A Nineteenth-Century Ontario and Quebec Case Study,' *Histoire sociale/Social History*, 16, 21 (May 1983)

21 Marta Danlyewycz and Alison Prentice, 'Teachers, Gender and Bureaucratizing School Systems in Nineteenth-Century Montreal and Toronto,' *History of Education Quarterly*, 24, 1 (spring 1984)

22 Theobald, 'Women and Schools in Colonial Victoria'; Marion Amies, 'Home Education and Colonial Ideals of Womanhood,' Ph.D. thesis, Monash University, 1986

23 Jo Anne Preston, 'Female Aspiration and Male Ideology: School-Teaching in Nineteenth-Century New England,' in Arina Angerman *et al.*, eds., *Current Issues in Women's History* (London: Routledge 1989); Dina Copelman, ' "A New Comradeship between Men and Women": Family, Marriage and London's Women Teachers, 1870–1914,' in Jane Lewis, ed., *Labour and Love: Women's Experience of Home and Family, 1850–1940* (New York: Basil Blackwood 1986)

24 Marta Danylewycz and Alison Prentice, 'Teachers' Work: Changing Patterns and Perceptions in the Emerging School Systems of Nine-

teenth- and Early Twentieth-Century Central Canada,' reprinted in this volume.

25 Martin Lawn, 'What Is the Teacher's Job? Work and Welfare in Elementary Teaching, 1940–1945,' in Lawn and Grace, *Teachers*

26 B.K. Hyams, 'The Battle of the Sexes in Teachers' Organizations: A South Australian Episode, 1937–1950,' *ANZHES Journal* 3, 2 (1974); A.D. Spaull, 'Equal Pay for Women Teachers and the New South Wales Teachers' Federation,' *ibid.*, 4, 1 (1975). Both articles are reprinted in A.D. Spaull, ed., *Australian Teachers: From Colonial Schoolmasters to Militant Professionals* (Melbourne: Macmillan 1977).

27 Cherry Collins, 'Regaining the Past for the Present: The Legacy of the Chicago Teachers' Federation,' *History of Education Review*, 13, 2 (1984); Harry Smaller, ' "A Room of One's Own": The Early Years of the Toronto Women Teachers' Association,' paper presented to the Canadian History of Education Association, London, Ontario, Oct. 1988, and 'Teachers' Protective Associations, Professionalism, and the "State" in Nineteenth-Century Ontario,' Ph.D. thesis, University of Toronto, 1988; and Wayne Urban, *Why Teachers Organized* (Detroit: Wayne State University Press 1982). Marîse Thivierge, in 'La Syndicalization des Institutrices Catholiques, 1900–1959,' in Nadia Fahmy-Eid and Micheline Dumont, eds., *Maîtresses d'maison, maîtresses d'école : Femmes, famille et l'éducation dans l'histoire du Québec* (Montreal: Boréal Express 1983), has analysed the associational history of Catholic women teachers in Quebec. For an excellent introduction to the history of teacher unionism generally, see *History of Education Review*, 14, 2 (1985), special issue on the subject edited by Andrew Spaull.

28 Urban, *Why Teachers Organized*; Alison Prentice, 'Themes in the History of Women Teachers' Association of Toronto, 1892–1914,' in P. Bourne, ed., *Women's Paid and Unpaid Work* (Toronto: New Hogtown Press 1985). Smaller, ' "A Room of One's Own," ' portrays an early radicalism that was muted by the second decade of the twentieth-century.

29 Judith Biddington, 'The Role of Women in the Victorian Education Department, 1872–1925,' M.Ed. thesis, University of Melbourne, 1977; Katherine M. Ashford, 'The Status of Women Teachers in the Victorian Education Department at the Turn of the Century, 1888–1914,' M.Ed. thesis, Monash University, 1981; R.J.W. Selleck, 'Mary Helena Stark:

The Troubles of a Nineteenth-Century State School Teacher,'
reprinted in this volume.

30 Marjorie R. Theobald, 'Women Teachers' Quest for Salary Justice in
Victoria's Registered Schools 1915–1946,' in Imelda Palmer, ed., *Melbourne Studies in Education 1983* (Melbourne: Melbourne University
Press 1983)

31 Danylewycz and Prentice, 'Teachers' Work'; Bergen, 'Only a Schoolmaster'

32 Prentice, 'Themes in the History of the Women Teachers' Association';
Pat Staton and Beth Light, *Speak with Their Own Voices: A Documentary History of the Federation of Women Teachers' Association and the
Women Elementary Public School Teachers of Ontario* (Toronto: Federation of Women Teachers' Association of Ontario 1987)

33 Collins, 'Regaining the Past for the Present'; Sarah King, 'Feminists
in Teaching: The National Union of Women Teachers, 1920–1945,'
reprinted in this volume.

34 For a discussion of the importance of focusing on women's perspective
on their own history, see Gerda Lerner, 'Placing Women in History,'
Feminist Studies, 3, 1 and 2 (fall 1975). Geraldine Clifford, 'Home and
School in 19th-Century America: Some Personal-History Reports
from the United States,' *History of Education Quarterly*, 18, 1 (spring
1978), takes the same stand with respect to teachers. See also Scott,
Gender and the Politics of History.

35 See, for example, Polly Welts Kaufman, *Women Teachers on the Frontier* (New Haven: Yale University Press 1984); Nancy Hoffman, *Women's True Profession: Voices from the History of Teaching* (New York:
Feminist Press and McGraw-Hill 1981); and A. James Hammerton,
*Emigrant Gentlewomen: Genteel Poverty and Female Emigration
1830–1914* (Canberra: Australian National University Press 1979).
See also J. Lyons, 'For St. George and Canada: The Fellowship of the
Maple Leaf and Education on the Prairies, 1919–1929,' in J.D. Wilson,
ed., *An Imperfect Past: Education and Society in Canadian History*
(Vancouver: University of British Columbia Centre for the Study of
Curriculum and Instruction 1984).

36 Geraldine Jonçich Clifford, 'Lady Teachers and Politics in the United
States, 1850–1930,' in Lawn and Grace, *Teachers*; Nellie McClung,
Clearing in the West (Toronto: Thomas Allen and Son 1975): Veronica
Strong-Boag, ed., *'A Woman with a Purpose': The Diaries of Elizabeth
Smith, 1872–1884* (Toronto: University of Toronto Press 1980). See

also Farley Kelly, 'The "Woman Question" in Melbourne, 1880–1914,'
Ph.D. thesis, Monash University, 1982.

37 Marilyn Kryger, 'The Mid-Victorian Woman School Teacher and Male
Officialdom: Image vs. Reality,' MA thesis, University of Toronto, 1989,
p 43; John Abbott and Alison Prentice, 'French-Canadian Women and
the New Social History: Some Suggestions for Archival Research,'
Canadian Women's Studies/Les cahiers de la femme, 7, 3 (fall 1986),
11. See also John Abbott, 'Accomplishing "a Man's Task": Rural
Women Teachers, Male Culture, and the School Inspectorate in Turn-
of-the-Century Ontario,' *Ontario History*, 78, 4 (Dec. 1986).

38 Sandra Gaskell's dissertation, 'The Problems and Professionalism
of Women Elementary Public School Teachers, 1944–1954,' Ed. D.
thesis, University of Toronto, 1990, documents the way in which
a women teachers' federation supported the battles of individual
teachers for their rights in the period after the Second World War.

39 See, for example, Selleck and Sullivan, *Not So Eminent Victorians*,
especially the essay by Judith Biddington, 'The Weekes Family.' For
college women in the United States and Great Britain, see Patricia A.
Palmieri, 'Here Was Fellowship: A Social Portrait of Academic Women
at Wellesley College, 1895–1920,' reprinted in this volume, and Martha
Vicinus, ' "One Life to Stand Beside Me": Emotional Conflicts in
First-Generation College Women in England,' *Feminist Studies*, 8, 2
(fall 1982).

40 Joan Lindsay, *Picnic at Hanging Rock* (Melbourne: Penguin
1967)

41 Joan M. Burstyn, 'Catharine Beecher and the Education of American
Women,' *New England Quarterly*, 47 (summer 1974); Kathryne Kish
Sklar, *Catharine Beecher: A Study in Domesticity* (New Haven: Yale
University Press 1973); Anne Firor Scott, 'The Ever Widening Circle:
The Diffusion of Feminist Values from the Troy Female Seminary,
1822–1872,' *History of Education Quarterly*, 19, 1 (spring 1979);
David F. Allmendinger, 'Mount Holyoke Students Encounter the Need
for Life-Planning, 1837–1850,' *History of Education Quarterly*, 19, 1
(spring 1979); Helen Lefkowitz Horowitz, *Alma Mater: Design and
Experience in the Women's Colleges from Their Nineteenth-Century
Beginnings to the 1930s* (Boston: Beacon Press 1984)

42 Joan Burstyn, 'Women's Education during the Nineteenth Century:
A Review of the Literature, 1970–1976,' *History of Education*, 6, 1
(1977), 13. On proletarianization, teaching, and gender, see also the

work of Michael Apple, for example, 'Work, Class, and Teaching,' in Ozga, *Schoolwork*.

43 Wayne Urban, 'New Directions in the Historical Study of Teacher Unionism,' paper presented to the American Educational Research Association, San Francisco, 1989: published in *Historical Studies in Education/Revue d'histoire de l'éducation*, 2, 1 (spring 1990)

44 University of Toronto Archives, B74-020, Mossie May Kirkwood Interview, conducted by Elizabeth Wilson, 1973

45 Vicinus, ' "One Life to Stand Beside Me" '

46 Patricia Albjerg Graham, 'Expansion and Exclusion: A History of Women in American Higher Education,' *Signs*, 3, 4 (summer 1978)

47 This more scholarly analysis has already begun. See, for example, Mary J. Oates, 'The Professional Preparation of Parochial Schoolteachers, 1870–1940,' *Historical Journal of Massachusetts*, 12 (Jan. 1984), and Mary J. Oates, ed., *Higher Education for Catholic Women: An Historical Anthology* (New York: Garland 1987).

48 See Marta Danylewycz, *Taking the Veil: An Alternative to Marriage, Motherhood, and Spinsterhood in Quebec, 1840–1920* (Toronto: McClelland and Stewart 1987).

49 The classic statement of the continuation of the traditional approach to women's work in an industrializing society, in this case nineteenth-century France, is Louise A. Tilly and Joan W. Scott, *Women, Work and Family* (New York: Methuen 1987). For a discussion of the intersection of traditional practices and modern industrial development in Canada, see Gail Brandt, ' "Weaving It Together": Life Cycle and the Industrial Experience of Female Cotton Workers in Quebec, 1910–1950,' *Labour/Le Travail*, 7 (spring 1981). For a case study of women teaching in family situations, see Marjorie R. Theobald, 'Women's Labour, the Family and the State: The Case of Women Teaching in an Elementary Schooling System in Australia 1850–1880,' in Marjorie R. Theobald and R.J.W. Selleck, eds., *Family, School and State in Australian History* (Sydney: Allen and Unwin 1990).

50 See, for example, the recent study by Jean Barman, 'Birds of Passage or Early Professionals? Teachers in Late Nineteenth-Century British Columbia,' *Historical Studies in Education/Revue d'histoire de l'éducation*, 2, 1 (spring 1990).

51 Studies addressing the question of teachers' sexuality are now beginning to appear. See, for example, Marjorie R. Theobald, 'Discourse of Danger: Gender and the History of Elementary Schooling in Australia, 1850–1880,' *ibid.*, 1, 1 (spring 1989); Alison Oram, ' "Embittered,

sexless or homosexual": Attacks on Spinster Teachers, 1918–1939,' in Angerman *et al.*, *Current Issues in Women's History*.

52 See, for example, Linda M. Perkins, 'The Black Female American Missionary Association Teacher in the South, 1860–70,' in Jeffrey J. Crow and Flora J. Hatley, eds., *Black Americans in North Carolina and the South* (Chapel Hill: University of North Carolina Press 1984), and 'The History of Blacks in Teaching: Growth and Decline within the Profession,' in Warren, *American Teachers*.

53 On women and teacher training, see Frances Widdowson, *Going Up into the Next Class: Women and Elementary Teacher Training 1840–1914* (London: Hutchison 1980); Jurgen Herbst, 'Nineteenth-Century Normal Schools in the United States: A Fresh Look,' *History of Education*, 9, 3 (1980), and *And Sadly Teach: Teacher Education and Professionalization in American Culture* (Madison: University of Wisconsin Press 1989); Alison Prentice, ' "Friendly Atoms in Chemistry": Women and Men at Normal School in Mid-Nineteenth-Century Toronto,' in David Keane and Colin Read, eds., *Old Ontario: Essays in Honour of J.M.S. Careless* (Toronto: Dundurn Press 1990); Noeline Kyle, *Her Natural Destiny: The Education of Women in New South Wales* (Sydney: New South Wales University Press 1986).

WOMEN TEACHING IN THE PRIVATE SPHERE

Schoolmistresses and Headmistresses:
Elites and Education in Nineteenth-Century England

Joyce Senders Pedersen

Ladies who kept private schools attended by young ladies are familiar figures in Regency and Victorian novels: ridiculous ladies, such as Miss Pinkerton, who kept a rather elegant establishment in *Vanity Fair*; sensible ladies like Mrs Goddard, whose more modest school was attended by Jane Austen's *Emma*; scheming ladies such as Mrs Kirkpatrick, who set her cap for Molly Gibson's father in Mrs Gaskell's *Wives and Daughters*. Memorable mostly for their personal quirks, their qualities of character, these ladies all fit comfortably in the framework of the domestic drama.

Accounts of real-life ladies who kept fashionable private schools in the early nineteenth century are more difficult to come by. A handful of biographies and autobiographies of such schoolmistresses exist, and they figure now and then in studies of eminent women who happened to attend their schools.[1] Early feminists and other proponents of educational reform occasionally analyzed and deplored their circumstances.[2] However, the only approach to a systematic survey of their conditions and opinions was that made by the Taunton Commission, which issued its report on the state of secondary education in England in 1867–8.[3] In the reports of those diligent assistant commissioners who attempted to visit ladies' schools and pestered them with written forms a multitude of private schoolmistresses were at least briefly mentioned, although individuals were not named. They emerged momentarily, sometimes reluctantly, into the glare of publicity, and for once the complaints and practices and aspirations of large numbers of them became a matter of the public record. However, this was extraordinary. Generally such ladies clung to the gentilities of private life and shunned the public eye. As one schoolmistress complained, denying a member of the Taunton Commission entry to her school, 'I am extremely sorry to find that Ministers [i.e. the government] have nothing better to do than pry into the ménage of private families, as I consider my establishment.'[4]

Beginning in mid-century, with the movement to establish women's colleges and public schools for girls and to open public examinations and university degrees to women,[5] a new category of female teacher appeared – the public school headmistress. These women did not figure prominently in the fiction of the time. However, at least so far as their working lives were concerned, their aims and activities were much more open to public scrutiny than those of the private schoolmistresses. The public school heads saw to it that their professional aspirations and achievements *were* publicly aired. The professional organizations they established debated educational issues and forwarded resolutions to public agencies. Their representatives testified before investigative bodies attempting to formulate public educational policy. The work of the headmistresses within their schools was evaluated by publicly recognized authorities.[6] And, as the century wore on and a college education became a precondition for garnering a desirable public school post, the teachers' own academic achievements increasingly became a matter of public record.

Very few of these women achieved renown as individuals. Among those who did were Frances Mary Buss of the North London Collegiate and Camden Schools for girls and Dorothea Beale of the Cheltenham Ladies' College, both of whom have been the subject of several biographies.[7] The achievements of these and a few other such teachers have been thought of sufficient general interest at least to merit a line or two in some surveys of the period or to figure in a biographical dictionary.[8] The personal histories of the great majority of the public school heads remain obscure, but owing to their institutional connections, they are in matters relating to their professional lives more accessible than the private schoolmistresses. Headmistresses figure in professional membership lists. Some appear in college registers. And, unlike the private schoolmistresses, whose schools seldom survived them and were usually soon forgotten, some public school heads are remembered in histories of their institutions.

The disparity in the sources that survive for studying the two types of teachers reflects the different roles they sought to play. Whereas the private schoolmistress aspired to a leisured, amateur role in a secluded, quasi-domestic setting, the public school heads aimed rather to secure professional recognition and sought distinction in the public sphere. The two types of teachers were animated by different values. Guided primarily by ascriptive social concerns and private interests, the fashionable private schoolmistress aimed to play and groomed her pupils for a largely leisured role suited to a private setting. The public school heads, on the other hand, considered themselves professional people and placed more emphasis on academic achievement. They claimed to serve not just private but also public ends and attempted to train their pupils for a public role.

Both types of teachers aspired to elite status, desiring to dissociate themselves from the mass of the middle classes. However, the two sorts of teachers defined the roles and values appropriate to a 'lady' somewhat differently. The private schoolmistresses' aspirations were of a piece with that gentle tradition with roots stretching far back in the pre-industrial era which stressed good birth and a leisured life-style as prime components of high social status.[9] The public school headmistresses' conception of their role represented a modification of this ideal. They redefined the components of elite status so as to give more weight to academic achievement and less to a leisured life-style. In their demand for professional recognition, the teachers stressed the values of expertise and public service in a non-traditional way.[10] But they retrained the vital distinction between low-status, profit-oriented employments and gentle occupations.

II

Along with family governesses and paid companions, ladies who kept private boarding or mixed boarding and day schools[11] in early nineteenth-century England were members of that anomalous social category – poor ladies obliged to work for pay.[12] The social position of such women was ambiguous, for ladies were usually not poor and did not engage in paid employment. While gentlemen might undertake certain categories of paid employment and yet retain their claim to gentle status in the mid-Victorian era, a lady was still almost by definition a leisured woman, who led a sheltered life amidst her family, her social contacts largely limited to her social equals and dependents.[13]

Insofar as private schoolmistresses could claim elite status, their claims rested primarily upon their ascriptive characteristics. Such prestige as they enjoyed derived mainly from those traditional patterns of status in which the hereditary rank of the two parties took precedence over the nature of the service rendered in determining the status of an employment. It was in the first instance the circumstance that she was supposed to have been born a lady and was thereby presumed fit to associate with other ladies that entitled the lady who taught to a certain consideration.[14] The lady-teacher's skills (her artistic and linguistic accomplishments, her mastery of etiquette) were obviously not irrelevant to her status. However, whereas modern professional groups have based their claims to elite status in the first instance on their possession of skills and techniques acquired through a course of intellectual training,[15] the connection between the lady-teachers' skills and status was rather tenuous and indirect. Often it seems such teachers' accomplishments were valued more for the indication they gave that the woman in question was well-born than for any promise they held of her effectiveness as an educator.[16] Further, so long as there were no recognized examinations and degrees for students or for teachers, it was difficult to judge a lady's attainments or her skill in imparting them to others with much precision.

Career patterns within the occupational group reflected the values of the ladies who taught. Since their leisured ideal defined paid employment as degrading rather than enhancing their status, ladies were said to turn to teaching only from economic necessity.[17] Unwillingly recruited to their work, they tended to retire if an opportunity arose.[18] Ladies who taught in early nineteenth-century England had undergone no special course of training for their work. No training institutions existed for such teachers. There were no nationally recognized degrees. Since in their case prestige attached to amateur status, to have educated these women in some unconventional way would have been to unfit them for their work in setting them apart from other ladies.

When contemporaries explained why ladies who were obliged to work preferred teaching to most other paid employments, they did not emphasize the ladies' economic prospects. These, it was agreed, were generally gloomy.[19] A few fortunate mistresses of highly fashionable schools (concentrated in London and the resort towns of southern England) made quite handsome profits, perhaps occasionally up to £1000 per annum for at least some years.[20] The good fortune of these lucky few helps to explain the continuing prestige of the occupation despite the fact that the great majority of private schoolmistresses were said to live at best a precarious existence on the fringes of gentility.[21] Even successful mistresses of select provincial establishments could seldom hope to earn much more than £300 a year[22] – barely enough for several sisters or a mother and daughter who kept a school to support the genteel life-style they had to maintain if they were to attract a select clientele.[23] It was not so much their pecuniary hopes as their preference for 'the gentilities of private life' that was thought to attract ladies who had to work to teaching.[24] Ladies, it was said, preferred to live in a secluded setting, surrounded by their social equals.[25] So far as possible, then, ladies who kept private schools attempted to order their affairs in conformity with the standards of those ladies who could afford to live protected, truly leisured lives amidst their families.

The family was thus the model for the small private school. A Miss Clarke recommended her London establishment in the following terms: 'The arrangements of the School are as much as possible like those of a Private Family and home-like habits and ways are carefully maintained.'[26] Another schoolmistress, denying a member of the Taunton Commission permission to visit her school noted: 'I think, sir, you have entirely mistaken the character of my establishment, which is not so much a school as a home for young ladies.'[27] The Sewell sisters, a former pupil recalled, 'were very indignant if "Ashcliffe" [their school] was called a school. It was a family home.'[28] Architecturally, at least, schools such as Ashcliffe were indistinguishable from truly domestic establishments. Such schools were lodged in substantial private dwellings adapted to the purpose.

The more fashionable the private school, the more closely it approximated the familial ideal. Boarding schools were deemed superior to day schools. They were more private in the sense that the external world intruded less upon the school. They were also more profitable and generally attracted a more select clientele. If a lady wished to upgrade her school, she attempted to attract boarders, slough off her day scholars, and raise her fees.[29] She did not attempt to expand her school greatly. The schools were small, usually with no more than twenty students, often fewer.[30] As one investigator reported to the Taunton Commission, private schoolmistresses did not wish to have large schools. They aimed rather to attract a small number of pupils of high social rank whom they could charge high fees.[31] Just as ladies in private life secured their social position by keeping a select, rather than a large and heterogeneous company, so ladies who taught sought to advance their position and that of their institutions not by making their schools large and comprehensive but by attracting a small but ever choicer clientele.

The content of the education they gave was in keeping with both the privatistic values and the private interests of the ladies who taught and reflected their leisured ideal. The accomplishments that dominated the curriculum were also the most profitable subjects to teach.[32] The two core subjects, music and French, were supplemented with a great variety of others, the number of subjects offered generally increasing with the rank of the school.[33] In addition to English subjects, history, geography, arithmetic, needlework, and religious instruction, the better provincial schools offered drawing, dancing, the piano and vocal music, German, and some sort of scientific lectures, while in highly fashionable establishments in London and southern England instruction in Italian and the harp was also commonly found. Not only was much the larger portion of the students' study time devoted to the more decorative studies, but also the teachers treated potentially serious subjects of scholarly inquiry in such a way as to make them seem merely ornamental. Critics lamented, for example, the unscientific way in which French was usually approached, with no regard being paid to general principles of grammar, and complained that as it was taught the subject had little value as an intellectual discipline.[34] Perhaps most remarkable was the scientific instruction most often offered in these private schools – the so-called 'use of globes.' Students were taught gracefully to manipulate spheres representing the solar system, often without being introduced to any of the principles of physics or astronomy. It was a curious adaptation of Newtonian physics to strictly ornamental ends.

That these accomplishments rather than reading, writing, and arithmetic dominated the curriculum was in keeping with the teachers' leisured, ornamental ideal. They aimed to fit their pupils to adorn a drawing room, not to spend time in the kitchen or behind a shop-counter. For purposes of shining in polite society and attracting a husband who could afford to give her a leisured life, a facility in music, dancing, and French was seemingly more functional to a young lady than great skill in computation or an easy familiarity with the nicer points of English grammar.

The curriculum reflected and reinforced the amateur character of the lady who taught. Since the number of subjects attempted in these tiny schools was very large and ladies who taught seldom specialized,[35] it could scarcely be hoped that these women would possess more than a passing acquaintance with the various subjects offered. But this was not expected. As one contemporary explained: 'What we ... seek for our children is not a learned machine stamped and ticketed with credentials ... but rather a woman endowed with that sound principle, refinement, and sense, which no committee of education in the world could ascertain ... all parents of sense must be aware that no governess can teach an ... accomplishment like a regular professor, and that her vocation is rather the encouraging and directing her pupils in such pursuits than the positive imparting of them.'[36] The function of the lady who taught was not, then, so much to transmit expert knowledge as to serve as a model of elegance and moral rectitude for her pupils. It was not primarily for her learnedness or expertise, but for her moral character, her charm, and refinement, in short for those personal attributes especially prized in private social concourse that the lady-teacher was primarily valued. She was, in effect, supposed to be a 'new corte-giano'[37] – a versatile, virtuous amateur who would, by the force of her example, gently win her pupils to the ways of virtue and familiarize them with the usages of polite society.

The essence of the lady-teacher's role was in fact quite simply to be a lady – to personify the well-bred, leisured woman. When, for example, the Sewell sisters' students learned deportment, one of the sisters acted as hostess and graciously received them. The more fashionable and successful the schoolmistress, the more nearly she tailored her activities to those of other truly leisured ladies. At the most fashionable establishments, the mistress of the school herself generally undertook no teaching duties.[38] Instead, she confined herself to supervising the efforts of resident governesses and visiting masters, much as the lady of a household would oversee the governesses and tutors of her offspring.

The aura of sentiment which prevailed in the small private schools was in keeping with the familial ideal. Teachers seem not to have hesitated to cultivate affectionate ties with their pupils, such as that which developed between Mary Ann Evans and Miss Lewis (the principal governess at one of the schools attended by George Eliot).[39] Given the familial ambience, it is not surprising to find schoolmistresses adopting a rather maternal tone towards their pupils; indeed, one private schoolmistress referred to ladies who taught as 'those unfortunate foster-parents.'[40] To enforce discipline, the schoolmistresses tended to rely on affective devices. Asked what she did when her students misbehaved, one schoolmistress replied, 'I say that I don't love them, that is always enough.'[41]

Private schoolmistresses generally rewarded pupils for their good behavior, for the effort they put forth, rather than for their objective achievements.[42] In the absence of a substantial peer group and any sort of public examinations, an individual pupil's progress was rather difficult to assess. In any case, it was not the function of the private teacher to judge her charges by some impersonal public standard and sort out the academically able. Rather she aimed to inculcate those social graces and qualities of mind and manner valued in the private sphere of life and to train her students for a domestic role.

Ladies who kept small, private schools were in a most difficult position. The very circumstances that sustained their claim that they were quite like other ladies undercut their status. The tiny size of their establishments, while in keeping with the familial ideal, limited their profits and placed them at the mercy of their small clientele. The polite fiction was that a lady who kept a school met her pupils' parents as an equal – as a lady receiving other ladies' daughters as a favor in her home. In fact, the private schoolmistress was in a distinctly subordinate position, obliged to defer to parental demands in ordering her establishment. Parents often treated the teachers shabbily, presenting and withdrawing their daughters at will, often with no prior notice, dickering over fees, interfering in curricular questions, exercising a veto over the schoolmistresses's admissions, and sometimes bullying them quite shamelessly.[43]

The fact that she was an amateur (while suggesting her affinity with other ladies) also undermined the private schoolmistress's authority in dealing with her pupils' parents. Unlike the elementary schoolmistress, who taught the children of the laboring poor and was usually better educated than her students' parents, the lady who taught could not claim deference from her clients on the basis of a superior expertise. Her amateur character further weakened the lady-teacher's economic position in that it encouraged a glut within the occupational group. Any woman could set herself up as a schoolmistress, and in the absence of any nationally recognized system of examinations or degrees it was not always easy to distinguish the competent from the incompetent. Complaints were voiced in the middle decades of the century that 'under-bred,' under-educated women – shopkeepers' and farmers' daughters were the groups usually specified – were taking to teaching and spoiling the market for the better-born, better-educated lady who taught.[44]

III

The movement to reform women's secondary and higher education was initiated in part as an effort to improve the position of such ladies.

Queen's College, founded in London in 1848, was one of the first reformed institutions for girls to be established.[45] The college grew out of a scheme to certify qualified governesses. When the ladies presenting themselves proved quite unable to pass an examination, a decision was made to offer lectures for their benefit. However, since it was considered undesirable to segregate ladies who taught from other ladies, from the beginning the college admitted young ladies other than practising or intending teachers.[46] Along with Bedford College and classes offered to women at University College, London, Queen's provided the highest education available to women until the Oxbridge women's colleges were founded, beginning with Girton and Newnham at Cambridge in 1869 and 1871. By 1894, when the Bryce Commission concluded its educational survey, four women's colleges had also been established at Oxford and two more in London.[47] Women had been admitted to all the degrees of the University of London in 1878 and to all those except medicine at Victoria University in 1884.[48] Gradually, in the 1880s and 1890s, Oxford and Cambridge opened their honors degree examinations to women, but women were denied degrees until the twentieth century.[49]

In the field of secondary education, girls had been admitted to the so-called Local Examinations conducted by Cambridge University on an experimental basis in 1863, formally in 1865, and to those of Oxford in 1870.[50] By 1894, there were over two hundred endowed and proprietary schools for girls, virtually all of them created or recreated in the period after 1850, the majority dating from after 1870. Most of the new girls' public schools were founded by local committees acting either independently or in concert with one of the national school companies.[51] In addition, some ancient foundations were reorganized by the Charity Commissioners, who also arranged endowments for newly founded institutions, and a few ambitious private schoolmistresses managed to transform their private schools into public institutions.[52]

'Public schools' were distinguished first in that they were not the private property of individuals and were not conducted primarily for private gain. The work done in them was scrutinized by publicly recognized authorities. Contemporaries further pointed to the liberal and advanced character of the instruction given in girls' schools preparing students directly for university and claimed that this, too, entitled such schools to be considered feminine analogues to the great male public schools.[53] In addition, public schools were sometimes distinguished by the 'public spirit' they were said to foster.[54]

The new girls' public schools were conceived as model societies.

Unlike the private schoolmistresses, who turned to familial metaphors in describing their establishments, public school teachers characterizing their institutions turned to the public sphere for analogues. One compared the government of a girls' public school to that of a 'constitutional monarchy.'[55] Another remarked with satisfaction that the introduction of elected form captains in her school had 'made the school more like a civic organization.'[56] A third, writing of the house system at St Leonard's School, St Andrews, referred to the 'loyalty and public spirit developed by this joint life of small communities [the houses] within a large one [the school].'[57]

Acting in their new, more public setting, reforming headmistresses aspired to a professional, rather than a private, leisured role.[58] As the president of the Association of Head Mistresses informed a conference of that body, 'The time had come when teachers should take their place as a learned profession.'[59] Whereas the private schoolmistresses' amateur character helped sustain their claim to elite status, the reforming headmistresses demanded deference in the first instance on the basis of their special intellectual expertise: 'Parents have to realise that the teacher is an expert professional and is entitled therefore to the deference shown to the skilled professional opinion of the doctor, lawyer, or architect.'[60] Beyond this claim to an authoritative, independent position based on special expertise, the headmistresses' idea of a professional was sometimes tied to an ethic of disinterested public service, as opposed to the pursuit of private gain. According to her biographer, Frances Mary Buss, for instance, desired 'that teaching should cease to be a mere trade ... and take its true place as foremost among the "learned professions," in which excellence of work, and not work's reward is the object of ambition.'[61] As professionals, then, headmistresses claimed a status superior to that of those engaged in trades on the basis of an assumed ethical superiority. Beyond this, the teachers' professional ideal was sometimes linked to a distinctive personal style. Their learnedness was to be expressed in an authoritative, reserved demeanor, in their restrained, well-disciplined, unostentatious appearance and behavior.[62]

IV

The professional claims of the reforming heads were sustained by the new institutional framework within which they functioned. Their institutional setting enabled the teachers to emancipate themselves from their clients' control, as they had to do if they were to claim and enjoy a status superior to that of mere purveyors of knowledge. As professionals, the teachers acted independently. They used their expert knowledge to determine what was in the best interest of their pupils; they did not merely carry out the dictates of their pupils' parents. Unlike the private schoolmistress (who totted up her bills like any tradesman and was the direct beneficiary of all manner of housekeeping and extra educational fees), the public school headmistress (whose school's fees were fixed and who sold no educational 'extras') was at least somewhat removed from the profiteering aspect of the private school enterprise and during her tenure of office enjoyed relative economic security. This favored the development of an independent outlook in these women. Generally, headmistresses were guaranteed a fixed salary which was supplemented with capitation fees. The headmistresses' professional incomes averaged very roughly £400 but rose as high as £2000 and even £3000 in exceptional cases.[63] They were congruent with the headmistresses' professional claims and lent a certain dignity to their position.[64] Together with the larger size of their schools (which ranged from less than one hundred students to over one thousand in the case of the Cheltenham complex by the turn of the century) their greater economic security freed the headmistresses from that immediate, total dependence upon a small circle of clients which placed the private schoolmistress at the mercy of her pupils' parents. Head mistresses could afford to take a more independent line, sometimes placing educational considerations before those of profit.[65] Gradually, the headmistresses emerged as the authoritative partner in the teacher-client relationship, with the teachers determining the conditions under which students would attend their schools.[66]

In addition to their new institutional setting, new educational and career patterns developing within the occupational group and participation in professional organizations encouraged headmistresses to assume a more professional role. Perhaps most crucial for their development as a group were the teachers' experiences in the new women's colleges. While some public school heads undertook and promoted special training courses in the field of education, the critical education for a public school teacher which ultimately determined her professional chances was the undergraduate education she received. By the 1890s, only a teacher with university training had any hope of professional advancement, and preference was apparently sometimes given to Oxbridge students when headships were to be filled.[67] Furthermore, an assistant teacher with first class honors usually stood to gain a higher salary than one with a second class degree.[68] Whereas the status of ladies who kept private schools in early nineteenth-century England was but tenuously related to their intellectual skills and training, the public school teacher's status was thus linked very directly to her academic achievements.

The provision of institutions of higher education for women in effect served a dual function, barring not just the inadequately educated but also the improperly socialized from the upper reaches of the teaching profession. Once advanced education became a prerequisite for securing a plum teaching post, the pool of possible candidates was limited to those who could obtain the proper training. A study of the registers of the early Oxbridge women's colleges (attended by about a quarter, perhaps more, of the women who joined the Head Mistresses' Association during its first two decades)[69] indicated that these institutions, at least, catered primarily to the upper middle class, especially to the daughters of professional people. At the four earliest female colleges at Oxford and Cambridge, of the students entering in or before 1894 whose father's occupation is reported in the college registers, 64 per cent were professionals' daughters, 25 per cent the daughters of business or tradesmen, as may be seen in Table 1.[70] A few poor but able girls, such as Sara Burstall, whose case is mentioned below, did enter the universities and went on to teach. However, the main effect of these advanced educational institutions upon recruitment to the upper ranks of the teaching profession was to give an edge to those women whose family's financial means and intellectual commitments encouraged and enabled them to obtain advanced academic training.[71] While scholarships were granted at the women's colleges, they seldom covered the full fees, so that except in unusual cases a man with several children would have had to be rather well-to-do in order to take advantage of the assistance offered.[72]

At the new women's colleges, the prospective teacher might obtain a professional education in the broadest sense, acquiring not only the intellectual skills but also the attitudes and style deemed appropriate to her future work. She might gain, as one early Girton student (the daughter of a mine owner) said she had gained, 'some appreciation of the scholarly, as distinguished from the man-of-business way of looking at things.'[73] At the Oxbridge colleges a girl apparently found herself largely in the company of professional men's daughters, engaged in a routine which emphasized plain living and high thinking. The aristo-

TABLE 1
Occupation of students' fathers in four female Oxbridge colleges through 1894
(percentages within parentheses)

	Professional[a]	Business and tradesmen[b]	Other[c]	Total known	Unknown	Total
Girton	250 (58)[d]	133 (31)	50 (11)	433	97	530
Newnham	121 (60)	63 (31)	17 (8)	201	749	950
Lady Margaret Hall	78 (93)	1 (1)	5 (6)	84	116	200
Somerville	43 (77)	–	13 (23)	56	185	241
Total	492 (64)	197 (25)	85 (11)	774	1,147	1,921

SOURCE: This table, which records the occupations of students' fathers as reported in the college registers from the founding of the colleges through 1894, was compiled from Christine Anson, ed., *Lady Margaret Hall Register 1879–1924* (Oxford 1928); *Newnham College Register 1871–1950* (Cambridge 1963); *Somerville College Register 1879–1938* (Oxford 1939); and *Girton College Register 1869–1946* (Cambridge 1948).

For Girton, in addition to the published *Register*, I was able to see the Admissions Book, which, beginning in 1884, listed the students' fathers' occupations. Although a much larger proportion of the Girton students' origins were thus discovered than in the case of Newnham (which I was informed kept no such records in the early years), the proportion of professional to business and trades people turned out to be quite similar in both cases.

a Professional occupations included: clergy 182, academic/scholar (some in holy orders) 91, medicine 57, law 56, India/civil/ other government service 29, military officer 28, engineer 15, artist 10, journalist/editor 5, accountant 4, architect 3, poet 3, musician/composer 3, librarian/archivist 2, surveyor 2, shorthand writer to House of Commons 1, veterinarian 1
b The categories of business and tradesmen with ten or more members were: merchant 61, manufacturer 33, director/head/manager of a company 12, banker 11, agent 10, draper 10
c The larger groups in this miscellaneous category were: self-styled 'gentlemen' (presumably men of independent means) 21, titular aristocrats for whom no occupation was listed 18, and farmers 16
d Percentage of known students to the nearest per cent

cratic sets, which played an important, if diminishing role in some of the male colleges and whose tastes tended in the opposite direction, were never prominent in the women's colleges. The students' rooms were spacious but not luxurious. The prevailing style of dress was simple and retiring.[74] The meals were excessively plain. The daily routine presupposed a certain disinterested intellectual commitment and self-discipline. Study, lessons, cocoa parties, walks, student societies (for debate, literary discussion, and so on), and beginning in the 1880s, organized games – these were the main activities.[75] It was obviously not a routine calculated to appeal to a young lady aspiring to a life of high fashion.

A large proportion – over half – of the early Oxbridge women students did teach,[76] and women who entered college with no idea of teaching sometimes determined while there to embark on a teaching career although they were under no economic compulsion to do so.[77] This suggests the influence of the colleges in altering the idea of teaching from that of the last resort of the destitute gentlewoman to that of a desirable profession meriting, finally demanding, advanced academic training.

Having left college, the aspiring headmistress had an apprenticeship to serve as an assistant teacher. Groomed by a successful head, the young teacher had a further opportunity to acquire the skills and habits and the outlook suited to her professional group or be denied further advancement. In effect, the public school headmistresses assumed at least a partial responsibility for regulating their membership, first in deciding which students to recommend for financial assistance at school and at college, later in determining which assistant teachers to recommend for hiring and promotion. Along with the new educational requirements, the system of 'sponsored mobility'[78] developing within the occupational group made it highly unlikely that, whatever her family origins, a woman who deviated significantly from the professional academic norm would gain entry into the higher ranks of the teaching profession. Few nineteenth-century headmistresses seem to have been memorable for their eccentricities. Such oddities as they did display seem minor and tended in the direction of extra plain living and high thinking, rather than the reverse.[79]

Sara Burstall is a case in point.[80] She was the daughter of a London builder. Although not destitute, the Burstalls were poor and their lifestyle was not genteel. They could not afford books or regular holidays or public schools for their sons. They drank small beer with their meals, a habit, writes Miss Burstall, that the children later despised.[81] Sara was first sent to the Camden School (a so-called 'middle school,' which educated girls only to about age fifteen), where, proving an exceptionally able student, she was singled out for special instruction and won a scholarship to the North London Collegiate School, where more advanced teaching was available. From there, with a scholarship which covered almost all her fees, she proceeded on to Girton, where she learned how to do mathematics and drink strong tea. Returning as an assistant teacher to the North London Collegiate, she was groomed for a headship by Miss Buss. Miss Buss not only encouraged her assistants to improve their proficiency in their special fields of study but also helped favored members of her staff extend their cultural horizons in other directions, inviting them to attend the theater and to accompany her on trips abroad. Thus a woman such as Miss Burstall, whose family's means had not permitted her such advantages as a girl, might be encouraged to develop the tastes and life-style of the upper middle-class. In 1898 the efforts of Miss Buss and her protégée were rewarded when Miss Burstall was appointed headmistress of the Manchester High School for Girls.

Participation in professional organizations further served to foster the headmistresses' conception of themselves as a professional group. Local schoolmistresses' associations began appearing in the 1860s, first in London, then in other cities and towns. National organizations followed. In 1874, the Association of Head Mistresses of Endowed and Proprietary Schools was founded, followed by the complementary Association of Assistant Mistresses in Secondary Schools in 1884. These two organizations cooperated with a third, the Teachers' Guild, established in 1885, which included all grades of teachers in its membership and aimed among other things, 'To obtain for the whole body of Teachers the status and authority of a learned profession.'[82]

Like most professional organizations the teachers' associations attempted to improve their members' competence. Discussion meetings and conferences were held. The London Schoolmistresses' Association went on record as favoring some sort of registration of schools and teachers in order to distinguish the competent.[83] The Head Mistresses' Association urged the opening of university examinations to women.[84]

Beyond encouraging their members to consider themselves as experts and to improve their expertise, the teachers' associations promoted their development as a social group with a distinctive style and distinctive values. At a meeting of the London Schoolmistresses' Association, for example, it was remarked that jewelry was worn too much by older students and sometimes by assistant teachers as well. Further, 'It was observed that girls who care most for dress are those who care least for study & general culture insensibly lessens the love of display & love of ornaments.'[85] Thus a connection was drawn between a sober (professional) appearance and a commitment to certain values which gave priority to love of learning as opposed to the display (and implicitly the pursuit) of wealth. In a somewhat similar vein, the Head Mistresses'

Association passed resolutions aimed at protecting its members from appearing to have a direct financial interest in their dealings with their clientele. Teachers, the association resolved, ought not to accept gifts from their clients and ought to discountenance the use of monetary fines as penalties for misbehavior as far as possible.[86]

v

Unlike the successful private schoolmistress, who generally dissociated herself from the actual business of instruction, public school headmistresses usually taught. Most often they seem to have taught the upper forms within their schools. This suggests a rough correlation between status and level of academic expertise developing within the profession and signals a further shifting away from the amateur ideal.

Curricular reform in the new schools was usually initiated by the headmistresses, often in the face of some parental opposition.[87] The content of the new education was a piece with the reforming headmistresses' professional claims, their shift away from exclusively privatistic aims and interests to a more public-oriented ideal. The accomplishments, dancing, drawing, and the like, gradually disappeared from the curriculum or were relegated to a minor place, as a more rigorous academic course was introduced, the content of which was backed by publicly recognized authorities – the universities. The main emphasis in most girls' public schools was literary but, in addition, more attention was given to mathematics and the natural sciences than was usual in the small private schools.[88] The teaching was more thorough, the subjects were carried further in the new public schools than had generally been the case. In the lower public school forms, pupils routinely acquired the basic arithmetic and literary skills required for the conduct of virtually all sorts of public business. In the higher forms, students might attempt the more arcane linguistic and mathematical subjects – including Latin, sometimes Greek, trigonometry, and calculus – required for university work and professional pursuits.

The headmistresses' view of the culture they were to transmit was Arnoldian, embracing the individual in both his private and his public roles.[89] They spoke of the dual aim of education: 'The perfection of the individual and the good of the community.'[90] Headmistresses might differ in the relationship they perceived between individual perfection and public improvement, but they seem generally to have considered the two ends as mutually compatible rather than conflicting. Echoing

John Stuart Mill, Miss Beale thought of public progress as the sum of individual improvement: 'it is not by starving the individual life, and merging it in the general, but by developing each to perfection that the common good will be secured,' she wrote.[91] Another headmistress, Mrs Woodhouse (head first of the Sheffield, then the Clapham High School), saw the two processes as somewhat more integrally related. Quoting the Oxford idealist T.H. Green, she contended that 'through civic institutions alone is it possible for the idea of moral perfection to be realized by human beings.'[92] Although the public schools were, of course, elitist institutions that did not cater directly to the general public,[93] the headmistresses considered that indirectly they promoted the general weal in attempting to train a generation of civic-minded women who would, so it was hoped, be mindful not just of their individual or familial needs but also of the public interest. Just as their own claim to elite, professional status rested in part on their contention that they did not simply pursue their private interests but also served a larger, public good, so the headmistresses sought to pass on cultural values which emphasized the individual's public as well as private role.

In a variety of ways, headmistresses sought to foster public interests in their pupils, to prepare them to play a public part. Headmistresses instituted student governments in their schools and watched the establishment of school debating and other special interest societies with a sympathetic eye. At the North London Collegiate School, Miss Buss lectured her students on 'Public Spirit.'[94] When in the 1880s organized games began to be an important part of girls' public school life, these were prized by some headmistresses for the corporate spirit and public virtues they supposedly instilled, for 'the development of powers of organisation ... a knowledge of corporate action ... the effort of loyally working with others for the common good.'[95]

Unlike the private schoolmistresses, who attempted to govern by affective tactics, the public school heads, as befit the leaders of model societies, sought to rule by law. Students, Miss Beale contended, must 'not do right for love of you [the teacher] but because it is right.'[96] Discipline was not to be achieved through appeals of a personal or affective nature. ('There should not be equal friendship and familiarity between teacher and taught,' another headmistress warned. 'This is only weakening for both.')[97] Nor were teachers and students to be linked by emotional ties, as unique individuals to one another. Instead, teacher and pupil were bound by a common obligation to respect moral and intellectual standards which made no exceptions as to persons.

'The chief good of school lies ... in the absence of special exemptions,'[98] wrote one public school head.

In contrast to the private schoolmistress, who judged her pupils almost exclusively in terms of their unique, personal merits, rewarding the 'effort' they put forth rather than their objective achievements, the public school heads also applied impersonal, public standards to their pupils. Prizes were given for achievement within the schools.[99] Students were put in for public examinations, to which scholarships were sometimes attached. In deciding which students to send in for examinations, which to recommend for financial assistance both within their schools and at the women's colleges, the headmistresses in effect assumed what was for them a new public function – that of sorting out the academically able pupils. Further, in influencing students in their decision to go – or not go – on to university, perhaps to obtain professional training, as they sometimes did,[100] the public school heads assumed a measure of responsibility for allocating pupils to their future social roles.

The new ethic of the public school heads expressed itself in the novel sorts of public work they undertook. Whereas private schoolmistresses clung to the gentilities of private life, reforming headmistresses sought distinction in the public sphere. Few had so distinguished a public career as Dame Frances Dove (headmistress of St Leonard's School, then of Wycombe Abbey), who was elected to the Wycombe town council, served as justice of the peace, and was created DBE in 1928, but numbers of headmistresses did severe in local government.[101] Eminent headmistresses frequently sat on the governing boards of educational institutions.[102] Some were active in settlement or other types of civic work.[103] Headmistresses acted as experts. They testified before royal commissions, joined learned societies, wrote books and articles on educational questions or in their special disciplines.[104] Undertaking a variety of the forms of public service, the public school heads expressed their rejection of the amateur ideal and privatistic values which informed the activities of the private schoolmistress and demonstrated their commitment to a professional ideal which stressed the merits of expertise and assumed an obligation to serve the public good.

VI

The headmistresses' assumption of what was for women a new social role and their elaboration of a corresponding set of values should probably be viewed as one facet of the movement by which in the mid and late Victorian period, partly through the medium of the public schools and universities, elite status was secured for the offspring of successful business and professional men who were unable or unwilling to be assimilated to the older, leisured gentle tradition. Like the public school headmasters whom they emulated (from whom, indeed, they took their name[105]), the headmistresses were the carriers of a new, professional, meritocratic ideal.[106] Attempting to win elite status for their group, the headmistresses defined their status claims in such a way as to place more emphasis upon academic achievement and institutional affiliation, less upon ascriptive characteristics and a leisured life style than had traditionally been the case. They rejected the privatistic values which governed the curricular offerings and institutional arrangements of the private schoolmistress and the amateur role she played. Instead they chose to assume a more professional mien, claiming to be guided by an ethic of public service, rather than one of private gain. Like other modern professional groups, the headmistresses sought to free themselves from direct dependence upon individual patrons, to gain an independent position based on their special expertise.[107] Their new institutional setting, with its expanded clientele, offered the teachers an avenue of escape from the ambiguous, distressed, dependent position of the private schoolmistress.

The headmistresses were not alone responsible for the reforms in women's education. The teachers found allies in other groups: parents mindful of status concerns, who wished their daughters to receive an education which would distinguish them from the mass of middle class females; male academics committed to providing a liberal education for women; and feminists who wished girls to be prepared for an extended range of public employments.[108] However, the headmistresses did play a vital part in establishing and shaping the 'new model' schools for girls, attempting to create an institutional environment which accorded with their professional values. Headmistresses in some cases founded or assisted in the initial organization of their institutions, and it was usually the teachers who initiated curricular and other reforms within the schools. Without the teachers' professional vision to structure the reforms, girls' secondary education might well have developed rather differently than it did in the mid and late Victorian years.

The headmistresses' activities are of special interest as they relate to the increasing participation of well-born English women in organized public life in the late nineteenth and early twentieth centuries. In keeping with their more public-oriented ideal, the reforming headmistresses encouraged their students to assume more public roles than had been thought consonant with good breeding in the case of women in early nineteenth-century England. The connection between the reforms made in women's secondary and higher education and women's entry into public life needs further investigation, but it seems likely that the public schools which the reforming headmistresses helped create provided one setting in which young women could acquire not only intellectual skills but also values which enabled and encouraged them, when other circumstances were propitious, to attempt public roles previously not within the purlieu of their sex.

NOTES

This article is from the *Journal of British Studies*, 15 (Nov. 1975), 135–62, published by the University of Chicago Press. © 1989 by The North American Conference on British Studies. Reprinted with permission.

  This essay is based on research done for a doctoral dissertation, 'The Reform of Women's Secondary and Higher Education in 19th Century England: A Study in Elite Groups,' University of California, Berkeley, June 1974. I am much indebted to Sheldon Rothblatt for his generosity in sharing his ideas and kind encouragement. I am also grateful to the Association of Head Mistresses of Endowed and Proprietary Schools, the Girls' Public Day School Trust, and Girton College for permitting me to use their archives and to the University of California, Berkeley, which supported my research.

 1 These include Phyllis D. Hicks, *A Quest of Ladies: The Story of a Warwickshire School* ([London] 1949); Eleanor L. Sewell, ed., *The Autobiography of Elizabeth M. Sewell* (London 1907); and Anna M. Stoddart, *Life and Letters of Hannah E. Pipe* (London 1908). Miss Pipe was a transitional figure who participated in some aspects of the reform movement but remained rather conservative in her general outlook. Winifred Gerin's *Charlotte Bronte: The Evolution of Genius* (Oxford 1967) includes information about the Misses Woolers' establishment, where Charlotte was a pupil and a teacher.

 2 Rev. G. Butler, 'Education Considered as a Profession for Women' in *Woman's Work and Woman's Culture*, ed. Josephine E. Butler (London 1869), 49–77; Emily Davies, *Thoughts on Some Questions Relating*

to Women, 1860 – 1908 (Cambridge 1910); [Bessie Rayner Parkes],
'The Profession of the Teacher: The Annual Reports of the Governesses'
Benevolent Institution from 1843 to 1856,' *The English Woman's
Journal*, I (1858), 1–13; [Elizabeth Sewell], *Principles of Education,
drawn from Nature and Revelation, and applied to Female Education
in the Upper Classes* (New York 1870). Unlike the other reformers cited
here, who had feminist sympathies, Miss Sewell was a conservative
educational critic who wished girls to be given an improved education
along traditional lines.

3 *Schools Inquiry Commission Report* in *Parliamentary Papers*, 1867–68
(Cd. 3966): hereafter *SIC*

4 *Ibid.*, VII, 69

5 The largest single body of data about the nineteenth-century reforms
is that found in the *Report of the Royal Commission on Secondary
Education* in *Parliamentary Papers*, 1895 (Cd. 7862): hereafter *Bryce*.
This includes some information about women's higher as well as
secondary education. It may be noticed that '1894' appears later in this
essay as the cutoff date for some other data gathered. The date was
chosen so that the data would tally with those gathered by the commission, which concluded its survey that year. The best general account of
the reforms remains Alice Zimmern's *The Renaissance of Girls' Education in England: A Record of Fifty Years' Progress* (London 1898).

6 The Oxford and Cambridge Schools Examination Board, formed in
1873, examined both girls' and boys' schools which gave evidence of
providing an education of the highest grade. Also, students were sent
in for public examinations conducted under the universities' auspices.

7 The biographies include Sara A. Burstall, *Frances Mary Buss* (London
1938); Josephine Kamm, *How Different from Us; A Biography of Miss
Buss and Miss Beale* (London 1959); Annie E. Ridley, *Frances Mary
Buss and Her Work for Education* (London 1895); Elizabeth Raikes,
Dorothea Beale of Cheltenham (London 1910); Elizabeth H. Shillito,
Dorothea Beale (London 1920); and F. Cecily Steadman, *In the Days
of Miss Beale* (London [1931]).

Other early headmistresses for whom full-fledged biographies and
autobiographies exist include Sara A. Burstall, *Retrospect and Prospect*
(London 1933); Elsie Bowerman, *Stands There a School: Memories of
Dame Frances Dove, D.B.E., Founder of Wycombe Abbey School* (Brighton [1966]); Lilian M. Faithfull, *In the House of My Pilgrimage* (London
1924); Frances R. Gray, *And Gladly Wolde He Lerne and Gladly Teche*
(London 1931); Mary E. James, *Alice Ottley: First Head-Mistress of the*

Worcester High School for Girls, 1883–1912 (London 1914); and
Agnes S. Paul, *Some Memories of Mrs. Woodhouse: Sheffield High
School 1878–98, Clapham High School 1898–1912* (London 1924).

8 Among them G.M. Young's *Victorian England: Portrait of an Age* (London 1936) and R.C.K. Ensor's *England 1870–1914* (Oxford 1936). But more often the movement in women's education has been ignored in social histories of the period.

Of the 202 women who joined the Association of Head Mistresses of Endowed and Proprietary Schools from 1874 through 1894, only two, Dorothea Beale and Dame Frances Dove (headmistress first of St Leonard's, then of Wycombe Abbey), found their way into the *Dictionary of National Biography*.

9 Peter Laslett discussed the components of gentle status in pre-industrial England in *The World We Have Lost* (New York 1965), chap. 2; G. Kitson Clark, *The Making of Victorian England* (New York 1967), 258–65; W.L. Burn, *The Age of Equipoise* (New York 1964), 253–67; and Geoffrey Best, *Mid-Victorian Britain 1851–1871* (New York 1971), 245–56, analyzed how the concept of gentility was modified in the mid-Victorian era, noting the new importance given a public school education and the inclusion of professional status as a hallmark of gentility.

10 Philip Elliott in *The Sociology of the Professions* (New York 1972), esp. pp 20–2, argues plausibly that unlike modern professional groups, professional men in the pre-industrial period were accorded gentle status less because they performed a professional function or possessed a special expertise than because they associated with a high status clientele, could live a leisured, cultured life, and (since the professions provided some younger sons of the gentry with a living) fit into a society in which status was largely governed by family position and inherited wealth.

11 Only certain categories of private schoolmistresses concern us – those who kept boarding or mixed boarding and day schools, attended for the most part by the daughters of the gentry and upper middle-class. Girls of lower middle class – shopkeepers' and clerks' and farmers' daughters – were usually educated in private day schools. The women who kept these schools, which were not considered 'genteel,' do not concern us. *SIC*, IX, 794, 821, 823, 826–7

12 This section is very much indebted to M. Jeanne Peterson's 'The Victorian Governess: Status Incongruence in Family and Society,' *Victorian Studies*, XIV (1970), 7–26.

13 As Peterson observed, the association of high status with leisure lingered on longer in the case of women than with men, and a gentleman's own elite status was expressed in part in his ability to support his wife and daughters in a leisured state. *Ibid.*, 9, 14

14 Standards varied and were seldom carefully defined, but when contemporaries *did* draw the line of gentility in the mid-Victorian era, they seem most often to have placed tradesmen's daughters who kept day schools catering primarily to tradesmen's and farmers' daughters beyond the pale. See James Bryce's classification of schools and schoolmistresses, *SIC*, IX, 794, 821–7; [Elizabeth Eastlake], '*Vanity Fair* and *Jane Eyre* and the Governesses' Benevolent Institution,' *Quarterly Review*, LXXXIX (1848), 153–185, 176, 180.

15 Such is the opinion of A.M. Carr-Saunders and P.A. Wilson, *The Professions* (Oxford 1933), 295.

16 When, for instance, a young lady noticed that Jane Eyre's accomplishments were unusual in an elementary schoolmistress, it was the social rather than the academic implications of the discovery that intrigued her. She thought Jane a '*lusus naturae*' as a village schoolmistress and decided Jane was 'clever enough to be a governess in a high family.' It was not just Jane's accomplishments in their own right but also the fact that they indicated that she must be well-born which made her think Jane suited to teach the daughters of the upper classes. Charlotte Bronte, *Jane Eyre* (New York 1961), 416–17

17 'Most of them have been driven by misfortune ... accidents of all kinds, more or less unexpected, into tuition.' *SIC*, VIII, 394. Parkes, 'Profession,' *The English Woman's Journal*, I, 1

18 *SIC*, I, 561. The Misses Woolers' case seems to have been typical. When their father's death brought the sisters 'greater independence,' they soon considered selling the goodwill of their school, although the eldest sister was then only in her mid-forties and the youngest in her early thirties. Gerin's *Charlotte Bronte* gives some details.

19 Unfortunately, no systematic information about the private schoolmistresses' incomes exists. The Taunton Commission was not empowered to compel the teachers to provide such information and was largely thwarted in its attempts to inquire into monetary matters. It was noted that differences in housekeeping expenditures among private boarding schools made any guesses highly unreliable, and the commission did not venture estimates of the incomes of persons keeping such schools. *SIC*, IX, 683. The commission's investigators and witnesses were, however, agreed in their impression that the overwhelming majority of

private schoolmistresses were anything but prosperous. *Ibid.*, IX, 819; VIII, 479; Emily Davies' Testimony, V, 246, 11363.

20 Fees in such schools might range from 120 to 150 guineas a year. *Ibid.*, VII, 70. Such schools were small, usually with less than twenty pupils, and overhead costs were high. For their seven students, the Sewell sisters, for instance, kept a domestic staff of eight or nine, and in instructing the students the three sisters were assisted by two nieces who lived with them and by visiting masters. Mrs Hugh Fraser, *A Diplomatist's Wife in Many Lands* (London 1911), I, 204 gives the details. Further, it might take some years to establish such a school to run at a profit and meanwhile debts might be incurred. Such was the Byerly sisters' experience. It took them some thirteen years to establish their very successful school securely. Despite the fact that the eight sisters were the beneficiaries of one bequest of £800 and another of £200 apiece, they had to turn often to their cousin Josiah Wedgwood (son of the famous potter) for loans in the early years. Hicks, *Quest*, pp 55, 70–1. While all these circumstances limited profits, a woman with fifteen or twenty boarders paying from 120 to 150 guineas would have realized substantial profits, even with the most generous allowance for housekeeping and tuition expenses.

21 As one investigator reported to the Taunton Commission, 'a lady may toil her whole life long in the service of the country gentry and clergy and yet her savings will be barely sufficient to secure for her, when she is too old to work, a small annuity.' *SIC*, VIII, 479

22 Fees in the best provincial boarding schools, most of them mixed day and boarding establishments, averaged around £70 for boarders and £20 to £30 for day scholars. *Ibid.*, IX, 800–1; VIII, 239. With twenty pupils, even the more exclusive of these schools would seldom have given a profit of much over £300, and many must have given less.

Fees in the cheaper day schools ranged from £3 to £10, which meant that a woman with twenty students would have had a gross income of from £60 to £200 from which she must deduct rent, repairs, taxes, and the cost of an assistant or two. Such schools would scarcely ever have yielded a profit of much over £100 and must often have given much less. *Ibid.*, IX, 800; VIII, 239.

23 J.A. Banks, *Prosperity and Parenthood* (London 1965), 41–5, 115, cited contemporary discussions as to whether £300 per annum would suffice for a newly married couple to keep a genteel life-style in the mid-Victorian years, and noted the case of Anthony Trollope who, a bit earlier, in the period 1830–40, found it impossible to live like a gentle-

man in London on a salary ranging from £90 to £140 a year without going into debt. James Bryce classified 'persons whose incomes range from £150 to £600 per annum (excluding the professional men)' as 'lower' (as opposed to upper) middle class, *SIC*, ix, 823, 826–7. Best quoted a contemporary statistician who considered £500 an 'upper middle class' income and concluded that '£300 did not carry a family man far up the slopes of gentility.' *Mid-Victorian Britain*, 90

24 Parkes, 'Profession,' *The English Woman's Journal*, i, 10

25 *SIC*, viii, 480

26 Girls' Public Day School Trust Archives, letter from Miss Clarke to Mrs Grey, 29 Aug. [c. 1870]

27 *SIC*, vii, 211

28 Fraser, *Diplomatist's Wife*, i, 204–5

29 This pattern of upward mobility is nicely illustrated by the case of Hannah Pipe, who began by opening a small day school with her widowed mother in their Manchester home in 1848. Gradually, the ladies acquired boarders who were charged thirty guineas a year. In 1856, the ladies moved their establishment to London. Here they accepted no day pupils and the boarders were charged eighty guineas per annum. In 1860, they moved to a grander London establishment, where it seems the fees were one hundred guineas. While highly successful, the school remained small, with twenty-five girls in 1862. Stoddart's *Life of Pipe* gives the details.

30 Private girls' schools were estimated to average around twenty pupils. *SIC*, vii, 114; ix, 281, 794. Since it was doubtless easier to locate large schools than very small ones, the estimates may well be high.

31 *Ibid.*, ix, 282. The Sewell sisters, for example, could evidently easily have enlarged their popular school, for parents put in their daughters' names for places years in advance. But during the forty years the sisters kept the school, the students numbered only from six to ten. Sewell, *Autobiography*, 117; Fraser, *Diplomatist's Wife*, i, 205

32 The basic tuition fee generally covered only instruction in the English subjects and (in the more exclusive schools) French, while lessons in music, drawing, dancing, and so on were charged as 'extras.' It was especially on the 'extras' that a mistress made her profits. The amount charged for the basic course of instruction was generally only about one-third or two-thirds of the amount parents paid for instruction in the accomplishments. *SIC*, ix, 282–3

33 Information about the curricula in different sorts of girls' schools is sprinkled throughout the Taunton Report; see esp. *ibid.*, vii, 199–200;

VIII, 507–8, 585–612; IX, 803. Music was especially emphasized: 'At present music occupies pretty nearly as much of a girl's life as classics do of a boy's,' reported one investigator. *Ibid.*, IX, 815

34 *Ibid.*, IX, 292

35 The female teachers who did specialize seem most often to have done so in music or modern languages. Unfortunately, the censuses are not as helpful as they might be in indicating the numbers. The 1851 Census listed four categories of female teachers: Music Mistress (2,296); Schoolmistress (39,619); Governess (20,058); and other Teachers (4,936). The 1861 Census listed eight categories, but music teacher was not among them. The largest group of female specialists listed in 1861 were the 982 language teachers.

36 Eastlake, *'Vanity Fair,'* *Quarterly Review*, LXXXIX, 184–5. The author was criticizing a scheme being mooted by the founders of Queen's College, London (one of the first schools to be established along reformed lines for girls) to offer certificates to qualified governesses.

37 G.M. Young developed the idea that educated women were heirs to the Renaissance ideal in 'The New Cortegiano,' in *Victorian Essays*, ed., W.D. Handcock (London 1962), 202–16.

38 *SIC*, VII, 70. Sometimes the assistant mistresses in such schools did not teach either, and all instruction was left to visiting masters, but this was unusual. Generally, the male teachers would just visit a school once or twice a week to give special, advanced instruction in the accomplishments, always in the presence of a governess.

39 J.W. Cross, *George Eliot's Life as Related in her Letters and Journals* (Boston 1884), I, 16 gives an account of the friendship and their correspondence.

40 Sewell, *Principles*, 386

41 *SIC*, IX, 817

42 *Ibid.*, VII, 214

43 One investigator observed that 'the first noticeable fact in ladies' boarding schools is the subjection of the teacher's will in every instance to the wishes of the parents, in many instances to the whims of the pupils ... in their anxiety to exclude from schools patronized by themselves all girls of an inferior class, [parents] exercise a control over schoolmistresses which is often very oppressive and tyrannical.' *Ibid.*, VIII, 478–9

A pupil of the Sewell sisters recalled that these ladies had circularized their students' parents (apparently gentry and professional people)

before venturing to admit a businessman's daughter to their school.
Fraser, *Diplomatist's Wife*, I, 208

44 Eastlake, '*Vanity Fair*,' *Quarterly Review*, LXXXIX, 180; *SIC*, VIII, 43-4;
Sewell, *Principles*, 439

45 Histories of the College include Rosalie Glynn Grylls, *Queen's College
1848-1948* (London 1948); Elaine Kaye, *A History of Queen's College
(Harley Street)* (London 1972); Mrs Alex Tweedie, ed., *The First College
Open to Women. Queen's College, London. Memories and Records of
Work Done 1848-1898* [n.p., n.d.].

46 Rev. Frederick Denison Maurice, 'Queen's College, London: Its Objects
and Method,' in *Introductory Lectures Delivered at Queen's College
London* (London 1849), 5

47 These were Somerville and Lady Margaret Hall (both 1879), St Hugh's
Hall (1886), and St Hilda's (1893) at Oxford; Westfield (1882) and
Royal Holloway (1886) in London.

48 Victoria University consisted of Owen's College, Manchester; Yorkshire
College, Leeds; and University College, Liverpool.

49 The universities' reluctance to grant degrees to qualified women
stemmed partly from the fact that degrees carried with them the
privileges attendant upon full membership in the universities, such as
eligibility for participation in university administration. Oxford
granted qualified women degrees in 1920. Cambridge granted them the
titles of degrees in 1921, denying them degrees until 1948.

50 The Preliminary, Junior, and Senior Local Examinations (for students
under the ages of fourteen, sixteen, and nineteen) had been established by Oxford and Cambridge in 1857 and 1858 respectively. Each
university appointed a special syndicate which supervised the examinations, held at various local centers where students might present
themselves.

51 The largest of these were the Girls' Public Day School Company and
the Church Schools Company. Guaranteed local support in the form
of shares taken locally, these companies would assist in founding and
administering schools. E. Moberly Bell, *A History of the Church
Schools Company 1883-1958* (London 1958); Laurie Magnus, *The
Jubilee Book of the Girls' Public Day School Trust 1873-1923* (Cambridge 1923); and Kathleen D.B. Littlewood, *Some Account of the History of the Girls' Public Day School Trust* [London 1960].

52 Most notable of these private schoolmistresses were Frances Mary Buss,
whose North London Collegiate School was widely used as a model by

later public schools, and the Lawrence sisters, whose Rodean School
rose to great prominence, but remained under private ownership until
the 20th century. For the latter, see Dorothy E. de Zouche, *Rodean
School 1885–1955* (Brighton 1955).

53 'A Public School is a school ... not carried on for private profit. This is
the primary ... meaning of the name, but it has come to be applied
only to schools which lead on their pupils directly to University.' Gray,
And Gladly, 77–8

'We [the Girls' Public Day School Company schools] claim to corre-
spond to ... Eton ... and schools of that sort ... inasmuch as there is no
other class of public school which gives a higher education than we do.'
Bryce, W.H. Stone's Testimony, II, 171, 1684

54 Thus Alice Zimmern, *Renaissance*, 161–2, thought that 'true' public
schools were those in which students helped administer the school's
government.

55 Dorothea Beale, Lucy H.M. Soulsby, Jane Frances Dove, *Work and Play
in Girls' Schools by Three Headmistresses* (London 1898), 22

56 Quoted in Olive Carter, *History of the Gateshead High School,
1876–1907 and Central Newcastle High School 1895–1955* [n.p.,
n.d.], 43

57 Zimmern, *Renaissance*, 156

58 This section is much indebted to Sheldon Rothblatt's *The Revolution
of the Dons, Cambridge and Society in Victorian England* (New York
1968), esp. 90–3. Rothblatt stressed that for those reforming dons who
claimed professional status the professional ideal was more than an
occupational category based on special expertise. It also encompassed
both a broader social ethic (that of disinterested service, as opposed to
the pursuit of private profit) and a reserved personal style by which
professional men might hope to distinguish themselves from the lower
order of flashy, bumptious men of trade.

59 Association of Head Mistresses, *Annual Conference Minutes*, II, 20 June
1891, 151

60 Burstall, *Retrospect*, 161. Miss Burstall was headmistress of the Manchester High School for Girls.

61 Ridley, *Frances Mary Buss*, 91

62 Thus the headmistresses tended to favor a severe sartorial style and
sometimes enforced this on their assistants as well. At Central Newcastle, the headmistress Miss Moberly prescribed a coat, a skirt with
a shirt blouse, a stiff collar, and a tie for herself and her assistants.
Carter, *Gateshead and Central Newcastle*, 35. Miss Beale's biographer

writes of her 'half-expressed' wish that the Cheltenham staff wear black to express their sense of vocation. Raikes, *Dorothea Beale*, 250

63 'GIRLS' SCHOOLS WITH SPECIAL REGARD TO SALARIES OF HEAD MISTRESSES AS RECOMMENDED BY THE ENDOWED SCHOOLS COMMISSION,' *Journal of the Women's Education Union*, IV (1876), 96, lists possible minimum and maximum salaries, including capitation fees. These ranged from £110 to £190 given the head of the Dolgelly School, Wales to £1100 to £2000 projected for the head of St Paul's School for Girls and averaged about £400.

In 1894, the thirty-five heads of Girls' Public Day School Company schools received the following salaries: six earned £250; twelve £250 to £400; thirteen £400 to £600; two £600 to £700; and two a little over £700. (Calculated from numbers give in the Girls' Public Day School Trust, *Minutes of Council and Committees for 1895*, 19.)

Some heads supplemented their salaries with profits from boarders and private pupils. Miss Buss, said to be one of the most successful women of her times, reportedly had an income of 'not less' than £2500 from boarders and private pupils in addition to the £800 to £1300 she received as headmistress of the North London Collegiate. Ridley, *Frances Mary Buss*, 94. Her income was thus similar to that received by headmasters of the great public schools, such as Arnold, who is said to have had an income of over £4000 at Rugby. T.W. Bamford, *The Rise of the Public Schools: A Study of Boys' Boarding Schools in England and Wales from 1837 to the Present Day* (London 1967), 127

64 Average professional earnings at a somewhat later date, 1913–14, have been calculated for barristers (£478), solicitors (£568), general practitioners (£395), and clergymen (£208) by Guy Routh, *Occupation and Pay in Great Britain, 1906–1960* (Cambridge 1965), 64.

65 As, for instance, when Miss Benton arranged the transfer of a gifted student from her South Hampstead High School to the North London Collegiate, where more advanced mathematical teaching was available. Girls' Public Day School Trust Archives, ms. account of Mary Sophia Benton's life, perhaps by Miss Stead.

66 Headmistresses, for instance, gradually established the rule that girls would conform to the school calendar and would normally absent themselves from school only with their permission. Miss Beale recalled that in the early days at Cheltenham girls would miss the first term so that the family could prolong their holiday, but that 'when the College grew more independent, we refused to re-enter those who played this trick.' Dorothea Beale, *History of the Cheltenham Ladies'*

College 1853–1904 (Cheltenham [1904]), 25. When a girl absented
herself without leave from the King Edward vi High School to attend
a wedding, the headmistress, Miss Creak, expelled her. Winifred I.
Vardy, *King Edward VI High School for Girls, Birmingham, 1883–
1925* (London 1928), 49

67 *Bryce*, Mary Gurney's Testimony, ii, 173, 1713, suggests this was so
   in the case of the Girls' Public Day School Company's schools.
68 *Ibid.*, Mary Gurney's Testimony, ii, 174, 1717–18
69 Of the 202 women who joined the Head Mistresses' Association from
   its founding in 1874 through 1894 the educational backgrounds of
   seventy-four were ascertained: at least forty-six received their advanced
   education at Oxbridge colleges; five at University College, London; six at
   Queen's College, London; four (and probably more) at London women's
   colleges which came to be of university rank; two at the North London
   Collegiate; two at Cheltenham; two at other public schools; and seven
   were educated at home or in private schools.
      The Oxbridge college registers contain biographical information
   about some students, often including schools where they taught, and
   it was easy to match these with the lists of new members (and their
   schools) found in the *Minutes* of the Headmistresses' Association.
   In the case of the early London colleges and University of London degree
   lists which do not give biographical details everything became much
   more difficult, since it was impossible to know whether a Miss Clarke
   who attended Bedford was the same Miss Clarke who appeared in the
   Headmistresses' *Minutes* without independent corroboration, which
   was hard to come by.
70 The pattern is similar to that found by Hester Jenkins and D. Caradog
   Jones, 'Social Class of Cambridge University Alumni of the 18th and
   19th Centuries,' *British Journal of Sociology*, i (1950), 93–116, 99,
   although professionals' and business and tradesmen's daughters com-
   prised a larger proportion of the Cambridge women college students of
   known origin than did the sons of such men in the university as a whole.
71 Unfortunately, it proved possible to discover the fathers' occupations
   of only twenty-two of the 202 women who joined the Head Mistresses'
   Association between 1874 and 1894, to whom may be added a twenty-
   third women, a widow whose husband's occupation was established:
   seventeen were professionals (ten clergymen, two doctors, two artists,
   one army officer, one schoolmaster, and one engineer); five in business
   or trades (a chemical manufacturer, a merchant, a manager and partner
   of a clay company, a tailor, and a commercial traveler); and one a planter.

Although these women constitute a mere 10 per cent of the group and may well not be representative, it is noteworthy that their composition is similar to that of the Oxbridge women students of the period, both as regards the proportion of professional to business backgrounds and the large proportion of clergymen's daughters within the professional group.

72 At Girton, for instance, where the fees were £105 per annum, of thirteen scholarships noted in the Admissions Book as awarded in 1894, one was worth £100 per annum, one £75, two £60, two £52 10s, one £50, two £45, one £30, two £27, one £21.

73 Quoted in Barbara Stephen, *Girton College, 1869–1932* (Cambridge 1933), 235

74 'The style of dress here is certainly *not* elegant,' a new Newnham student wrote in 1885. Victoria Glendinning, *A Suppressed Cry: Life and Death of a Quaker Daughter* (London 1969), 73
    'I see in memory spectacles, cropped but otherwise undressed hair, stiff stand-up linen collars and inconspicuous dress as characteristic of many [students],' an Oxford resident recalled. Margaret Fletcher, *O Call Back Yesterday* (Oxford 1939), 76

75 Constance L. Maynard in her memoir, *Between College Terms* (London 1910), 192, described a typical day at Girton College in the 1870s.

76 *Bryce*, v, 186, 191

77 Maynard, *Between Terms*, 181; Stephen, *Emily Davies*, 226. Miss Maynard entered Girton without intending to teach but then taught at St Leonard's School and later became principal of Westfield College.

78 Ralph H. Turner, 'Modes of Social Ascent through Education: Sponsored and Contest Mobility,' Reinhard Bendix and Seymour Martin Lipset, eds., *Class, Status, and Power: Social Stratification in Comparative Perspective* (New York 1966), 449–58

79 There was the case of Miss Benton, for example, headmistress of the South Hampstead High School, remembered for having no memory for names (a most acceptable, even stereotypical eccentricity in a high-minded scholar) and her odd style of dress. Apparently, she invariably wore a well-cut coat and skirt, a plain shirt with a stiff collar and a tie, and a Homburg hat. The effect is said to have been 'certainly individual and rather masculine.' Article by M.M. Barber in the Girls' Public Day School Trust *Newsletter* (1956), 27. While doubtless mildly remarkable, her dress seems but an exaggerated version of the plain styles affected by many women college students, and her appearance was surely not disturbing to the values of an academic community in

the way that a bejewelled, bedizened headmistress erring in the opposite direction would have been.

80 The details are related in her autobiography, *Retrospect*.

81 *Ibid.*, 36–7

82 *The Teachers' Guild of Great Britain and Ireland. Constitution &
Objects of the Guild, together with a Report of the General Meeting,
held ... on Monday, April 17th, 1893,* 8

83 London Association of Schoolmistresses, *Minutes*, I, 31 May 1870

84 Association of Head Mistresses, *Minutes of Annual Conferences*, I,
22 Dec. 1874, 5

85 London Association of Schoolmistresses, *Minutes*, I, 12 Dec. 1873

86 Association of Head Mistresses, *Minutes of Annual Conferences*, I,
4 Feb. 1876, 21

87 Dorothea Beale, for instance, related how very carefully she went about
introducing curricular reforms at Cheltenham so as not to alienate
too many parents in 'Girls' Schools Past and Present,' *Nineteenth Century*, XXIII, (1888), 541–54, 547

88 Information about the curricula in some girls' public schools is given
in *Bryce*, IX, Appendix, 416–23; VI, Appendix D, 207.

89 See Matthew Arnold, *Culture and Anarchy*, esp. chap. 1, 'Sweetness
and Light,' for his concept of culture.

90 Beale, *Work and Play*, 2

91 *Ibid.*, 3

92 Quoted in Paul, *Mrs. Woodhouse*, 29

93 A study of the social origins of students in nine girls' public schools
indicated that these schools, at least, catered primarily to the upper
middle class, especially to professional people, in the nineteenth century. Pedersen, 'Reform', chap. IX

94 Grace Toplis, ed., *Leaves from the Notebooks of Frances M. Buss* (London 1896), 122

95 Jane Frances Dove, 'Cultivation of the Body,' in *Work and Play*, Beale
et al., 400–1

96 Quoted in Raikes, *Dorothea Beale*, 256

97 Lucy H.M. Soulsby, *The Religious Side of Secular Teaching* (London
1907), 16–17

98 Lucy H.M. Soulsby, 'The Moral Side of Education,' in *Work and Play*,
Beale *et al.*, 386

99 Even early headmistresses who initially opposed applying a competitive
principle in their schools gradually came round. Raikes noted that

Miss Beale at first opposed entering students for competitive examinations. (*Dorothea Beale*, 147). However, Cheltenham girls were soon being prepared for examinations, and Miss Beale pointed with pride to their successes in her *History of Cheltenham*, 44, 102–4. Also see James, *Alice Ottley*, 95.

100 For instance, it was reported to the Bryce Commission that headmistresses sometimes combined with girls to induce reluctant parents to permit their daughters to go on to university. *Bryce*, vi, 298

101 For example, Jane Beggs (head of Tottenham High School) served on the Tottenham District Council: Ethel Conder (head of Milton Mount College) was a committee member of the Gravesend Borough Council; while Ethel Gavin (head of Shrewsbury, then Notting Hill, then Wimbledon High School), Edith Hastings (head of Nottingham, then Wimbledon High School), and Alice Woods (head of the Junior Division of Clifton High School, then principal of the Maria Grey Training College) all served on local education authorities.

102 Miss Buss's taste for gubernatorial activities seems to have been almost insatiable. She sat on the governing bodies of at least thirteen institutions in addition to being a governor of the two schools she founded. Ridley, *Frances Mary Buss*, 288

103 For instance, Miss Conder worked for the Canning Town Women's Settlement; Isabel Bain (head of the Carlisle High School) later became inspectress of schools in Madras, probably after her marriage to James Brander.

104 Miss Beale and Miss Soulsby, for example, wrote numbers of educational tracts, some of which have been cited above, while Helena Powell (head of the Leeds High School, then principal first of the Cambridge Training College, then of St Mary's College) wrote history books.

105 Although the mistresses of girls' schools had not traditionally been called 'headmistresses,' the Association of Head Mistresses chose the title because it was the feminine analogue of 'headmaster.' Ridley, *Frances Mary Buss*, 246

As the academic and clerical worlds began partially to sort themselves out in the latter half of the nineteenth century, dons and public school masters (who could no longer automatically rely as a group on a clerical connection to define the prestige and character of their office) were themselves casting about for a new professional identity. See Rothblatt, *Revolution*, esp. chaps. 6 and 7.

106 Harold Perkin's construct of a professional middle class ideal seems to

tie in well with the values espoused by the public school heads. See his section on 'The Forgotten Middle Class' in *The Origins of Modern English Society 1780–1880* (Toronto 1972), 252–70.

107 Capitalizing on an expanded market for their services, as urbanization and rising living standards extended their potential clientele, modern professional groups typically have attempted to free themselves from the bonds of personal dependency which in pre-industrial times tied the professional (or pre-professional) practitioner to his patron, but which in an age which valued independence were felt to be irksome and demeaning. *Ibid.*, 254–5; Elliott, *Sociology*, 24, 94–5. Elliott views the autonomy accorded the professional practitioner as the distinguishing feature of modern professional practice.

108 Pedersen, 'Reforms,' chaps. iii and ix

'Mere Accomplishments'?

Melbourne's Early Ladies' Schools Reconsidered

Marjorie R. Theobald

Orthodoxy locates the beginnings of worthwhile secondary and higher education for English women in the establishment of the Governesses' Benevolent Institution in 1843, and the people and institutions associated with this reform movement have been well documented.[1] Under the auspices of Christian socialist Professor R.D. Maurice and other lecturers at King's College, the Governesses' Benevolent Institution became Queen's College which provided a model for the new high schools for girls which quickly followed.[2] Foremost among these were Frances Buss's North London Collegiate School and Dorothea Beale's Cheltenham Ladies' College, both founded in the 1850s.[3] The sisters Emily Shirreff and Maria Grey established the Girls' Public Day School Trust in 1872 which by 1891 had thirty-six schools.[4] The Tauton Commissioners, who were persuaded to include the education of girls in their enquiry into secondary education in the 1860s, focused public attention on a movement which was already underway, and endorsed the work of the new headmistresses and their schools.[5]

Hand in hand with the restructuring of secondary education for girls went demands for the right to public accreditation and admission to the formal institutions of tertiary education and the professions. In 1863–4 the Cambridge local examinations were opened to girls. As early as 1862 London University rejected an application for the admission of women, but the decision was not reversed until 1878. Oxford and Cambridge accepted women grudgingly by means of a series of concessions. This movement by women for access to 'masculine' forms of secondary and tertiary education is customarily linked with an emerging feminist consciousness in the second half of the nineteenth century which fuelled demands for the right to paid employment and the reform of laws relating to women.[6] The vote was a later, more bitterly disputed, demand.

In Victoria the orthodoxy of historical interpretation dates the beginnings of rigorous and systematic secondary education for girls from the establishment of Presbyterian Ladies' College in 1875 and Methodist Ladies' College in 1882.[7] The matriculation examination of the University of Melbourne was opened to women in 1871 although a further ten years passed before they were admitted to the University itself.[8] The absence of women as active agents of these changes in Victoria has passed virtually unremarked.[9]

In both England and Australia this consensus on the beginnings of secondary education for girls has been in large measure constructed in the process of centennial celebration. Understandable corporate pride in survival has led the historians of schools such as Queen's College, London, Presbyterian Ladies' College, Melbourne, and the Otago Girls' High School, New Zealand, to claim the spoils of the victor and blacken the reputation of the girls' schools and teachers who went before them.[10]

Nevertheless the efficacy of nineteenth-century reforms in the education of women has now been called into question. Feminists have pointed to the economic disadvantages suffered by women today in a still largely sex-segregated work force, their underrepresentation in parliament, in the upper echelons of the professions, the universities and the business world. Historians like Joyce Senders Pedersen, Sara Delamont and Carol Dyhouse have begun to reappraise concessions granted to women in the nineteenth century.[11] Dyhouse questions the 'standard assumption ... that the provision of these new kinds of schooling represented the achievement of feminists bent on widening opportunities available for women in public and professional life.'[12] Pedersen argues that the respectable middle-class men who stepped in to administer organizations such as the Girls' Public Day School Trust would hardly have done so if such schools had seriously challenged the patriarchal values of Victorian England. Others have also questioned whiggish assumptions of progress by characterizing the rise of social Darwinist theory and its prescription of domestic education for women as a backlash against concessions granted in the nineteenth century.[13]

A reappraisal of the early ladies' schools and their accomplishments curriculum is a necessary part of this revisionist enterprise.[14] They have shared the fate of much womanly enterprise in the past, reduced by the attrition of time and neglect to an unflattering stereotype. They are deemed to have been ephemeral and marginal, inhabiting a nether world of education by default. They are portrayed as costly and pretentious, teaching deportment and a smattering of 'mere accomplishments' to prepare the daughters of the upwardly-mobile middle classes for the marriage market. Their proprietors are said to have been 'starched and prim ladies of uncertain age,' widows and spinsters down on their luck or failed Continental gold seekers with dubious qualifications and morals. It is also assumed that they had the decency to fade away upon the advent of the new high schools for girls. Yet polemicists from Hannah More in the 1790s to Sara Ellis in the 1840s complained that girls educated in ladies' schools were conceited, selfishly absorbed in their newly acquired accomplishments and disinclined to take on the traditional role of women – an educational outcome which, if it had been allowed to get out of hand, would have caused a social *bouleversement* more radical than that proposed by the Chartists.[15]

That these small, private girls' schools proliferated in England and Australia throughout the nineteenth century may be verified by reference to any newspaper or local directory. Over seven hundred self-styled ladies' schools advertised in the Melbourne *Argus* between 1850 and 1875 and some may have richly deserved the scorn of posterity. The same may be said of any form of education. It is not the present purpose to cavil about the standards of individual schools. Rather it is intended to disinter, in the Australian context, a tradition of female education which has fallen victim to male/bureaucratic definitions of education and professionalism; to reinterpret its language, symbols and forms; and to reconsider its importance to women as teachers and pupils.

The accomplishments curriculum emerged as the dominant mode of education for middle-class girls in Britain in the late eighteenth and early nineteenth centuries. This programme of general and cultural studies proved a hardy transplant to Australian colonial soil where it flourished unchallenged until the 1870s. So complete has been the focus of historians upon later reforms that this earlier transformation of female studies has been overlooked. Although Jane Austen's Mr Darcy reckoned few English women to be truly accomplished, it was sufficiently well established as a coherent pedagogical form to be noted by the acerbic Sydney Smith in 1810: 'A decided and prevailing taste for one or another mode of education there must always be. A century past, it was for housewifery – now it is for accomplishments.'[16] The term 'accomplishments' in the context of female education combined an exhortation to excellence in music, modern languages and painting with an understanding that female achievement must not be used in the public sphere. The emergence of the term 'mere accomplishments' later in the century signalled a further shift in fashion rather than a valid appraisal of standards.

The ladies' schools were initially a response to this consensus on the accomplishments as the proper focus of female education. Small groups of young women gathered in the home of an aunt or family acquaintance to receive lessons from visiting masters of modern languages, painting and music. Although the ladies' schools retained the reassuring image of the private family throughout the nineteenth century many developed into far more ambitious institutions. By the middle of the century most offered English language and literature, history and geography, science, arithmetic, religious studies, needlework and physical education as well as the 'accomplishments' of modern languages, music and painting.[17] In the cryptic language of shared tradition this was rendered as: 'A sound English education with the usual accomplishments.' The 'masculine' subjects of Latin, Greek, mathematics and commerce were missing. Housewifery had indeed suffered an eclipse, an omission which may have worked to the detriment of the ladies' school as reaction to the feminist movement provoked a cry for domestic education later in the century.

For twenty-five years the East Melbourne Ladies' College run by Julie and Lewis Vieusseux rivaled the public schools for boys in the middle-class landscape of Melbourne.[18] The Vieusseuxs were among the first wave of immigrants drawn to the colony by the news of Australia's new-found wealth in gold. Elegant, cultured and cosmopolitan, they were both of Huguenot stock. Julie was born in 1820 in Holland, the daughter of Catherine, née van de Winkle and Louis Matthieu, a captain in the Belgian army. She regarded herself as a native of French Flanders and was educated in Paris in the traditional accomplishments. Lewis was born in 1824 in England of Swiss parents from Lausanne. He was educated at the Enfield Grammar School near London and trained as a civil engineer, architect and surveyor in Europe. He was fluent in English, French and German and a scholar in the literature of all three languages. They married in England and arrived in Victoria with their two infant sons aboard the *Fortitude* in early 1852.

The Vieusseuxs' skills were eminently saleable in a British colony and in the biographical minutiae of their early lives in Melbourne may be traced the evolution of a ladies' school. Julie Vieusseux established herself first as a portrait painter and art dealer, working from their first home in Kyte's Buildings, an early enclave of fellow European scientists, artists and musicians who dominated the scientific and cultural life of Melbourne in the decades following the gold rushes. She had some success (the influential and ambitious Hugh and Emily Childers were among her clients) and surviving works confirm that she had received classical training in oils and portraiture.[19] As early as 1853 her advertisements carried the postscript: 'Drawing and Painting Classes for Young Ladies, who can enjoy the advantages of French conversation.'[20] Lewis tried his luck on the goldfields and upon his return to Melbourne did not prosper in his profession. As more and more young women beat a path to Julie's studio the Vieusseuxs decided to turn their cultural and capital assets to account in a more systematic way.

The Ladies' College opened amid considerable fanfare in July 1857 in Victoria Parade, Fitzroy. It fared well in the decades of prosperity following the discovery of gold, weathering the slight economic recession of the early 1860s which sent Geelong Grammar School and St Patrick's College reeling amid financial scandal. Between 1857 and 1882 the Vieusseuxs enrolled 886 girls and their meticulous register of pupils is a profile of emerging power and privilege in the colony.[21] As gate-keepers to the elite they charged high fees, requested references and gave them in return. Among the influential citizens who lent their names to the school were the Rev. Henry Handfield of the nearby St Peter's Church, the ubiquitous à Beckett family, the merchant families of Grice and Sargood, and the lawyer and politician Sir Archibald Michie. Most had daughters in the school. Within three years the school had outgrown its original home and moved to the corner of Clarendon and Albert streets overlooking the newly planted Fitzroy Gardens. Its new home, an extensive Georgian terrace indistinguishable from the surrounding homes of its clientele, suggests that capital investment in the Vieusseux family enterprise was considerable. By 1863 the enrolment had reached 103 and the proprietors were obliged to erect two new classrooms and a lecture hall/gymnasium in the grounds.[22] Even so, the school moved to Brighton from 1868–71 to allow the complete rebuilding of the Clarendon Street premises. Nevertheless the headmaster of Melbourne Grammar School, the Rev. Dr John Bromby, privately reserved his judgment on the Continental goldseekers. He noted in his diary: 'Mr Vieusseux notwithstanding his French name is a Yorkshireman, and looks it. His profession properly that of an engineer; but having married a lady of French Flanders has turned his name to profitable account, by producing the idea that the ladies educated at (their) ladies' College would have the same advantages as if they had been sent to Paris. They have realized a goodly fortune.'[23]

The philosophy and curriculum of the Vieusseuxs' Ladies' College were representative of middle-class female education of the time. The aims of the school were: 'To impart a solid and superior education which comprehending, with the development of the Intellectual Faculties and high Moral and Religious Training, those graceful accomplishments proper to ladies, shall result in qualifying them for the thorough fulfil- ment of those important duties which fall to the lot of womanhood.'[24] Under the rubric of an English education the prospectus grouped English studies (reading, writing, grammar and English literature), history (scriptural, ancient and modern), geography (mathematical, physical and political), science (botany, astronomy, object lessons and natural science) arithmetic, needlework and bible studies.[25] The accom- plishments subjects were music (vocal, instrumental, harmony and musical composition), drawing and painting in oils and water colours, perspective and object drawing, French and German. Craftwork, danc- ing and calisthenics were also offered.

When the matriculation examination of the University of Melbourne was opened to women in 1871 the Vieusseuxs added a matriculation class and the 'masculine' subjects of Greek, Latin and mathematics entered the college curriculum. Their son Edward, a graduate of the University of Melbourne who had been teaching at the Geelong Gram- mar School, became master in charge of the matriculation class. This adaptation of potentially radical means to conservative ends Lewis Vieusseux explained in his speech day address of 1873: 'So much has been said ... of the inefficiency of our private girls' schools, that they ought to be the subject to some public test, so that parents might have some guarantee that their daughters were properly taught; and therefore, as soon as this University test was open for young ladies, we availed ourselves thereof, to show to all, that if the boys' schools were doing their duty by their pupils so were the girls' schools doing theirs.'[26] Of the 113 women who presented for matriculation before Presbyterian Ladies' College sent its first candidate in 1875, ninety-five came from the early ladies' schools of Melbourne.[27]

Julie and Lewis Vieusseux taught full time, taking the language and literature classes in English, French and German. Madame Julie also taught drawing, painting and craft classes. The staff included the cream of Melbourne's artists and musicians, among them landscape painter Eugen von Guerard, soprano Fanny Simonsen and composer Charles Horsley. Scientist John Macadam and journalist and writer David Blair taught at the school. Madame Julie supervised the boarding house which she characterised as 'a well regulated family, Mrs Vieusseux associating with her young friends, and paying the utmost attention to their well-being, dress, manners, and habits.'[28] She emerges from the recollections of her pupils as the accomplished woman presiding in the private sphere:

I think of her always as the most elegant, dignified and graceful woman I have ever known. To see her enter and walk across a room was a lesson in deport-ment. Her hands had been used as models for those of an Angel in a picture that used to hand in the College drawingroom; I never tired of looking at it, chiefly on account of the lovely hands. Her objection to any display of finery or any gaudiness in dress was pronounced, and when some of the wealthier girls began the habit of wearing gorgeous and costly jewellery, suddenly the edict went forth that no jewellery whatever was to be worn to school, beyond a simple brooch at the neckband. Unpalatable as this was to some, none dared disobey. Madame's word was law, her graceful dignity, in and out of school, holding us all in deep reverence and awe.[29]

Nevertheless, the symbolism of the mother/daughter relationship and the accomplished women legitimated an institution which antici-pated the later high schools for girls: it was large by the standards of the day; it was primarily a day school; its internal organization turned upon classes, specialist teachers and orderly progression through an articulated programme of studies and regular examinations; and, after 1871, it came under the influence of public examinations.[30] It nevethe-less lacked the vital mechanism of succession; as the school had grown up around Madame Julie's cultural and entrepreneurial skills, so it did not long survive her death in 1878. The Ladies' College closed in 1882 although the family continued their involvement with education.[31]

The Vieusseux Ladies' College was not unique and survived amid fierce competition in fashionable East Melbourne. The Talbot Lodge Ladies' College in Grey Street was run by sisters Mary Evans and Claudia Permezel.[32] Like Julie Vieusseux they had been educated in Paris and were talented linguists and musicians. In partnership at the school was Claudia's husband Edouard Permezel, a French lawyer and graduate of the University of Melbourne who taught modern languages at many schools and institutions in Melbourne. Mary Evans and Claudia Permezel were under consideration for the principalship of Presbyterian Ladies' College in 1874.[33] Scottish novelist and journalist Caroline Ponsonby conducted her Scotch College for Young Ladies in nearby Elmbank Terrace, and her skills as a publicist were such that it was sometimes assumed to be the official sister school for Scotch College.[34] Ponsonby's pamphlet entitled *Education: The Scotch System* is one of the few professional statements by a colonial lady-principal.[35] The London-trained school teachers Sarah and Edmund Samson opened their Torrington House Day and Boarding School for Young Ladies in South Fitzroy.[36] In 1871 they campaigned for the admission of women to the matriculation examination although they believed that girls should be examined in subjects 'best suited to the domestic and social position that in the natural order of things they will be called upon to occupy in their later position in life.'[37] Around the corner in Nicholson Street was Philippa James's Grantown House.[38] As a single woman and as a widow she ran ladies' schools in Melbourne for half a century, at various times under the patronage of professors from the University of Melbourne and the Anglican establishment led by Bishop Charles Perry and his successors. Also in Nicholson Street, a few doors north, was the Academy of Mary Immaculate, a Catholic ladies' school opened by the Mercy Order in 1857.[39]

It has been accepted as a truism that voluntarist enterprise in education attracted the halt, the lame and the blind. As teaching was the only female calling compatible with gentility it also attracted talented women for whom the ladies' school became a focus of economic, intellectual and professional aspirations. It is therefore a paradox that mastery of the accomplishments, intended as they were for the private sphere, also constituted professional preparation for women in the nineteenth century. The professional evolution of the Singleton sisters, owner-principals of Ormiston Ladies' College from 1872–1912, is a case in point. A medical doctor, John Singleton purchased the East Melbourne school for his daughters in 1872 and thereafter it housed his consulting rooms and provided him and his wife with a home in their old age. This remarkable mesh of the public and private domains he disposed of in one bland, autobiographical sentence: 'For close on twenty years I have lived with my two unmarried daughters at their Ladies' College ... and I have had the same unremitting, loving attention and unwearied care their dear mother experienced – our very wishes being anticipated.'[40]

John and Isabella Singleton were part of the Anglican ascendancy

and its busy network of philanthropic and moral crusaders, and Elizabeth and Anna were nurtured in an atmosphere of missionary zeal and
high purpose – a configuration of evangelical fervour and intellectual
endowment which led men into the church and women along the prescribed path to the ladies' school. Their resolution was strengthened
by the spectacle of an unhappily married sister and family tradition
has it that they made a conscious decision not to marry.

Both parents were concerned about the education of their daughters.
John Singleton was one of those arch-conservative proponents of the
rights of women who are sometimes inadvertently more helpful than
their more radical friends. In 1885 he took up the cause of Dr Laura
Morgan, an American physician who was refused registration by the
Medical Board of Victoria, employing her at his Collingwood Free Medical Centre. Singleton took his stand on the essentially conservative
grounds that morally and temperamentally women were suited to the
medical care of women and children. He viewed the success of the
early women graduates and the 'patience, perseverance, gentleness, and
attention' displayed by women in new areas of employment such as
telegraph and post offices as 'evidence of woman's adaptability for
many sources of emolument ... hitherto held by men exclusively.'[41] He
wanted his daughter Mary to be a doctor but she entered instead
upon the marriage which so distressed her sisters. Their mother had
encountered the indigent gentlewomen of Melbourne in her philanthropic work and she too insisted that her daughters be as well educated
as her sons.[42] Anna and Elizabeth were sent as boarders to Ormiston
Ladies' College when it was owned by the Ainslie family in the 1860s.

They were in their early twenties when Helen Nimmo bought the
school from the Ainslie family in 1869 and they remained there in
that limbo between parlour boarder and articled pupil satirized by
Thackeray in the person of Becky Sharp.[43] Helen Nimmo enjoyed the
advantage of being the daughter of the parsonage and her father, the
Rev. David Nimmo, was incumbent of the Victoria Parade Congregational Church in Fitzroy throughout her four years as owner-principal
of Ormiston Ladies' College.[44] Educated at Queen's College, London,
she was among the emerging elite of teachers who claimed precedence
by virtue of attendance at the new high schools for girls. Her presence
in this small, antipodean girls' school points to a continuity which has
been overlooked. Many of the beneficiaries of the new educational
opportunities went back into the ladies' schools, among them the Chambers sisters of Faireleight, the Day sisters of Cromarty and the Wilson

sisters of Hadleigh.[45] The experience of the Singleton sisters at Ormiston Ladies' College underscores the potential of the ladies' school to nurture its own traditions and expertise. Helen Nimmo chose her own successors and inducted them into the profession. Over thirty years later, when the Teachers and Schools Registration Board enquired of Anna Singleton her experience and training she replied tersely: 'Thirty-three years' experience, privately trained.'[46]

While the ladies' schools provided legitimate space for female education and professional and entrepreneurial roles for women, they were also institutions which reproduced a vital component of ruling class culture. Speech, manners, social ritual and the right connections were vital in an era of family-based capitalist enterprise.[47] The gatekeepers of power and privilege looked to women of their own class to educate their daughters in the ways of gentility. For nearly forty years Elizabeth Macarthur conducted her school within the proprieties of class and gender. She established her school in the Port Phillip District in 1838 when Melbourne was little more than tents and crude huts, and the school may be traced to Clyde Girls' School which amalgamated with Geelong Grammar School in 1976.[48] Born Elizabeth Kirby in 1803, the eldest daughter of Edinburgh physician Jeremiah Kirby and Jane Kennedy of Romana, Perthshire, she married Donald Gordon Macarthur, a surveyor, and in 1835 came with her husband's family to New South Wales. She established her first Australian school in Sydney where her daughters Elizabeth and Helen were born.

Elizabeth Macarthur and her brother-in-law David Charteris Macarthur became the mainstays of the family economy. When he was appointed founding manager of the Bank of Australasia in the Port Phillip District in 1838 the entire family accompanied him. Her husband Donald did not prosper and the marriage ended in one of those discreet separations common when divorce was neither a legal nor a social possibility for most people. He died in 1871.[49] The fortunes of David Macarthur rose steadily. He became 'a squire in the Heidelberg hills,' the confidant of governors, politicians, bishops and merchants.[50] In a close-textured and intimate society this was the constituency which nurtured Elizabeth Macarthur's school. She was always first and foremost 'sister-in-law of David Charteris Macarthur'; she served on philanthropic committees with notables such as Sophie La Trobe, Frances Perry and Lydia à Beckett; her daughters married into the wealthy and influential Docker and Were families.[51]

By 1847 the enrolment at her school on the corner of Flinders Lane and Russell Street exceeded that of the two leading boys' schools, William Brickwood's proprietary Port Phillip Academical Institution and Richard Hale Budd's private classical school.[52] With fees at forty guineas per annum for boarders (a modest charge by the standards of the day), eight guineas per annum for day pupils, and a quarterly fee of two or three guineas for each of the accomplishments, her gross income must have exceeded 1,000 guineas per annum.[53] Macarthur's success was reflected in her public announcement of 1851: 'Notice of removal. Mrs. D.G. Macarthur begs to intimate to her friends, and the parents of her pupils, that instead of removing to St. Kilda as formerly intended on the 1st April, she has in consequence of the present unhealthy state of Melbourne, made arrangements for immediately removing there.'[54] Elizabeth Macarthur became the first of many proprietors to follow her clientele from the centre of Melbourne to the first ring of prestigious suburban developments. In Robe Street, St Kilda, she built Belle Vue House, sufficiently imposing to be used as a landmark by entrepreneurs subdividing the coastline. In 1867, when Robe Street had become a busy thoroughfare, the school moved again to Romana, named for the place of her mother's birth, in the then more secluded Alma Road, St Kilda. In 1875 she sold the school to Alice and Florence Chambers.

Elizabeth Macarthur's obituarist had no doubt about the nature of her contribution to ruling class culture: 'She had the training of the wives of many of our leading colonists, and it is not too much to say that to her intelligence, and her motherly affectionate discipline, we are indebted for much of that leaven of better domestic life which distinguishes the class representing what we may call the historic residents in Victoria.'[55] The shaping of the self to the proprieties of womanhood runs deeper than lessons in deportment and elocution. The letters of Charlotte Docker to her mother from Belle Vue House in the 1850s reflect the structure of everyday life in the ladies' school.[56] The world of Belle Vue House is rendered in the intimate language of the private sphere. Mrs. Macarthur and the music governess, 'my dear Miss Forsyth,' are 'such dear Creatures, so very kind and so very strict too.' The lady-principal is omnipresent in the letters; her relationship to Charlotte is personal and immediate. She shops for her pupil at Buckley and Nunn, takes her to Dr Macadam's evening lectures on chemistry, plagues her about a quarterly account outstanding, presses her to stay another term at school and calls upon her socially at the home of a friend during the vacation. While Charlotte's brothers at

Geelong Grammar School might contemplate the enchancement of their self-esteem and personal autonomy by means of orderly progression through public examinations, elevation to the office of prefect, or participation in the meritocratic fraternity of football and rowing, Charlotte's standing was dependent upon her acceptance of the role of dutiful and affectionate daughter in the Macarthur household. In March 1856 she wrote to her mother: 'I received your ... kind and welcome letter last Wednesday, and it is with pleasure I now answer it, thanking you kindly for giving me permission to be a parlour boarder, it is more like home having tea and breakfast with Mrs. McArthur [sic].' The manner of Charlotte's apocalyptic preferment in the community of symbolic daughters is significant. It is won not by excellence on her part but by arrangement between parents and principal. Its reward is not enhanced personal autonomy or power within the school community but greater intimacy with the lady principal.

The letters document the circumscribed domestic routine of the ladies' school: music practice, lesson preparation, walking out, small repairs to her wardrobe, games in the late afternoon and informal dancing after supper. In the summer months the girls were taken to bathe in the sea. The solemn and conscientious Charlotte wrote to her mother: 'I had a delightful bathe this morning and I will try to go every other day, so that I may look well, as people say bathing is good for the health.' Otherwise her relationships with the outside world were limited to the womanly rituals of church going and formal visiting.

The home and hearth of Elizabeth Macarthur did not win the dutiful Charlotte. Her emotional dependence upon her family remained intact. She parted from them in tears each January to undertake the trying and often hazardous coach journey from Bontharambo Station to Melbourne. Her letters have the anxious tone of an outcast. Her ambivalence towards an education bought at such expense is apparent: 'I think it is only throwing away money to send me there for I do not think I improve very much and you know I try to do my best.' Although her pupil is happy to go home Elizabeth Macarthur does not stand exposed as a charlatan: 'I regret that I have not fifty (daughters), that I might have the pleasure of placing them all, in succession, under your charge,' wrote Joseph Docker to Elizabeth Macarthur. Neither saw Charlotte's stay at Belle Vue House as a decisive break in the pattern of her life, unlike the symbolic removal from the care of women to the care of men which began her brothers' progress into the public sphere.

Those who enter the schools of the past with their own set of preconceptions should tread warily, since the individual outcomes of such an education varied greatly. Charlotte Docker returned with alacrity to help keep house in her father's home until her marriage. Yet the feminists Annette Beare Crawford and Alice Henry received part of their education in ladies' schools. Nellie (Mitchell) Melba became the greatest soprano of her time, a shrewd entrepreneur, a divorcee and a cosmopolitan larrikin of great charm. She received a typical musical education at home, at Mrs. Wigmore's Leigh House ladies' school and at Presbyterian Ladies' College. Educated at her mother's Lawn House ladies' school, and briefly at Presbyterian Ladies' College, Lilian Alexander became a pioneer woman doctor in Melbourne. Melian Stawell attended Talbot Lodge ladies' school and later became a classical scholar at Newnham College, Cambridge and a socialist.[57]

The complex relationship between women and knowledge in the nineteenth century is illustrated in the life of Catherine Deakin. Born in Adelaide in 1850 the daughter of William and Sarah Deakin (née Bill), she was the archetypal accomplished woman. Her mastery of the French language was complete and there is abundant testimony that she could have been a concert pianist. She was extremely well read, particularly in literature and politics and, as one of her biographers comments, 'at 84 ... could well have contributed invaluable comment and criticism at any newspaper's editorial conference on the international scene.'[58] She sometimes taught, but for the greater part of her life used her accomplishments in the private sphere and in the service of others. Catherine had several suitors but did not marry. The focus of her emotional and intellectual life was her brother Alfred Deakin, six years her junior and three times prime minister of Australia.

Alfred Deakin's biographer J.A. La Nauze is perceptive about the importance to the public man of the covey of adoring women (mother, wife, sister, daughters) who attended Deakin all his life.[59] His correspondence with his sister Catherine, the beloved K of his diaries, suggests that she was the most important person in his life.[60] She nurtured him emotionally as a child and adult and deployed her formidable intellect in the advancement of his intellectual and political career. She educated his three daughters, eventually accompanying them to study in Europe.[61] She was, in nineteenth-century parlance, Deakin's wifely help-meet.

In the education of Catherine Deakin two influences are customarily noted: her family circle and the Presbyterian Ladies' College. As with Nellie Melba and Lilian Alexander, the college is proud of Catherine

Deakin, as the sister of Alfred and as the only student to pass the matriculation examination of the University of Melbourne (with honours) in 1875 – the school's first year of operation.[62] In the following year she became the first of many past pupils to return as a member of staff. The school's historian notes that the college could hardly take full credit as she was twenty-five years old and had attended for only one year, but there is no reference to her former education. A descendant of the Deakin family with access to restricted papers placed considerably more store by her stint at Presbyterian Ladies' College: 'Catherine was privately educated and did not have a chance of formal schooling until Professor Pearson ... helped to establish the first major secondary school for young ladies – the Presbyterian Ladies' College in East Melbourne in 1875. Pearson ... probably had more influence on Catherine's development and thinking than anyone outside her father and brother.'[63]

Yet access to private papers is not necessary to discover that for ten years she attended a ladies' school run by Edith and Louisa Thompson. Her autobiographical notes state that she attended the school in the central Victorian town of Kyneton from 1858–62 and when it moved to the Melbourne suburb of South Yarra from 1863–5.[64] In the absence of testimony to the contrary it may be assumed that her fluency in modern languages, her musicianship and her appetite for intellectual pursuits were fostered during her ten years with the Thompsons. Miss Louisa, who had studied piano with a professor of the Royal College, London, was her music teacher.[65]

The Thompsons and their school fare better at the hands of J.A. La Nauze because Alfred also attended before he went to Melbourne Grammar School.[66] La Nauze provides scattered evidence that the Deakins held them in high esteem, although he rarely mentions them by name. He concludes that the Deakin family's move from Fitzroy to South Yarra in 1863 was to be near the school which Catherine was attending rather than to be near Melbourne Grammar School. The date is consistent with the arrival of the Thompsons in South Yarra. He notes that on £300 per annum William Deakin gave his children the best education available. When Catherine was a boarder in Kyneton the basic fees were forty-five guineas per annum.[67] La Nauze observes that Catherine was born too early to attend university 'for which she was well qualified by intelligence and interests, but she had a good grounding at her school.' He quotes Deakin's recollection of his sister as 'too much alone at school and after – serious – religious – introspective proud and sensitive. Very successful at school and in music which was her forte.'

Although the Thompson family school retained a toehold in the historical record because of their relationship to the Deakin family, biographical details are sketchy. They were the sisters of John Henning Thompson, a master at Melbourne Grammar School in Deakin's time and owner-principal of the private Kew High School from 1875–1909.[68] Catherine Deakin was in love with him but her family did not approve of the match. History does not record which member of the family disapproved. The Thompsons arrived from London in 1856 and by the following year the Kyneton Ladies' School was at Lauriston House, a two-storey bluestone home which still stand in Piper Street, ill-proportioned and crowded forward to toe the footpath as if additions were contemplated at the rear.[69] In 1863 the Thompsons moved to South Yarra where they had obtained a lease on the home of Colonel William Anderson on the site now occupied by Melbourne Church of England Girls' Grammar School. Masters from the nearby Melbourne Grammar School lectured daily at the South Yarra Ladies' College and leading Melbourne musicians like the Italian tenor Cesare Cutolo and the organist George Tolhurst attended as visiting masters.[70] Catherine Deakin's cryptic diary provides evidence that she remained close to the Thompson sisters after her school days ended, possibly teaching music at the school until in 1870 it became Lawn House and continued under the proprietorship of Mrs Alexander.[71]

The ladies' school tradition in the education of nineteenth-century women raises questions concerning the complex relationship of ideology to reality, of educational intent to educational outcome. The ladies' schools were institutions which helped to reproduce the dominant culture in its dimensions of class and gender. The ideal female type (dependent, chaste, domesticated and cultured) was vital in the maintenance of capitalist and patriarchal relationships. The hothouse world of the ladies' school withheld 'male' knowledge and replicated the confined moral space of women. It may be that the rapid growth of the ladies' schools forestalled a social revolution which is only now getting underway. J.S. Mill would have taken this view.[72]

Yet the notion of the accomplished woman was compatible with educational excellence. Within the confines of their time women created schools which pushed at the boundaries of female professionalism and learning. The self-proclaimed harbingers of the new order, Presbyterian Ladies' College and Methodist Ladies' College, were schools run by men for women and in the context of Victoria they had no immediate imitators. The lady-principals continued to dominate the education of middle-class girls, adapting, chameleon-like, to changes from the admission of women to the matriculation examination in 1871 to the new educational theory at the end of the century. Could this degree of economic and intellectual independence have contributed nothing to the women's movement which the Victorian era both created and contained?

NOTES

This article is from the *History of Education Review*, 13, 2 (1984), 15–28. Reprinted with permission. A version of the paper was given at the 1984 Australian Historical Association Conference in Melbourne.

1 The most comprehensive account is in Margaret Bryant, *The Unexpected Revolution* (London: University of London Institute of Education 1979).

2 E. Kaye, *A History of Queen's College, London* (London: Chatto and Windus 1972)

3 J. Kamm, *How Different from Us* (London: Bodley Head 1959)

4 J. Kamm, *Indicative Past: A Hundred Years of the Girls' Public Day School Trust* (London: George, Allen & Unwin 1971)

5 *British Parliamentary Papers, Schools Inquiry Commission Report*, Education General, Irish University Press Series (Taunton Commission) chap. 6, Girls' Schools, P.A. Hall, 'The Taunton Commission – A Study in Revolutionary Conservatism?' M.Ed. thesis, Monash University, 1977, chap. 5. 'Not in Accordance with the Fitness of Things – The Education of Girls and the Taunton Commission'; Sheila Fletcher, *Feminists and Bureaucrats* (Cambridge: C.U.P. 1980)

6 For a chronology of acts relating to custody of infants, divorce, prostitution, married women's property and suffrage, see Bryant, 13–15.

7 Kathleen Fitzpatrick, *P.L.C. Melbourne: The First Century 1875–1975* (Melbourne: Presbyterian Ladies' College 1975); M.O. Reid, *The Ladies Came to Stay*, (Melbourne: Presbyterian Ladies' College 1960); Ailsa G. Thomson Zainu'ddin, *They Dreamt of a School* (Melbourne: Hyland House 1982)

8 Ailsa G. Thomson Zainu'dinn, 'The Admission of Women to the University of Melbourne 1869–1903, in R.J.W. Selleck, ed., *Melbourne Studies in Education 1973* (Melbourne: M.U.P. 1973), 50–106

9 In a public lecture on the education of women delivered at the University
   of Melbourne in 1983, Gwyneth M. Dow pointed out that almost all
   of the men who campaigned to have women admitted to that university
   had large numbers of daughters, many of whom availed themselves
   of the new opportunities. This indirect influence is hard to document.
10 See for example Fitzpatrick, 24. The New Zealand experience is related
   in E. Wallis, *A Most Rare Vision: Otago Girls' High School – The First
   100 Years* (Dunedin: John McIndoe Ltd. 1972)
11 J.B.S. Pedersen, 'The Reform of Women's Secondary and Higher Education in Nineteenth-Century England: A Study in Elite Groups,' D. Phil.
   thesis, University of California, Berkeley, 1974. See also Pedersen
   'Schoolmistresses and Headmistresses: Elites and Education in Nineteenth-Century England,' reprinted in this volume, and Pedersen, 'The
   Reform of Women's Secondary and Higher Education: Institutional
   Change and Social Values in Mid and Late Victorian England,' *History
   of Education Quarterly* (spring 1979), 61–92; Carol Dyhouse, *Girls
   Growing Up in Late Victorian and Edwardian England* (London:
   Routledge and Kegan Paul 1981). See also Dyhouse, 'Social Darwin-
   istic Ideas and the Development of Women's Education in England,
   1880–1920,' *History of Education*, 5 (Feb. 1876) 41–58; S. Delamont,
   'The Domestic Ideology and Women's Education,' in S. Delamont and
   L. Duffin, eds., *The Nineteenth Century Woman: Her Cultural and
   Physical World* (London: Croom Helm 1978)
12 Dyhouse, *Girls Growing Up*, 57
13 Carol Bacchi, 'Evolution, Eugenics and Women: The Impact of Scientific Theories on Attitudes towards Women 1870–1920', in Elizabeth
   Windschuttle, ed., *Women, Class and History: Feminist Perspectives
   on Australia 1788–1978* (Melbourne: Fontana 1980), 132–56; Farley
   Kelly, 'The Woman Question in Melbourne 1880–1912,' Ph.D. thesis,
   Monash University, 1983; Alison Mackinnon, 'Educating the Mothers
   of a Nation: The Advanced School For Girls, Adelaide,' in Margaret
   Bevege *et al.*, eds., *Worth Her Salt* (Sydney: Hale and Iremonger 1982),
   62–71; Jill Matthews, 'Education for Femininity: Domestic Arts Education in South Australia,' *Labour History*, no. 45 (Nov. 1983), 30–53
14 A revisionist assessment of dame schools and preparatory schools is
   also underway. See J.H. Higginson, 'Dame Schools,' in *British Journal
   of Educational Studies*, 22, no. 2 (June 1974), and D.P. Leinster-
   Mackay, 'Dame Schools: A Need For Review' *ibid.*, 24, no. 1 (Feb.
   1976)
15 Hannah More, *Strictures on the Modern System of Female Education*

(London: Cadell and Davies 1801); Sarah Stickney Ellis, *The Daughters of England* (London: Fisher 1842). For an example of this stereotypical view of the ladies' school, its proprietor and the accomplishments curriculum, see Beverley Kingston, *My Wife, My Daughter and Poor Mary Ann* (Melbourne: Nelson 1977), 78–9.

16 Sydney Smith, *Essays Social and Political* (London: Ward Lock and Co. 1882), 187

17 This profile of the curriculum in girls' schools is compiled from newspaper advertisements and prospectuses included in family papers.

18 Details on the Vieusseux school are from the family papers unless otherwise stated. See also Marjorie R. Theobald, 'Julie Vieusseux' in Marilyn Lake and Farley Kelly, eds., *Double Time* (Melbourne: Penguin 1984)

19 Her portrait of Eugen von Guerard is reproduced in Marjorie Tipping, *Eugen von Guerard's Australian Landscapes* (Melbourne: Lansdowne 1975).

20 *Argus*, 4 Nov. 1853, p 9

21 The register of pupils is in the family papers.

22 *Prospectus*, 1863

23 J.E. Bromby papers, MS 8847 La Trobe collection, State Library of Victoria, diary of Dr J.E. Bromby, 15 July 1869, p 32

24 *Prospectus*, 1862

25 *Prospectus*, 1862

26 *Prospectus*, 1873

27 Matriculation entries, University of Melbourne, 1871–5

28 *Prospectus*, 1862

29 *Southern Sphere*, 1 Dec. 1911, p 11

30 For the organization of classes, synopsis of examinations, awarding of prizes etc. see *Prospectus*, 1863.

31 It is not clear whether the school was sold or closed down. Another school claimed to be a continuation of the Ladies' College but did not appear in the official returns of private schools for the year 1883. For Edward Vieusseux and the Berwick Grammar School see the article by Ailsa G. Thomson Zainu'ddin reprinted in this volume.

32 Permezel family papers unless otherwise stated. In 1882 the school moved to St Kilda and took the name La Rochelle, closing during the depression of the 1890s.

33 This family tradition is supported by the *Prospectus* which reprints the relevant testimonials.

34 For Alexander Morrison's denial see *Argus*, 21 Jan. 1861, p 8
35 Caroline Ponsonby, *Education: The Scotch System: What It is; With strictures on its Adaptation to the Education of Young Ladies* (Melbourne: George Robertson 1861). The *British Museum General Catalogue of Printed Books*, 192, p 746, lists seven novels by Ponsonby written between 1841 and 1860. She also edited and wrote for the *Christian Family Advocate* in which the advertisements for her Edinburgh school appear.
36 Victorian Public Record Series 892, Special Case Files, 528, 76/9671. E.A. Samson to the minister of education applying for a position of elocution teacher to the Victorian Education Department.
37 Quoted in Zainu'ddin, 'The Admission of Women,' 65
38 F. Frazer and N. Palmer, eds., *Records of the Pioneer Women of Victoria 1835–60* (Melbourne: Osboldstone 1937), 136; *Argus*, 7 May 1934, p 10; *Victorian Churchman*, 26 May 1911; *Age*, 17 Feb. 1962. Grantown House still stands opposite the main gates of the Exhibition Buildings in Nicholson Street.
39 Maree G. Allen, Mother Ursula Frayne in Colonial Melbourne 1857–85, B.A. Hons thesis, University of Melbourne, 1976
40 J. Singleton, *A Narrative of Incidents in the Eventful Life of a Physician* (Melbourne: Hutchinson 1891), 360; *The History of Ormiston Girls' School, 1849-1964* (Melbourne: Ormiston Girls' School 1964); M. Kent Hughes, *Pioneer Doctor: A Biography of John Singleton* (Melbourne: O.U.P. 1950)
41 Singleton, *A Narrative*, 412–13
42 She was a founder of the Governesses' Institution and Melbourne Home, and the Society for the Assistance of Persons of Education.
43 W.M. Thackeray, *Vanity Fair*, chap. 1
44 *History of Ormiston*, 15–16
45 The Chambers sisters attended Cheltenham Ladies' College, London, the Day sisters attended Methodist Ladies' College.
46 VPRS 10061, Teacher registration files, 6397 and 6398
47 Two writers who develop this theme are Leonore Davidoff, *The Best Circles: Society, Etiquette and the Season* (London: Croom Helm 1973), and Elizabeth Windschuttle, 'Educating the Daughters of the Ruling Class in Colonial New South Wales, 1788–1850' in S. Murray-Smith, ed., *Melbourne Studies in Education 1980* (Melbourne: M.U.P. 1980), 105–33.
48 Frazer and Palmer, *Records*, 164; *Australasian*, 7 Dec. 1878, p 712;

J.B. Cooper, *The History of St Kilda* (Melbourne: Printers Pty Ltd. 1931, p 378–9; Olga May, *Chronicles of Clyde* (Melbourne: Brown Prior Anderson 1966), chap. 2.

49 For D.G. Macarthur's unsuccessful career as a public servant see VPRS 19. Superintendent Port Phillip District Inwards Registered Correspondence, 43/575, 43/2157, 44/1407, 45/1031, 46/872, 46/1079, 47/260.

50 Douglas Pike, ed., *Australian Dictionary of Biography* (Melbourne: M.U.P. 1974), 5, p 122. 'David Charteris Macarthur,' S.J. Butlin, *Australia and New Zealand Bank* (Melbourne: Longmans 1961)

51 Helen Macarthur married Matthew Docker, squatter, of Bontharambo Station in 1874. Elizabeth Macarthur married Jonathon Binns Were, business man, in 1880. Both daughters taught in the school and both married widowers comparatively late in life.

52 VPRS 36. Returns of Schools, Port Phillip District, 1847

53 *Argus*, 13 Dec. 1849, p 3

54 *Argus*, 18 Jan. 1851, p 2

55 *Australasian*, 7 Dec. 1878, p 712

56 Docker Papers, MS 10437 La Trobe collection, State Library of Victoria, 1342/4

57 For Alice Henry see Bede Nairn and Geoffrey Serle, eds., *Australian Dictionary of Biography* (Melbourne: M.U.P. 1983), 9. pp 264–5. For Nellie Melba Alexander see Marjorie R. Theobald, *Ruyton Remembers 1878–1978* (Melbourne: Hawthorn 1878), 32. For Melian Stawell, see her father's testimonial, *Argus*, 28 Sept., 1868, p 3. Farley Kelly drew my attention to Annette Beare Crawford's education at East Leigh ladies' school.

58 Rohan Rivett, 'Deakin's Confidente' in *Overland*, 69 (1978), 49

59 J.A. La Nauze, *Alfred Deakin: A Biography* (Melbourne: M.U.P. 1965), 1, p 15

60 Rivett, 'Deakin's Confidente,' 46–7

61 Deakin's daughters were Ivy Brookes, Stella Rivett and Vera White.

62 Fitzpatrick, *PLC*, 53–4, 66, 104

63 Rivett, 'Deakin's Confidente,' 46–7

64 Frazer and Palmer, *Records*, 65

65 *Kyneton Observer*, 29 Sept. 1857, p 1

66 La Nauze, *Deakin*, 1, pp 8–14

67 *Kyneton Observer*, 29 Sept. 1857, p 1

68 La Nauze, *Deakin*, 18–20. He does not mention the connection between the Thompson sisters and John Henning Thompson.

69 G.A. Bremner, *A Tour Brochure of Kyneton and District With Historical Background* (Kyneton: Kyneton Guardian 1973), 7

70 *Argus*, 2 Jan. 1864, p 8

71 Catherine Deakin Papers MS 4913, Australian National Library, diary of Catherine Deakin, box 2, folder 9

72 J.S. Mill, *The Subjection of Women* (London, 1869)

'The poor widow, the ignoramus and the humbug':

An Examination of Rhetoric and Reality in Victoria's 1905 Act for the Registration of Teachers and Schools

Ailsa G. Thomson Zainu'ddin

In 1906 the establishment in Victoria of a Registration Board brought into effect the Act to provide for the Registration of Teachers and Schools. Registration, although not quite in the form finally enacted, had been advocated for over a decade by members of the Independent Association of Secondary Teachers of Victoria, representing self-styled public schools on the English model and large private schools. It had been opposed by Catholic authorities resisting government intrusion into the non-aided educational system they established after the passing of the 1872 Elementary Education Act. It was feared by proprietors of smaller schools as a threat to their very existence in an era when small was increasingly suspect and big assumed to be beautiful. In its final form it provided for compulsory registration of all schools and teachers other than those in the Education Department, clearing the way for the newly reformed, centralised department under its first director, Frank Tate, to introduce government secondary schools. The first of these, under the guise of a Continuation School, opened in 1905.[1]

The legislation marked a further stage in the institutionalisation and standardisation of education following the 1872 Elementary Education Act. By 1876 the implementation of that act had led to some state supervision of private schools to police its compulsory clause. Proprietors and principals of private schools were obliged to submit an annual return to the Ministry of Public Instruction, a chore resented by some, ignored by a few, but generally accepted without complaint. The new legislation of 1905 required registration as a prerequisite for the existence of non-government schools or the remuneration of teachers in them. This led to the formal definition of the criteria which were to distinguish primary from secondary education. The effects of the legislation weighed particularly heavily on many women proprietors, forcing their small private schools either to conform to a particular emerging pattern or to close.

In introducing the bill to the Legislative Council in 1905 the Hon. A.O. Sachse claimed that 'not the most crusted Conservative would dispute the point that everyone who taught children should at least have some qualification for that work. The object of the Bill was merely to satisfy this one point. At present in Victoria anyone, even a person without the faintest possible education, could open a school to teach children.'

He referred to the Royal Commission on Technical Education which, in 1901, had advocated registration for teachers and had argued that 'facilities for the training of teachers of private primary and secondary schools would require to be provided by the Education Department and the University.' He also mentioned the moves by private schoolmasters and departmental officers to have such legislation introduced. Various deputations 'all desired registration, and also that teachers should be possessed of some qualifications.' The legislation had been drafted by a sub-committee drawn from University members and heads of leading Protestant and Catholic schools, men of substance and of learning whose schools were seen as the leading ones because they were the largest in Victoria. They had been 'met in their investigations by the biggest enemy they had – the poor widow. It was held by some very kindly disposed people that when a woman could not earn her living at anything else, she should be allowed to open a school where she could distort the minds of children. A more mistaken form of charity it was impossible for him to imagine. It would pay the State very much better to give that poor lady a good income and prevent her from blocking up any of the channels of education.'[2]

In the deputations to which he referred and on which there were no women, the 'poor widow' had already come under consideration. Equally nebulous plans had been suggested to accommodate her. In 1903 Professor Tucker, who held the chair of Classics at Melbourne University, had said: 'There was no proposal to eject from a livelihood persons in that position, but after a certain date no one should either set up a school or be a teacher in a school unless they had the qualifications. It was not fair to say that because one must find a livelihood they must get it from teaching. If the Government must provide positions for such people they might be appointed pupil teachers in the State schools.'

L.A. Adamson, the Rugby-educated English bachelor who had become headmaster of an antipodean public school, Wesley College, Melbourne, was a co-founder of the Independent Association of Secondary Schools of Victoria and a key figure in deputations regarding registration of teachers. Even when he was co-proprietor of University High School, a large, successful school for both boys and girls, women were on the periphery of his all-male world. While his main interest was the preservation of the public schools from undue competition with either state or private schools he also expressed concern at the 'unfair competition of the unqualified female teachers.' This, he claimed, when interviewed by Sachse in 1901 'at the request of the latter,' 'interfered with the chances of the efficient teachers to such a great extent that it was very hard for a lady who had taken her degree and was a properly qualified teacher to obtain any opening for a proper and decent living.'

On that score registration was not necessarily a solution, as will be demonstrated. He thought the 'poor widow' need not 'be required to pass an examination but she should be required to prove to the council that she had studied the principles of education.' What would be held adequate proof and where she could have studied, assuming that certification was required, were not considered. It was barely fifteen years since the first woman had been admitted to Melbourne University.[3]

Sachse had developed the 'poor widow' stereotype in some detail during discussion with the various delegations and, in the House, came out with a most revealing jumble of notions which show the 'poor widow' to be a rhetorical device. 'There seemed to be some principle underlying the British idea that the young people's education was best carried out by women. For the teaching of babbling infants starting say from three to four years and working up to eight years, it did not seem to him (Mr Sachse) that any very high qualification was required ... there might be the case of a very refined widow who through force of circumstances had to take up a school for a livelihood. It seemed cruel to send that woman up to matriculate before she could be allowed to earn her living if she intended to teach very young children.'

Clearly the concern of the minister, as of the schoolmasters and proprietors forming the delegations, was with secondary rather than elementary education. The terms required definition as, on one hand, elementary schools extended the range of their teaching and, on the other, select schools extended preparatory work downward. Adamson, in 1901, had expressed a fear that 'If the door was opened to primary teachers to teach elementary French, etc. it would break down the whole registration scheme. A great deal of mischief was done by the teaching of secondary subjects by unqualified teachers.' The minister also assumed that refinement and the undertaking of matriculation studies by women conflicted. His assumption reflected a community attitude which was to have quite serious implications for girls' secondary schools when the content and concept of 'secondary education' were being defined and codified by those who took the curriculum of boys' schools as the norm.

When the minister addressed a delegation representing the university, University Colleges and headmasters, the 'poor widow' had become 'a big enemy they had to fight.' To this Sir John Madden, university chancellor, responded that 'the poor widow, the ignoramus and the humbug would do their best to influence Parliament.' While the ignoramus and the humbug may well have been represented, or even present, in Parliament, the poor widow was unlikely to have any influence at all on a Parliament for which women did not even have the franchise prior to 1908. As it happened Parliament showed very little interest in the bill and, at the committee stage, 'there were only eight or nine members present,' hardly odd because it was the middle of the night.[4]

Although he was prominent in the legal world, Sir John Madden's main contact with schools was as speaker at various Speech Day celebrations. He urged that 'there should be nothing in the bill to allow a horde of these unqualified persons to come in.' Adamson was more realistic (and more revealing) in remarking that 'there were people turning to teaching because there was nothing else to do or until they could obtain an opening in some real profession.' Uncommitted male teachers could use teaching as a stepping stone to the 'real' professions but access to other recognised professions, despite the admission of women to the Medical School in 1887 or the Sex Disqualification Removal Act of 1903 allowing them to practise as lawyers, provided no practical alternatives for the 'poor widow' or for most other members of her sex.[5]

The solutions offered by Sachse and Tucker for the objects of their solicitation were quite unrealistic and not serious programmes of action. Sachse claimed that it would pay the state better to give a good income to 'that poor lady' but it was more economical still, having debarred her from teaching, to leave her to fend for herself. Tucker's proposal that poor widows become pupil teachers in the state system revealed an abysmal ignorance of the excess of pupil teachers in state schools, surprising in someone regarded as an educational expert. Any cursory glance at the *Australasian Schoolmaster*, journal of the teaching profession, during the preceding decade should have indicated the impracticality of looking for openings for poor widows there. By the end of the century the gradual reorganisation of the colonial teaching service had confined women to the lower levels of the classified rolls and, during the course of retrenchment in the depression years of the 1890s, departmental regulations had effectively excluded women from senior teaching positions as well as compelling them to retire upon marriage. It was also increasingly difficult for any women to move from private to government teaching.[6]

The protestations of concern for the mythical 'poor widow,' the association of the poor widow with the ignoramus and humbug as one of a trio, the fear expressed toward her as the 'chief enemy' are reminiscent of the Walrus who, while deeply sympathizing with the plight of the oysters, yet managed to demolish 'those of the largest size.' The legislation created hurdles of increasing height not, as one contemptuous parliamentarian expressed it, for 'any second rate washerwoman who failed to make a living at washing' but for many women whose commitment to teaching was fully professional. Some may even have chosen independence in the preference to the precarious lottery of marriage, believing with Miles Franklin, that marriage could be 'the most horribly tied-down and unfair-to-women existence going' and preferring to economic independence of a home-based family enterprise.[7]

The allegations against the poor widow were not substantiated by supporters of the act but, because of the generalised nature of the stereotypes, such charges were impossible to refute. To link her with the ignoramus and the humbug was to suggest guilt by association. Ambiguity in the use of 'poor,' conjured up someone in financial need because inadequately provided for by any male protector but also implied a sense of inadequacy, a 'poor performance,' and a degree of condescending pity for the 'poor woman.' The implied denigration resembled similar references to 'mere' accomplishments and, given the contemporary emphasis on the educational value of big schools, the small school of the 'poor widow' is also under attack.

Such stereotypes, accepted then reinforced by such acceptance, are passed on by general historians. An example occurs in Geoffrey Blainey's *History of Camberwell* (1964). 'By 1886 Camberwell had three private schools with nearly a hundred students,' he wrote. 'It was then possible for any idle dame or dissolute scholar to open a school, and some of their Boroondara schools lasted one year and some two.' Later, in reference to half a dozen girls' schools, he commented, 'All have vanished ... In fact all Camberwell's early private schools were overshadowed by the larger schools only a mile or two to the West.' He has, by the use of 'their,' allowed the reader to assume that the proprietors of Boroondara educational institutions were idle dames or dissolute scholars running ephemeral schools. A closer look at this account, now that more work has been done on the history of private schools, illuminates the relationship between rhetoric and reality. Of the three private schools listed in the 1886 returns, the first year in which returns from the district are recorded, one may have lasted only another year, or more probably, four. Another, the High School for Girls, continued until 1906, a twenty year span. The third, which became Camberwell Grammar School, has outlasted all those 'larger private schools to the west' of which Blainey speaks – Hawthorn Grammar, Hawthorn College, and Kew High School. The only ones in Kew to survive to the present are Xavier College and Methodist Ladies' College, church corporate bodies recognised as Public Schools in the English sense, and Ruyton Girls' School, whose founder might even have been described in Sachse's phrase as 'a very refined widow who through force of circumstances had to take up a school for a livelihood.' Newnham (Ladies') College, despite its elaborate and extensive advertisements in the local press and a name linking it with higher education for women in the United Kingdom, lasted only from 1893 to 1897 before its headmaster, Frank Wheen, BA, was forced to close it. In contrast, Milverton Ladies' College, owned by the Misses Burke, former students of Wheen when he was headmaster of MLC, lasted another thirty years, closing in 1927. Hessle Ladies' College, founded by Miss Ada Gresham, BA, in 1888, continued until 1913.

One suspects that Blainey, in nominating the 'strong' schools, was unconsciously influenced by their one common feature – their headmasters – and by the strength of their advertising. The women's schools, designated as 'too poor to attract many good teachers, too small to provide the stimulus of competition in the schools and too young to leave a name comparable with the older schools' were being judged anachronistically by modern criteria based on public school education for boys. The evidence contradicts the implication that idle dames or dissolute scholars ran ephemeral schools in Camberwell, nor does Blainey's account recognise the effects of the 1905 legislation on small private schools.[8]

Available evidence is inadequate for estimating how many poor widows closed schools between the passing and the promulgation of the act. The complete list of registered teachers and schools published in 1907, indicates no rush or hordes of them into teaching. The Closed Schools Files generated by the 1905 legislation provide consolidated information about the private schools of Victoria in 1906. The remainder of this paper is based on a preliminary exploration of this material looking particularly at the effects of the act on small secondary schools run by women. These represented a tradition of education which, at its worst, was easily caricatured and in need of reform but, at its best, had much to offer. Although Sachse maintained that the bill sought 'merely to satisfy this one point' that everyone teaching children 'should at least have some qualification for that work,' one effect of the act was to make it more difficult for small family schools, run by women autonomously, to survive as an alternative form of secondary education, even when the proprietors were well-qualified and experienced women.[9]

Sachse quoted Professor Tucker as 'a leading educational authority' (although not as Sachse claimed, 'the most unbiased authority in Victoria') on the subject of small secondary schools. The university, with rapidly declining numbers at the turn of the century, was vitally anxious to obtain more students, to improve and extend their preparatory grounding at secondary level and to feed them into the dwindling student population of the Arts Faculty in which Tucker was professor of Classics. Tucker claimed that 'within ten miles of the Melbourne Post Office there were four hundred schools and that a great proportion of those schools were being conducted by people who were ... ignorant.' His figures were impressionistic and exaggerated. The number finally registered within ten miles of the GPO was closer to 360 schools. At least 100 passed the quite stringent tests for secondary registration, another seventy-five were religious schools, mainly Catholic, ten were coaching colleges or private coaches and another five were orphanages or institutions. Among the remaining 170 schools proprietors (less than half the total) some may have aspired to a secondary status they were not qualified to maintain or have claimed it on the assumption that any non-government school was by definition secondary. But some were hardly 'a great proportion.' Of the 152 applications for secondary registration by girls' schools in Melbourne and its suburbs ninety-one

(60 per cent) were ultimately granted. One effect of the act was to clarify the definition of secondary education, tying that definition closely to the requirements of the university where women were a newly admitted minority in a predominantly male world.[10]

The search for the 'poor widow' in the real world is rendered difficult by the lack of relevant evidence. Of at least 327 women proprietors in the city and suburbs of Melbourne forty used the title 'Mrs' and at least three of them are known to have had husbands still living. In the country another six married women were school proprietors. Ten married women in the city and one in the country were granted secondary registration. Thirty-four other women were proprietors of country schools. There were almost as many unmarried sisters in partnership as there were married proprietors. In some cases, such as the Misses Dare of Stratherne, they may have been partners with, or successors to, a widowed mother but such evidence is mostly unavailable. In thirty-three city or suburban schools two, three or four unmarried sisters held joint ownership; in another thirty-four schools one sister was the proprietor and one or more other sisters made up the rest of the staff or took charge of boarders. In the country there were a further five partnerships along with six proprietors who employed other relatives. This accounted for seventy-two unmarried women in the city or suburbs and another seventeen in country areas, almost twice the number of married women with or without husbands. Even had all the remaining married women been widows they would still have been a minority among women proprietors of schools. Nor does any evidence suggest that widows were necessarily unqualified, though they may well, like some English counterparts, have been poor. Emily Davies, in urging endowments for girls' schools in England, referred to 'those who would be thought poorest of all – widows of professional men with small incomes, having children whose education they could less afford to pay for than many working men could for theirs.'[11]

Joyce Pedersen, writing of women teachers in nineteenth-century England, distinguishes between the private schoolmistress who 'aspired to a leisured, amateur role in a secluded, quasi-domestic setting' and public school headmistresses seeking professional recognition in the public sphere. The former stressed 'good birth and a leisured life-style' as the main elements in high school status. Public school headmistresses gave 'more weight to academic achievement and less to a leisured life-style.' The former preferred boarding schools as 'more private ... more profitable,' catering for a more select clientele. Such a proprietor served as a 'model of elegance and moral rectitude for the pupils,' although academically she was likely to be both amateur and dilettante. The new type of 'public school' for girls, with Cheltenham Ladies' College and the North London Collegiate School for Girls as prototypes, dated from the 1870s. Pedersen argues that the headmistresses of such public schools sought professional not amateur status and could 'emancipate themselves from their client's control' in a way in which smaller schools could not. The relatively greater economic security resulting from increased size enabled head teachers to determine the conditions under which pupils attended their schools and to demand regular attendance.[12]

By 1906 three girls' schools in Victoria claimed, and were accorded, the status of 'public school' in the English sense: Presbyterian Ladies' College, founded in 1875, Methodist Ladies' College, founded in 1882 and Melbourne Church of England Girls' Grammar School, which came under Anglican auspices in 1904, having evolved from a private school, Merton Hall, established by a Newnham graduate in the 1890s. Each, in varying degrees and combinations, drew on both the traditions outlined by Joyce Pedersen. Victorian public schools were all church-backed institutions, the boys' schools established on land granted by the government, the girls' schools established without government aid or endowment, but accorded public school status by an extension of the original English definition and by modelling their teaching to some extent on the secondary education provided for boys. The three girls' public schools were not large by English standards and only MCEGGS had a headmistress. The other two were under the dual control of a clergyman principal and a male headmaster. The women who taught there lacked the autonomy of their English counterparts in schools of the Girls' Public Day School Company nor could there have been any equivalent of the Headmistress' Association formed in England in 1874.

A number of other smaller privately owned schools, in choosing the name 'Ladies' College,' seem to have aspired to similar status with varying degrees of optimism. Several such schools preceded the girls' public schools in providing academic secondary education for girls once the Matriculation examinations of Melbourne University were opened to women in 1871. Only three of those still in existence in 1906 had 100 or more pupils while another twenty had between thirty and ninety-five. The typical private school, primary or secondary, had fewer than thirty pupils.[13]

With the introduction of the 1905 legislation, implemented just as the Board of Education in England and Wales was abandoning its attempt to maintain a register of teachers, the conditions under which pupils attended schools were determined less by the proprietors of the schools than by the Registration Board established by the state legislature. This prevented the development of any varying types of school. The small private schools described and defended by Ken Clements were forced, if they wished to survive by qualifying for secondary registration, to accept that 'the quality of the education given at a secondary school could only be measured by the number of passes and honours gained at Matriculation,' an examination designed for and governed by university entrance requirements. The standardisation of the secondary curriculum in relation to the matriculation examination thus involved admission into the male world of higher education on terms and conditions devised by men for their male heirs and successors. Initially girls had been grudgingly admitted to the examinations in 1871 but, until 1880, denied the right to matriculate when successful. Now the situation was reversed. Pressure was being placed on schools hitherto free of examination restrictions to enter candidates or else forfeit the right to claim secondary status.[14]

One of the first schools closed as a direct result of the 1905 act was Camberwell High School for Girls, owned by Mrs Susan Lewis who had, in the early 1880s, established a school at Carmarthen, Wales, 'where there was really no opening for one' because she 'had to maintain herself and child by her own exertions.' The rural dean of Carmarthen, in a testimonial, said she 'held the appointment of Teacher of Music at the Carmarthen High School and has conducted most successfully a Private school for many years' which three of the dean's own children had attended. He had 'no doubt of her success at Melbourne as soon as her ability and efficiency are known.' Her advertisement in the *Carmarthen Journal* of September 1884 referred to 'vacancies for a few daily pupils. Terms £4.4s. per annum. Tuition in English, French and Latin.' Dancing was taught by a visiting mistress. By April of the following year she was advertising it as a 'School for Young Ladies Only' with no fees mentioned and had made 'special arrangements to receive four young ladies as boarders.' To prospective parents she offered 'references to parents of former pupils,' with confidence borne out by the testimony already quoted and more which accompanied it. In February 1886 her 'Preliminary Advice' in the *Argus* indicated that 'Mrs F.D. Lewis who has several years experience as Principal of an

Educational Establishment in Wales intends shortly to OPEN A LADIES' SCHOOL at Camberwell for boarders and day pupils. Particulars in a future prospectus.' By 1900 the school 'was in a most flourishing state with as many as fifty pupils at times' but by 1906 it had only twelve day pupils and no boarders, with one other permanent member of staff and visiting teachers for piano, violin and elocution. The decline in numbers in the previous five years she claimed was due to a serious illness during which, as the vicar of Camberwell substantiated, she 'lost many of her pupils to other rival schools.' As one requirement for secondary registration related to the number of pupils passing matriculation in the previous five years, this unfortunate illness counted against her.

She was granted secondary registration on appeal but in the following year wrote sharply to the registrar, 'I have the honour to inform you (for the second time) that I gave up my school before Easter, principally because my name had not been printed on the roll of Registered Teachers though I had been ranked as a Secondary teacher.'

Whether through a misunderstanding of the requirements or the loss of her application she was clearly a victim of the new legislation, though her return to Melbourne in 1886 with her young son suggests neither the stereotype of a 'poor widow' nor of an 'idle dame.'[15]

Other women, whatever their marital status, also had difficulty in producing evidence to satisfy the Registration Board. Miss Minnie Strickland of Merton Ladies' College in Armadale, founded in 1885, had Miss Miriam Merfield, MA, an experienced graduate matriculation teacher as an assistant in 1906. Miss Strickland wrote: 'As is so constantly the case with smaller private schools we have entered to us girls whom the parents absolutely refused to have put through public examination either from some delicacy on the part of the pupil or the parents' views as to the danger of cramming rather than solid education ... the registration is the matter of most vital importance to a school of such long standing at the present juncture.'

The Misses Rudd owned Strathclyde in Toorak. Two of them had been among the earliest girl matriculants presented from Geelong Ladies' College, one of the oldest private schools for girls in Victoria. Elizabeth Rudd had matriculated in 1874 and Jane in 1875. They wrote that the standard they taught was the equivalent of matriculation. 'This standard we have always maintained but the parents of our pupils – with two exceptions – whilst requiring this standard at our hands absolutely refuse to allow their daughters to present themselves for Public Examination ... Our parents ask for a wide range of subjects, up-to-date general information and many accomplishments ... an education more fitted to the life that lies before their daughters.' Both these schools, in the fashionable suburbs of Melbourne, were granted secondary registration on appeal.

Less fortunate was the proprietor of Blinkbonnie, a school founded in Moonee Ponds, on the less favoured western side of the city, in 1894. Miss Marian Morris had six girls studying for matriculation but two did not enter because of ill-health, two went to city schools (one to PLC) and two left. She commented that 'There seems to be a strong tendency now for girls to leave school at fifteen in order 1) to enter in a business college; 2) to study for examinations in music; 3) to learn a business, and very few girls seem to wish to study to become teachers.'[16]

Milverton Ladies' College, established in 1894, was owned by the Misses Frances and Hannah (Effie) Burke. Miss Frances Burke, educated at MLC, was not allowed to present for matriculation owing to ill-health but 'at the same time, as co-principal of a very successful secondary school she considers herself entitled to register as a secondary teacher,' although the board did not agree. Miss Effie Burke, who had matriculated from MLC in 1890 with honours in English, History and French, and Milverton Ladies' College were both granted secondary registration without difficulty. It was possibly one rival school taking girls from Camberwell Girls' High School during the illness of Mrs Lewis. 'During the past five years,' wrote the Misses Burke, '17 passes at matriculation have been gained, 25 separate honours, including ten places in the class lists, and the Botany and Physiology Exhibition (1904, December).' In 1907 they opened a branch school in Union Road, Surrey Hills. As this was after the initial period for the registration of existing schools, they raised a problem regarding its classification which had wide implications. 'If schools are only to be classed by results, no new school can ever show these. It is then intended for the future that no new school can be commenced as secondary?' they enquired. This intention may have been in the minds of some supporters of the act but they would not have wished attention to be drawn to it. As the Misses Burke pointed out 'the school which has yet to win its laurels, will be foredoomed to failure if it is under obligation to announce itself as primary only ... As all the teachers we are employing are secondary, our outlay in salaries and other directions is much greater than if we were only aiming at primary standard.' The issue raised was significant, compounded for many private schools by the entry of the state into secondary education, first through the establishment of the co-educational Melbourne Continuation School in 1905 and, after the Education Act of 1910, through University Practising School in the city and District High Schools in the country.[17]

The act of 1905 covered three main aspects, all desirable in themselves. 'Effective and regular instruction' was to be provided in healthy and suitable school buildings and premises by registered teachers only. School proprietors who coped satisfactorily with the first and third of these requirements faced, in later years, an increasing standard for instruction and registration. In 1909 the *Australasian Schoolmaster* reprinted the *Age* comment that 'The Registration Act is evidence of the determination to protect the public from itself, and from the evils of free trade in education ... it is at present an offence to employ an unregistered teacher and after the end of the current year the requirements for registration will be more stringent than at present.' Private school proprietors, both men and women, also faced rising levels of expectations as to what constituted healthy and suitable buildings and the financial outlay necessary to provide these rose in consequence.[18]

In 1913 the president of the Council of Public Education, a position held *ex officio* by the director of education, Frank Tate, prepared a memorandum to counteract 'statements ... to the effect that the qualifications demanded by the Education Department from state school teachers are inferior to those required by the Council of Education from teachers of registered schools.' While true of the qualifications *actually* required during a period when teacher supply exceeded demand, there were no *legal* requirements for state school teachers, expressly excluded from the operation of the act. Tate did not mention the requirements regarding 'healthy and suitable school buildings and premises' which were certainly more stringent than those in state schools, exempt from Health Department inspection.[19]

The Closed Schools Files contain many examples of women caught between Health Department requirements and the reluctance of the landlord leasing the accommodation to make the required alterations. It is easy to understand the resentment and bitterness of school proprietors whose landlords were often slow-moving boards of trustees of church halls who believed these to be perfectly satisfactory for Sunday schools. They resented the implied criticism of their premises, especially when the Victorian State Schools' Teachers' Union was drawing attention to 'the very serious position of teachers in country schools, owing to the entire absence – in many instances – of any sanitary arrangements.' In the inner city at the Faraday Street State School 'tons of refuse ... had been stowed under the galleries by means of trap doors let into the sides.'[20]

Brunswick High School for Girls, like the Faraday Street school, was in an older suburb where all public buildings pre-dated the laying down of Health Department standards for private schools. Since 1890 it had been owned by Mrs Elizabeth McCowan, family breadwinner in lieu of her husband, assisted by four of her daughters. In 1909 the school was sold to Mrs Halloran. Neither fitted the accepted stereotype of wife or widow. Mrs McCowan, as Elizabeth Philpott, had been headmistress of a London girls' school from 1869 to 1871 and had then taught history and physical geography at Stockwell Training College, London, for two years. Her certificate from the Privy Council on Education had favourable reports from Her Majesty's Inspectors, Matthew Arnold, Mr J.D. Morell, and Canon E.D. Tinling, while Alfred Bourne, principal of the college, in accepting her resignation and wishing her much happiness and prosperity in the future, expressed 'the regret of the Ladies at losing a governess so able, conscientious and ladylike.' A widow, Mrs Halloran (formerly Bella Guerin), the first woman graduate of Melbourne University, had taught at Loretto Convent, Ballarat, the Ballarat School of Mines, St Vincent's College (Sydney) and at her own University College, Bendigo. As the High School was changing hands it had to be re-registered. Its three large schoolrooms and two classrooms failed to meet the standards laid down by the Board of Health. From 1910 to 1914 Bella Lavender (no longer a widow as she had remarried later in 1909) was in constant trouble with the Board of Health as she moved from hall to hall in Brunswick, seeking premises to meet its requirements, only a few years after Brunswick State School, with its overcrowded galleries, large classes and harsh discipline, caused one beginner to need a year's absence from 'brain fever.'

Mrs Lavender moved from the Congregational Hall to the Lyceum Hall. The Trustees argued that their hall was already well-ventilated and that the Board of Health requirements meant that 'people at our Sunday evening services are greatly complaining of the draught and keep away in consequence.' The Masonic Hall was no better although no worse than the St Augustine Sunday School Hall which, uninspected, the state school hired for its overflow classes. Finally, after a prolonged correspondence with the Inspector of Registered Schools, Martin Hansen (not a man who responded well to intelligent, articulate and highly qualified women), she bowed to the inevitable and wrote in 1917 that 'the number of children is too small' – they had dwindled to four – 'to make it payable for me to continue the school.' Her husband appears in the electoral roll as a gentleman of independent means. Why should she, however well qualified, be running a school instead of depending on his support?[21]

When state high schools were given parliamentary sanction in 1910, matriculation as the goal of secondary studies was further reinforced. By 1914 twenty-one schools with secondary registration had closed, two-thirds of them owned and staffed largely or entirely by women. From 1907 to 1914 only one new, short-lived, secondary school was opened (by a man for girls) and four secondary business colleges. As the Misses Burke had predicted, the problems of starting a new private secondary school were well-nigh insuperable.

Some men teachers were also caught at a disadvantage by the act's requirements. Two examples of proprietors of small country schools demonstrate the reaction of men to an act which they had never imagined would impede *them* in their professional lives. The first, Edward A. Vieusseux, was the son of the well-known educational family in Melbourne which had been a pioneer of higher education for girls. He was attempting to provide an alternative form of education for boys at Berwick Grammar School, a small country boarding school near Melbourne but out of reach of the temptations of city life. It was established in 1882. In 1906 it was refused secondary registration. Vieusseux wrote: 'It is very hard that one who has devoted a lifetime to scholastic pursuits and has always held an acknowledged position among his fellow teachers, should find himself suddenly reduced in status and his means of living considerably curtailed by the action of the Board.'[22]

The second was the Rev. Frank Wheen whose Melbourne teaching career had also begun in 1882 when he became first headmaster of the newly opened Methodist Ladies' College, Kew. When retrenched eleven years later he established the short-lived Newnham College already mentioned and shortly afterwards took a step not then available to women by entering the Congregational ministry. In December 1906 he bought St Andrew's College, Bairnsdale, a small country school for boys. He wrote to the registrar objecting to being asked for a transfer fee as his proprietorship dated from 1906. He even argued further that such a fee was *ultra vires* and also requested dispensation from the requirement to erect a noticeboard. 'If they could see the place they would agree that the erection of a board would benefit no one but the carpenter and painter,' he claimed. The first point was granted, thus avoiding any dispute on the validity of the transfer fee; the second refused. He commented, 'Years ago I was actively engaged in the movement for the Registration of Secondary Schools for Teachers, but it was never intended *then* that all sorts of 'pinpricks' should be devised for the vexation of qualified teachers who are trying (1) to do the State a service (2) to eke out a living.' Years ago he had viewed the matter from the vantage point of a headmaster of a public school for girls and was active in advocating registration but was understandably less enthusiastic when suffering vexatious pinpricks as proprietor of a small country school. Certainly the legislation was hard on these men, who saw themselves as part of the educational establishment. For them it was unthinkable that they should be classed with poor widow, ignoramus or humbug.[23]

Yet how much more was at stake for Miss Annie Rohs! Born 3 April 1866, daughter of Margaret Bowen from Ireland and Peter Rohs, a successful Bendigo businessman who had emigrated from Germany, she was, in 1880, the first girl in the colony to win a government scholarship. This took her from Gravel Hill State School in the Sandhurst Corporate High School where, at the age of fifteen, she sat successfully for Matriculation. In 1883 she took the Classics Exhibition and was placed equal first among that year's matriculants. By 1889 she had completed her MA with honours in classics and philology and had begun teaching. After two years in the Education Department she taught at country private schools until 1897 when she became principal and head teacher of Geelong Ladies' College. At Speech Day in 1905 the Rev. J.V. McNair (whose daughter was dux of the school that year), in reading the principal's report on her behalf, remarked, by way of introduction, on the new Church of England Girls' Grammar School to be established in Geelong in the coming years: 'If the new school was a success (and he did not wish it otherwise) he sincerely trusted it would not be at the expense of that institution and he hoped that no parents would dream of taking their children away ... Whatever new schools might be started, denominational or otherwise, it was quite certain that as long as Miss Rohs was head of the Ladies' College, it would retain its position as one of the leading schools in the State.' The school had two graduates and three matriculated teachers, all women, on the permanent staff and another four women on the visiting staff.

His prophesy was not fulfilled. In 1909 Miss Rohs wrote to the registrar informing him that she had closed the school and inquiring if any vacancy on the teaching staff of a Continuation School would be available to her. She mentioned that 'the foundation of the C.E. Girls' School and the intention of your Department to open a Continuation School have resulted in the closing of a hitherto successful school.' The registrar, dissociating himself by implication from her reference to 'your department,' replied that 'With reference to your obtaining employment as a teacher in a Continuation School you should make application to the Secretary, Education Department.' If she did so the application was unsuccessful although in the 1930s, living privately in retirement at Bendigo, she still had a formidable reputation as a coach of classics.[24] Dr Leeper, warden of Trinity College, Melbourne University, the first affiliated college to provide residential accommodation for university women, was one of the early members of the Registration Board. He claimed, 'I think you might say we closed scores of schools by that Act' and boasted that 'We were denounced for taking the bread out of the mouths of young women.' Annie Rohs, Headmistress of Geelong Ladies' College, had been one of his early students at Trinity Women's College and holder of his Warden's Scholarship. She was forty-four and her school a decade older when it closed. She was a highly qualified professional woman, head of a school older than the majority of English-style boys public schools in Victoria. The Registration Act, which paved the way for the state's entry into education, combined with the expansion of Anglican education for girls to spell the doom of Geelong Ladies' College and the end of the career of Annie Rohs as an autonomous headmistress.[25]

The stereotype of the 'poor widow,' the enemy who 'distorted the minds of children,' helped salve the consciences of the men who legislated for the registration of teachers. They discussed improbable alternatives to aid her in her plight. The closing of some schools may have been, on the available evidence, an educational advance. Some of them may have fitted and therefore reinforced the stereotype. The change from the small private secondary school to the large secondary school, government, 'Public' or private, was a result of extended and redefined secondary education. Yet it was the educated, competent, autonomous woman who stood to lose most as new state requirements destroyed her livelihood, her life's work and her autonomy. She was unlikely to be able to escape into some 'real profession.' There was not even a place for her in the new state high schools. She had, perforce, to find her proper place in the private sphere where women were expected to remain.

NOTES

This article is from the *History of Education Review*, 13, 2 (1984), 29–42. Reprinted with permission. It is based on a paper given at ANZHES, Adelaide 1976. I am indebted to Bob Gidney and Win Millar for their valuable assistance in reading and commenting on the original paper. The tables which accompanied that paper are available from the author upon request.

1 For a succinct account see R.J.W. Selleck, 'The Directors – F. Tate ...' in C. Turney, ed., *Pioneers of Australian Education*, 3 (Sydney University Press 1983), 20–1; for a fuller account see Selleck, *Frank Tate: A Biography* (Melbourne University Press 1982), 153–65; for a detailed discussion see M.A. (Ken) Clements, 'Relationships between the University of Melbourne and the Secondary Schools of Victoria,' Ph.D. thesis, University of Melbourne, 1979, pp 211 ff.

2 For Sachse in the Legislative Council, see *Victorian Parliamentary Debates*, 14 Nov. 1905, pp 2620, 2671; for the various delegations see Victorian Public Record Series (Special Cases File), Papers on Registration of Teachers, (Laverton).

3 For Adamson see *Australian Dictionary of Biography* article by M.A. (Ken) Clements and also G. Blainey *et al., Wesley College: A Centenary History* (Melbourne: Robertson and Mullens 1978), *passim*, esp. chap. 5.

4 For Madden see R. Campbell, *A History of the Melbourne Law School, 1857–1973* (Faculty of Law, University of Melbourne 1977), 82–4; for the committee stages of the bill see Vic. *P.D.* 8 Dec. 1905, p 3621; the comment by Mr Hutchinson when the council refused to accept the assembly amendment excluding 'any school conducted by a teaching order of any denomination.' In this way state school teachers who wished to be included were excluded and the teaching orders who wished for exemption were included.

5 For an example of Adamson's claim see VPRS 10300 No. 461, school held at the Central Fire Brigade Eastern Hill by Charles John Lowe (later Sir Charles Lowe, Chief Justice of Victoria, then of Selborn Chambers) until 1914. For admission of women see G. Blainey, *Centenary History of Melbourne University* (M.U.P. 1957), chap. 9; A.G.T.

Zainu'ddin, 'Admission of Women to Melbourne University ...' in S. Murray-Smith, ed., *Melbourne Studies in Education* 1973; Farley Kelly, *Degrees of Liberation: A Short History of Women in the University of Melbourne* (The Women Graduate Centenary Committee of The University of Melbourne 1985)

6 See 'Position Past and Present of Female Teachers' from the 24th Annual Report of the Victorian Lady Teachers' Association in *Australasian Schoolmaster*, 1 Dec. 1908, pp 114–15. The marriage bar was not removed until 1956. For a widow in the Education Department see A.G.T. Zainu'ddin, 'The Corr Family' (Minnie Catford) in R.J.W. Selleck and M. Sullivan, *Not So Eminent Victorians* (Melbourne University Press 1984); for the difficulty in moving from private to government teaching see *ibid.* (Alice Corr).

7 The washerwomen/teacher as a further note of rhetoric has an echo in Wales where the 'dame' who began Parade Row School, Carmarthen 'began school when ill-health disabled her as a washerwoman.' M. and E. Lodwick, *The Story of Carmarthen* (Carmarthen: St Peters Press 1972), 98; Miles Franklin, *My Brilliant Career* (1901), 47.

8 Blainey, *Centenary History*, 28, 72. Figures on private schools (1878–93) are published with the Annual Reports of the Minister of Public Instruction 1878–1893. As the minister was interested only in the number of pupils attending, other details can be misleading. A centenary history of Camberwell Grammar School has been written by Ian Hansen (1986). For Xavier College see G. Dening, *Xavier College* (Melbourne: Old Xaverians 1978); for M.L.C. see A.G.T. Zainu'ddin, *They Dream of a School* (Melbourne: Hyland House 1982); for Ruyton Girls' School see M.R. Theobald, *Ruyton Remembers 1878–1978* (Hawthorn, Victoria: Hawthorn Press 1978); for Frank Wheen and Newnham College see A.G.T. Zainu'ddin, 'The Career of a Colonial Schoolmaster: Frank Wheen Esq. in S. Murray-Smith, *Melbourne Studies in Education* (1981), esp. 82–6. He was emphatically *not* dissolute. See also M.A. (Ken) Clements, 'Some Aspects of the Private Schools and the Smaller Catholic schools in Victoria in the Beginning of the 20th Century' (Roneoed paper, Monash Education Faculty 1975); Milverton Ladies' College see VPRS 10061 Files 97, 1135, 1169; Hessle Ladies' College, *ibid.* File 312

9 Vic. Govt *Gazette*, Jan.–Apr. 1907, pp 207–538; May–Aug. 1907, pp 3780–3860 for register of teachers. Other more diffuse sources can also reveal much detail about such schools. See also Theobald, '"Mere Accomplishments"?' reprinted in this volume.

10 Clements, 'Some Aspects,' Vic. *P.D.* 1905, p 2621

11 For Stratherne see Zainu'ddin, *They Dreamt of a School*, 82; Emily
Davies (1872) quoted in S. Fletcher, *Feminists and Bureaucrats* (Cambridge U.P. 1980), 74. There were in England wealthy widows such as
Mrs Reid, founder of Bedford College, London but they had no equivalent in Australia.

12 Joyce Pedersen, 'Schoolmistresses and Headmistresses: Elites and Education in Nineteenth-Century England,' reprinted in this volume.
They ranged in size from under 100 to over 1000 students by the turn
of the century. Victoria's largest girls' school had 247 girls in 1906.

13 K.E. Fitzpatrick, *P.L.C.: The First Hundred Years, 1875–1975;* Zai-
nu'ddin, *They Dreamt of a School;* M.C.E.G.G.S., Jubilee History, *Nisi
Dominus Frustra* (Melbourne Church of England Girls Grammar
School 1953). For date at which the school came under Anglican auspices
see VPRO 10061 No. 4639. For the boys' public schools in Victoria see
I.V. Hansen, *Nor Free Nor Secular* (Melbourne O.U.P. 1971). There
is scope for a closer comparison between the registration movements in
Victoria and in Great Britain. For the latter see J. Milburn, 'The
Secondary Schoolmistress: A Study of Her Professional Views and Their
Significance in the Educational Developments of the period 1895–1914,'
Ph.D. thesis, London University, 1969, pp 198–213.

14 Clements, 'Small Schools,' 16. Anne McGrath, 'Some Convent School
Traditions in Victoria,' M.Ed. thesis, Melbourne University, 1964,
examines this in relation to Catholic girls' schools. (Tables 1 to 4
of my original paper give further details.) The better staff/student
ratio in girls' schools can partly be explained in terms of lower salaries
for women – more staff for less outlay – and partly by the higher
number of visiting staff and greater provision for sub-primary teachers
than at boys' schools which did not, in many cases, even have primary
registration.

15 VPRS 10300 No. 440 for testimonials. For her Carmarthen school, *Carmarthen Journal* (Colindale) 1884–5. First advertisement 19 Sept. 1884,
second 24 Apr. 1885. Her final advertisements 'MRS FRANK LEWIS has
made special arrangements to receive FOUR YOUNG LADIES AS BOARD-
ERS. Next term commences Tues. Sept. 1' ran from July 1885 to 8 Jan.
1886 without alteration, suggesting she had already closed the school.
For her preliminary advice *Argus* 2 Feb. 1886. C1.4(3) of Act 2032 1905
read: 'The absence of the name of any person or of any school from
such printed list ... shall be evidence until the contrary is made to appear
that such person is not a registered teacher'. In Carmarthen the

household in 1881 consisted of herself, then 34, her Victoria-born son, then aged 5, and a 14 year old domestic servant. Gr.Br., Public Records Office, RG 11/5398.

16 Merton L.C. VPRS 10300 No. 740. The school closed in 1910; Strathclyde VPRS 10300 No. 667, closed in 1912; Miss Marian Morris VPRS 10061 No. 4646 and Blinkbonnie VPRS 10300 No. 506. It continued until 1920. Ormiston VPRS 10300 No. 696. The Misses Singleton sold the school in 1913. It continues as the Camberwell C.E.G.G.S. Junior Branch. For Miriam Merfield see Zainu'ddin, 'Admission of Women.'

17 Milverton L.C. VPRS 10300 No. 97 and No. 833. VPRS 10061/813, 815/818. For State High Schools Act No. 2301 Geo v, Jan. 1911, Pt III.

18 *Australasian Schoolmaster*, 10 Mar. 1910. The *Age* was strongly protectionist in policy.

19 *Education Gazette and Teachers' Aid* published the details. (This was the departmental rival and successor to the *Australasian Schoolmaster*, another example of the government taking over a former educational activity maintained initially by private initiative.)

20 *Australasian Schoolmaster*, 15 Jan. 1908

21 Details of Mrs McCowan's qualifications come from VPRS 10061/4844 and Pauline B. Burren, 'Mentone Girls' Grammar School and Its Forerunners 1899–1974: A study in Continuity,' M.Ed. thesis, Monash University 1982, pp 126–7; Bella Halloran VPRS 10061/2869 and for Brunswick Girls' High School VPRS 10300/534, 1014, 1039. On 16 March 1913 she wrote 'I do wish some *modus ventilandi* could be arranged so as to suit them (the Trustees) and your Board, as I am placed in a very awkward position.' Hansen was unamused and unmoved. For Brunswick State School 1901, ms. Memoirs of Thelma B. (Roberts) Thomson, in possession of the writer, her daughter.

22 VPRS 10300/774. He was the son of the owners of Vieusseux Ladies' College. See M.R. Theobald, 'Julie Vieusseux' in F. Kelly and M. Lake, *Double Time* (Penguin 1984) and '"Mere Accomplishments"?' The school closed when he died in 1919.

23 Zainu'ddin, 'The Career of a Colonial Schoolmaster' 60–97

24 Geelong L.C. VPRS 10300/660. Further information from VPRS 10061/6026; Matriculation Entries 1881, Trinity College Calendar, 1889, *Australasian Schoolmaster*, May 1895.

25 De Leeper's comment was reported at an interview with Misses Valentine and Molly Leeper, 24 July 1976.

WOMEN TEACHING IN THE PUBLIC SPHERE

'Daughters into Teachers':
Educational and Demographic Influences on the Transformation of Teaching into 'Women's Work' in America

Geraldine Jonçich Clifford

'The old prejudice against remunerative labor for women has not wholly died out,' lamented Miss Whitney of the Vassar College faculty, in 1882, 'and in many families the daughters go home, after their school-days are over, to live parasitic lives upon busy fathers and mothers; giving a little domestic assistance, perhaps, but, upon the whole, filling no really empty place and doing no essential duties.'[1] Some daughters did find an empty place and essential duties but still went home without satisfaction. One such was Isabella D. Godding, Mount Holyoke Female Seminary class of 1857 and teacher at Girls' High School in Brooklyn from 1869 to 1902. 'One has everything to select from in New York,' she recalled to her classmates. 'Nature, Music, Science, Art. My Sundays were spent in Plymouth Church listening to Henry Ward Beecher and Lyman Abbott ...'[2] Miss Godding reluctantly returned to Gardiner, Maine, to care for her father – 'who since my mother's death has been at the mercy of various housekeepers. The arrangement seems to be giving him a happy old age for at 92 he has a keen enjoyment of life while I find the change in my own surroundings very limited when compared to my life in New York. My associations there were with delightful women in the corps of teachers and the students were girls of most interesting Character ... It was not an easy thing to do when I thus turned away from the privileges and delights which had been mine thirty-three years.'[3] The 'family claim' – to use Jane Addams' conception – had reclaimed Isabella Godding.[4] Would women born later escape or redefine it?

   In 1926 the liberal monthly, the *Nation*, began publishing a commissioned series of anonymously authored autobiographical essays by women – women who were, in their several ways, representative of rebellious feminism.[5] The series' stated purpose was 'to discover the origins of their modern point of view toward men, marriage, children, and jobs.' The seventeen women were born between 1868 and 1896. Seventy per cent were or had been married, a lower figure than the national average of 92 per cent but much higher than available statistics for college-educated women of their generations.[6] A recurring theme of their autobiographies was 'My mother bore too many children.' 'A vague smell of olive oil and mama in bed – this combination always meant a new baby,' was one women's way of registering her regret.[7] Only five of the *Nation*'s women bore any children. Disapproval of their fathers – for childlike selfishness, romantic impracticability, thought-less irresponsibility – was another common but not universal element in their life histories.

Kate Gregg recalled her father's behaviour when she took her savings from three years of teaching and left for the university:

He sulked in the barnyard and refused to say goodbye. He was indignant to see me throwing away my money. But three years later when I returned I was astonished to know that he was proud that I had graduated and indeed was giving himself some credit for this higher education in the family.[8]

II

Most of these women were journalists and professional writers but twelve of the seventeen had personal or family connections with the movement of women into teaching. Seven were or had been teachers; three others had teacher mothers; an additional two mentioned teacher aunts.[9]

However much fathers (like Kate Gregg's) might doubt the worth or wisdom of schooling women, the fact remains that changes in the family itself promoted it and, furthermore, encouraged its extensions to employment in teaching. For most of the nineteenth century women had been getting education, including what amounted to preparation for paid work outside of the home. By 1926, the year of the *Nation* series on the new woman, women were 53 per cent of America's public high-school students, over 56 per cent of those graduating from high schools, and 47 per cent of the nation's college and university undergrad-uates.[10] Would they use that education in the labour force? *Why? Where? For how long?*

My research into the intersections of the domestic, educational, and labour histories of women suggests four social conventions by which family roles, women's schooling, and women's labour-force participation may be 'harmonized.' Each convention operates today, but with economic and social change over the past 180 years, one has succeeded another as the most important system of accommodating and legitimating the economy's need for women's labour and women's own employment needs and desires.

First, women may contribute to the economy by working in and for the family corporation: the family farm, trade, or business. Except among some recent immigrant groups, in the United States this model has lost its former importance.

Second, women have found paid work for employers outside the family circle, in work perceivable as traditional women's work, as useful preparation for their ultimate domestic careers, and as appropriate supplements to home duties. Piece work done at home and employment in textile mills and garment factories exemplify different versions of this model. So, too, do nursing and social work.

Third, women in a diversity of occupations may be employed until marriage or pregnancy retires them from the labour force. Such work need not prevent women from pursuing their 'true profession' as homemakers. Arguably it could even enhance family formation by widening a woman's contacts with marriageable men and directing her earnings toward a dowry or a 'nest egg' for the young couple.

Fourth, woman's labour-force participation, even after marriage and child-bearing, may be legitimated by its material contributions to family welfare and cohesion. The counterpart of the single woman worker of the nineteenth century whose paycheck went to her parents to cover the cost of her keep or helped pay for the schooling of siblings, is, today, the married woman whose earnings go to 'help make ends meet,' or put a husband through a graduate or professional course of study, or pay school tuition bills.

As a form of income-generating work for women, teaching was being pursued under all the foregoing conventions. First, schoolkeeping was frequently a family business in which daughters, sisters, and wives gave instruction. Second, teaching was argued for as 'within woman's sphere' – an extension of the maternal role as the child's first and most important educator. The gradual replacement of subscription and dame schools by church-sponsored and endowed private schools and, especially in America, by public schools would have meant the *loss* of work opportunities to nineteenth-century women had they not been able to move into the newer sectors.

Third, teaching was considered an appropriate way for the educated young woman to occupy her time until she married and began her family. The short duration of the average woman's career in school teaching was explained by the call of matrimony. An 1857 survey of Wisconsin's teachers, for example, found the lifetime 'career' in teaching averaged eighteen months – or about four terms.[11] Importantly, this turnover itself vacated schools for other aspiring women teachers.

Fourth, in the past half-century or so, the married woman teacher, with children, has become the modal public school teacher. Despite the Depression-fueled campaigns against married women workers during the 1930s, most intensely directed against teachers, married women increased: from 17.9 per cent of all women teachers in 1930 to 22 per cent in 1940.[12] By 1975, nearly 80 per cent of all women teachers were or had been married.[13]

III

Teaching represents the largest field for women in the Department of Labor's category of 'professional and technical occupations.' In 1973, of all women college graduates working at a job, 59 per cent were working in education, mostly as teachers. Moreover, at no time between 1870 and 1970 did teaching fall below fifth place on the list of the ten leading occupations of all women in the labour force. And teaching recruits broadly from the social spectrum. Early stereotypes of women teachers emphasized downward social mobility, as educated women were forced by family reverses to take pupils. The 'reduced gentleman's daughter,' someone like Miss Jane Fairfax in Jane Austen's *Emma*, illustrates the type: the granddaughter of a country vicar whose widow lived in 'a very small way,' enabled by generous friends to acquire 'every advantage of discipline and culture' in order to support herself in a 'career of laborious Duty.' The orphaned Jane Eyre, a member of 'an anathematized race' of governesses in the eyes of Mr Rochester's friends, further illustrates an increasingly common figure in the nineteenth-century novel.

However prevalent were the *downwardly mobile* among governesses and other teachers in earlier periods, their ranks were being swelled in

England and America by the *upward-looking* of the nineteenth century. The profession of teacher was a place where, Bessie Parkes wrote in 1865, two classes of women met: 'the one struggling up, the other drifting down.'[14]

In his study of the women textile workers of antebellum Massachusetts, Thomas Dublin comments on the abandonment of mill work by the single daughters of native-born farm families. The attraction of schoolkeeping was one cause. Between 1835 and 1850 teaching expanded at a greater rate and its wages improved relative to mill wages. In the same period, the number of women teachers in Massachusetts grew by 80 per cent.[15]

As America became more ethnically diverse, so did teachers. Young women from the working class were evident among Poughkeepsie, New York teachers by 1860. In 1910 the native-born daughters of the foreign-born were already 27 per cent of all women teachers, and the 1920 Census ranked teaching fifth among the occupations held by women of foreign or mixed parentage.[16] To a Brooklyn school child in the 1930s it must have seemed that genteel young Irishwomen 'from Upstate' were the largest component among his teachers. Irish Catholic women had already captured the Boston public schools, and Jewish teachers carved out a stronghold in New York City's high schools, challenging the hegemony of the Irish and Germans. The 1920 Census also showed that teachers ranked *seventh* among all black women workers – recognition of the fact that racially segregated schools in the North and South generated career opportunities for the graduates of the system.[17] At a time in the mid-nineteenth century, when education did not provide upward social mobility for working-class males, it functioned in this way for young women by enabling them to become teachers. Unlike working-class women generally, teachers were better positioned to 'marry up' as a consequence of their greater visibility, geographic mobility, and genteel image.

While the working class sent some of its daughters into teaching, so did the middle and upper classes. A 1929 study of the backgrounds of a large sample of women attending fifteen non-elitist teachers colleges concluded that however provincial and circumscribed their backgrounds, most were daughters of owners or managers of farms or small businesses – quite representative of the broad, heterogeneous American middle class.[18] The better educated Minnesota parents who sent their daughters to the Winona Normal School in the last third of the previous century probably did so for similar reasons: that they might receive some advanced schooling and be trained for a profession should fate require them to be self-supporting.[19]

College-educated women represented even more of an intellectual and social elite. In 1896 it was reported that 90 per cent of employed women college graduates were teachers. Examining questionnaires returned by the 1912 graduates of five socially prestigious Eastern women's colleges, Mabel Robinson found 54 per cent in the teaching profession – ranging from Vassar's rate of 31 per cent to Mount Holyoke's 74 per cent. Subsequent studies have shown that elite colleges continued to send the largest proportions of their women graduates who entered the labour force into teaching.[20]

IV

The movement, first of single women and, then, of married women of varied origins into teaching can be explained by – to employ currently fashionable jargon – both *demand-side* and *supply-side* factors. On the demand side, public schooling could not have become so quickly a universal institution had it not admitted women into teaching in massive numbers. First for religious and social reasons, reformers urged the improvement and expansion of common schools. Working men's associations, politicians, and businessmen joined the chorus. Where were the men to staff schools in labour-short America? A writer in the *American Journal of Education* in 1826 commented that 'So many opportunities are open for industrious enterprise, that it has always been difficult to induce men to become permanent teachers.'

In the first 200–250 years of European settlement on the North American continent, when men were the majority of public and private school teachers, the brief teaching careers of most men were lamented but expected. Teaching was something a man did as a slack-season supplement to farming or to help finance his further education, to await a call to minister to a congregation or something in which he 'marked time' while he found his real occupational direction. In an era when a man might work at many jobs before settling into an occupation, teaching reasonably could fill several years of one's youth.

For women brief careers were considered natural but for different reasons. Marriage was quite universally regarded as the destiny of all normal women, most (90 per cent or more) could expect to marry, and neither teaching nor other employments should deflect woman from her 'true career.' Teaching was not to compete with marriage and, lest they forget that, prohibitions against retaining women as teachers if they married become commonplace in the later nineteenth century. When teacher Henrietta Rodman led the Feminist Alliance into the battle on behalf of suspended married women teachers in 1914, the existing regulation specified that New York City could not hire married women unless they had been separated from their husbands for three years or more. When the smoke of the battle cleared, dismissed teachers had been reinstated and even maternity leaves granted.[21] In California the legal question on the married woman's occupational rights was not settled in teaching until 1929, in a court case involving a tenured woman teacher who subsequently married, refused to resign her position, and was punitively reassigned to teach children in a tubercular hospital; her suit to void the School Board's action was upheld and marriage was there effectively ended as a formal disqualification to teach.[22] As late as 1931, however, the National Education Association reported that 60 to 75 per cent of a large sample of the nation's school districts dismissed the woman who married or refused to hire married women teachers. The tide in the other direction was inexorable, however. The compatibility of the school calendar and the hours of work with domestic responsibilities, especially with child-bearing, has been a 'selling point' of teaching for generations of women high-school and college students thinking about careers. And the shortage of men, able or willing to teach, continued. The only surplus of manpower was womanpower – single or married womanpower.

Historians of education, including feminist historians, make much of two factors as causes of women's coming into numerical dominance in teaching. One is the ideology of a 'woman's sphere' that was broadened to include school-keeping as an extension of the domestic role. The rhetoric of woman's 'natural mission' as teacher, Jim Wallace suggests, may have served primarily as a 'moral lubricant' – removing some of the friction that might otherwise have hampered the change from men to women teachers.[23]

The second traditional explanation is the lower wages commanded by women teachers, a powerful inducement to financially strapped school trustees. In a study of Massachusetts teachers from 1840 to 1860, Wallace concludes that the combination of high male earnings in competing occupations and a desire by town officials to minimize school costs was the single most important cause of shifts to women teachers.[24] By employing women 'to a far greater extent than they have hitherto been, without any detriment to our schools,' argued New York's Alonzo Potter in 1842, 'our schools might be lengthened one fourth or one half.'[25] Nor should women rebel at the wage, for, as the *Connecticut Common School Journal* explained it in 1841, the woman teacher sees her reward primarily 'in the secret depths of her own soul, in the convictions of an approving conscience, and in the approbation of Him, whose eye seeth in secret, and whose approving sentence will reward us openly.' That nineteenth-century women could be secured to teach for 40 to 50 per cent of the male wage, and in such great numbers, requires better explanation than messianic self-sacrifice, however.

Despite the strong religious motivations that animated many women to teach, we must look at other elements in the *supply-side of the equation* to see what conditions pushed or drove women from home to schoolroom. I will confine myself to outlining two interrelated sets of factors: (1) the contributions of the educational system itself to creating a large and willing pool of prospective teachers and (2) demographic changes that were reducing women's reproduction duties and possibilities, swelling the numbers of women on the ragged margins of the domestic ideal.

v

At the outset it was noted that girls and women became heavily engaged as consumers of schooling during the nineteenth century. The beginnings of that go back to the late eighteenth century when, for reasons not yet well understood, the town schools of New England began to relax their formal prohibitions and restrictions on female students. As tax-aided town and district schools spread westward, it appears that, from the outset, they did not limit the access of girls as students. This was probably, in part, evidence of a parental ambivalence at work: a desire, as taxpayers, to realize some personal benefit for their daughters as for their sons. Furthermore, by possessing a common schooling, girls were made eligible to teach common schools.

As the American public acquired more years of schooling, its teachers were asked only to stay a little ahead. When Julia Richman, daughter of Jewish immigrants, completed grammar school in Manhattan about 1867, she enrolled in the five-year course of the Normal College (later Hunter College) and graduated, ready to teach before she was quite seventeen years of age.[26] Indiana, in 1907, was the first state to require even that teachers be high-school graduates. While normal schools proliferated in the later nineteenth century, and were upgraded to state teachers' colleges after 1930 or so, many persons still went directly from the high schools into teaching. High schools had a mandate to recruit and prepare teachers dating from their earliest expansions in the 1880s. Wisconsin high schools were required to offer instruction in the theory and art of teaching by an 1883 law.[27] A study of the 1914 graduates of forty-seven Kansas high schools found the largest percentage (29 per cent of the graduates) directly entering teaching, and only 6 per cent headed for teacher training in the normal schools. In New York State, in the same period, the number of graduates attending normal schools was virtually the same as that of high-school graduates going immediately to teach.[28] Further to bridge the needs of the schools for teachers and their graduates' desires to enter the profession, many high schools continued to offer normal courses. According to data received by the United States Bureau of Education in 1926, every state but one had high schools with teacher-training courses; over 48,000 pupils were enrolled. Seven states – including New York, Ohio, and Michigan – also offered normal courses in high schools as postgraduate work.[29]

Minimal as were educational demands leading towards professionalism, they were too much for most *men*. Longer school terms (made possible by women teachers' lower wages), the requirement to attend institutes and prepare for more stringent and centrally supervised certification, the raised minimum age for teaching – together increased what economists call the 'opportunity costs' for men beyond what most would tolerate; it was becoming too difficult to combine even temporary teaching stints with other occupations. Although male teachers could look ahead to higher salaries, to promotions, and to entering the growing school administration superstructure, men were still reluctant to teach.[30]

Not so with women given their limited and unattractive choices. When her father died in 1869, relatives urged her mother to take Eliza Cooper from school and put her in the cotton mills. Mrs Cooper instead entered Eliza in the Girls' Normal School of Philadelphia to prepare herself to teach. Unlike many women Eliza Cooper Blaker made her career in education.[31] Luella Boelio took six weeks of study after her junior year in high school to prepare to get the third-grade certificate that let her teach in a one-room Michigan school. Her earnings helped finance her course at Ypsilanti Normal College, which she entered in

1901 – in spite of the admonition of her grandfather 'that sending her to college would be a waste of money since she very likely would marry soon.' Grandpa was correct: Luella married Claude Bower in 1905 and retired to housewifery. But she returned to teaching as a widow with five children, seeing all through a college education and raising three to be teachers.[32]

In his book *Schoolteacher: A Sociological Study*, Dan Lortie describes the process of training and recruiting for teaching as one of 'eased entry.'[33] Minimal requirements for preparation, the practice of giving local laymen discretion in examining and hiring teachers, providing briefer and less specialized training than required by the other learned professions, the development of cheap, accessible, and unselective public high schools, normal schools, and state teachers colleges in which to get teacher preparation – by all these means entry into teaching was made relatively easy, a sort of compensation for the low pay and relatively low prestige which the work offered as a career. But since teaching was not expected to be a career for most of its incumbents, bound as they were for *homemaking*, society's limited investment in teacher training 'made sense' to most teachers, to public officials, to public opinion. The situation remained like the one revealed in testimony in England before the Commissioners of Popular Education in 1851: namely that 'Fathers will not expend capital in training girls as teachers, or in any other profession; it is not a good investment of capital they think, as the girl may marry and leave her profession after exercising it a short time, or before exercising it at all.'[34]

This family-oriented view extended and persisted beyond Victorian England, even as it was stretched to cover the fact that more women *would* be employed. 'Most families of a certain income fit their daughters for self-support,' explained a teacher writing for the mass-circulation magazine, *World's Work*, in 1909. 'It is convenient to have them earn something through several years; it may even become necessary, and a modern independence prompts the girls to make use of their training.' Small wonder that, in his 1910 study of New York high-school students, Van Denberg found that nearly twice as many graduates chose teaching as chose all other occupations combined. The reason seemed clear: 'For teaching, the way is open through free training schools to actual positions attractively paid. No initiative is required, but merely the compliance with certain scholastic standards ... Until a girl marries she finds in teaching a gentle position with apparently short hours and long vacations. Moreover, most girls are very fond of their teachers and the impulse to emulate them is very strong indeed.'[35] The woman teacher was one of the few models of the working woman with whom school girls had protracted and direct experience. 'I have forgotten everything the schools every taught me,' claimed a one-time student of the New York City schools. 'But the glamour of the lady teachers, shining on the East Side world, I shall never forget.'[36]

VI

Education has been a necessary but not a sufficient condition in accounting for women's movement into teaching. Profound changes in the demographic profiles of the American population, especially in the nineteenth century, affected both women's education histories and their employment histories. Historians of education have heretofore given little attention to demographic factors.

The experience of Miriam David Colt is not typical but illustrative, in one life, of several of the demographic shifts that profoundly affected life experiences and shaped consciousness in the nineteenth century. Miriam David was born in 1817 in Essex County, New York, in the Adirondack Mountains. Her parents were natives of New Hampshire who had migrated in the hope of being able to keep their growing family around them in a more prosperous country – although their new home was also destined to lose population to places further west. Miriam's mother bore seventeen children, ten of whom died in early childhood. By age fourteen, Miriam, the twelfth child, was the oldest left at home. Attending the winter school irregularly, she was sometimes kept from the summer session by the need to help her mother at home or to keep house for the young family of a widowed brother. She remembered that:

What caused me to shed many tears in my early life, was that I could not have the opportunity of getting an education, and I almost coveted the advantages that some girls had of being sent away to attend an academy school; so I could wish that my father (a tanner) was rich enough to board, clothe, and pay my tuition, somewhere at a high school. But what I crave must be gained by my own effort; I felt a determination to clothe and educate myself ... The height of my aspirations were to attain the position of school teacher, and I hoped that some day I should have a pair of scissors hanging by my side, fastened with a large scissor hook to my silk apron strings ... and walk to school with a score or more of little urchins calling me school-ma'am; this would constitute my beau ideal of attainments and honors.[37]

Miriam David did teach school, from ages eighteen to twenty-six, alternating it with some study at an academy, paid for by her wages earned at school and at house-keeping in a hotel. She married a fellow teacher in 1846 and they farmed until 1856 when the family of four became part of the emigration to Kansas. Mrs Colt returned to New York State a year later with her daughter, to a lonely future on a hard-scrabble farm, her forty-year-old husband and three-year-old son left in graves in Missouri.

The first general trend, one magnified in Mrs Colt's case, is the falling birthrate in the United States. It represents a nationwide secular trend of decline from the first Census of 1790 to the present, reversed by the post–Second World War 'baby boom' years, but now back on track. Historian Carl Degler calls the decline in family size 'the single most important fact about women and the family in American history.'[38] Think of the divergent educational and occupational implications for women born in different periods in American history. An early group of women, American Quakers born before 1788, had on average a childbearing stage lasting 17.4 years, and they survived the marriage of that last child by just four years. Among American women born during the 1880s, however, their childbearing stage was 11.3 years (i.e., 6.1 years or three to four pregnancies shorter) and they survived departure from the home of the last child by twenty years.[39] Records for the town of Sturbridge, Massachusetts, show that cohorts married in the eighteenth century had a model family size of eight children ever born; the figure for cohorts married in the first half of the nineteenth century was five.[40] Put more generally, among women who ever bore children (but excluding consideration of miscarriage, abortion, and still birth), the birthrate dropped in the United States from 7.04 live births in 1800 to 3.56 in 1900. The largest proportional decline was in rural areas, where most of the population lived and where school attendance rates were often higher in the nineteenth century than they were in urban areas.

What consequences flow from such a change? Fewer children and less time and effort spent in pregnancy, parturition, and nursing meant better maternal health and strength; less risk of maternal death and orphanhood; and lighter child care duties for mothers and daughters.

Remember that, in earlier times, a great deal of childcare devolved not on mothers but on daughters ('Mother's little helper') and on spinsters and widowed relatives living in the household. The great age range between the oldest and youngest child – often more than twenty years – furthered this allocation of duties.

In recognition of the fact of their having household duties, it was a regulation of the Boston School Committee in the mid-nineteenth century that girls be given no school homework. Such rules became increasingly unnecessary with a lessened place for household manufacture, with smaller families, more vigorous mothers, and the free public school itself coming to function as a universal childcare institution. Urbanization limited the time spent on the production and processing of foodstuffs, for as late as 1920 farm families produced two-thirds of the foods they consumed.[41] The reduction in the urban middle class of the once widespread practice of taking in boarders and lodgers also lightened daughters' domestic duties. A 1901 United States Labor Department interview study of 25,000 families found that nearly 24 per cent, however, still had paying guests; other studies reported even higher figures.[42] The gradual introduction of farm machinery reduced the numbers of farm hands for whom women cooked and laundered. Many girls responded by staying in school longer and attending more regularly – which increased their educational qualifications to teach and strengthened their 'identification' with the institution of the school. By their earnings they acquired more independence and the means, if they wished, to purchase advanced schooling or professional training in another field, or to remain single. 'The ability of women to earn their own living has put out of existence a class of people whom we meet in the novels of fifty years ago, "the poor relation," "the indigent female," "the elderly spinster," who works for her board in the home of some prosperous relative, treading softly, echoing the opinions of those who feed her, wearing decent shabby black, as becomes her humble condition ... marrying for the sake of getting a living.' The author of this 1914 statement, a teacher at New York City's Washington Irving High School, added 'That sort of dependence is not good for the woman who takes it, or for the one who gives it.'[43]

A second demographic change that occurred during the years when women were becoming more accepted as teachers, and then taking most of the positions, was the rising age of first marriage. This is a factor thought by many demographers to account for more of the decline in the birthrate than was contributed by the direct practice of the several known methods of birth control. The age of first marriage of Sturbridge women had risen from 20.7 years for those married between 1730 and 1759 to 24.4 years for the 1820–39 marriage cohort.[44] Another study of Massachusetts women in the ninety-year period between 1830 and 1920 found that more than 95 per cent in each birth cohort were still single when they reached age twenty.[45] For the 1830 female birth cohort (i.e., those participating in the push that made women the majority of Massachusett's teachers), the single were 71 per cent of those twenty to twenty-four, 44 per cent of those twenty-five to twenty-nine, and 29 per cent of those ages thirty to thirty-four.[46]

Under conditions that postponed or prevented marriage, some possibilities of relief came to women equipped to teach; they could be self-supporting and decently occupied while waiting. They might go West as teachers, help to found a public-school system and perhaps marry the men who had preceded them West. Enough did so that the lady schoolteacher became a staple figure in legends of the frontier. A six-county census report for Texas in 1850 listed only three women by occupation: Elizabeth Baker and Mrs J. W. Latimer, Dallas County schoolteachers, and a 'suspect professional' euphemistically recorded as a 'lone grass woman.' After the outbreak of the Civil War the American Missionary Association urged unmarried women to go South to offer enlightenment to the freedmen, abandoning their positions as 'ornaments in their fathers' parlors, dreaming, restless, hoping, till some fortunate mating shall give them a home and a sphere.'[47]

Although they could not know the actuarial realities, as early as the colonial period the fact is that American men who survived childhood and women who survived childhood and maternity had almost as long a life expectancy as do their descendants in the late twentieth century. Postponing marriage meant reducing a woman's pregnancies and materially improving her life chances – something women knew experientially very well. Remaining single was the best protection of all. The third important change in life-cycle data was the growth of a permanently single population of American women.

Look for a moment at two more Mount Holyoke Seminary graduates. Both taught school from 1851 to 1859, before their careers diverged. The former Helen Gorham (Mrs J.J. Warren of Stamford, Connecticut) wrote to her classmates in 1870: 'To the unmated portion of the Mount Holyoke Class of 1851 – I wish it might be that you had done as many of us have – devoted yourselves to more particular and less general cares. I rejoice heartily with each one as she accepts a good husband.'

To this the editor of the class letter replied: 'Thanks for your good wishes, sister. But what would become of the rising generation if the "40,000 surplus women" were supplied with that rare specimen of the *genus homo*, a "good husband"? ... No, it won't do to pack off all the old maid school ma'ams and "useful aunties" to homes of their own. Why the country would certainly relapse into barbarism.'[48]

The life situations of both the later-marrying like Helen Gorham and the never-to-marry like Sarah Bigelow were in the minds of those men and women who spoke in the nineteenth century of female 'redundancy.' Never-married women like Catharine Beecher and Mary Lyon urged that educational and employment opportunities be expanded for women so that they might find a productive place in the society. 'Of those who speak so bitterly of women engaging in some pursuit now conducted by men, we would inquire, What would you have destitute single women do, by which to earn their bread?' Virginia Penny asked rhetorically during the Civil War that hastened women's entry into the labour force: 'Many men would banish women from the editor's and author's table, from the store, the manufactory, the workshop, the telegraph office, the printing case, and every place, except the school room, sewing table, and kitchen.'[49]

Inspired by British essays on 'female redundancy,' a former teacher and founder of the American woman suffrage paper, *The Agitator*, Mary Livermore, developed a lecture – 'Superfluous Women' – which she delivered around the United States, beginning in the 1870s. She noted that single women exceeded single men in sixteen of the United States, on the Atlantic seaboard and Gulf coast. Therefore, she recalled, 'All women do not marry, and cannot, and we are, for many reasons, entering an era when a large minority of our most gifted, scholarly, and useful women will decline marriage. My lecture was a plea that women should receive so complete a training, that, married or unmarried, they should have firmness and fibre, and be able to stand on their own feet, self-supporting, happy in themselves and helpful to the world.'[50]

VII

The work of 'social reproduction' represented by the instruction of the young in schools was an obvious and rather rapidly accepted answer to the enforced idleness of the schooled daughters of the middle class and those parents and daughters or the working class with aspirations to rise. And, whereas in 1850 only one mother in five witnessed the adulthood of all her children, there were now more fathers and mothers surviving to their own middle-age years. These were parents able to think about and plan for their children's futures, even to contemplate how their daughters might contribute to their parents' old-age security, as well as to be self-supporting if such were required.

For many of the New York City parents Van Denberg studied in 1910, schooling was part of a 'grand struggle upward,' the means whereby their sons could climb the occupational ladder to a more secure and respectable position. From the girls would come teachers, sales clerks, and stenographers – able to support themselves or assist their younger siblings and aging parents. The middle-class family, especially, felt weighed down by the prolonged dependency caused by the extended schooling and later marriages of its children, also by the absence of pension and (until 1935) social-security systems, by increased reliance on purchased consumer goods, even by the workings of the existing home-mortgage system. Then there was the knowledge that sickness, death, divorce, economic panics could blast away the security of one's married daughters and one's grandchildren. By providing adequate education and encouraging work experience for their female children, families erected hedges against such contingencies. Perhaps, in this new society, the very survival of the family would depend on the married woman *at work*, rather than exclusively at home.

There were always those, of course, who believed that women's education, like women's employment, threatened marriage and the family. In 1919 an Italian-American university student of architecture, whose sister worked in a factory, commented that few Italian-American girls went to college. He added, 'Well, I guess it is just as well they don't, for girls who go to college always stay single.'[51] The low marriage and fertility rates of the earlier graduates of the women's colleges, and even of the coeducational universities, seemed to confirm the worst fears of those who saw – especially in higher education and professional employment – the un-sexing of American womanhood.[52]

Nonetheless, it appears that after 1910 or so the majority of college women, even in the elite, rejected voluntary spinsterhood. Marriage rates went up, and the proportions (and sometimes the absolute numbers) of women physicians, professors, and scientists went down. If Frank Stricker is correct, educated women had decided *not* to choose between marriage and career but to try to have both.[53] And teaching presented them the smoothest path, the way having been cleared and made straighter by the hundreds of thousands who went bravely or timidly out before them.

NOTES

This article is from the *History of Education Review*, 12, 1 (1983), 15–28. Reprinted with permission. It is from a paper prepared for the annual meeting of the History of Education Society, New York University, October 1980.

1 'Scientific Study and Work for Women,' *Education* (Sept. 1882), 64

2 Typescript report for 1905. In 1857 Class letters. College History Collection and Archives, Mount Holyoke College Library, South Hadley, Massachusetts

3 *Ibid.*

4 I am indebted for the Addams' term to Joyce Antler,"'After College, What?" New Graduates and the Family Claim,' *American Quarterly*, no. 4 (fall 1980), 409–34.

5 Republished in Elaine Showalter, *These Modern Women: Autobiographical Essays from the Twenties*, (Old Westbury, New York: Feminist Press 1978)

6 For example in Frances M. Abbott, 'Three Decades of College Women,' *Popular Science Monthly*, LXV (Aug. 1904), 350–9

7 Showalter, *These Modern Women*, 111, 127

8 *Ibid.*, 77

9 *Ibid.*, 37, 106

10 'Statistics of Public High Schools, 1925–1926,' United States Bureau of Education *Bulletin 1927, No. 33* (Washington, DC: U.S. Government Printing Office 1927), 8, 11

11 Lloyd P. Jorgenson, *The Founding of Public Education in Wisconsin* (Madison: State Historical Society of Wisconsin 1956), 156

12 Lois Scharf, 'Even Spinsters Need Not Apply: Teachers in the Depression,' in *To Work and to Wed: Female Employment, Feminism, and the Great Depression* (Westport, Conn.: Greenwood Press 1980), 76, 85

13 'Women as Teachers,' *Educational Review*, 2 (Nov. 1891), 361; 'Facts on American Education,' *National Education Association Research Bulletin*, 49 (May 1971), 47

14 Bessie Rayner Parkes, 'The Profession of Teacher,' in *Essays on Wom-*

an's Work (London 1865). Quoted in A. James Hammerton, *Emigrant Gentlewomen: Genteel Poverty and Female Emigration, 1839–1914* (London: Croom Helm 1979), 32

15 Thomas Dublin, *Women at Work: The Transformation of Work and Community in Lowell, Massachusetts, 1826–1860* (Columbia University Press 1979), esp. 13, 139

16 Clyde Griffen and Sally Griffen, *Natives and Newcomers: The Ordering of Opportunity in Mid-Nineteenth-Century Poughkeepsie* (Harvard University Press 1977), 241; Lotus Coffman, *The Social Composition of the Teaching Population* (Teachers College, Columbia University 1911), 35. See also the essays of Selma Berrol, James W. Sanders, and Lana Muraskin in Diane Ravitch and Ronald K. Goodenow, eds., *Educating an Urban People: The New York City Experience* (New York: Teachers College Press 1981)

17 Howard N. Rabinowitz, 'Half a Loaf: The Shift from White to Black Teachers in the Negro Schools of the Urban South, 1865–1890,' *Journal of Southern History*, 565–94

18 M'Ledge Moffett, *The Social Background and Activities of Teachers College(s) Students* (Teachers College, Columbia University 1929)

19 George E. Bates, Jr., 'Winona Normal School Student Profile, 1860–1900,' *Journal of the Midwest History of Education Society*, 7 (1979), 17

20 Kate H. Claghorn, 'The Problem of Occupation for College Women,' *Association of Collegiate Alumnae Publications*, Series II, No. 21 (1897); Mabel Robinson, 'The Curriculum of the Women's College,' United States Bureau of Education *Bulletin 1918, No. 6* (Washington, DC: USGPO 1918), 120. See also Adele Simmons, 'Education and Ideology in Nineteenth-Century America: The Response of Educational Institutions to the Changing Role of Women,' in Berenice A. Carroll, *Liberating Women's History: Theoretical and Critical Essays* (University of Illinois Press 1970), 115–26

21 June Sochen, *Movers and Shakers: American Women Thinkers and Activists, 1900–1970* (New York: Quadrangle Books 1973), 41–3

22 Dutart V. Woodward (1929), 99 *District Court of Appeals of the State of California Reports*, 736, 279, p 493

23 James M. Wallace, 'The Feminization of Teaching – A Case Study: Massachusetts, 1840–1860,' unpublished paper, Lewis and Clark College, March 1973 (courtesy of the author), p 3

24 Wallace, 'Feminization,' 9–10

25 Alonzo D. Potter and George B. Emerson, *The School and the School-master* (New York: Harper and Brothers 1842), 204

26 Selma C. Berrol, 'Julia Richman: Agent of Change,' *Review Journal of Philosophy and Social Science*, 2, no. 2 (summer 1977), 130

27 Jeff Wasserman, 'Wisconsin Normal Schools and the Educational Hierarchy, 1860–1890,' *Journal of the Midwest History of Education Society*, 7 (1979), 4

28 An additional 2 per cent were postgraduate high-school students preparing to teach; 19 per cent were headed for the liberal arts colleges. Contrary to what might be expected, those heading straight for teaching were scholastically the superior, while those normal-school bound were below average. F.R. Aldrich, 'The Distribution of High-School Graduates in Kansas,' *School Review*, 24, no. 8 (Oct. 1916), 610–16; Guy-Wheeler Shallies, 'The Distribution of High-School Graduates After Leaving School,' *School Review*, 21, no. 2 (Feb. 1913), 81–91

29 'Statistics of Public High Schools, 1925–26,' 9

30 Thomas Morain, 'The Departure of Males from the Teaching Profession in Nineteenth-Century Iowa,' *Civil War History*, 26, no. 2 (June 1980), 161–70

31 Emma Lou Thornbrough, *Eliza A. Blaker: Her Life and Work* (Indianapolis: Eliza A. Blaker Club and Indiana Historical Society 1956), 5

32 Luella Boelio Bower, in Delta Kappa Gamma of Michigan Collection (Box 2), Schiesinger Library, Radcliffe College, Cambridge, Massachusetts

33 Dan C. Lortie, *Schoolteacher: A Sociological Study* (University of Chicago Press 1975), esp. 17–19

34 Quoted in Hammerton, *Emigrant Gentlewomen*, 38

35 Anonymous, 'The Confessions of a Successful Teacher,' *World's Work*, 9, no. 1 (Nov. 1909), 12221–2; *Secondary Schools of New York City* (Teachers College, Columbia University 1911)

36 Catharine Brody, 'A New York Childhood,' *American Mercury*, 14, no. 53 (May 1928), 62

37 Miriam David Colt, *Went to Kansas* (Watertown, NY: L. Ingells and Co. 1862; Ann Arbor, Michigan: University Microfilms 1966), 236–7

38 Carl Degler, *At Odds: Women and the Family in America, from the Revolution to the Present* (Oxford University Press 1980), 181. Chapter 8 is a lucid and non-technical review of the formative studies of economic and other demographers. Cf. Rudy Ray Seward, *The American Family: A Demographic History*, (Beverly Hills, California: Sage Publi-

cations 1978). See also Richard A. Easterlin, 'Factors in the Decline of Farm Family Fertility in the United States: Some Preliminary Research Results,' *Journal of American History*, LXIII, no. 3 (Dec. 1977), 600–14.

39 Robert V. Wells, 'Demographic Change and the Life Cycle of American Families,' in Theodore K. Rabb and Robert I. Rotberg, *Families in History* (New York: Harper and Row 1973), 85–94

40 Nancy Osterud and John Fulton, 'Family Limitation and Age of Marriage in Sturbridge, Massachusetts, 1730–1850,' *Population Studies*, 30, no. 3 (Nov. 1876), 483

41 'Housewives as Workers,' in Ann H. Stromberg and Shirley Harkess, eds., *Women Working: Theories and Facts in Perspective* (Palo Alto, California: Mayfield Publishing Co. 1978), 395

42 Cited in Martha Norby Fraundorf, 'The Labor Force Participation of Turn-of-the-Century Married Women,' *Journal of Economic History*, 31, no. 2 (June 1979), 402

43 Edith M. Tuttle, 'Vocational Education for Girls,' *Education*, 34, no. 7 (March 1914), 454

44 Osterud and Fulton, 'Family Limitation,' 484

45 Peter R. Uhlenberg, 'A study of Cohort Life Cycles: Cohorts of Native Born Massachusetts Women, 1830–1920,' *Population Studies*, 23, no. 3 (Nov. 1969), 409

46 The corresponding figures for the 1920 birth cohort were ages 20–24, 68 per cent; 25–29, 23 per cent; 30–34, 16 per cent – all figures rounded. *Ibid.*, 420

47 Blaine T. Williams, 'The Frontier Family: Demographic Fact and Historical Myth,' in Howard M. Hollingsworth and Sandra L. Myares, eds., *Essays on the American West* (University of Texas Press 1969), 58; 'Woman's Work for the Lowly,' in James M. McPherson, *The Abolitionist Legacy: From Reconstruction to the NAACP* (Princeton University Press 1975), 165

48 1870 Class Letter, in Class of 1851 letters, Mount Holyoke College Library. Helen Gorham, teacher in New Jersey and Connecticut; married 1859, 3 children; died 1910. Sarah Bigelow, teacher in Tuscaloosa, Alabama (1861–66), Pennsylvania, Massachusetts, New York, Boston, Milwaukee, Chicago (1871–74), Wellesley College (1876–77), died 1901. *One Hundred Year Biographical Directory* (1837–1937) (South Hadley, Massachusetts: Mount Holyoke Alumnae Association 1937), 70

49 Virginia Penny, *The Employment of Women: A Cyclopaedia of Women's Work* (Boston: Walker, Wise, and Co. 1863), vi–vii

50 Mary Livermore, *The Story of My Life* (Hartford, Connecticut: A.D. Worthington and Co. 1897), 493

51 Louise C. Odenkrantz, *Italian Women in Industry: A Study of Conditions in New York City* (New York: Russell Sage Foundation 1919), 255–6

52 Data on women graduates of the University of Michigan show patterns of low marriage and high percentages in teaching, like those reported for the women's colleges. In Roberta Frankfort, *Collegiate Women: Domesticity and Career in Turn-of-the-Century America* (New York University Press 1977), 111–15.

53 Frank Stricker, 'Cookbooks and Lawbooks: The Hidden History of Career Women in Twentieth Century America,' *Journal of Social History*, 10, no. 1 (fall 1976), 1–19

Teachers' Work:
Changing Patterns and Perceptions in the Emerging School Systems of Nineteenth- and Early Twentieth-Century Central Canada

Marta Danylewycz and Alison Prentice

The contract of Miss Ellen McGuire, dated 1 June 1880, spelled out government teachers' duties as they were understood at that time in the province of Quebec. As mistress of District School No. 3 in the township of Lowe, she agreed to

exercise an efficient supervision over the pupils attending the school; to teach such subjects as are authorized and to make use only of duly approved school books; to fill up all blank forms which may be sent her by the Department of Public Instruction, the Inspectors or Commissioners; to keep all school registers required; to preserve amongst the archives of the school such copy books and other works of the pupils which she may be ordered to put aside; to keep the school-rooms in good order and not to allow them to be used for any other purpose without permission to that effect; to follow such rules as may be established for discipline and punishment; to preserve carefully the *Journal of Education*; in a word to fulfill all the duties of a good teacher; to hold school every day, except on Sundays, and festivals and on the holidays authorized by the Commissioners or granted by proper authority.[1]

Miss McGuire's contract stated that it was 'in conformity with' the Quebec School Act of 1878 and, like many teacher contracts of the period, was on a printed form provided by the Quebec Department of Public Instruction. Her duties, as spelled out in the printed engagement, were those put forward by the department as the standard for any government schoolteacher in the province.

In subsequent years, provincial regulations and contract forms included further detail. Indeed, the very next year, the contract of Philomène Lachance of the parish of St Croix, St Flavien, already stipulated that it was the teacher's duty to supervise pupils, whether they were in or out of class, as long as they were 'under her view.' It was further agreed that Mlle Lachance would keep the school register and children's books in a cupboard especially designed for that purpose. The teacher was expressly forbidden to use any of the schoolrooms to entertain unauthorized visitors. The contract also sounded a cautionary note regarding the use of corporal punishment, which was to be discouraged. Finally, the teacher was to be properly dressed and to set a good example of 'cleanliness' and 'savoir vivre.'[2]

Teacher contracts such as those of Ellen McGuire and Philomène Lachance outline the major areas of teachers' work in state-supported elementary schools in the latter part of the nineteenth century. They deal with the subjects to be taught, the paperwork, and the discipline of both pupils and the teacher herself. They speak, if only briefly, of the teacher's duty to take care of the schoolroom and its property. On the other hand, the contracts say nothing about the responsibility of the school commissioners towards the teacher and the school. Although they failed to mention class size, the state of school buildings, heating and cleaning arrangements, or even the locations of schools, these factors too affected teachers' work. Teacher's contracts, therefore, left much unsaid.

They nevertheless serve as a useful starting point for examining the history of teachers' work in a vital period of transition. The following discussion, which is part of a larger, ongoing study of Quebec and Ontario public school teachers, focuses on the crucial years in the nineteenth and early twentieth centuries when state school systems were in the process of being established and teacher work forces were becoming disproportionately female across both provinces. We have probed elsewhere some of the major problems addressed by our explorations in this history, such as teachers' class and ethnic origins, the question of their changing ages, marital, and household status, and the overwhelmingly important issue of gender as it affected all of these questions, or was addressed by school reformers and teachers of the time.[3] In this exploratory essay, our focus is on the actual work of teachers in the schoolroom, as this appears to have been understood and as this understanding changed during the crucial years of school system development in the nineteenth and early twentieth centuries. It is taken as a given that, increasingly, the teachers we are studying were women.

As we analyzed the history of teachers in this period, we were struck by two interesting lacunae in most previous historical considerations of the subject. Educational historians have tended on the whole to treat turn-of-the-century school mistresses and masters as incipient professionals or, more disparagingly, as professionals 'manqués,' shying away from any concrete consideration of the work that they actually did. The story has often been told as a tragedy: an account of the failure of teaching to become a 'genuine profession.' In one Canadian analysis, this failure was explicitly attributed, at least in part, to the influx of inexperienced and malleable young girls into the occupation and the resulting devaluing of the work of experienced and well trained males. Equally, labour historians have not seen teachers as part of the changing work force that needs to be examined in their analyses of the emergence of industrial capitalism. As Graham Lowe has shown to be the case with clerical workers, teachers also have not fitted very well into the classic model of workers perceived to be men doing manual, as opposed to intellectual or managerial, work.[4] Teachers, on the contrary, have been seen and portrayed as 'brainworkers'; and as either actually or ideally the managers, at the very least, of children if not of other adults. In addition, they were very clearly not working *men*, since so many, as time went on, were in fact women. Thus, teachers *as workers* have been left out of nineteenth- and early twentieth-century labour history, just as they have been ignored in the history of education. Recently, investigations by Michael Apple on the position of twentieth-century American teachers, and Barry Bergen, Jenny Ozga, and Martin Lawn on their late nineteenth- and twentieth-century British counterparts, have called into question both the tendency to focus exclusively on teachers' status as either incipient or failed professionals and the tendency to ignore them as workers. By looking carefully at the meaning of changes in teachers' work and working conditions, and by introducing the concept of gender, these studies begin, rather, to develop a convincing argument for the 'proletarianization' of the teacher labour force.[5]

Our task, in the light of these considerations, was to try to come to grips more concretely than has been the case in the past with what teachers did in their daily work and how this work changed during the period of state school system construction in central Canada. As our concern was to try to get a general picture, we have ignored many details and interesting comparative questions, perhaps blurring very real differences between teachers' work in Quebec and Ontario, in Catholic and Protestant, or rural and urban schools. Nor have we focused very sharply on emerging differences between the roles of teaching assistants and principal teachers or even between those of men and women. Our concern, rather, has been to look at what was going on in nearly all nineteenth-century state-supported elementary schools, in both provinces, in all their regional, religious, and ethnic variety, to try to find the common denominators that seemed to have been affecting nearly all teachers, whatever their backgrounds or places in schools and school systems. In a reading of the annual reports of the Ontario and Quebec provincial departments of public instruction, the reports of the Montreal Catholic School Commission and the Toronto Public School Board, the *Journal of Education for Upper Canada*, and the *Educational Record of the Province of Quebec*, as well as a sampling of the correspondence of the two provincial education departments and other scattered sources, we in fact discovered a number of recurring themes. These included the introduction of new subjects and new teaching methods into nineteenth- and early twentieth-century schoolrooms; the introduction and phenomenal growth of paperwork; and a growing emphasis on discipline and hierarchy, as well as on uniformity of practice and routine. Pupil and teacher health and the question of the physical maintenance of schools and classrooms also emerged as important questions for analysis. Documents of the period make it clear, in other words, that an understanding of teachers' work must include a consideration not only of their tasks, but also of the changing conditions under which they performed them. Finally, teachers' work was affected by less tangible factors. Their own perceptions, and the perceptions of their employers, regarding the economic and social position of schoolmistresses and schoolmasters, as well as assumptions about what work was compatible with that position, also played a role. Here great tensions were generated, tensions that explain the contradictory policies pursued by the women teachers' associations which emerged at the turn of the century, as they sought to improve their members' conditions of work and to define the position of women teachers in the labour force.

NEW SUBJECTS, MORE TEACHING

Despite the profound differences in the organization and structure of the Ontario and Quebec public school systems, both were settling into an era of consolidation and growth by the 1880s. Having weathered the storms of local opposition to the intervention of central authorities in the establishment of schools, and having asserted their dominance over teacher certification and classroom instruction, provincial educational leaders were now in a position to expand the functions of the institutions they increasingly controlled. The lengthening of the period of formal schooling and the broadening of the public school curriculum were part of that expansion and both developments directly affected the work of teachers. As children remained in school longer, class sizes and schools grew proportionally; and as students had to master a broader range of subjects, the workload of many teachers increased.

The 1871 Ontario School Law, which made schooling compulsory for children between the ages of seven and twelve, also called for the addition of agriculture and drawing to the long established elementary school programme of reading, writing, arithmetic, geography, and grammar. The 1880s saw the introduction in Ontario of hygiene, temperance, and calisthenics into the curriculum, and the turn of the century brought in manual training and domestic science. The annual reports of the Department of Education recording the number of children learning the new subjects following their introduction attest to the widening of teachers' responsibilities during the last quarter of the nineteenth century. The number of children studying drawing, for example, increased eight fold between 1870 and 1900; the number taking hygiene increased six fold; and the number taking drill and calisthenics increased three fold between 1880 and 1900.[6]

Similar developments occurred in Quebec, producing comparable alterations in the work of teachers. Although compulsory education was not legislated until 1940, a rise in school attendance, owing to growing enrollment and the lengthening of the period of formal schooling, was evident by the last quarter of the nineteenth century. Moreover, as was the case in Ontario, so too in Quebec were agriculture, drawing, hygiene, calisthenics, and domestic science beginning to be integrated into the public elementary school curriculum during the closing decades of the nineteenth century.[7]

In both provinces curricular reform created much consternation among teachers. Not having been consulted about or forewarned of changes in elementary school programmes, they were frequently overwhelmed by the new demands being made of them. 'Can anyone tell us where we are drifting to in this matter of additional text-books and increasing number of subjects?' asked one Montreal teacher of a teachers' journal. It was this teacher's hope that the editor would throw some light on the 'impossible goal' towards which teachers were 'expected to hasten.'[8] Teachers such as this correspondent were often troubled by their lack of preparation to teach the new subjects. Many responded by simply ignoring the pressure to introduce them, arguing that this was justified as long as the central authorities did not provide proper instruction manuals or opportunities for teacher retraining. Because both provinces were slow in helping teachers out of the conundrum the new subjects created, such resistance endured.[9]

Central authorities, for their part, may have counted on the high turnover rate among teachers to flush out the older and ill-equipped masters and mistresses who would, they must have reasoned, eventually be replaced by normal school graduates trained in the teaching of the new subjects. But normal school training remained the exception rather than the rule in both Ontario and Quebec. The majority of teachers moved into the occupation through other channels, generally by attending model or convent schools and then presenting themselves to local boards of examiners. Moreover, within the teaching corps there were increasing numbers of persisters or career teachers whose training pre-dated curricular reform. If in the early days educational authorities satisfied themselves by assuming that such teachers would train themselves in the new subjects or by reminding the recalcitrant that 'the *clever* teachers' would be able to master them 'without the aid of a manual,'[10] by the last decades of the nineteenth century they began to supply some assistance. During the holidays, after school, and on weekends, schoolmistresses and masters were urged to attend provincially or locally organized classes and institutes, to learn not only the new subjects but the more modern methods of instruction and classroom management popularized by the 'new education' movement of the period. These extracurricular courses, ad hoc at first, soon became a regular part of teachers' work.[11]

PAPERWORK

If new subjects added to the teacher's workload, so did the rapidly growing mounds of paperwork. As early as 1847, the chief superintendent of schools for Upper Canada had foreshadowed this work when he wrote to a local school officer to the effect that what was not put in writing did not, for the purposes of the school system, exist. What was communicated 'verbally,' he commented then, could not be considered 'official.' In this brief remark, tossed off so casually to an obscure Upper Canadian educator who must have failed to put some information crucial to his purposes on paper, the chief superintendent enunciated a principle which was to haunt teachers as well as the officers of school systems from then on.[12]

It may have been the local school officers who were legally required to fill out the forms demanded by provincial authorities – and by the 1860s in Ontario, local trustees' reports covered over a hundred different items – but it was usually the teacher who had to supply the basic information. And of the 'blank forms' mentioned in the Quebec teachers' contracts of the early 1880s, the most time-consuming, as well as the most vital, was probably the individual class or school register. In Canada West the daily attendance register seems to have made its appearance as early as the 1840s. In 1850 it took on a crucial role for local schools, and parents and taxpayers, for after that date the Upper Canadian school grant was distributed on the basis of average attendance rates, with the highest grants going to the schools with the best attendance. Woe betide the teacher who did not keep an accurate daily account of pupils' presence or absence in the school, for falsification of the attendance register, according to the chief superintendent's report for 1859, met with 'punishment.' Failure to keep it altogether jeopardized the entire school grant to the section.[13]

By the 1880s in Quebec, it was clear that individual teachers had paperwork that went beyond the compiling of the daily registers. A correspondent to the *Educational Record* explained the methods whereby teachers could compute the averages from their daily records for half-yearly reports.[14] Rural Quebec teachers reported to local commissioners rather than to boards of trustees for individual schools, and an 1883 report from the county of Soulanges is evidence of some of the information that they had to include. This document, dated 19 February 1883, came from the pen of Marie Argonie Viau, *institutrice* of a school in the sixth *arrondissement* of the *Municipalité Scolaire de St Joseph*. It was two pages in length. One page listed the scholars in the school, along with their ages and the numbers of boys and girls who were studying various subjects or reading particular books. The other page consisted of a letter introducing this material, explaining its deficiencies, and requesting that the commissioners supply the teacher with a notebook so that she could comply with the requirement that an ongoing record be kept of inspectors' and commissioners' visits to her school.[15]

In the city of Toronto, the annual reports of the Public School Board are evidence of the reporting tasks that could be added to the work of urban teachers as school systems grew larger and more complex. In

1872, in addition to the statistical summaries of their schools' registers that were periodically required, headmasters and mistresses were asked to provide monthly lists of absentees for that month, along with the reasons for their non-attendance. In 1881, it was announced that every teacher had to keep a written record of all homework assigned to pupils. Finally, in 1891, written assessments of individual students' progress were added to the teachers' work. At the end of the school year, every teacher had to produce a 'mind chart' for each pupil, along with his or her recommendations regarding the individual pupils' promotions.[16]

If reporting to their superiors produced one kind of paperwork for teachers, the advent of written tests and examinations produced another. Gone was the era when everything depended on the oral questioning of both pupils and teachers. Examinations for teacher certification on the one hand, and the correction and assessment of students' workbooks and examinations on the other, loomed ever larger in the work of schools. Another part of the teachers' work lay in dealing with the anxiety that examinations inevitably produced. On the occasion of the introduction of provincial examinations in Quebec in 1895, a sarcastic letter from 'Amicus' appeared in the Educational Record, revealing the extent to which one correspondent, at least, felt that schoolmistresses and masters in Ontario had already become slaves to the unreasonable central authorities who controlled such exams. Amicus produced a list of injunctions which reflected what this author clearly believed were the sins the Ontario examiners had all too often committed. Failing to phrase questions simply or arrange them clearly, or to proofread the printed copies of the examinations were only a few among many. Moreover, it was really the teachers who were being examined, not their pupils. What provincial examiners wanted, Amicus seemed to imply, was confusion and anxiety – in short, more work for the people who were actually on the firing line in the schools, their already overburdened teachers.[17]

THE WORK OF SUPERVISION – AND BEING SUPERVISED

Both Amicus and Marie Argonie Viau outlined the difficulties teachers had in complying with the control mechanisms set in place by provincial schoolmen, and their comments reveal how wide the gulf could be between the expectations of central authorities and the realities teachers faced on the local level. If the laws and departmental or local regulations were problematic, even the pressures generated by reformers' supposedly helpful suggestions could have a disquieting effect. A teacher writing to the *Educational Record* in the mid-1880s captured the anxiety of many. The *Record*'s advice was good, the letter implied, but hard to follow in this teacher's country school. The *Record* had suggested a school museum, but that was impossible. The 'scholars would likely kill one another with the mineral specimens.' Even the more standard activities of needlework and scripture reading were counted 'a loss of time' in this teacher's school, where pupils no doubt continued the tradition of attending only when farm or domestic work permitted them to do so: 'You have never taught schools in this country. I feel as I felt one summer when I rode for a month a very vicious horse, coaxing him a little, yet not too much, lest he should think, or rather find out, that I feared him, for then he would be sure to run away with me.'[18]

Individual teachers were caught between the exigencies of local conditions and the demands of their superiors, and both fell heavily on them. In the 1840s it had been possible for an elderly rural teacher from the Upper Canadian District of Gore to lie on a bench and allow the pupils to read out loud to him as they gradually drifted into the school over the course of the morning. But the district superintendent, on observing this approach to school teaching, had been shocked. As he related to the chief superintendent of the province, when all the pupils were assembled he had lectured both teacher and taught on the importance of punctuality; later on he had seen to it that the old man's certificate to teach was not renewed.[19] The situation of the teacher from Gore anticipated that of his successors for, as the nineteenth century wore on, the teacher's role in matters like punctuality was increasingly emphasized. One graphic illustration of how important such issues became was the astonishing drop from 69,456 cases of 'lateness' reported for Toronto board schools in 1874 to only 5,976 cases in 1880. This constituted a great improvement in the eyes of the city's newly appointed school superintendent, James Hughes; how it had been achieved was not explained. Clearly, though, classroom teachers must have been involved in Hughes' campaign to reduce tardiness.[20]

Teachers were also increasingly expected to take responsibility for the behaviour of students outside the classroom. This included pupils 'on their way to and from school' as well as during lunch hours and school breaks. Recognizing the fact that some parents sent children to school when they were sick, the Toronto board required each school to appoint a teacher to stay inside with such pupils during recess. All other teachers, according to a new regulation of 1879, had to be in the schoolyard during that period.[21] The supervision of children outside of the classroom, most educators believed, involved not just one's presence but also setting a good example. Thus an 1885 *Educational Record* article entitled 'Noontime' exhorted teachers to eat 'decorously' and use a napkin when having lunch with their pupils. After a short lunch-time rest, they were also encouraged to organize games for the children to keep them happy and occupied.[22]

As school officials increasingly used teachers to tighten the reins of control over students, they also introduced measures to insure that the teachers themselves performed their work as specified in the regulations. Through local institutes teachers were instructed in matters as personal as their tone of voice and as trivial as how many times to pull the rope when ringing the school bell, as well as in matters more clearly related to academic instruction.[23] But the more obvious controls were exerted by the visits of school inspectors and, where schools were growing larger, by principals or head teachers. The frequency and character of rural school inspection depended on a variety of factors, ranging from the personality of the inspector to the location of the school. Schools that were hard to reach were sometimes missed altogether when the inspector made his rounds.[24] Conversely, urban teachers were inspected more regularly than rural teachers and were subjected to more systematic and closer controls. In Toronto, for example, Public School Board teachers were visited by an increasing number of 'specialists,' who supervised the teaching of subjects like drawing, domestic science, and drill. Schoolmistresses and some masters who taught for large urban boards were also visibly compartmentalized in the lower rungs of growing educational bureaucracies which subjected them to several levels of inspection, beginning with the school principal and ending with the district and provincial superintendency.[25]

WORKING FOR BETTER HEALTH

The superintendency concerned itself not just with teachers, of course. It was also part of the inspector's job to supervise the local school boards themselves, with a view to enforcing the laws requiring decent school accommodation. Ontario authorities, for example, specified in 1871 exactly how much land, floor space, and air each school should have, depending on the number of pupils. Requirements governing fences, ventilation and heating, drinking water, school privies and equipment were vaguer, stating only that these items should be 'sufficient' or 'suitable.'[26] But whether they were specific or vague, the regulations were hard to enforce and teachers all too often found their employers delinquent in these matters. As a result their work frequently had to be performed under the most trying conditions.

In a typical letter, dated 23 March 1883, a local inspector described to his superiors in the Quebec Department of Public Instruction the failure of the commissioners for St Jean de Rouville to provide proper accommodation for their village school. The school, he reported, was exactly as he had found it the year before, despite promises to repair and renovate it. The building was so cold that parts of it were uninhabitable; the rooms were so small that some of the children were literally 'crushed one against the other.' The inspector clearly felt that only provincial pressure could bring about an improvement and he buttressed his case by referring to the feelings of the school's two teachers. These schoolmistresses not only suffered considerable 'malaise' because of the conditions in their school, but, according to the inspector, were reluctant to complain because when their predecessor had done so, he had been reprimanded and forced to retract his complaints by the St Jean de Rouville commissioners.[27]

In Montreal, teachers employed by the Catholic School Commission did not even need to submit a grievance to be reprimanded. City health inspectors might achieve the same result, as in the case of Mlle Thibodeau in 1877. Because they found the conditions in her two-room school 'injurious to the health of the pupils' and reported that finding to her employers, Thibodeau's subsidy from the commission was cut off. This teacher, her employers decided, would be reinstated only after the required renovations were made or after she found a new building to house her 150 pupils.[28]

Thibodeau's predicament was not an isolated one in the history of Quebec schooling. Many Montreal women teachers toiled in poorly ventilated, ill-equipped, insufficiently lit, and overcrowded classrooms. When health inspectors presented a damning report, they and not their employers, the commissioners, faced the consequences, because schoolrooms and buildings were their responsibility.[29] Thibodeau was laid off for a month and a half; she needed that much time to find more suitable accommodation for her school. In the meantime, she and others like her suffered the loss of their salaries while moving from one site to another. Thibodeau, like many other teachers, also suffered from poor health, fatigue, and physical breakdown as a result of her working conditions, and eventually had to resign.

Clearly, if the health of the students was endangered by the poor condition of many schools, so too was that of their teachers. Léocadie Généreux, a contemporary of Thibodeau and mistress of a neighbouring school, requested a leave of absence in 1879 due 'to the precarious state of her health.' It was granted along with a $50.00 bonus in recognition of fifteen years of service to the school commission.[30] Généreux returned to the classroom one year later, to take up the front line in the battle against small pox, diphtheria, and tuberculosis being waged by school officials and public health reformers. In the wake of scientific findings that many of the contagious diseases could be contained by vaccination and proper diet, late nineteenth- and early twentieth-century teachers increasingly found themselves instructing their pupils in hygiene and correct eating habits, insuring that they were vaccinated, inspecting them for contagious diseases, and sending the ill to the school clinic or home.[31]

The combination of poor working conditions and exposure to a variety of contagious diseases debilitated teachers, forcing many to take periodic leaves of absence. In recognition of this fact, the Toronto Public School Board in the 1870s began to hire 'occasional teachers' to replace those on sick leave.[32] While from the students' and employers' point of view substitute teachers were a solution to the absent teacher problem, they were hardly the answer as far as the ailing schoolmistresses were concerned. Their only recourse at times of sickness was family, kin, or charitable institutions. In this regard their situation was no different from that of nineteenth-century labourers, who also relied on these traditional, albeit frequently inadequate, support systems.

At the same time, however, teachers were pressuring provincial governments to make amends to pension funds (established in 1853 in Ontario and in 1856 in Quebec) in view of the ill effects working conditions had on their health. Individual and isolated requests of schoolmistresses like that of Eliza Pelletier from L'Islet, Quebec, for an early retirement with a pension due to her anemic condition, became by the turn of the century collective demands voiced at meetings of teachers' associations.[33] The associations of Protestant and Catholic teachers of Montreal stood united in the early 1900s in an effort to pressure the provincial government to lower the age of retirement for women teachers from 56 to 50. Reasoning that 'the great majority of women teachers break down before reaching the present retiring age, and are utterly unfit to follow other occupations,' they demanded revisions to the pension fund scheme as well as, at least implicitly, a recognition by school officials that the work of women teachers was far more exacting than that of the men.[34]

In the same vein, women teachers began to publicize their concerns about health and working conditions through the medium of the press. Whenever the occasion presented itself, and it did in turn-of-the-century Montreal with the founding of the *Ligue d'enseignement*, they pleaded their case with the public.[35] They also rejoiced when support for their cause or recognition of the difficulties under which they laboured appeared outside their own circles. In 1891 the *Educational Record* reprinted an article from one of the province's newspapers that had taken notice of the teacher's plight and outlined ways in which teachers could prevent fatigue, anemia, or mere discouragement.[36]

SCHOOL MAINTENANCE AND HOUSEKEEPING

If poor working conditions and health care were dominant themes for teachers in the second half of the nineteenth century and carried on unabated into the early twentieth, a related and muted theme was the teacher's continuing role in the physical maintenance of the school. The school had once been located in the teacher's home, a rented house, or a room in someone else's house; then, as provincial school systems were put into place, in most locations the school house became public property and, in theory, the responsibility for its maintenance shifted to local boards of trustees or commissioners. But, for the women who taught under the Montreal Catholic School Commission, as we have seen, this theory did not even begin to be put into practice. And for a long time the boundaries of responsibility for the maintenance and upkeep of school property remained blurred in other regions as well. Often school boards insisted that at least the minor work of school maintenance still belonged to teachers.

In Ontario, debate on the subject can be traced back to the 1840s. Queries to the office of the chief superintendent of schools suggest that Upper Canadian trustee boards and their teachers had already entered into dispute in two areas: who should lay the fires in schools and who should clean the schoolhouses. In 1848, Egerton Ryerson wrote that these were matters for negotiations between teachers and trustees, the law not specifying who was responsible for the work of school maintenance. He suggested that the trustees could give the teacher a higher salary in return for the work, grant a special allowance for the purpose, or agree to it being done by the pupils under the teacher's direction.[37] But arguments on the subject continued to reach the chief superintendent's desk, as trustees pressed the housework of the school on reluctant teachers who clearly regarded such tasks as 'extra' work, or beneath their dignity. By 1861 the provincial Education Office took a stronger stand on behalf of such teachers. The housekeeping work of the school, Egerton Ryerson now argued, was no longer a matter for negotiation; such work, he implied, did not belong to the men and women whose employment educational reformers were trying so hard to define as 'professional.' Under the heading 'Official Replies of the Chief Superintendent of Schools to Local School Authorities in Upper Canada,' the *Journal of Education for Upper Canada* published the following brief statement: *'Teachers are not required to make Fires.* The Teacher is employed to teach the school, but he is not employed to make the fires and clean the school house, much less repair the school house.'[38]

Provincial educational authorities' pronouncements did not necessarily sway local school boards, however, and in an 1863 trustees' minute book for School Section No. 1, North West Oxford, building fires as well as ringing the school bell were explicitly laid out as the teacher's contracted work. In 1865, however, the superintendent from Oxford County reported that the more common solution in the country schools under his jurisdiction was to hire a lad to do the 'extra work' or to press it onto the pupils.[39]

Anna Paulin, who taught in the Quebec parish of Ste Marie de Manoir Rouville in the 1880s, engaged to keep the school clean and the path to the school clear, according to her contract.[40] But in Quebec as well, such work was subject to debate. Under the heading 'Enquiries,' the *Educational Record* dealt with the topic in 1885. Was it 'part of the teacher's duty' to light the school fires each morning? The answer was unequivocal: 'Certainly not. The trouble and expense of lighting the fires must be provided for by the school commissioners through the school manager of the district.'[41] In 1889 the *Educational Record* argued that it was the teacher's job, with the help of her pupils, to keep the schoolroom neat and clean, but only provided that a proper caretaker cleaned it thoroughly once a week. The issue was of sufficient importance to merit attention once again in an 1893 editorial on how teachers could improve their position in society. School mistresses and masters were advised to see to it that their contracts were signed and sealed and that no one dictated to them on the subject of where they should board. Last but not least they were told to arrange 'if possible, with the trustees to make someone look after the cleaning of the schoolroom and making the fires.'[42]

If these issues continued to be problematic for rural teachers as late as the 1890s, in the cities they were less often debated. At least wherever urban schools were larger than one or two rooms, the need for a separate staff of caretakers was generally recognized. By 1876 the Toronto Public School Board employed nineteen caretakers; fifteen years later their number had almost tripled. City school caretakers in the nineteenth century frequently lived on the school property; indeed it seems often to have been a family occupation and even a job for women. Wages compared favourably with those of teachers: in 1889 the top annual salary for a male caretaker was $600, for a woman $375. In 1891, nine women were among the board's fifty-three caretakers. Two of these women were succeeded, when they died, by their sons.[43]

If the heavy work of school cleaning and laying fires was a thing of the past for city schoolteachers, this did not mean that their jobs were entirely free of housekeeping tasks. Urban and rural teachers alike were exhorted to keep their schoolrooms tidy and to 'beautify' them.[44] Even the Montreal daily, *Le Canada*, in its support for the 'new education' movement, decried the unattractive appearance of Quebec schools compared to American ones: 'Our [schools] are devoid of decoration, while in the public and catholic schools of our neighbours, professors and students pride themselves on giving their schools as beautiful an appearance as possible.'[45] Schoolroom tidying and decorating, indeed, gradually moved in to replace the more mundane tasks of sweeping and dusting for late nineteenth-century teachers.

Tidying became important for both rural and city teachers because of the growing stock of globes, maps, and other material goods that modern schools required. In the city of Toronto as well as in rural and urban Quebec, school documents express concern about this work. As one of them put it, now that the teacher was responsible for school property it was only fair that each school or classroom should contain a cupboard for its safekeeping. In Toronto, the school board recognized in 1873 that teachers occasionally needed extra time for the work of tidying and organizing the schoolroom and its contents. That year, at least, the day before the Christmas holidays was set aside for teachers to put their rooms 'in good order.'[46]

The advent of caretakers also meant another kind of work for urban teachers: the work of negotiating when their interests and those of the caretakers clashed. Such a conflict occurred when the women employed in Toronto schools noticed that the oil used by the caretakers on the floors soiled the hems of their skirts. If it was part of the teacher's work to set a good example by looking clean and presentable – and Ellen McGuire's 1880 Quebec contract was not the only one to state explicitly that this was the case – then a measure initiated to reduce costs or caretakers' labour in maintaining floors had resulted in increased costs and labour for the women who taught in Toronto public schools.[47]

RESISTANCE AND PERCEPTIONS OF THE WOMAN TEACHER'S
AMBIGUOUS POSITION

It was this issue, along with those of their wages, that the Women Teachers' Association of Toronto brought to the trustees of the city twenty years after their organization's founding in 1885. Indeed, these were the problems, along with other long-standing concerns about health, working conditions, and the reorganization of the pension fund in light of the particular needs and experiences of women teachers, that eventually drove schoolmistresses to band together and establish protective associations. In central Canada, Toronto led the way with Montreal and then, somewhat later, rural teachers in both Ontario and Quebec follow suit. By the turn of the century, urban women teachers were speaking with collective voices, not only echoing the grievances their predecessors had so frequently raised in individual exchanges with their local and provincial superiors but also winning some concessions from their employers. In Toronto for example, organization helped to bring the women teachers a salary scale based on seniority rather than grade level and the election of a woman to the school board.[48] In Montreal the associations of Catholic and Protestant women teachers succeeded in persuading the provincial government to make the pension plan more favourable to women teachers and to raise the annual pension by 50 per cent. The Catholic association also guaranteed ill or unemployed teachers some assistance during times of need.[49]

When schoolmistresses should be allowed to retire and the presence of women on school boards were hardly the major concerns of those promoting school system development and professionalism among teachers in the nineteenth and early twentieth centuries. The former were of such profound interest to Ontario and Quebec women teachers, on the other hand, that eventually they began to view themselves as a class apart from their male colleagues and state school employers. A sense of separateness, nourished by years of working conditions harsher than those endured by men (who generally could look forward to administrative positions or at least teaching the more advanced grades) and of a shared experience of inequality in salary and opportunity for advancement in the occupation, led many of the career women teachers to express their particular demands and grievances increasingly openly. As part of her contribution to the pension debate, a Quebec schoolmistress, who had 'roamed professionally' from one rural county to another for nearly twenty years, remarked in no uncertain terms that she, as a teacher, did 'more work for [her] country than some of our politicians.' This conviction prompted her to ask why no provision could be made for 'the few women' who made elementary teaching 'their life-work' and to offer the provincial government a list of suggested improvements. 'I would suggest that our government provide a work house for superannuated female teachers, taxing highly-salaried teachers and school inspectors for its support. Another suggestion I beg leave to make is that women be eligible for the office of school inspector. It would be a comfortable berth for some of us that have been too long on starvation salaries.'[50]

Such sentiments were behind the founding of separate women teachers' associations in both Ontario and Quebec. The frustrations and aspirations expressed by teachers making suggestions of this kind were also a reflection of the transition teachers' work had undergone in the period since 1840. Prior to the establishment of government school systems as well as during the early years of their creation, schoolmistresses and masters worked within informal, more personal, and less hierarchical structures. Centralization and the development of provincial elementary school systems brought about a major change in the form and content of schooling. Athénais Bibaud, the principal of Marchand Academy in Montreal, noted in 1911 that in the past 'the programme of studies was not as heavy,' leaving time for frequent breaks and 'cordial chats between teachers and pupils, chats which were very useful because they *shed light on everything*.' But, as she further remarked, as all things go, this type of interaction between student and teacher had come to an end, and not just in her own school. Discipline had become 'more severe,' pupils and teachers alike 'worked a bit harder,' and younger mistresses were now supervised by the older, more experienced ones. By this time, too, the Montreal Catholic School Commission exercised more control over the academy.[51]

The reorganization of time, work, and discipline in the school did not improve the lot of the teacher. 'One thing that did not keep pace with the changing times,' added Bibaud in her reflections, 'were the salaries of teaching assistants.'[52] A similar observation of the disjuncture between the enduring regime of low salaries and the changing mode of schooling led Elizabeth Binmore, a founder of the Montreal Protestant Women Teachers' Association, to speculate on the nature of the woman teacher's work in the public schoolroom and its relationship to her status in society. Did her employment fit with the title 'lady teacher' which was still so much in use? Elizabeth Binmore seemed to think not.[53] Her work was not leisure; therefore it was not appropriate to refer to the schoolmistress by using a term implying that it was. 'Lady teacher' belonged to a genteel past which by the turn of the century was but a dim memory to the vast majority of overworked and under-paid women teachers in Montreal.

While Binmore was able to make such a statement in the mid-1890s, a moment when Montreal teachers' salaries, owing to depressed economic conditions, may have been at a particularly low ebb, she and her colleagues in the three women teachers' associations that late nineteenth-century conditions spawned in Quebec and Ontario nevertheless had great difficulty grasping permanently a vision of themselves as workers. Wayne Urban has argued that in the three American cities he studied, the women teachers who organized were aware of their interests and fought mainly as interest groups rather than as incipient professionals, although their approaches varied according to local conditions.[54] It is very clear that Canadian women teachers, like their American counterparts, also formed their associations with bread and butter issues such as wages, working conditions, and pensions chiefly in mind. Yet, unlike the most radical Americans, Canadian teachers were reluctant to ally themselves with working-class organizations or identify with working-class groups that had comparable problems. In Toronto, the Woman Teachers' Association toyed with a labour affiliation in 1905, but backed off.[55]

Perhaps the key word here is 'comparable.' For, with hindsight, we can now see that the position of turn-of-the-century women teachers was similar to that of beleaguered industrial workers but, as the women teachers of the time perceived, it was also different. Women teachers had not necessarily been 'deskilled'; on the contrary, new skills were constantly being demanded of them. Nor were they necessarily subjected to seasonal unemployment and layoffs to the same extent as labourers, especially those who worked in the light manufacturing industries. Moreover, their work was supposedly intellectual and not manual, a division which, at least according to Harry Braverman, was 'the most decisive single step in the division of labour' taken by industrial capitalist societies.[56] Yet as 'brainworkers' they also at times toiled manually, beautifying their schools, keeping the path to the schoolhouse clear in the winter, and inspecting pupils for contagious diseases. They spent hours on the busy work of maintaining school records and looking after the objects that increasingly filled their classrooms. In fact, in their work they straddled both sides of Braverman's great divide and laboured on the margins of both. As far as their working conditions and salaries were concerned, however, they did share the plight of nineteenth-century workers.[57]

It was the uncertainty of their position in the labour force that helps to explain how women teachers could flirt with the mystique of professionalism while at the same time their members referred to themselves as the exploited or as toilers and hirelings. In recalling their double bind one returns, finally, to feminists' recognition of the need for a more nuanced analysis of work and a less dichotomous vision of the social order if we are to understand the work of women.[58] Elizabeth Binmore began to glimpse these truths in the mid-1890s. Teachers, she saw, were not 'ladies.' Nor, however, could they fully see themselves as workers, in spite of the poor wages and difficult working conditions they endured.

Michael Apple has rightly argued that teachers' 'deskilling and reskilling, intensification and loss of control, or the countervailing pressures of professionalization and proletarianization' that have affected the occupation, and continue to affect it to this day, are complex processes. They cannot be explained solely in terms or the sexual division of labour. Nevertheless, as he also contends, that division has been an essential component in these processes.[59] This brief study of central Canadian teachers during the period of state school system formation confirms Apple's contention. Turn-of-the-century women teachers in Ontario and Quebec were increasingly aware of their special problems and some were already aware of the ambiguity of their position. Many also knew that a major source of their difficulties was the fact that they were women in school systems largely designed for and controlled by men.[60]

NOTES

This article is from *Labour/Le Travail*, 17 (spring 1986), 59–80. Reprinted with permission.

The first draft of this paper was written in February and March 1984, for the American Educational Research Association meetings that spring. Its writing followed a wonderful research trip to Montreal and Quebec, which I shared with Marta, and during which we discovered together the richness of the Quebec Department of Public Instruction records deposited in the *Archives Nationales*, among other treasures of interest to historians of teachers. That fall, Marta and I wrote a detailed proposal for the funding of further research, another more theoretical and historiographical paper for the Social Science History Association meetings in Toronto, and submitted 'Teachers' Work' to *Labour/ Le Travail*. Marta was looking forward with special interest to the criticisms of *Labour*'s readers because, of all our joint endeavours, this was probably the paper that excited her the most. Although she never heard the news of our paper's acceptance by the journal, the writing and talking that we did that fall were invaluable to me when revising it for publication. I am also grateful to the Social Science and Humanities Research Council, to Atkinson College, York University, and to the Ontario Institute for Studies in Education, for institutional support; and I wish to thank Ian Davey, Ruby Heap, Greg Kealey, Andrée Levesque, and Veronica Strong-Boag for their critical suggestions and their sympathy, which greatly lightened the task of revision. [Alison Prentice]

1 Engagement of Ellen McGuire, 1 June 1880, Education Records, E 13, Archives Nationales du Québec (hereafter ANQ)
2 Engagement of Philomène Lachance, 11 July 1881, E 13, ANQ
3 Alison Prentice, 'The Feminization of Teaching in British North America and Canada, 1845–1875,' *Social History/Histoire sociale*, 8 (1975), 5–20; Marta Danylewycz, Beth Light, and Alison Prentice, 'The Evolution of the Sexual Division of Labour in Teaching: A Nineteenth Century Ontario and Quebec Case Study,' *ibid.*, 16 (1983), 81–109; Danylewycz and Prentice, 'Teachers, Gender and Bureaucratizing

School Systems in Nineteenth Century Montreal and Toronto,' *History of Education Quarterly*, 24 (1984), 75–100

4 André Labarrère-Paulé, *Les Instituteurs laiques au Canada français, 1836–1900*, (Quebec 1965). J.G. Althouse, *The Ontario Teacher: A Historical Account of Progress, 1800–1910* (1929; Toronto 1967) focuses on the 'rise' of the professional teacher, but avoids discussing the question of gender. Graham S. Lowe, 'Class, Job and Gender in the Canadian Office,' *Labour/Le Travail*, 10 (1982), 11–37

5 Michael W. Apple, 'Work, Class and Teaching,' in Stephen Walker and Len Barton, eds., *Gender, Class and Education* (New York 1983), 53–67; J.T. Ozga and M.A. Lawn, *Teachers, Professionalism and Class: A Study of Organized Teachers* (London 1981); Barry H. Bergen. 'Only a Schoolmaster: Gender, Class and the Effort to Professionalize Elementary Teaching in England, 1870–1910,' *History of Education Quarterly*, 22 (1982), 1–21

6 *Annual Reports of the Chief Superintendent of Schools for Ontario*, 1870–1900

7 *Ibid.* and *Annual Reports of the Superintendent for the Province of Quebec*, 1879–1900

8 *Educational Record of the Province of Quebec*, 13, 1 (1893), 28

9 *Educational Record*, 9, 12 (1889), 324. Resistance to curricular reform in Quebec can be traced in a variety of sources. For references to complaints coming from rural schools, see the letters in Education Records, E 13, 615–44, 614–50, 615–200, and 615–82, ANQ.

10 A reference to parent resistance to too many new subjects, and the fact that the Toronto Public School Board supported the complaint against their introduction by the provincial government, may be found in the *Annual Reports of the Toronto Public Schools Board*, 1872 and 1873. Reports for the remainder of the 1870s and 1880s record the work of special subject masters hired to deal with new areas like music, drill, and drawing, including the introduction of after-hours classes to train the teachers. The tone of the special subject masters' reports suggests that many urban teachers were as slow as rural teachers to accept the new subjects.

11 Miss Reid, 'How to keep the Little Ones Employed,' *Educational Record*, 2, 10 (1882), 413

12 Egerton Ryerson to C. Gregor, 5 May 1847, Education Records, RG 2, C-1, Letterbook C, 355, Public Archives of Ontario (hereafter PAO). On the role of the Ryerson administration in the increase of paperwork in Ontario schools, see Alison Prentice, 'The Public Instructor: Egerton

Ryerson and the Role of the Public School Administrator,' in Neil
McDonald and Alf Chaiton, eds., *Egerton Ryerson and His Times*
(Toronto 1978), 129–59.

13 *Annual Report of the Chief Superintendent of Schools for Ontario*, 1859,
16–17
14 *Educational Record*, 6, 3 (1886), 81–2
15 Report of Marie Argonie Viau to the commissioners, 19 Feb. 1883, E
13, ANQ
16 *Annual Reports of the Toronto Public School Board*, 1872, 12–5; 1881,
16; 1891, 28ff
17 *Educational Record*, 15, 3 (1895), 91–3
18 *Ibid.*, 5, 2 (1885), 57
19 Patrick Thornton to Egerton Ryerson, 22 Jan. 1849, RG 2, C–6–C, PAO
20 *Annual Report of the Toronto Public School Board*, 1880, 11
21 *Ibid.*, 1873, 66; 1879, 29
22 *Educational Record*, 5, 1 (1885), 7–8
23 *Annual Report of the Toronto Public School Board*, 1886, 18–19
24 J-P. Nantel to Hon. Surintendent de l'Instruction Publique, 29 March
1884, E 13, 637–50, ANQ
25 *Annual Report of the Toronto Public School Board*, 1891, 33ff.,
describes the addition of an assistant superintendent and four 'supervi-
sory principals' to the Toronto administration.
26 *Annual Report of the Chief Superintendent of Schools for Ontario*,
1870, 59
27 J.B. Delage to Gédéon Quimet, 23 March 1883, E 13, ANQ
28 Registre des délibérations du Bureau des Commissaires, Vol. II, 27
April, 4 May, 19 June 1877. Archives de la Commission des Écoles
Catholiques de Montréal (ACCM)
29 The Montreal Catholic School Commission was unusual in requiring
women teachers to find accommodation for their own schools. The commission did not, until the 1900s, build schools for female teachers and
students. A discussion of its policies may be found in Marta Danylewycz,
'Sexes et classes sociales dans l'enseignement: le cas de Montréal à la
fin du 19e siècle,' in N. Fahmy-Eid and Micheline Dumont, *Maîtresses
de maison, maîtresses d'école* (Montreal 1983), 93–118.
30 Registre des délibérations, Vol. II, 5 March 1879; Généreux worked for
the commission until her death in 1890, ACCM.
31 For a discussion of public health reform and the role of teachers in it
see Neil Sutherland, *Children in English-Canadian Society: Framing
the Twentieth Century Consensus* (Toronto 1978).

32 Teachers were permitted to take sick leaves of up to one month. For longer absences they had to pay for the substitute teachers out of their own pockets. See *Annual Reports of the Toronto Public School Board*, 1872, 98, and 1874, 85–90.

33 Eliza Pelletier to V.T. Simard, 19 Jan. 1884, E 13, 637–12, ANQ

34 'Miss Ferguson's Address to Convention on Pension Act,' *Educational Record*, 28, 12 (1903), 392

35 See the following in *La Patrie*, 'Causerie – Une Grande Fondation,' 6 Dec. 1902; 'Autour de l'école,' 11 Oct. 1902

36 *Educational Record*, 11, 1 (1891), 4–12

37 Egerton Ryerson to John Monger, 26 Dec. 1848, RG 2, C–1, Letterbook D, 360

38 Letters of inquiry on the subject include C.W.D. De l'Armitage to Egerton Ryerson, 27 June 1849; Meade N. Wright to Ryerson, 26 June 1859; and Teacher to Ryerson, 1 April 1859, RG 2, C–6–C, PAO. 'Official Replies ...' *Journal of Education for Upper Canada*, 14, 3 (1861), 40

39 North West Oxford Trustees' Minute Book, School Section No. 1, 15 Jan. 1863, RG 51, 10816, No. 1, PAO, and *Annual Report of the Chief Superintendent of Schools for Ontario*, 1865, Appendix A, 53

40 Engagement of Anna Poulin, 1 June 1882, E 13, 826–13, ANQ

41 'Enquiries,' *Educational Record*, 5, 7 and 8 (1885), 199

42 *Educational Record*, 13, 10 (1893), 286

43 *Annual Reports of the Toronto Public School Board*; see especially 1876, Appendix 1, 10, and 1891, 14–15 and 37–9

44 See *ibid.*, 1876, 18; and 'Something for Country Teachers,' *Educational Record*, 4, 2 (1884), 51–3

45 'Les écoles primaires à Montréal et aux États Unis,' *Le Canada*, 26 Aug. 1903

46 *Annual Report of the Toronto Public School Board*, 1873, 87

47 Wendy Bryans, 'The Women Teachers' Association of Toronto,' paper presented to the Canadian Association for American Studies, Ottawa, 1974

48 *Ibid.*

49 Marie Lavigne and Jennifer Stoddart, 'Women's Work in Montreal at the Beginning of the Century,' in Marylee Stephenson, ed., *Women in Canada* (Toronto 1977), 139; Marîse Thivierge, 'La Syndicalisation des institutrices catholiques, 1900–1959,' in Fahmy-Eid and Dumont, *Maîtresses de maison*

50 'Correspondence,' *Educational Record*, 11, 9 (1891), 241–2

51 Athénais Bibaud, 'Nos écoles de Filles,' *Revue Canadienne*, 2 (1911),

138–9. In 1905 the Marchand Academy had been listed as 'receiving subsidies,' but not 'under the control' of the Montreal Catholic School Commission. By 1909, the Catholic School Commission had replaced the former school with a new one built by itself and now directly under its control. Many girls' schools in Montreal underwent a similar transformation at this time.

52 *Ibid.*, 139

53 Miss E. Binmore, 'The Financial Outlook of the Women Teachers of Montreal,' *Educational Record*, 13, 3 (1893), 69–74

54 Wayne Urban, *Why Teachers Organized* (Detroit 1983). The three cities studied were Chicago, New York and Atlanta.

55 Bryans, 'The Women Teachers' Association of Toronto,' 13–14. See also Alison Prentice, 'Themes in the History of the Toronto Women Teachers' Association,' in Paula Bourne, ed. *Women's Paid and Unpaid Work* (Toronto 1985). The most radical Americans were the women leaders of the teachers' association in Chicago.

56 Harry Braverman, *Labor and Monopoly Capital* (New York and London 1974), 126

57 Michael W. Apple has argued that twentieth-century teachers are 'located simultaneously in two classes,' being members both of the petite bourgeoisie and the working class. See his 'Work, Class and Teaching,' 53.

58 Joan Kelly, 'The Doubled Vision of Feminist Theory,' in Judith L. Newton, Mary Ryan, and Judith Walkowitz, eds., *Sex and Class in Women's History* (London 1983), 259–70

59 Apple, 'Work, Class and Teaching,' 64

60 Prentice, 'Themes in the History of the Toronto Women Teachers' Association'; Bryans, 'The Women Teachers' Association'; John R. Abbott, '"A Man's Task": Women Teachers and the Turn-of-the-Century Public School Inspectorate in Ontario,' paper presented to the Canadian Historical Association annual meeting, Montreal, 1985

Mary Helena Stark:
The Troubles of a Nineteenth-Century State School Teacher
R.J.W. Selleck

A witness giving evidence to a Royal Commission on Education in Melbourne in August 1882:

Will you state to the Commission what your opinion is as to females having the charge of schools? – I have had no experience of it, but I think myself that a female is not competent to manage a school beyond a certain number of children, and a certain age of children.
What do you think should be the maximum age in that case? – The ladies in America profess to be able to manage boys of any age.
As they do not happen to administer the Act in Victoria, what about the ladies in Victoria? – I have never met one yet that would undertake to manage grown boys – there may be some.
If a woman is a head teacher of a school she must take those who come; they can come up to the statutory age? – Yes.
Is that your objection to women being head teachers? – Yes.

These are not the views of a hardened conservative, but those of a relatively liberal man – Patrick Whyte, headmaster of the Old Model School and father of Margaret Whyte, one of the first women to graduate from the medical faculty of the University of Melbourne. When the well-disposed were so tentative, it is easy to understand the difficulties faced by women teachers in nineteenth-century Victoria.[1]

It is all the more remarkable, therefore, that less than a decade after Whyte had given this evidence, *Melbourne Punch* wrote of an 'heroic young lady' who at first

had only against her the Education Department; but when she got Dr. Pearson on his knees and was about to despatch him, the Treasurer and the Attorney-General, with their whole host of retainers, rushed to the assistance of their fallen colleague and held their shields over him. Then the battle waxed more and more furious. She beat them in argument. She beat them in law and equity. She beat them before the Single Court and the Full Court. She beat them in Parliament. And she has wound up by beating them before the highest court in the whole British Empire. If Dr. Pearson and Messrs. Gillies and Wrixon are not black and blue after the course Miss Stark has just put them through, they must have very thick skins indeed![2]

Mary Helena Stark, the 'heroic young lady,' had beaten Duncan Gillies (the premier), H. J. Wrixon (the attorney-general) and Charles Henry Pearson (the minister of public instruction) in a dispute over the classification which she had been awarded when the first classified roll of teachers was published in 1885. Though her case is still referred to in legal discussions, the main concern of this essay is not with the legal issues, but with the light which the case sheds on the political, social and educational attitudes of the time.[3] Mary Stark's story also provides a mirror in which are reflected some important contemporaries – Dr. Pearson and Messrs Gillies and Wrixon, of course, but also George Higinbotham, Sir Bryan O'Loghlen, Drs W. N. Maloney and James Beaney, David Gaunson and Sir Frederick Sargood. It is even possible to obtain a brief glimpse of Tommy Bent.

Mary Helena Stark was born in Dublin on 6 March 1850 to Malcolm Stark and his wife Ellen, née Bannon. When she was about four years old the family migrated to Australia, perhaps in search of gold or of better health for Malcolm. The Starks brought three children with them (a son Malcolm and two daughters, Mary and Annie Victoria) and either went direct to Victoria or moved there soon after their arrival in Australia. From 1860, or perhaps earlier, they lived in the vicinity of Hotham (North Melbourne). Malcolm senior worked as a decorative artist, but he did not have a long career: in 1860 he died of tuberculosis and was buried in the Melbourne General Cemetery after receiving the rites of the Roman Catholic Church, of which the Starks were members. His journey to the Antipodes had brought him neither riches nor health.[4]

Ellen Stark and her children faced a stern financial struggle. She seems to have worked at home while Mary, from the age of fourteen, brought in a Common-School teacher's low salary, and Annie the scanty and fluctuating rewards of a private music teacher. Malcolm junior, who was nineteen when his father died, was employed as a legal clerk at the Court of Petty Sessions or as a registrar of the County Court, nearly always in acting or relieving positions. As a result he was frequently away from home, moving around city and country districts, sometimes close to Melbourne (Anderson's Creek, Heidelberg, Eltham and Healesville) and sometimes further away (Yarrawonga and St Arnaud). From about 1866 the Starks lived at 2 Leveson Street, Hotham, in Walworth Terrace, a newly built and respectable dwelling which they rented from Allisons, the funeral directors. Probably their financial situation was one of genteel poverty, a grim condition, which Ellen would have found no easier to bear for having, in Ireland, been the daughter of a barrister-at-law.[5]

On 1 November 1864, amid these difficult circumstances, Mary Stark began her career as an assistant teacher at St Francis school in Melbourne. She had passed the examination, conducted by the well-known inspector Arthur Bedford Orlebar, for the second division of the certificate of competency. In January 1865 she moved to another Catholic school, St Mary's in West Melbourne. The headmaster Peter Madden was an Irish Catholic, at least an acceptable and probably a very good teacher, and a fussy man who would like to have been a stern authoritarian, if only he could have managed it. In 1873 he can be found asking the secretary of the Education Department for an answer to certain questions:

1. Is an assistant teacher acting wrongly when during the hours set apart for secular instruction, he sits down opposite his class, and writes letters about his private affairs although told by the Head Master he should not do so?
2. Is an assistant not wrong in sending boys out of the school on private messages without the sanction of the Head Master?
3. Is it correct that an assistant should just only say to the Head Teacher – I am going to a funeral and walk off; or I am going down town on business, and walk off fifteen or thirty minutes before the closing of the School – without waiting or caring to know whether it be agreeable to the Head Teacher?

Madden asked that the reply should be 'so worded that I can definitely say to the person in the face of attempted justification or excuses, he must not do it, or he shall be reported to the Minister of Instruction.'

The Education Department sidestepped Madden's request by informing him that the matter was one for the local committee.[6]

After the passage of the 1872 Education Act state aid was withdrawn
from church schools, and in 1877 St Mary's was struck off the departmental roll. Stark refused an appointment at a state school in West
Melbourne, and did not teach again until January 1879, when she was
appointed to state school 1252 Lee Street, Carlton, then called the
Stockade School. She informed the department that she was hoping for
something better and in particular for a 'vacancy in Hotham where I
reside.' Her brief stay at Lee Street provided the first official indication
of the ill health which was to trouble her constantly throughout her
life. She took leave in May 1879 with 'congestion of the lungs,' made
worse, she claimed in July, because of her travelling during the 'severe
winter' from Hotham to North Carlton. Her leave was extended until
mid-September, and she became ill again early in October. Fortunately
she had some powerful friends to plead her cause. Her medical certificates were sometimes signed by W.N. Maloney, soon to be a Labor
parliamentarian; and a letter of support which stated that 'the poor
girl is very ill' came from George Collins Levey, who was involved with
the organization of Melbourne's 1880 international exhibition.[7]

In November 1879 Stark was appointed to state school 307 Hotham,
where she remained for the rest of her career and where she rejoined
Peter Madden, who had become headmaster of the school in 1876. His
change of school had not changed his habits, and in 1880 he sent a
set of regulations to the Education Department. They required all
assistants and pupil-teachers 'unless where the Head Teacher has
expressly given permission' to arrive before 9 o'clock, to send no child
out of the school except in very special circumstances, and (among
other things) to remain 'each in their turn during dinner-recess to take
charge of the buildings and playground.' He asked the department to
confirm the regulations 'by sending me an official letter containing
their substance, or sign what I have drawn.' Such a response would
'strengthen me to carry out things as they ought to be done.' He was
informed that teachers were expected to be punctual and to assist in
supervising children during the mid-day and other recesses. His
other suggestions were described as 'matters of detail with respect to
which it scarcely seems necessary for the Department to lay down
general rules.'[8]

The fastidious Madden, who never came to terms with the little, brief authority which is bestowed on headmasters, soon found that Mary Stark was troubling him again. In July 1880 she took a month's leave for congestion of the liver, and a teacher who called to see her reported to Madden that 'she was very ill indeed.' When she was granted leave on half-pay she obtained a meeting with the minister, and protested; but, undeterred by the temerity of this lowly female teacher, the minister held to his decision, particularly when he learned of the leave she had been granted in 1879. Not long after she had resumed duty she applied for more leave because of illness, and then sorrow. On 27 August 1880 her mother Ellen died of Bright's disease (nephritis) after months of illness. Pressing for leave, Mary Stark insisted: 'After fifteen years, surely with all deference to you [the minister] I can claim this small request.' She was supported by David Gaunson, an aggressive member of Parliament who had just led an attempt to prevent the hanging of Ned Kelly and who, when his own time for death came, numbered among his pall-bearers John Wren and Tommy Bent. Stark was given leave, but at this time (October 1880) Madden remarked that she 'did not seem well when she came and since, and as far as having a good assistant in her is concerned, I might as well have a junior pupil teacher, as she scarcely ever stands, or talks or controls the children as a proper assistant ought to do.' Madden had made his position even clearer when earlier he had written to the department:

I cannot do less than say that I do not think this same Miss Stark works as *briskly* or *energetically* as she might do, and moreover, I am sorely puzzled at times to tell whether she really is so ill as she says.

At the present moment I do not wish to make a charge against her – but I wish I could *conscientiously feel* that she *does all she could do* for the State and which her profession demands.[9]

More illnesses perhaps helped to increase suspicions that she was malingering. In June 1881 Madden informed the department, 'I cannot boast about the quantity of work she performs for the State. I am much afraid that her health is not equal to the strain or amount of energy given by the other teachers to their professional duties.' The inspector Samuel Ware visited the school and reported that 'Miss Stark' had left during the morning 'owing to weakness.' Madden had informed him that she was suffering from 'disease of the heart' and Ware decided to ascertain if this were the case. After speaking to Stark he reported that she did not seem 'to have enough energy to control a class' and during individual work 'she did not keep the attention of more than two or three at a time and yet appeared satisfied with the state of the class.'[10]

In September 1881 Madden reported Stark for insubordination. Inspector Thomas Brodribb, who conducted the consequent inquiry, interviewed Madden, Stark and other teachers and reported on the two principal allegations: disobedience, because she had refused to assist in bringing girls from the playground into the school, and unpunctual attendance at the opening of morning and afternoon school. Brodribb noted Stark's admission that 'she has *always* refused to assist in bringing in the children into school and pleads ill-health as the reason' – on the occasion which led to Madden's charge she had claimed to be recovering from an attack of mumps. Brodribb was willing to accept this claim, but he held that it was not 'a sufficient excuse for her declining *always* a simple school duty that every other teacher and pupil teacher is required to undertake.' Of the charge of unpunctuality, Brodribb remarked (truthfully) that she lived only a quarter of a mile away and, judged by her own entries on the timesheet and the comments of some teachers questioned in her presence, she was frequently late. He reported that Stark 'dwelt on the idea of the Head Teacher persecuting her,' but he found no evidence of such treatment and acquitted Madden of dealing with her harshly, remarking that 'few teachers would have shown equal moderation.' Nevertheless Brodribb was worried. 'I am most anxious,' he said, 'that every due consideration should be made for Miss Stark ... There is no doubt that her health is very infirm, and that she is away from duty so frequently and for such long periods, through ill health, as to make her absence detrimental to the interests of her school.'

Having expressed pity for Mary Stark's ill health (which, he remarked, 'has perhaps somewhat sharpened her temper') Brodribb faced the awkward question he was called upon to answer: 'forced to the alternative that she is either *unwilling* or *unable* to fulfil her duties thoroughly, I am reluctantly driven to believe her *unwilling*. The circumstances of the case lead me to think that Miss Stark does not, after making full allowance for her state of health, render that loyal and efficient service which the Head Teacher has a right to expect.' He recommended that she be required to be punctual, that she undertake the supervision duties and that, because of her 'inharmonious' relationship with Madden, she be exchanged 'for some weak assistant in any neighbouring school.' The obsessive Madden was not content with his victory. He sent the department a letter from some pupils who claimed that they had heard Stark say to him 'that "she would not go out to assist in the playground for him or any other man." ' He asked that the inquiry be reopened so that he might refute some claims which Stark had made. The department took no action.[11]

During the next few years the depressing inspectorial reports on Stark's teaching continued:

Does not seem to have enough energy to keep her class in order and at work (Ware, 1881).
Weak physically, and not thorough in her work (Brodribb, 1882).
Did not impress me favourably, seemed rather a weak teacher (Carmichael, 1884).
Appears to be a fair teacher (Carmichael, 1885).

The ill health also continued. In the twenty-two months between May 1879 and March 1881 Stark had been absent for more than eight months; in following years absences, though not as frequent, were still common. She seems at this time to have been under the medical care of the ebullient Dr James Beaney, who supplied the department with the required medical certificates. At least one pressure was removed from Stark at this time: to the dismay of some parents, Madden was transferred to Footscray in 1882.[12]

This, then, was the Mary Stark who made life difficult for Dr Pearson and Messrs Gillies and Wrixon: an inadequately educated, Irish-Catholic, female migrant who was afflicted with ill health, a fussy authoritarian headmaster, difficult financial circumstances and family sorrows. Yet she had some influential friends and, through her mother and her brother, sufficient acquaintance with the law to be unafraid of it. And as her clashes with Madden and her willingness to press her rights even to ministerial level suggest, she had an uncompromising and defiant temperament which troubled the authorities but which might also have helped Mary Stark to make her own winters.

The first classified roll of Victorian state school teachers, published on 1 January 1885, followed the passage of the 1883 Public Service Act. In drawing up the roll the classifiers had little alternative but to base it on the appointments which teachers currently held, though in many cases these appointments had been secured with the aid of the political patronage which the Public Service Act aimed at abolishing. Complaints and appeals flooded in, and in June 1885 two hundred and forty-two teachers, including Stark, sent a petition to the minister asking that the lot of some particularly disadvantaged women teachers be improved. During the disputation some women teachers, already disturbed by the Education Department's attitude, established the Lady Teachers' Association in an effort to protect their interests.

One of the difficulties facing the Lady Teachers' Association was made evident in April 1886, when some women accompanied a deputation to the minister from the Male Teachers' Association. The women claimed that the men had so monopolized the minister's time that they had been prevented from stating their case adequately, and led by Alice Weekes, an important and neglected figure, they successfully asked for another meeting. Pearson informed them that it was relatively easy for the department to attract female teachers, though often it did not obtain full value from them. Male teachers could be sent anywhere in the colony but, 'in the case of the ladies ... not only did they refuse to go [to the country], but the department was compelled to accept their objections.' The Lady Teachers' Association, for its part, stressed that 'both as Head Teachers ... and Assistants, women have proved themselves quite able to keep pace with, if not go beyond, men.' They complained that 'the undeserved degradation of Female Teachers' had struck a blow at the Education Act. Girls attending state schools were 'destined to be the wives and mothers of the future generations' and it was essential that they 'should be under the immediate supervision of an educated woman; and *that* woman's position in the School must be next the Head Teacher, at least.' When Stark complained about the treatment she had received, she was one of many angry and disappointed women teachers.[13]

What was her complaint? Before the passage of the Public Service Act she had been an assistant teacher at Hotham. She believed that she should have been classified at least in the third sub-class (the lowest sub-class) of the fifth class (the lowest class) of female teachers. Instead, she had been relegated to the position of junior assistant, a new and still lower category which was occupied mainly by women and which had not existed before the Public Service Act. She appealed against her classification (later it was denied that she had) but her appeal was rejected, as were most appeals; then on 24 March 1886 she fired the first shot in what was to be a bitter and protracted battle. F. J. Stephen, her solicitor, wrote to the department enclosing a copy of an opinion received from Dr John Madden, one of the colony's leading barristers, which stated that Stark should have been placed in one of the three sub-classes of the fifth class. The letter was referred to the attorney-general (Wrixon) who decided that the classifiers were empowered to classify Stark as a junior assistant. 'The matter is not free from doubt,' he said, 'but looking to the important interests involved I would not advise that A.B.'s [i.e. Stark's] claim be admitted unless there should be a judicial decision in support of it.' When the department replied to Stephen, there was no suggestion of doubt: the attorney-general had given an opinion that Stark was 'a junior assistant in the fifth class and is not entitled to claim to be put into one of the sub-classes of that class.'[14]

However, apparently the department was uneasy for, in November 1887, when a Bill to Amend the Public Service Act was introduced (it did not grow out of the Stark case), the opportunity was taken to tidy matters up. Clause 48 read: 'Junior assistants shall constitute a separate division of the fifth class and shall not be entitled so long as they hold the position of junior assistants to be placed in any sub-class.' Teachers, irritated by several of the bill's provisions, forced some concessions, including the promise of an amendment which ensured that those who were now called 'junior assistants,' and who had been employed before the 1883 act, could receive the increments which would be denied them if they remained in the category of junior assistants. Then, mainly because of pressure of business at the end of the parliamentary session, the bill was withdrawn. Two days later, on 8 December 1887, Stark obtained from the Supreme Court of Victoria an order calling on the classifiers to show cause as to why she should not be put in one of the classes or sub-classes of the classified roll.[15]

On 22 and 23 March 1888 the new head teacher of state school 307 (with whom Stark's relations seemed to be reasonable) noted that she was absent at the Supreme Court, and on 28 March the chief justice, George Higinbotham, gave judgment in her favour. He argued that, as Stark was a teacher permanently employed in a state school at the time the Public Service Act was passed, she was entitled to be classified in accordance with that act. He pointed out that the term 'junior assistant' was used for the first time in the act, which neither defined the term nor listed the qualifications of those described by it. He assumed that it referred to 'a body of supernumeraries,' some of whom may have been temporarily employed before the act, and were therefore not entitled to be included on the roll of classified teachers. Obviously, teachers with a right to classification (that is, those such as Stark, who were permanently employed before the passage of the act) would not be satisfied by the inclusion of their names in the list of junior assistants. The court directed the classifiers 'to classify the applicant in some one or other of the sub-classes' mentioned in the act.[16]

On 5 April 1888 T.H. Templeton, who was chairing the third annual conference of the State School Teachers' Union (which had done little to help Stark), remarked: 'I am sure that you are all prepared to rejoice with me that the junior assistants, or rather those hitherto illegally styled junior assistants, are now in a fair way to secure their long-withheld rights ... and though we do think the department entitled to our consideration on the outbreak of such an earthquake, yet we trust that no fatalities will occur, and that the office will speedily be restored to its equilibrium.' 'We honour Miss Stark,' Templeton said, 'for so successfully standing in the breach for the juniors.'

It speedily became clear, however, that the rejoicing was premature. Pearson announced that there would be an appeal to the Privy Council in England and that Stark, though placed in the fifth class, would be paid neither the increment to which that classification entitled her nor the arrears which had accumulated while the case was being decided. The department's intransigence was made still clearer when it became known that W.H. Nicholls, the teachers' representative, had refused to sign the classified roll of 1888 – he differed from his two fellow classifiers, who accepted the department's argument that the junior assistants whose cases were similar to Stark's should not be classified. To obtain classification, each junior assistant would have to fight a separate case.[17]

It cannot be said that Pearson and his department adopted this position unwillingly. On 7 May, only five weeks after the Supreme Court decision, Henry Hodges, the department's counsel in the case, gave an unequivocal opinion – Stark and all the junior assistants were entitled to classification and to an increment. The *Australasian School-master* accepted the *Daily Telegraph*'s view that Gilbert Wilson Brown, the department's secretary, was 'a fighting man'; certainly he was known to take a hard and sometimes authoritarian line with teachers. Brown, acting at the request of Gillies, asked Wrixon for another opinion, and on 4 June Wrixon advised that the Supreme Court's decision was 'at variance with the Act' and that no increment should be paid until the Privy Council had made its views known. In the meantime F.J. Stephen had unsuccessfully asked for the arrears of salary to which he believed Stark was entitled – £78 was his calculation. The decision to send the case to the Privy Council, the involvement of the premier, the refusal of classification to the other junior assistants, and the seeking of a new opinion when Hodges's was unsatisfactory suggest that the Stark case had assumed importance in the eyes of the authorities. Why were they so determined to fight over what appeared to be a relatively trivial problem involving a none-too-effective female teacher?[18]

The answer to this question became clearer in June and July 1888 during Parliamentary debate. The Gillies–Deakin coalition which came into power in 1886 was showing signs of strain by mid-1888. The country members, nearly all of whom supported the government, were restive, as were some Liberals, either for reasons of personal ambition or because they though that Deakin was conceding too much to his conservative coalition colleagues. The opposition was not well led (Tommy Bent was ill during 1888 and was beginning to reel from the financial blows which drove him into temporary disgrace), but it did make use of the Stark case. A series of questions, one of which was asked by Bent, probed at the government's position. Wrixon came close to deception when he informed Parliament in answer to Gaunson, the most persistent questioner, that no case had been submitted to counsel and no opinion received from counsel 'with reference to an appeal against the decision of the Supreme Court in favour of Miss Stark.' Strictly speaking, this was true – Hodges's opinion had been confined to classification and payment of the increments, but Wrixon was making a conveniently limited interpretation of Gaunson's wide-ranging question.[19]

Matters came to a head on 25 July when Sir Bryan O'Loghlen, an opposition spokesman, introduced a petition in which eight women asked for classification in accordance with the Supreme Court judgment. During the debate which followed Pearson remarked that the House should be governed 'by considerations of equity, and even of generosity, rather than of technical justice.' He insisted that he 'was never more astounded in my life' than when he heard the court's decision which he thought to be 'in contravention of the clear letter and spirit of the Act.' Though he claimed that he was not looking at the matter 'from a money point of view,' he argued that the cost of meeting the teachers' demands was excessive: £40 000 for the arrears and £14 000 per annum for the increments. His figures were challenged by the opposition, and the next day Pearson explained that he had quoted from memory and that the true figures were £15 000 and £4750. It was not a reassuring incident.[20]

Throughout the discussion Pearson insisted that those responsible for the 1883 act had intended that junior assistants should not receive an increment. This was true; but the point of Stark's argument and of the Supreme Court's decision was that she and her colleagues ought not to have been classified as junior assistants in the first place. A more effective objection, perhaps the crux of Pearson's case, also derived from the 1883 act. Pearson and Wrixon drew attention to a statement made by the then premier, James Service, when defending the act: 'if junior assistants in large schools were allowed increments, their salaries would grow larger than those of head teachers in some of the country schools, and they would not take charge of schools in country districts. The object of not giving increments was to secure a supply of teachers for the country schools.' Pearson pressed this argument strongly, informing the members that 'unless they desire to see the children in the country districts condemned to absolute ignorance, simply because female teachers don't like to be removed from the comforts of town – they must come to the help of the Education department.' It was a familiar problem for Australian educational administrators, the staffing of remote rural schools.[21]

The department exempted many women from teaching in the country – twelve hundred in the previous two years, Pearson claimed. At the same time some women did teach in very difficult circumstances in remote rural districts (they were living in 'perfect shanties' one member said). Seen in this context the act was an attempt to ensure that teachers such as Stark who had not gone to the country should suffer a financial penalty, the loss of increments. By their decision the classifiers had supported this attempt, and by her challenge Mary Stark had attacked departmental discipline – its control over teachers was at risk. To put Stark's case at its worst (as Pearson did): 'teachers are asking for what they were never intended to have, and what they can only get, if they can get it at all, by a technical interpretation of the law.' When Stark secured that interpretation, Pearson feared that departmental discipline might be undermined. As the *Age* remarked: 'Probably the department attaches more importance to the effect which the recent Supreme Court decision may have on the discipline of the service than to the amount of money involved.'[22]

However, Pearson's case would have been more impressive if he had not agreed to the compromise amendment to the withdrawn 1887 act. This would have enabled at least some of the junior assistants to receive increments, and presumably their salaries would have become larger than those of the head teachers of country schools. But, if Pearson's argument was inconsistent, it was politically effective: the debate on the petition was adjourned on the motion of a country member who felt that Parliament was in a mood to support the Supreme Court decision. He stated bluntly: 'If it means that I am to have fifteen or twenty schools empty in my district, I am prepared to defend my people.' Mary Stark had become a victim of one of Australia's enduring conflicts – that between city and country.[23]

Before the debate ended Mary had become the victim of an older and more desperate conflict. The discussion had begun in a dispassionate and rational way, and Pearson even complimented O'Loghlen for having presented his case 'in a singularly calm and weighty manner.' Then, after the motion for adjournment had been moved, Duncan Gillies, who had not been present during the debate, entered the chamber and began an extraordinary and unprovoked attack on those who 'desire the destruction of the Education Act – those who desire that a certain body in this colony shall have a special expenditure for its own benefit, and for the behalf of its church.' O'Loghlen, loyal to both Ireland and Irish Catholicism, immediately rose to the bait. He spoke of Catholics getting 'their own taxes back which they have paid. They have as much right as you have.' 'Now we are beginning to understand the position,' said Gillies. Roman Catholics, he claimed, had 'insisted on religious instruction on its own account.' 'And ... will have it,' O'Loghlen interjected, and he continued: 'The justice of the country will give it.' 'Now we know whereon we stand,' was Gillies's comment. They did indeed; and it was a very old battle ground. Gillies, whose budget had been introduced the previous night, had rallied his wavering coalition by (in Geoffrey Serle's words) 'brazenly and blatantly raising the sectarian issue.' Gillies managed to inflate the Stark issue until he spoke of financially over-burdening the Education Act 'to such a degree as to break it down.' O'Loghlen retorted that Gillies's concern for the act had not prevented him from being absent during the debate, but the damage had been done, and his own quick and urgent response had helped to do it. Stark, whose Irish Catholicism was no assistance in the circumstances, had become a pawn in that centuries-old struggle in which religion, nationality and money are bitterly and inextricably intertwined. The fires of that struggle have always smouldered below the surface of Australian social life, there have always been politicians such as Gillies who are willing to feed the flames when it assists their efforts to clutch at or to cling to power, and there have always been the Mary Starks who are burnt by the flames.[24]

After the adjournment of the debate, the Stark case was hardly mentioned in Parliament until October 1888, when Pearson made another mistake and another compromise. His mistake was to claim that 'the Government had paid Miss Stark's expenses.' Stark, obviously following the debates with care, contacted an opposition member who informed Parliament that she had 'not received from the government one farthing' towards her legal expenses. Pearson promised that she would be repaid and later guaranteed that the expenses of the Privy Council case would be met by the government – as they were. Pearson's compromise was to offer to pay the increments provided that the teachers abandoned any claim to the arrears. He made the offer during the Estimates debate on 24 October, explaining that 'he got the consent of the Premier to that settlement' when the 1887 Amendment Act was under consideration, and he (Pearson) 'was quite prepared now to abide by what he promised then.' The following day a meeting of women teachers rejected his offer.[25]

Though the offer undermined departmental discipline in a similar way to the 1887 proposal, Pearson pressed ahead. On 30 November 1888 the one hundred and eighty-one teachers affected by the Supreme Court decision were sent a form of release and asked to sign it. It was not the action of a scrupulous minister. A group of poorly paid teachers, nearly all of them women, were asked to forego the arrears to which the Supreme Court had ruled they were entitled. Pearson, having first denied them both arrears and increment by his appeal to the Privy Council, had then, before the appeal was heard, offered the increment provided that the arrears were rejected. By November 1888 the teachers had waited nearly four years for classification, and the Privy Council decision was still an uncertain time in the future. It is hard to avoid the conclusion that by issuing 'this dishonourable circular' (as the *Daily Telegraph* was later to call it) Pearson was taking advantage of the financial weakness of the junior assistants. They were victims both of 'the law's delay' and 'the insolence of office.'[26]

To make matters worse there were suggestions that the teachers were placed under pressure to sign. Pearson had to admit that one teacher, Jane Wylie Davison, had signed under pressure, and he agreed to release her from the arrangement. He would not have found this decision any easier because Davison, who was active in the women's suffrage movement, taught at Hotham with Stark from 1882 to 1889. Accusations were made that W. H. Nicholls, the classifier elected by teachers, had tried to persuade teachers to sign the form of the release. Pearson brought Nicholls's denial before the House, but five women repeated their claim that he had 'on more than one occasion, sent messages to us, strongly advising us to sign.' Despite the department's pressure, the teachers proved reluctant. Of the one hundred and eighty-one involved, one hundred and twelve signed between 30 November 1888 (when the first official approach was made) and 30 January 1889. Another letter was sent out of 11 February and, by 8 March, twenty-two more had signed. In November 1889, a year after the first approach had been made, yet another effort was made to roundup the strays, and six more signed. At the end of this deliberate and prolonged campaign, there were still forty-one teachers refusing to co-operate. Of Stark's intransigence there was, of course, no doubt.[27]

To add a final touch of mismanagement to this sad affair Pearson discovered that he did not have the power to make the agreement, and a special provision had to be rushed into a Public Service Amendment Act in 1889. This was accomplished, though Pearson had to listen while an opposition member remarked that 'many of these so-called "junior assistants" were growing grey in the service' and asserted that Pearson 'could satisfy all their equitable claims at a cost not exceeding the expenditure which would be involved in the needless and unjustifiable appeal to the Privy Council.'[28] As the dispute had developed Pearson's demands had steadily hardened, and his concern for departmental discipline seems to have been overtaken by personal obstinacy. Perhaps he did not appreciate the fact that the trouble was caused by a struggling female teacher who had not benefited from 'the higher culture of women' of which he had spoken in the days when he was headmaster of the Presbyterian Ladies' College. Or, perhaps, as the *Australasian Schoolmaster* claimed, his decision was 'only another example of the policy of "pure cussedness" which seems to us to be traceable throughout so much of the recent action of the Education Department.' Certainly the desire to be generous, of which Pearson at first spoke, seemed to disappear rapidly.[29]

While the negotiations continued Stark remained at Hotham. She was no more impressive than in previous years. In 1888 Inspector Curlewis said: 'A fair teacher; not active, somewhat mechanical,' and the following year Inspector Holland reported that she 'taught 3rd well: the homework of her class good: discipline fairly good.' Despite her problems in the classroom Stark was active outside it, especially as a member of the Lady Teachers' Association. She went as one of the association's delegates to the annual conference of the State School Teachers' Union of Victoria in 1889 and 1890, and was therefore a witness of the continuing conflict between men and women teachers. An Education Act passed in 1888 made this worse by reducing women's salaries below the previously paid level of four-fifths of a male teacher's salary. The Lady Teachers' Association struggled to regain the four-fifths margin and, often against the opposition or the passive resistance of the men, to obtain more equitable working conditions. Stark's prominent position in the association suggests that her colleagues were willing to entrust her with more general causes than her own.[30]

On 16 May 1890, more than two years after the Supreme Court decision, her personal fight came to an end, or at least what appeared to be an end. John Main, who became the department's secretary when G.W. Brown retired in 1889 because of ill health, received a letter from the crown solicitor informing him of the fate of the department's appeal. The Privy Council had dismissed it in a blunt and forthright judgment: 'It seems to them [the privy councillors] that the conclusion of the Court below was right, and ought to be affirmed, and they will so advise Her Majesty.' Stark had won a striking victory. 'From court to court the luckless Minister has gone,' the *Daily Telegraph* somewhat spitefully remarked, 'and has been everywhere defeated.' 'What a stark-mad business that has been from the first,' said a member of the opposition.[31]

In history's harsh impersonal light Stark's struggle was a minor event, but her difficult life provides personal and social happenings in which late nineteenth-century Victoria can be caught off-guard: the effort of unlucky migrants to maintain a life of genteel poverty, the sometimes dispirited but not despairing efforts of women (particulary women teachers) to obtain their rights, the rivalry between men and women teachers, a government department's determination to discipline its employees and its willingness to exploit the weak, the country's suspicion of the city, the premier's deliberate fanning of anti-Irish feeling and its attendant class and religious prejudices, a tentative headmaster's search for authority, the advantage afforded by well-connected friends, the pettiness of powerful men, and the bravery of a sick and difficult woman.

The story does not end with the Privy Council's decision. In October

1890 Stark, determined to force home her victory, asked for the interest on the arrears for which she had now waited nearly five years. The ritual was repeated. The department asked the crown solicitor for his view and, though it was not clear cut, Stark seems to have been paid the interest. Meanwhile, Pearson insisted that the teachers who had signed the agreement to forgo their arrears should be held to it, even though the Privy Council's decision had confirmed their right to the arrears. Pearson argued, no doubt truly, that if the Privy Council had found against Stark, he would have heard nothing from the teachers who had signed. This, of course, did little to assuage their anger; they had reluctantly done what the department wished and now were being disadvantaged. Some claimed that they had signed only because they saw others gaining promotion ahead of them, and Jane Davison remained an awkward case for Pearson to explain. The papers were unimpressed by his attitude. A private employer who acted as he had done, the *Daily Telegraph* said, 'would be branded in all the debates of the Trades'-hall as the shocking example of capitalist tyranny.'[32]

Pearson responded to such criticism with bitterness. After the Privy Council decision he defended himself against the accusation that 'Miss Stark has been persecuted in some way, and that certain teachers were intimidated into entering a contract.' He claimed that Stark's costs were originally paid by some of the teachers and that in any case all her expenses had now been recovered. 'Her position is this,' he said: 'For two or three years she has been uncertain as to whether she would win a doubtful lawsuit; but she has not been put to one sixpence of expense; she has not been harassed; and she has been a sort of heroine in the press ... Anciently the Department had the power of bullying the teachers, although I do not believe that it was ever used ... But the mode of transfer and promotion is now fixed by Act of Parliament, and is regulated by two bodies which are perfectly independent of the Minister.'[33]

As resentment gathered around Pearson, Stark's health deteriorated. In November 1890 she was absent from school with gastritis and 'nervous shock.' In February 1891 she was suffering from paralysis brought on, according to her doctor, by 'mental worry.' She was given a month's leave, a further month's leave followed, then in mid-April another month. In May (and understandably) the department acted. The government medical officer was asked to examine Stark, and on 1 July he reported that her paralysis made her unfit for employment. John Main asked the Public Service Board whether it would make a recommendation which would enable the department to apply for an order in council 'calling on Miss Stark to retire.' On 3 July she was requested to forward an application to retire, but on 11 August her sister Annie wrote asking 'most respectfully but most earnestly' that retirement not be required. She suggested that Mary's be declared a special case 'as her health has certainly broken down under the severe mental strain she has had to undergo.' She pointed out that Mary was attending the Bethall Electric Medical Baths, that the doctor believed that there was some hope of recovery, and that 'the result of being enforced suddenly to retire would prove fatal' to her.[34]

Eight days later, growing desperate, Annie wrote to a friendly doctor pointing out that Mary's medical attendants believed that her illness 'was brought on by the severe mental strain she suffered in connection with the law suit Stark v The Queen.' She asked the doctor to see the minister Sir Frederick Sargood (the Deakin–Gillies government had fallen in October 1890) to explain how they were placed. She claimed that if Mary were compelled to resign 'it will cause our home to be broken up and it may be fatal to her after all she has had to suffer. I think if Sir Frederick Sargood only knew the great blow that has come upon our home through this he would re-consider her case and make her life less a burden.' She pointed out that their medical expenses in the past six months had taken all their income, that heavy expense was still required for attendance at the baths, and that there was hope of ultimate recovery. The doctor wrote to Sargood asking: 'can nothing really be done for the poor girl who is stricken with paralysis.' Sargood took no action.[35]

On 9 December 1891 the Public Service Board declared Stark unfit and recommended that her services be dispensed with. Six days later, and before this notice had reached her, she wrote to the secretary:

I have the honor through you to apprise the hon. the Minister of Education that it is my intention to resign my position as Assistant teacher in your Department. I also with great deference understand that I shall receive the usual retiring emoluments.

I have the honor to be
Your most obedient servant

Mary Helena Stark.

She died that day, 15 December 1891, but not before she had won a final grim victory: because she had resigned she was entitled to a gratuity of nine month's salary. 'And as she was now deceased,' a Treasury official noted in immaculate copperplate handwriting, 'the Gratuity [is] payable to such members of the family as the Honourable the Minister of Public Instruction might indicate.' Sargood indicated Annie Stark, and she received £89 5s, plus 19s 6d which was owing to her sister from some leave on half pay and for whose payment an order in council was required.[36]

Custom may have dulled the irony of the letter's ritualistic ending – and Stark had not been one of the department's most obedient servants. But, even in the desperate conditions under which she wrote the letter (it is in her ungainly handwriting), one expression may have caused her to reflect: 'I also with great deference ...' We shall never know whether or not she did stop to think, but we do know that, if the letter's formal ending is excluded, this was the last sentence that Mary Stark wrote to the Education Department.

NOTES

This article is from *Melbourne Studies in Education 1982*, ed. S. Murray-Smith (Melbourne University Press 1982), 141–60. Reprinted with permission from La Trobe University Press.

1   Minutes of evidence, p 107, Royal Commission on Education 1884, *Victorian Parliamentary Papers 1884*. Ailsa Zainu'ddin, 'The Admission of Women to the University of Melbourne, 1869–1903,' in S. Murray-Smith, ed., *Melbourne Studies in Education 1973* (Melbourne 1973), 97, 102

2   *Melbourne Punch*, 22 May 1890, p 321

3   I.K.F. Birch, *The School and the Law* (Melbourne 1976), 73

4   6 March 1850, the date given on the Teachers' Register entry supplied to the Board of Education when Mary began teaching, has been accepted as her birth date. Official records (death certificates for Malcolm senior, Ellen and Mary) give conflicting dates. There is also doubt about her name. She signed herself 'Mary Helena Stark' but 'Helena' was sometimes given as 'Ellen' and at times 'Theresa' was added. There is also uncertainty about Malcolm Stark senior's name, which in various records is given as 'Malcolm Alexander,' 'Malcolm John' and 'Alexander Malcolm.' The most likely date for the Starks' arrival in Australia is 1854, but the death certificates give dates ranging from 1854 to 1858. There is no record of their arrival at the Port of Mel-

bourne, though the death certificates suggest that they were always residents of Victoria. Perhaps they disembarked at Sydney or Adelaide and came quickly to Melbourne. Malcolm Stark's death certificate, 23 Oct. 1860, gives their address as 5 Chetwynd Street, North Melbourne. The same death certificate provides the details of his illness and burial and gives his occupation as decorative artist.

5 Entries in the *Victorian Government Gazette (VGG)* identify Malcolm Stark acting as Clerk of Petty Sessions at Hotham from 11 Dec. 1873, *VGG 1874*, p 94; the last entry, when he is a Warden's Clerk at Foster, is for 22 Oct. 1888, *VGG* 1888, p 3225. The *Sands and MacDougall's Melbourne and Suburban Directory* has one or more members of the family living at 2 Leveson Street from 1871 to 1896. The rate books, Borough of Hotham in the City of Melbourne, show the Starks renting this building from 1866 to 1896. (The rate books are held at the Melbourne Town Hall.) For Ellen's father's occupation – death certificate, Ellen Stark, 27 Aug. 1880.

6 For the details of Stark's career, Education Department of Victoria, Teachers' Register, no. 1968 (hereinafter, TR 1968). For Madden's letter, Education Department of Victoria, Correspondence, state school 600, 73/8955, Series 794, Box 30, Public Record Office of Victoria (P.R.O. Vic.).

7 Aid was withdrawn from St Mary's in 1877 because it was a capitation school (a school which was paid a government grant based on its attendance, but was left in the control of its local committee). After the passage of the 1872 Education Act such schools (often controlled by churches) were given a five-year winding down period before aid was withdrawn. For her appointments and illnesses, Education Department of Victoria, schools correspondence, state school 1252 (hereinafter SC 1252), 78/44237; 79/17939, 27284, 27285, 28450 (P.R.O. Vic.). For Levey, *Australian Dictionary of Biography (ADB)*, vol. 5, pp 81–2.

8 SC 307, 80/19255

9 SC 307, 80/25315, 25694, 32021, 34150, 35141, 37517, 33332

10 SC 307, 81/25736

11 SC 307, 81/41969, 42644, 42052

12 Inspectors' reports, TR 1968. For ill health, SC 81/41400. For Beaney, *ADB*, vol. 3, pp 124–6

13 85/18926 and 13847 in Education Department of Victoria, Special Case File, no. 864 (hereinafter SCF 864), P.R.O. Vic.

14 For Stark's classification, *VGG* 1885, p 69. The list of junior assistants who appealed is in SCF 896. The claim that Stark did not appeal is

made in 'Statement of the case of Mary Helena Stark' (hereinafter 'Statement'), scf 896. Stephen's letter is reproduced in *Victorian Parliamentary Debates* 1888 (hereinafter *VPD* 1888), p 1464. For Wrixon's opinion, 'Statement,' Attachment A; for the department's reply to Stark, 'Statement,' Attachment B. The 'Statement' is a useful summary of the Stark case.

15 For the 1887 bill, 'Statement,' Attachment C; the Wrixon amendment is Attachment E and also *Argus*, 6 Dec. 1887, p 5. For the withdrawal of the bill, *VPD* 1887, p 2495. For the 8 Dec. action, 'Case for the Respondent' [in the Privy Council], scf 896.

16 sc 307, 88/9017. *Regina* v. *Main and Others, Ex parte Stark, Victorian Law Reports*, vol. 14, 1888, pp 98–101; *Daily Telegraph*, 31 March 1888, p 6.

17 *Daily Telegraph*, 6 April 1888, p 7 (Templeton) and 3 July 1888, p 4 (Nicholls)

18 scf 896 holds Hodges's opinion (88/15263), Wrixon's (88/16574) and Stephen's letter (88/16574). For Brown, *Australasian Schoolmaster and Literary Review* (hereinafter *AS*), May 1888, p 169 and *ADB*, vol. 3, pp 257–8

19 For the state of the coalition, Geoffrey Serle, *The Rush to Be Rich* (Melbourne 1971), 318–27 and P. Loveday, A. W. Martin and R. S. Parker, eds., *The Emergence of the Australian Party System* (Sydney 1977), 50–5. For questions: *VPD* 1888, pp 130, 236, 347 (the Wrixon reply), 369, 401–2

20 *VPD* 1888, pp 568, 569, 587

21 *VPD* 1888, p 56; *VPD* 1883, p 1366 (Service); *VPD* 1888, p 570 (country teachers)

22 *VPD* 1888, p 572 ('shanties'), p 570 (Pearson). *Age*, 27 July 1888, p 4

23 *VPD* 1888, p 578

24 *VPD* 1888, p 568 (Pearson); pp 578–81 (Gillies and O'Loghlen). Serle, *Rush to Be Rich*, 320–1.

25 *VPD* 1888, pp 1466 and 1546 (the 'mistake'), p 1676 (the compromise). Also *AS*, Nov. 1888, p 265

26 'Statement,' Attachment G (form of release); *Daily Telegraph*, 19 May 1890, p 4

27 *VPD* 1890, pp 1300, 2458-60 and 90/35492 in scf 896 (Davison); Nicholls, *VPD* 1890, p 1467 and letter by Helen Johnson and four other teachers to Colonel W.C. Smith, 18 Sept. 1890, scf 896; for the details of those who signed, 'Statement,' scf 896

28 *VPD* 1889, pp 2082-3

29 For Pearson at PLC, Kathleen Fitzpatrick, *PLC Melbourne: The First Century 1875–1975* (Melbourne 1975), esp. pp 47–78. *AS*, May 1888, p 169

30 TR 1968 for reports; *AS*, May 1889, p 355, and April 1890 (Stark as representative of Lady Teachers' Association); for a dispute between men and women teachers, *AS*, May 1889, p 357

31 90/22167 in SCF 896 (Crown Solicitor's letter). SCF 896 contains a copy of the full text of the decision. *Daily Telegraph*, 19 May 1890, p 4; *VPD* 1890, p 82

32 For the interest claim 90/48007, 58036, 60655 in SCF 896. As no further argument took place it seems that Stark's claim was satisfactorily met. The teachers' anger is evident in the report of a deputation on 4 Feb. 1891, SCF 896. See also *VPD* 1890, pp 2451–60. *Daily Telegraph*, 19 May 1890, p 4

33 *VPD* 1890, pp 228–9

34 SC 307, 90/55327; 91/6739, 12107, 17026, 22641, 35157 and 40324

35 SC 307, 91/64474

36 SC 307, 91/65561

Feminists in Teaching:

The National Union of Women Teachers, 1920–1945

Sarah King

In 1919, the year after the vote had at last been granted to some women, the president of the National Federation of Women Teachers wrote of the 'all conquering women's movement'[1]: 'The NFWT is proud to have taken and be taking its very definite part in such a movement. Its existence has been ignored and its members have been maligned but its influence spreads and its powers grow.'[2] Yet Miss Dawson reminded members of her union that the fight was far from over. She called upon them: 'For the sake of the girl who is with us now and the women of England that is to be, let us take our trowel and build.'[3] Those members, women teachers in elementary schools, responded to the appeal. Throughout the interwar years they campaigned with immense vigour and dedication as part of an extensive feminist movement to challenge the oppression imposed upon women and the educational policies which perpetuated that subordination.

Yet their efforts have been forgotten, their ideals, outlooks and achievements ignored in historical and educational analyses. The feminist movement in which members of the NUWT participated so energetically has been written off as 'organisationally enfeebled, theoretically confused and disastrously fragmented,'[4] a feminism lacking glory and power. Although women have been numerically dominant among the staff of state schools throughout the twentieth century, their own perceptions of their role and the relationship of their world outlook to their employment has been disregarded. The NUWT has been particularly hidden, largely because the records of the organisation were lost for many years.[5] It has been assumed that during the twenties and thirties women teachers remained quiescent, worthy of analysis only in terms of their 'numerical dominance' and 'professional passivity.'

This paper will focus on the forgotten feminist teachers in the NUWT and their role within the women's movement during the interwar years. The important part which women teachers played in the vigorous, optimistic feminist network will be explored to suggest the strength of a movement which has been overlooked in most historical accounts. It will then be argued that the members of the NUWT perceived themselves above all as feminist educationalists and saw their work in and outside schools as very important in the struggle to achieve emancipation. Their definition and ideology of feminism shaped both their notion of the role of a teachers' trade union and their perception of the potential and objectives of girls' education. The beliefs of these feminists about the nature of women's subordination and the way in which institution-alised schooling contributed to that oppression will be examined to suggest the way in which they consciously connected their political outlook to the practice of teaching. They rejected the existing assumptions and practices of the education system and challenged other teachers' associations to do the same. These women teachers battled relentlessly in and outside the classroom to achieve a radical new vision of the role in society for which education should prepare girls.

When, in 1918, the much sought-after vote was finally granted to certain women, the suffragists who had campaigned so hard were well aware that much remained to be done. One leading feminist wrote that no women believed that, 'the freedom of women in society is either achieved or really stable.'[6] Yet this contemporary recognition that the sphere of feminist activity had to be extended has not been generally recognised by historians. The small amount of research which has been conducted into interwar feminism has presented it in disarray, fragmenting into single issue campaigns and critically divided between the 'old style' egalitarian feminists who sought 'liberal and absolute equality' and the 'new' welfare feminists who stressed reforms such as protective legislation which took account of the different nature of women's lives.[7] Although it has been argued that welfare feminism had the potential to become a new radical ideology if it had not diverted energy into general social reform, there have been virtually no positive assessments of egalitarian feminism or suggestions that this had a strong, potentially radical theoretical base.[8]

There was certainly an amazing multiplication of women's organisations during this period. Yet in spite of the fragmentation a vibrant *network* existed which, although operating in a very hostile social and political climate, remained theoretically strong and very active.[9] Feminism is an extremely difficult concept to analyse, particularly from the vantage point of secondwave, late twentieth-century feminism.[10] The concerns of feminism have always been historically specific, marked by contradictory ideas and this is particularly true of the interwar era. While recognising the continuities in women's lives, it is vital in any historical interpretation to accept the contemporary perceptions of the women involved and in the subsequent analysis the self definitions of individuals and organisations will be used to define feminism. The women of the NUWT constantly and consciously defined their ideals and actions as 'feminist' and this criterion must be recognised in any assessment of their philosophy and work.

The context in which these feminists operated was extremely hostile. The interwar years were not years of social and economic advance for women but a period of reactionary backlash against the perceived emancipation of women. As soon as war ended great efforts were made to ensure that females returned to traditional occupations, marked by inferior conditions and payment. This was certainly so for women teachers, for during this period their employment disadvantages were formally codified; the marriage bar was widely introduced, the payment of female to male teachers was fixed at a ratio of 4 : 5 and the sexual division of labour within the profession hardened. Vera Brittain summed up the atmosphere of conflict about gender roles when she wrote, 'The feminist movement of the present day is not very popular,' but she went on adamantly: 'Feminism still lives in England today because the incompleteness of the English franchise represents but one symbol among many others of the incomplete recognition of women as human beings.'[11]

Feminism did indeed still live. The great number of women's organisations which existed consciously united in 'the cause,' the 'women's movement.' There was a strong sense of hope, of optimism that feminists could, 'at this most critical time for all women,' alter women's lives in a radical way. Societies united in demonstrations and deputations, lobbying and public statements while most, like the NUWT, belonged to one or more of the 'umbrella' organisations. Feminists seem to have been very conscious of the need to present a consolidated front and they demonstrated unity regularly as in, for example, the 1929 deputation on Equal Rights to the prime minister and the 1933 Right of Married Women to Earn meeting. At the latter the hall was packed with women of all groups, even those disagreeing with each other on other issues. The strong sense of shared women's culture was demonstrated as usual by community singing. However, after a protest from the NUWT, the 'inappropriate' Land of Hope and Glory was replaced by the more suitable 'Blow the Man Down.'[12]

It was as part of this organised and vibrant network that the NUWT existed, seen by contemporaries as 'a true feminist body which is always to be found in the thick of the fight for equality.'[13] The union defined itself as 'a separate women's organisation ... to provide an avenue by which the women of the teaching profession may give clear and unmistakable expression to their opinion.'[14]

The organisation had started in 1904 as an Equal Pay League formed within the National Union of Teachers (NUT) and aiming to secure the principle of equal pay as official NUT policy.[15] In 1909 the League changed its name to the National Federation of Women Teachers (NFWT) and began to work as a separate body although officially still as part of the NUT. Its efforts to secure the adoption of support for women's suffrage and for equal pay continued to fail and relationships became increasingly strained. Miss Phipps was to comment that the 1913 Annual Union Conference demonstrated clearly that 'the men in that Union, like most men, really at times forgot that women existed.'[16] Support grew and in 1920 the federation became the National Union of Women Teachers. Although dual membership of the NUT and NUWT was formally banned only in 1932, the women's organisation became totally independent long before that. Hostility escalated with the formation of the National Association of Schoolmasters, a separate male elementary teachers' union formed to protect men's interests against the 'selfish women' motivated by 'sex hatred.'[17]

It is extremely difficult to discover the backgrounds of the women who joined the NUWT for records reveal very little of members' personal history. Although recent research has established that, in the pre-1914 period, elementary teaching increasingly became an occupation for the lower-middle-class girl,[18] uncertainty surrounds the class composition of women elementary teachers in the interwar years. It seems likely that it continued to be lower-middle-class females entering the profession while skilled working-class families provided the majority of male entrants. Evidence suggests that these women saw teaching as a relatively secure, long term career, not as a temporary job before marriage. Such expectations and backgrounds obviously affected the attitude these women brought to their employment and their demands of a trade union or professional association.

It is equally problematic to establish why certain women teachers chose to join the NUWT while the majority suffering the same disadvantages in employment, remained in the NUT.[19] These were strongly condemned by NUWT members: 'They must be ... women who will play the men's game, who will acknowledge the inherent superiority of man and be his abject follower.'[20] Recent research has shown that, in its efforts to achieve recognition as a professional association, the NUT offered no model for the role of its female members.[21] The Ladies Committee was not very active during the inter-war years and for a long time the union had no paid female officials. The NUWT was very aware that within the rival union, 'we may be quite sure that every effort will be put forward to intimidate the women, to bring them to heel, to stifle any independent act of expression.'[22]

The women who turned to the new organisation sought an alternative trade union to one whose role had been defined by men. They wanted an association which would reflect their political and educational outlooks and help them challenge the inequalities they perceived in society. Like the rest of the feminist movement, the NUWT was very aware of the minor part women were permitted to play in trade union affairs[23] and of the ambiguous policy of the Trades Union Congress (TUC) towards its women members. These teachers sought an alternative association which would 'really concentrate on women ... put us first and make us feel we mattered.'[24] Although the union did perform the 'normal' functions of a trade union, the outlook of its members meant that they sought more from a professional association. The NUWT was to be a support network to help women teachers in their everyday struggle for freedom and equality. It would operate as a 'pioneer among teachers' unions not only in questions particularly affecting the professional interests of women but also in social and educational affairs.'[25]

If recognition of the NUWT members' perception of its role as a union is important in any analysis of its educational work, so too is an understanding of the group's definition of 'feminism as we know it.'[26] The feminist ideology of these women formed a strong theoretical base not only for all educational policies but also for their teaching within the classroom. This ideology was rooted in the demand for total equality on exactly the same terms as men, above all for economic equality. They believed that women's lack of economic self-determination and men's control of financial resources were the roots of subordination. This idea shaped the attitude of these feminists to marriage, motherhood, men and the role of education in women's lives. In this, 'economic phase of the feminist struggle,'[27] it was vital for women to work in paid employment and to achieve, 'a right to work and be paid for the work done.'[28] This view fuelled their immense opposition to the marriage bar which not only affected members personally but was perceived as a concrete example of male power operating through an overt restriction on women's economic activities.

A corollary of the need to fight for economic liberation was the idea that male prejudice in refusing to 'allow' women equality in the home and in paid employment was the basic cause of oppression. Virtually every NUWT analysis of women's position made the point that 'we are still fighting feeling ... It is *feeling* which refuses us equal pay ... the feeling that men are superior to women.'[29] The constant argument was that men sought to control women's lives, believing it to be in their interests: 'men claim the right to approve or disapprove any enlargement of women's sphere.'[30] This concentration on patriarchal power relations is only explicable in the context of interwar Britain and the countless examples of men's patriarchal attitudes and behaviour collected by the NUWT. The contentious issue of protective legislation based on the sex of the worker was also seen as an example of male scheming confining women to certain jobs. Although restrictive legislation might make the lives of some women a little easier, to the NUWT women equality *per se* had to be the overriding priority. They agreed social reforms for all were desirable, but these teachers were realistic, recognising that women had to have equality with men *before* they could make a more radical challenge to the structure of society.[31]

The belief that economic self-determination would lead the way to ending men's domination of women was very apparent in the attitude of the NUWT towards marriage and motherhood. Although these women tactically could not and indeed probably did not want to appear to be challenging the family unit, they did want to challenge the division of labour within the home and the financial dependence on men of many wives. In 1937 an editorial in *The Woman Teacher*, the weekly journal of the union, stated: 'Inequality between the sexes has its roots in the marriage relationship ... (men know) the power of the purse is the most real kind of power.'[32] The 'solution' was not a rejection of marriage as such but the rejection of marriage as a trade and the constant advocation of continued paid employment after marriage. As will be examined, both these ideas featured strongly in the educational policies of the union as did the notion that marriage should be a partnership in which there was an equal division of household work. The employed wife should not have to fulfil a dual role: 'The old adage that women's work is never done should not be tolerated for the women of the future.'[33] Unlike the 'new' welfare feminists who assumed mothers should stay at home but be paid family allowances, the egalitarian feminists of the NUWT argued adamantly that a mother too should work outside the home for her own independence and for the good of her sex: 'There is something neurotic in the woman who is 'wife' and 'mother' and nothing else whatever ... The notion that motherhood totally incapacitates a woman for any work but tending a baby is untruthful.'[34]

If motherhood was seen as simply precluding a woman from paid employment the sexual division of labour would continue and harden. The question of how practically a working mother could cope was not entirely ignored although it did not receive great attention. In years of great criticism of working-class mothers, these teachers who daily came into contact with the mother's offspring do seem to have recognised the horrendous hardships many women suffered. Although, probably for tactical reasons, the union never advocated nursery schools simply so that women could continue in paid employment, they did plead for nurseries, especially in working-class districts, 'where mothers toil hard to make homes happy for husband and children and where they did marvellously but at the expense of health and leisure.'[35]

Organised feminists have long been berated for being middle-class and unaware of the realities of the lives of working-class women. Whatever their own backgrounds, the women of the NUWT did perceive society as being divided on social class lines as well as by gender. Moreover, they tended to assume that the much praised professional woman, employed as part of her quest for self-determination, was the norm rather than the industrial woman who worked to eat. Thus frequently in *The Woman Teacher* the view was expressed that a professional woman would not be a bad homemaker because she would never have to face housework: 'plenty of woman like doing these things, some do not'[36] and thus the latter group could employ someone else to do their chores. This ambivalence was part of these women's own experiences in a hostile society. However, recognition of the confusion and class-based outlook should not detract from their positive attitude towards *all* women and particularly the mainly working-class girls they taught. Many of the NUWT members were well aware of economic hardship and were supporting dependants. It may be argued that their beliefs about paid employment as a means to liberation also ignored the fact that there is nothing innately rewarding or emancipating in being given the opportunity to work within a capitalist economy.[37] Yet these feminists knew that women always worked, the relevant point was whether it was paid or unpaid work, low-status jobs or more skilled, secure employment. Above all, this group of teachers wanted all women to be able to shape their own lives: 'let us help ourselves and decide for ourselves what work is best for us.'[38]

It was this ideology which pervaded their critique of girls' schooling, their radical ideals for change and their educational work. Armed with these beliefs the union fought ceaselessly to achieve their aims, always conscious of being, 'of fullest possible service to the women's movement.'[39] Thus any differences within the feminist network had to be put aside in order to achieve a successful fight. As the NUWT motto proclaimed: 'she who would be free herself must strike the blow.' These teachers struck their blow by a great barrage of propaganda and constant public visibility – frequently in yellow and green dresses. *The Woman Teacher* was foremost in the education of public opinion. It was 'a women's paper written by women, controlled by women and above all read by women in order that the women's point of view shall no longer be submerged or distorted.'[40] The first issue made clear that there would be no fashion, cookery or advice on how to make bedroom suites out of packing cases – there would be 'too much propaganda for that.'[41] There was a strong sense of involvement and commitment within the union, as one member recalled: 'We were always kept informed ... you knew what to do.'[42] Young members were encouraged to speak in public and learn lobbying while an endless flow of correspondence between headquarters and local branches intensified the solidarity. A set of instructions sent in 1931 to all units stated: 'Are there mixed organisations in the district in which the women's point of view needs putting? ... every real branch of the NUWT should be prominent in everything but obsessed by nothing that does not lead directly to the goal of equality.'[43] The many social and cultural events added to the immensely important part of the union in its members' lives.

The activities of the NUWT within the feminist network are too extensive to recount in detail but a sample suggests the inordinate activity. This began immediately in November 1918 when the union mounted an election campaign in three weeks, financed and run entirely by members. Miss Phipps stood as an Independent in Chelsea and managed to retain her deposit. Political work continued with deputations, lobbying, questionnaires to MPs and the financial support of Agnes Dawson on the London County Council (LCC). Wherever possible, active support was given to bills such as the 1927 Married Women (Employment) Bill. The sheer volume of feminist events attended was enormous. In the late twenties there were frequently three or four open air meetings a week in London. In 1928, during celebrations of Equal Political Rights, *The Woman Teacher* commented that right until the end of the campaign, 'the NUWT continued the work, open air speaking every Saturday in Hyde Park and Wandsworth Common, lobbying, deputations, processions and mass meetings.'[44] In all publicity it was stressed that feminist teachers were operating as a part of a united movement 'cooperating with other feminist organisations ... with the object of spreading the doctrine and practice of equality.'[45]

Yet although the NUWT was thus involved in challenging every aspect of women's subordination it saw itself as 'pre-eminently an educational body,' the organisation for women who wished to 'combine feminist activity with inspired work in their profession.'[46] They sought, as the editorial of the first *Woman Teacher* stated: 'to proclaim from the housetops our judgement on things that matter vitally to the work of education.'[47] The women teachers of the NUWT recognised that in a society where the domestic ideology located women within the home, the opportunities of girls within institutionalised educational provision were likely to be restricted. Their resistance to this and efforts to combat discrimination were an integral part of their feminist outlook, for they saw education as another example of the platforms of male power which shaped women's lives. They had to guard the educational opportunities of women won by feminists in the past and ensure 'that all the remaining barriers be flung down.'[48]

This paper will now examine the feminist critique of the structure and curriculum of the state schools. Actual interwar educational policy certainly presented these women teachers with much to criticise, for the majority of elementary school girls continued to be perceived as headed for domesticity, only temporarily workers in unskilled, low paid employment.[49] Policies throughout the twenties and thirties stressed a 'feminine' curriculum and assumed that the educational requirements of boys and girls were not identical. Reports repeatedly stressed that the ultimate social role of the girl as a homemaker must determine schooling. The 1923 Report on the Differentiation of the Curriculum for Boys and Girls in Secondary Schools lamented that, 'old and delicate graces had been lost and individuality of womanhood has been sacrificed upon the austere altar of sex equality.'[50] During years of increasing awareness of the importance of vocational skills in future life, the influential Spens Report of 1938 virtually ignored girls. While it defined boys by aptitude for certain types of schooling, girls were defined only by gender, a homogenous grouping which should be taught how to use the many books published in the interest of the home.

It is important to recognise such trends in official policy both in order to understand the accepted educational ideology of the time and to comprehend how radical the views of the NUWT feminists were. They stood virtually alone in the educational world in renouncing underlying assumptions about girls in policy.[51] Their position was made more difficult and indeed more significant by the extraordinary hostility they faced in their arguments about girls' schooling. Attacks from other teachers' unions and society in general were extremely vicious. One incident in 1913, at the NUT Annual Conference, was typical of the opposition of the post-war years. Miss Cutten, a leading member of the NFWT, was listening to a speech by a Board of Education official: 'Lord Haldane was outlining the education of the future. *Boys* should have this, boys must have that but not one word about girls did he say ... At last, when it appeared that the education of the future generation of girls was to be overlooked altogether, Miss Cutten ventured to put the pertinent question, 'What about the education of girls?' Pandemonium followed. Men rose in the hall with their backs to the platform and shouted wildly: the organised stewards rushed upon Miss Cutten, seized her by the legs and dragged her from the chair on which she was standing.'[52] Attacks continued: these women teachers would feminise the nation, they were Bolshevists, they were jaundiced spinsters 'for whom a cold douche is the best treatment.'[53] One Willesden headmaster commented authoritatively that 'women's minds are always intent on sexual matters'[54] while another man worried about the effect of these teachers' 'damned up sexual urge' on pupils.[55]

Undaunted, the NUWT women remained convinced that education was women's strongest weapon and that their own sex must control the provision made for girls. 'This gives to the women opportunity for working out the kind of education which they consider most suitable ... it is up to them to see that such schemes fit the girl for the place in life which must be taken by the women of the future.'[56] They argued that unless the overwhelmingly male composition of policy-making bodies was changed, the needs of girls would continue to be, 'entirely overlooked or treated as of quite secondary importance.'[57]

Thus the union fought fiercely against the increasing amalgamation of single-sex schools into mixed establishments. They demanded that wherever possible, girls should be taught by women in separate schools for, 'under a headmaster the boys are likely to get more attention both in the curriculum and in the provision of sport.'[58] In arguing for women teachers for girls, professional concerns about members' increasing displacement from the higher-status jobs were, of course, considered, but it is clear that policy also reflected deeply-held feminist beliefs about the need of girls to be taught by females. Union records chronicle countless examples of the disadvantages to girls of a male-dominated structure of authority in schools, an aspect of the hidden curriculum which so concerns the feminist educationalists today. The union stressed that the continual subjection of women teachers to younger, often inexperienced male headteachers affected both girls and boys adversely: 'For a man to be at the head of a mixed school engendered in a boy a false idea that nature had destined him, the Lord of Creation, for positions of authority and it developed in the girl a cramping lack of confidence and ambition.'[59] A corollary of this was the argument that women teachers themselves were critically important as role models to teach girls to 'believe in themselves'[60] and to fight against the humility society imposed.

Such a feminist outlook shaped the organisation's stand on coeducation. Although it was seen as theoretically a progressive development, worthy of support by the most 'advanced feminists,'[61] the NUWT argued that mixed schools did not provide true coeducation since girls were subject to a gender-differentiated curriculum within them. No official pronouncements in favour of coeducation were ever made for the difficulty that 'feminists feared' was that the girl would be overshadowed in such schools.[62] The NUWT repeatedly contended that the whole matter of coeducation was closely bound to that of equal opportunities in society in general. Before it would earn feminist approval, coeducation had to offer, 'facilities for boys and girls alike and any differentiation in education should be based on the child's needs or aptitudes and not upon sex.'[63] Until this occurred, the NUWT continued, with limited success, to fight against mixed schools, their feminist educationalist concerns as central to their arguments as fears about their own promotion.

The critique of these women teachers of how the structure of schooling transmitted patriarchal power relationships and accepted gender roles extended to the curriculum, to the 'knowledge' transmitted within the classroom. They believed that in their daily work they were being required to impart a gender differentiated curriculum which vehemently reinforced traditional attitudes about and towards women. The challenge of the NUWT to this curriculum reflected two basic corner-stones of their feminism – the belief that women must be given exactly the same opportunities and be judged on the same terms as men, and the notion that women had to be prepared for paid employment to become economically independent and free. Schooling thus had to not assume all girls would become wives and mothers but equip them to forge their own destiny.

The overriding principle that these true 'egalitarian' feminists fought for within their individual schools and on a national level was to ensure that girls received identical lessons and opportunities to those of boys; so called 'equal but different' provision was dangerous as a 1928 article pointed out: 'The education given to the boy is designed and calculated to be that which will give him the best all round training of soul, mind and body. We claim for the girl an education which will equally give her the best all round training.'[64]

The NUWT thus relentlessly protested against the countless 'insidious forms of sex favouritism' apparent in the education system. These included the allocation of Local Education Authority scholarships to secondary schools to far fewer girls than boys and the fact that girls' schools taught botany as it required less expensive resources than physics. The syllabi of examination subjects also received heavy criti-cism for perpetuating detrimental stereotypes of women or ignoring them altogether. *The Women Teacher* pointed out in 1923 that, 'unwise examples in arithmetic occur as of a man earning more than a woman and there are books like John Halifax where the man is infallible and the woman weak and clinging.'[65] In answer to girls' supposed innate lack of mathematical ability, it was pointed out: 'if girls spend so many hours on needlework and domestic work while boys are studying maths the girls cannot possibly attain the standard in this subject achieved by the boys.'[66]

The union did not confine its concern entirely to one sex. These women teachers saw themselves as educationalists fighting for a 'pro-gressive' policy for all. They were well aware that they worked within a system divided on social class as well as on gender lines. The NUWT argued for the right of all to free secondary education and for the Raising of the School Leaving Age (ROSLA). Yet even on this latter general question the union was made only too aware of the need for their battle specifically on behalf of girls, a battle which these women teachers believed had to take priority over general reform. When it was proposed that ROSLA should take place in 1939, special provisions were made for some children to be exempt from remaining at school for an extra year. The terms made it easy for girls to be excused if they were 'needed' at home. Miss Dawson wrote angrily: 'How easy it would be under some Authorities for girls to get this exemption, earning nothing, adding nothing to their own status or dignity but just being the home drudge.'[67]

The greatest energies of the union were therefore directed at changing the domestic education which perpetuated the sexual division of labour and which denied girls other technical training for a variety of skilled work. Their attack on existing assumptions was radical, threatening both the accepted patterns of work and power within the home and the strict occupational segregation of the interwar economy. Throughout this period domestic subjects continued to take up a very large proportion of an elementary schoolgirl's hours at school. Official policy insisted on its national importance, on girls being 'trained to guard the home life and home keeping of the nation.'[68] There was also the consideration, despite frequent official denials, of directing girls towards domestic service, deemed suitably feminine work, particularly in years of servant shortage. Thus girls spent many hours on practical lessons in dusting, laundry and cooking.

The NUWT argued vehemently against such policy, above all against making domestic lessons compulsory for all girls from an early age. 'We protest against, we quarrel eternally with the view that girls in an elementary school are necessarily doomed to become household drudges and that they should be sidetracked into this position while they are still at school.'[69] Their quarrel was not with domestic subjects *per se* but with the facts that the lessons did not form part of a broad general education and that they took so many hours in girls' short school lives. The union accepted that limited domestic economy lessons did have some value – for both sexes. It was quite obvious, these feminists argued, that there should be, 'equal preparation for home life as between boys and girls by the giving of instruction to boys in the simple elements of domestic subjects such as needlework and cookery.'[70]

Similarly girls should learn about woodcraft, electricity and engines. The suggestion that boys should be given domestic lessons in exactly the same form as girls was official NUWT policy throughout the interwar years and was consciously a challenge to the traditional sexual division of labour and the 'assumption that the male worker is always to have someone to do such work for him but that the female is always expected to do two jobs, the one at lower pay than the male worker and the other for no pay at all.'[71] Although these women did want domestic labour to receive higher social and economic reward within society, they recognised that the existing status of housework placed, 'an unfair handicap on girls' education as compared with a boy for future wage earning employment.'[72] The corollary of this was that schooling should give girls the potential to enter a wide range of employment and to achieve economic independence and stability. 'Women are so handicapped now; they are *not* free to choose their own work for unless they adopt a career supposedly suitable for women they have no chance of acquiring skill.'[73]

The interwar years were a time of great debate about the links of education to industry and the economy. However, while facilities for boys were greatly extended, the provision for girls in junior technical, central and elementary schools perpetuated their disadvantages in the labour market by directing them towards stereotypically women's work, such as laundry work or dressmaking, characterised by low status and insecurity. The NUWT predicted that, in a time of economic depression, this would accentuate women's problems in the job market and create, 'an artificially large supply of half skilled or unskilled women's labour with a corresponding fall in wages.'[74] These feminist teachers adopted a number of strategies to combat this. The London Unit was particularly active in securing equality of treatment in London County Council technical scholarships and training schemes, seeing this work as part of the, 'educational, egalitarian and feminist aims of the NUWT.'[75]

The union was one of the few dissenting voices to speak out against the much-heralded Spens Report of 1938 which advocated technical schools for the less academic, more practically-minded secondary pupils but did not even mention girls in its discussion of the merits of such schools. Mrs McMillan, then president of the NUWT, tiraded that since these schools were 'based on the view that they provide the best type of education for pupils of certain abilities ... there can be no good reason for debarring girls from participating. Failure to provide girls with facilities equal to those of boys handicaps the girl at the outset.'[76]

The concern of the women teachers was accentuated by the widely acknowledged juvenile unemployment problem of the 1930s. The Junior Instruction Centres (JIC) set up to help alleviate this, worked to disadvantage girls by providing less grant per head to unemployed female adolescents.[77] Miss Fisher inquired of a Ministry of Labour official sent to placate the Central Council,[78] why the girls' centres received such meagre resources when they were supposed to function to maintain employability? Miss Fisher deplored 'the tendency to regard the needs of employment of girls less seriously than that of boys. Unemployed girls, she said, were as great a menace to the nation as unemployed boys and there was no reason to suppose that the home could ever provide every girl with adequate employment.'[79] Moreover, the curricula of JIC limited girls to hygiene and domestic science lessons. As Miss Coleman wrote to Miss Froud, having just read the ministry's 1934 publication, 'Junior Instruction Centres and Their Future': 'It seems that boys are the juveniles that matter – it looks like 78 Centres for boys and 25 for girls. It was ever thus!'[80]

The NUWT's concerns about and policies for girls' vocational education thus reflected their feminist beliefs about economic emancipation and the right of women to shape their own lives. Their analysis of why girls were confined to training in only low-status employment also reflected their theoretical perspective on the roots of women's oppression, their belief that male prejudice and patriarchy contributed greatly to women's subordination. Their archives contain many examples of men ,both employers and employees, forcing women out of certain jobs or refusing to allow them to train for skilled work. The union united with allies in the feminist network to fight this and to change technical education. In 1928 the NUWT participated in a deputation against women being forced to train for domestic service and in 1930 joined a conference on female unemployment. It worked most closely with the Open Door Council, particularly in 1937–8 when they together drew up a memorandum to send to the International Labour Office reaffirming the conviction that 'without full technical education women can never take their rightful place in industry.'[81]

Thus the feminist teachers of the NUWT recognised how the models of knowledge presented within schools, the subjects taught to girls and the lessons of which they were deprived, all operated to eventually disadvantage women as employees, citizens and in the home. Their feminist outlook and demand for change were inextricably related to the notion of the role for which education *could* prepare girls in an equal society. They perceived their fight for equality in schooling as part of the overall struggle for women's emancipation in all areas of life: 'the attitude towards the education of girls is merely a reflection of the attitude taken in the world in general to women's value as a person, to women's work and to women's remuneration.'[82]

The inability of the NUWT members to win changes in official policy is hardly surprising given the enormous weight of opposition in a society torn by confusion about appropriate gender roles. Yet lack of success does not diminish the importance of these women. Their achievement rests in their unrelenting feminist critique of the way in which institutionalised schooling was perpetuating gender inequalities. They knew that the struggle to achieve their alternative vision for girls' schooling would be hard but they believed that ultimately equality could be reached in state schooling. They could help bring about a 'different conception of woman.' As *The Woman Teacher* commented in 1930: 'To secure that end the members of the NUWT will devote their many talents, their wonderful energy and their great courage.'[83]

NOTES

This article is from Martin Lawn and Gerald Grace, eds., *Teachers: The Culture and Politics of Work* (London: Falmer 1987), 31–49. Reprinted with permission. Throughout the notes the place of publication is London unless otherwise stated.

1 The National Federation of Women Teachers changed its name in 1920 to the National Union of Women Teachers. It will hereafter be abbreviated to NFWT and NUWT in this work.

2 *The Woman Teacher*, 26.9.19, p 2

3 *Ibid.*, 31.10.19, p 45

4 D. Doughan, *Lobbying for Liberation* (LLRS Publications 1980) p 8

5 The NUWT was wound up as an independent organisation in 1961 and an embargo placed on its records for twenty years. When the archives became available to historians their whereabouts remained unknown for some years. They were finally located in the London Institute of Education but remain uncatalogued.

6 R. Strachey, ed., *Our Freedom and Its Results* (Hogarth Press 1936), 9

7 Until recently, with the exception of Jane Lewis, very few historians had conducted research into interwar feminism. See O. Banks, *Faces of Feminism: A Study of Feminism as a Social Movement* (Martin Robertson 1981); D. Doughan, *Lobbying for Liberation*; J. Lewis, 'In Search of a Real Equality – Women between the Wars,' in F. Glover-smith, ed., *Class, Culture and Social Change: A New View of the 1930s* (Brighton: Harvester 1980), 208–39.

8 See Lewis, 'In Search of a Real Equality,' for a full account of the 'new' feminist ideology.

9 For a much fuller account of the activities and interconnections of the interwar feminist network, see S. King, 'Our Strongest Weapon: An Examination of the Attitude of the NUWT towards the Education of Girls, 1918–39,' MA thesis, University of Sussex, 1986.

10 Oram has made this point. A. Oram, 'Sex Antagonism in the Teaching Profession, Employment Issues and the Woman Teacher in Elementary Education 1910–30,' Ph.D. thesis, Bristol University, 1983.

11 NUWT Archives Box 123, Why Feminism Lives – V. Brittain, 6 Point Group, n.d., p 1

12 NUWT Archives Box 60, Miss Pierotti to Miss Whateley, 13.11.33

13 *The Catholic Citizen*, 15.2.27, reported in *The Woman Teacher*, 4.3.27, p 172

14 *The Woman Teacher*, 16.9.29, Call to the Young Teacher

15 The National Union of Teachers was the trade union of the vast majority of elementary teachers at this time. See P.H.J.H. Gosden, *The Evolution of a Profession* (Oxford: Blackwell, 1972)

16 E. Phipps, *The History of the NUWT* (NUWT 1928), 22

17 Very little has been written about the relationship of the NAS to other teachers' groups but see M. Littlewood, 'Makers of Men,' *Trouble and Strife* (1985), 5, 23–9

18 F. Widdowson, *Going Up into the Next Class: Women and Elementary Teacher Training 1840–1914*, (WRRC 1980)

19 It must be remembered that the majority of women elementary teachers remained in the NUT. The NUWT never published membership figures but estimates suggest a total of 7,000–10,000 members during the interwar years.

20 *The Woman Teacher*, 28.11.19, pp 76–8

21 D. Copelman, 'Women in the Classroom Struggle: Elementary School-teachers in London 1870–1940,' Ph.D., Princeton University, 1985; B. Walker, 'Women and the NUT,' M.Ed., Bristol University, 1981

22 *The Woman Teacher*, 14.1.21, p 114

23 See S. Boston, *Women Workers and the Trade Union Movement* (Davis-Poynter 1983), 132–85, and S. Lewenhak, *Women and Trade Unions* (Benn 1977)

24 Mrs Anderson, interview with the author, 16.7.86. Mrs Anderson joined the NUWT in 1922.

25 *The Woman Teacher*, 21.9.28, p 336

26 NUWT Archives Box 73, Report of a Meeting of the National Council of Women, 9.11.29

27 *Ibid.*, 20.12.35, p 91

28 NUWT Archives Box 255, Report of the 1933 conference, presidential speech

29 *The Woman Teacher*, 11.4.24, p 220

30 *Ibid.*, 20.12.35, p 91

31 Although it is clear that a number of NUWT members were active socialists more research is needed into how they perceived the relationship of feminism to socialism.

32 *The Woman Teacher*, 12.3.37, p 203

33 *Ibid.*, 13.1.28, pp 113–14

34 *The Woman Teacher*, 12.3.37, p 203

35 NUWT Archives Box 255, speech of Miss Dawson recorded in press clipping, 14.6.19

36 *The Woman Teacher*, 12.5.22, p 244

37 Boston makes this point. Boston, *Women Workers*, introduction

38 *The Woman Teacher*, 16.1.20, p 130

39 NUWT Archives Box 144, Miss Pierotti to Miss Wharram, 21.11.31

40 *The Woman Teacher*, 7.11.19, p 50

41 *Ibid.*, 26.9.19, p 2

42 Mrs Anderson, interview with the author, 16.7.86

43 Suggestions for the Conducting of Local Associations, NUWT, 1931, p 15

44 *The Woman Teacher*, 13.7.28

45 *Ibid.*, 21.9.28, p 336

46 *Ibid.*, 15.5.36, p 269

47 *Ibid.*, 26.9.19, p 1

48 *Ibid.*, 28.5.37, p 283

49 There does seem to have been some recognition in educational policies of the fact that some girls would never marry and acknowledgement of the careers 'opportunities' of secondary school girls. However, recent research, currently being undertaken by Felicity Hunt and Penny Summerfield, has suggested ambivalence in the minds of policy makers about the extent to which girls should be prepared at all for paid employment.

50 *Report of the Consultative Committee on the Differentiation of the Curriculum for Boys and Girls Respectively in Secondary Schools* (HMSO 1923), p xiii. This report was concerned with secondary schools but the

ideas that it expressed were held to be applicable to girls' education in general given the official tendency to define girls as a homogenous group.

51 The Association of Headmistresses and the Association of Assistant Mistresses were concerned with the education of girls but confined their work to secondary schools.

52 Phipps, *History*, 11

53 *The Woman Teacher*, 30.1.20, p 150

54 NUWT Archives Box 123, The Policy of the Woman Teacher, n.d.

55 Alec Craig quoted in S. Jeffreys, *The Spinster and Her Enemies: Feminism and Sexuality 1880–1930* (Pandora 1985), 180

56 *The Woman Teacher*, 6.5.27, p 241

57 NUWT Archives Box 256, the 1927 Annual Report

58 NUWT Archives Box 129, note written by Miss Froud, n.d.

59 *Ibid.*, cutting from the *Daily Herald*, 3.1.35, Report of the Presidential Address at the NUWT Conference

60 *The Woman Teacher*, 14.1.21, p 114

61 *Ibid.*, 30.1.20, pp 148–9

62 Significantly, in the evidence to the previously mentioned 1923 Differentiation of the Curriculum Committee, only women witnesses spoke against coeducation.

63 NUWT Archives Box 129, letter from Miss Pierotti to Miss Orton, 13.12.43

64 *The Woman Teacher*, 20.4.28, p 217

65 *Ibid.*, 14.9.23, p 349

66 *Ibid.*, 14.2.36, p 177

67 *Ibid.*, 26.11.37, p 72

68 *Report to the Ministry of Labour of the Committee appointed to enquire into the present conditions as to the supply of Female Domestic Servants* (HMSO 1923), para 13

69 *The Woman Teacher* 20.4.28, p 216

70 *Ibid.*, 19.1.34, p 374

71 NUWT Archives Box 144, statement sent to Open Door International, Jan. 1939

72 *The Woman Teacher*, 19.1.23, p 122

73 *Ibid.*, 14.9.23, p 349

74 *Ibid.*, 27.2.20, p 181

75 NUWT Archives Box 306, London Unit Minute Book of Education Committee

76 NUWT Archives Box 121, speech by Mrs McMillan, 1938

77 All boys centres were granted 5s 10d per head, mixed centres 5s 6-½d and all girls centres 5s 3d.

78 The Ministry of Labour rather than the Board of Education controlled the centres, much to the NUWT's disgust.

79 NUWT Archives Box 121, Report of Miss Evans' visit, n.d.

80 *Ibid.*, Miss Coleman to Miss Froud, 2.11.34

81 NUWT Archives Box 144

82 *The Education of Girls*, NUWT, 1950, p 7

83 *Ibid.*

'I am ready to be of assistance when I can':

Lottie Bowron and Rural Women Teachers in British Columbia

J. Donald Wilson

On the morning of 14 November 1928 officials of the Cowichan Lake Logging Company came upon a grisly scene in the teacher's residence at Nixon Creek, an isolated logging camp on the southwest shore of Cowichan Lake on Vancouver Island. Upon entering the three-roomed dwelling they were horrified to find the body of the teacher, twenty-year-old Mabel Jones, stretched out on her back on the floor in the sitting room with a .22 rifle beside her. The post-mortem report coldly described 'a bullet wound of entrance on the front of the chest just to the left of the mid-line with about it a powder burn.'[1] A note was found. In a letter to the managing director of the logging company, which had that fall 'built and equipped an excellent school building' at Nixon Creek, Miss Jones wrote: 'There are a few people who would like to see me out of the way, so I am trying to please them ... I know this is a coward's way of doing things, but what they said about me almost broke my heart. They are not true. Forgive me, please. Say it was an accident.' The complaints registered against Mabel Jones by some parents (out of twenty-two children, the parents of only three were responsible for these criticisms) were enumerated as follows: the flag was continually flying; the children were allowed to march into school in a careless manner; schoolroom discipline was lacking; and the teacher was allowing the children to 'waste their scribblers.'[2]

Later in the month a coroner's inquest was held before which a number of witnesses appeared, both company officials and local residents. The verdict was straightforward: 'Mabel Estelle Jones came to her death whilst temporarily insane.' The jury added, however: 'we are further of the opinion that the mental state was the result of unjustifiable, unfeeling and underhanded criticisms of her work on the part of two members of the school board.' It recommended finding ways in future to free teachers in such small, isolated school districts 'from the gossip of irresponsible and petty citizens.'[3]

Public outrage about the Mabel Jones case was immediate. Typical of newspaper reaction was the Vancouver *Province*'s editorial which lamented the tragic death of 'poor little Mabel Jones' who 'took her own life because it had become intolerable to her in that lonely settlement in the deep woods of Vancouver Island.' But there was a positive side to this tragic affair, the newspaper continued, because 'her pitiful story has done more to arouse public interest in the problem of our rural schools than anything else that has been done or said in this province for years.'[4] Women's groups such as the influential Local Council of Women in Victoria were upset and Joshua Hinchliffe, the new Conservative minister of education, dismissed the Nixon Creek board, replacing it with an official trustee.

Ironically, only three weeks before Mabel Jones' death the school inspector for the area, A.C. Stewart, had complimented her on her 'good' work. Her school management and control were described as 'satisfactory,' the character of teaching, her grading of pupils, and her attitude to work as 'good.' In his previous report of January 1928 he described Jones as 'very interested in the welfare and progress of the pupils' and complimented her on their behaviour. In his 1927 report on his inspectorate as a whole, Stewart had pointed to the need for local communities to be charitable in their criticism of inexperienced teachers in remote situations. By the same token teachers had to learn to live with local criticism. 'We all have the same burden of human defects and need all the helpfulness, sympathy, and encouragement possible from the community in which we serve in order that we may rise in some measure and in some degree to the height of the service required and demanded of us. Whatever the baffling conditions, whatever the adverse and apparently unjust criticism, if we honestly and sincerely try and strive we shall at least enjoy the luxury of self-respect.'[5]

Hinchliffe launched an immediate investigation into conditions as they affected the lives of teachers in rural and assisted schools.[6] The investigators recommended a revision of rural school classifications, higher salaries for assisted school teachers, and a system whereby the provincial police would periodically visit teachers in isolated schools. While none of these recommendations was acted upon, Hinchliffe did take one positive step: he appointed a Rural Teachers' Welfare Officer whose duty was to 'visit the rural districts of the Province where the living and social conditions under which young female teachers are working are not found to be satisfactory.' To the one-room school teacher the welfare officer was to act as a 'friend and good counsellor who will ever be ready to respond to any call that may come for advice or assistance.'[7] The person chosen to carry out this important duty was Lottie Bowron, like Hinchliffe a staunch Anglican. Effective 1 April 1929, her title was fixed as Rural Teachers' Welfare Officer (Women) in the Department of Education. She began work, however, immediately after the Jones tragedy in November 1928, issuing her first report on 11 January 1929.[8]

Instead of choosing to make the structural changes he might have – revised school classifications, higher salaries, and police visits to teachers – Hinchliffe chose to shore up individual teachers by naming someone who could offer pastoral care to the troubled female teachers in the province's isolated areas. The appointee was a noted club woman rather than an experienced teacher, whose culture was one of sociability, service, and subordination. The decision to appoint Bowron was made, therefore, without intention to attack the rural school problem at its roots.

Lottie Mabel Bowron was born in Barkerville on 20 November 1879, the daughter of John Bowron, one of the original Overlanders in 1862 who had settled in the Cariboo the following year. She received her early education in Barkerville and later attended All Hallows School in Yale in 1891–2 and the Annie Wright School, a private girls' school in Tacoma, Washington.[9] In 1904 she was appointed clerk and stenographer in Conservative premier Richard McBride's office, beginning an association that lasted until his death in 1916. In 1909 she became his personal secretary, a post she held until December 1915 when McBride resigned as premier and assumed the post of British Columbia's agent-general in London. Bowron then became secretary to the provincial minister of mines, but departed for England on a leave of absence when the Liberals came into office late in 1916. In London she worked in the Admiralty from March 1917 till November 1918. On her return to Victoria the Liberal government under John Oliver showed her little consideration, offering her only, 'under pressure' as she phrased it, a temporary position as stenographer at half her salary with McBride. Work in the premier's office was specifically denied her.[10] Upset and disappointed, Bowron left the civil service and served as a public stenographer at the Empress Hotel and assisted for a brief period in the lieutenant-governor's office until her appointment as Rural Teachers' Welfare Officer under the new Conservative government of S.F. Tolmie in 1928.

After returning to Victoria in 1919 Bowron, now in her forties, became an active club woman. She was the founding president of the Kumtuks Club (Chinook word meaning 'to know, understand'), the forerunner of the Victoria Business and Professional Women's Club.[11] Later she was active in the Local Council of Women, the women's auxiliary of the Canadian National Institute for the Blind, assistant secretary of the White Cane Club, and a member of the BC Historical Society.

Given the large number of congratulatory notes she received upon her appointment as Rural Teachers' Welfare Officer, Bowron was well respected, certainly amongst elitist groups and organizations. Among her well-wishers were the Vancouver Club, the Native Daughters of British Columbia Post #1, the Imperial Order Daughters of the Empire and the Children of the Empire, the Victoria Local Council of Women, and many personal friends. One acquaintance, Maude Palmer, wrote: 'good for the Conservative Government they couldn't have chosen a more suitable woman to fill the bill.' Then she added, 'I certainly think that you will make the lives of those often lonely girls much brighter – and you will love doing it.' The president of the National Council of Women joined in: 'I think you are the first to hold such a position and I am delighted for I am sure that you will set a splendid precedent.'[12] Such comments underline the perceived service component of her task. Neither Hinchliffe nor Bowron herself imagined that her job would produce significant structural changes affecting the lot of rural teachers. Certainly fundamental improvements in rural education were not to be effected during his term of office.

II

The conditions that contributed to Mabel Jones' suicide were by no means unique to Nixon Creek. Hundreds of young female teachers in rural British Columbia in the 1920s faced similarly difficult circumstances. The following year, for example, at Lily Lake, a 'difficult place' south of Fort Fraser, the inspector reported that the teacher was a victim of 'petty persecution' from one of the families living in the district. Although the inspector was not specific about the nature of the problem, he expressed concern about the physical safety of the teacher and recommended the appointment of an official trustee. If 'serious consequences' should develop, he warned, he did not want to be held responsible for not acting on the situation. He and Lottie Bowron actually alluded to the similarities between this case and the harassment Mabel Jones suffered before taking her life.[13] Fortunately, nothing so serious transpired.[14]

Loneliness, isolation, difficult and unfriendly trustees, parents, and landlords confronted many teachers. Yet compared to domestic service, working in a cannery or factory, or even early marriage, teaching offered numerous attractions. It was certainly a genteel occupation offering sometimes the opportunity to meet respectable eligible members of the opposite sex. It paid not handsomely but reasonably well compared to other occupations open to women, and required little special skill or equipment. At a minimum, a high school graduation diploma and one term (four months) at normal school were sufficient, although by 1922 one year at normal school in Vancouver or Victoria was expected of all prospective teachers. The average weekly wage in Canada in 1931 was $22.56 for men and $12.01 for women.[15] At about the same time the average salary for a teacher at a rural assisted school was $1,080 per annum or $20.76 per week. So in terms of disposable income, rural female teachers, especially if single, were not badly off compared to women in other female occupations such as domestic servant, stenographer and typist.[16]

Despite the material difficulties presented by rural British Columbia, many female teachers thrived on the independence and modest social status afforded them. The economic opportunity to live away from home made teaching a desirable transition stage between schooling and marriage, the ultimate 'vocational' goal for most women of the time.[17] For a minority of women, however, teaching was 'less a preparation than a substitute for woman's divine calling in the home.'[18] For these women teaching became a vocation, in fact often a lifetime career. For some, rural school teaching satisfied a sense of adventure. As one such teacher reminisced: 'It sounds like teachers had a hard life in those days but we thought of ourselves as adventurers – like Olympic Torch-bearers in our gumboots and mittens.'[19] Finally, as work, teaching provided the challenge, satisfaction, and sense of accomplishment that came from reaching the minds and hearts of young children.

A word about the context of rural schools in British Columbia in the 1920s. Whether there was a school or not and whether the school was in good or bad condition, depended on local enthusiasm and support.

The building itself was a product of local initiative. Only after it was built and ten students enrolled did the government reimburse the building costs and supply a grant to pay the teacher. Consequently, even in the 1920s many schools were built of logs; almost all the rest were frame structures, as was true throughout western Canada. Unlike southern Ontario, where brick was commonly used by this time for rural schools, wood was the normal material of construction. The diversity in appearance of British Columbia's one-room schools belied Department of Education efforts seeking uniformity of design. The suggested 1911 Public Works designs for provincial one-room schools were a joke.[20] In reality, rural schools expressed community conditions, initiative, and reliance on local materials. They were manifestations of local, and particularly family, control. By contrast multi-roomed city schools dotting the landscape of Vancouver and Victoria represented state power, the architectural designs bespeaking a uniformity that extended beyond the structure itself. The rural school blended into the topography whether it be prairie, mountain valley, or west coast rainforest. In a culture where the family was central to everyday life and the family economy still persisted, it should not surprise us that the school was family-dominated. By the same token, as most regions were impoverished, the schools were poor and makeshift, materials were at a premium, and upkeep varied from loving attention to none at all.[21]

The way rural British Columbians organized their schools reflected their surroundings and what they valued in their lives and for their children. Localism ensured that rural schools would become distinctive and reflect the attitudes of the communities creating them.[22] The desire of settlements, even very small ones, to have their own schools led to a proliferation of schools. The process continued in the 1920s in the face of recommendations to the contrary emanating from the department and the likes of the Putman-Weir Report of 1925 on how to solve the perceived 'rural school problem' created by small, ill-equipped, one-room schools with inefficient teachers and lack of financial resources. One solution proposed was amalgamation or consolidation of these tiny schools into multi-roomed, urban-like structures, to shift the control from the individual community where it had resided for half a century to the Department of Education in Victoria and its officials, in particular to the inspectorate, the system's representatives in the field.[23] Although by legislation responsibility accrued to local trustees, they were, in the final analysis, 'creatures of provincial authority' and even 'subject to the constant scrutiny and, if warranted, intervention' of provincial officers.[24] Bureaucratic centralization raised the spectre of control by 'outsiders' and resistance to it persisted right up to the Second World War. In other words, rural parents supported basic schooling but resisted outside intervention.

For rural parents 'school' meant much more than the designation of a building; it signified a whole series of interactions inside and outside the building between teacher and students. Despite the pretensions of the central authorities, the very existence of a rural school depended primarily upon two factors: the teacher's ability to adapt it to community desires and parents' willingness to support the school by enrolling their children and seeing that they attended.[25] The existence of the school was what mattered, not the precise nature of its construction. Throughout the 1920s inspectors' reports continually recommended to local school boards school improvements that went unheeded. By 1920, while attendance rates in urban schools were much improved over prewar years, in rural British Columbia students, especially older ones, attended only when school did not compete with other, more pressing demands or when the weather was not inclement. Attendance was also affected by distance.[26]

By virtue of its focus on the Rural Teachers' Welfare Officer, this essay concentrates on the condition of rural rather than urban teachers and particularly teachers in remote and one-room schools; on female rather than male teachers (only one out of five rural teachers was male); and on female teachers in trouble rather than those who were coping well. Bowron's responsibility was confined solely to female rural teachers experiencing difficulties. One should not assume that male rural teachers did not experience problems in their rural schools and communities; they did.[27] Nor should one imagine that all female rural teachers had difficulty coping; they didn't. Although in the course of her visits Bowron did talk to teachers who were coping well she said little in her reports about them because the point of her job was to resolve as best she could problems women teachers faced in remote schools.

III

Now to return to Lottie Bowron's story. Tall, striking in appearance, and forty-nine years of age, Bowron set to work promptly in the new year of 1929 to visit schools. Her normal mode of operating was to choose an area of the province, such as the Peace River or the Bulkley/

Nechako valleys, and plan a visit to most of the one-room schools with female teachers in the area. She might stay at a school only a few minutes or at most a couple of hours since her main task was to chat with the teacher, not observe her class in progress. Bowron, after all, had never been a teacher. Sometimes, if her schedule allowed no more, she met her charges at a freight way station during a brief train stop or on a wharf. But at 'difficult' schools or in cases where her assistance had been requested (most often by the teacher herself), Bowron might stay up to two days sorting out a problem.[28] She usually met around 250 teachers each year.

Typical of Bowron's trips into the Interior was her visit to the Peace River Block in February–March 1931. As recorded in her diary, she left Victoria for Vancouver on 18 February and boarded the train for Edmonton via Kamloops and Jasper. While in Edmonton she went to the 'House' to hear the budget speech. The next day, 21 February, she took the Alberta Northern Railway to Pouce Coupe where she noted 'a great change' since her previous visit. Two days later she was 'still waiting for car to take me to Fort St John. Same old story of 18 months ago.' Finally she left late in the day, but unfortunately the car broke down on the way, and so she did not visit her first school in Fort St John until the afternoon of 24 February. Using this town as a base, she visited over the next week nearby schools, on the average two a day, including Fish Creek, Clayton, North Pine, Rose Prairie, Charlie Lake, Crystal Springs, Montney, and Taylor Flats. On 27 February she returned to Fort St John in order to attend in the evening a 'tremendous meeting of about 300, keen looking men – and women' including the mayor. The purpose of the gathering was to discuss the lack of 'fairness re roads this side of [Peace] River.' Resolutions were passed. She ended the entry cryptically with: '[met] a youngish type of man – afterward stayed to dance for a time.' On 4 March she returned to Pouce Coupe and from there over the next three days she visited schools at Dawson, Rolla, Roe Creek, Shearerdale, Landry, Sunset Prairie, Progress, Devereaux, Dawson South, and Saskatoon Creek. On Friday evening she attended 'Masons' banquet' at Rolla. 'Danced afterward. Got home about 1:30. Enjoyed it.' The last week of her stay in the Peace, again using Pouce Coupe as a base, she visited teachers at Swan Lake, Hays, 'missed Tupper Creek,' Riverside, East Pouce Coupe schools, Rolla, Sweetwater, and Arras. By the end of three weeks, Bowron calculated she had travelled nearly 900 miles in the 'Block.'[29]

Three weeks later Bowron set off again on a lengthy trip, this time to the Nechako and Bulkley valleys along the Grand Trunk Pacific west of Prince George and the Cariboo Country. On 9 and 10 April she attended a teachers' convention in Prince George where she gave a talk on 'Love of Country' in the afternoon, spoke at the banquet in the evening, and left for the hotel at 2:30 the next morning after staying for the dance. 'Such a nice lot of men and girl teachers,' she confided to her diary. While in Prince George she visited both socially and professionally with the district inspector Mr Gamble. On 14 April she began working her way along the GTP rail line visiting schools located along the line and making excursions to others north and south of it. The first week she got as far west as Decker Lake, just west of Burns Lake. The second week she worked out of Vanderhoof, visiting as many as five nearby schools in a day. Toward the end of the week she headed north by car to Fort St James. The trip took three and a half hours, but it was worth it: 'This is a most glorious site. The Hudson Bay Company and Indians facing the lake – most romantic.' The third week, having returned to Prince George, she drove south to Quesnel. Her chauffeur for much of this section was a police constable. Stops included Dragon Creek, Castle Rock, Bouchie Lake, Sister's Creek, Australian, and Alexandria. From Alexandria she took the Pacific Great Eastern to Williams Lake which became a base for the next two days' work. On 1 May she headed south by car over the 'old Cariboo Road' to Cache Creek, Savona, and Kamloops. From there she caught the train back to Vancouver.[30]

Bowron also made special trips to problem schools when asked to. Such was the case with the teacher at Nicomen Island in the Fraser River near Dewdney. 'Miss Martin had written to me,' Bowron reported, 'asking me to visit her as conditions were rather discordant.' She met her at the school together with the trustees and the two complaining parents who were upset about what they termed a lack of discipline. A solution was reached: the trustees concluded 'the parents were not to visit the school and complain to the teacher but were to send in writing to them [trustees] any remarks they had to make.' Another special visit, this time to Gabriola South, was also typical. The teacher, Jennie Szlater, had written Lottie Bowron asking for help. Two days later Bowron left for Gabriola. One or two parents had questioned the teacher's discipline, and wished to have a small boy expelled. In her meeting with the secretary of the board and one of the disgruntled parents she learned that the ratepayers wanted a new teacher. For her part Miss Szlater did not want to give up her job because she was helping her mother out financially. Declaring it was 'not an easy school for a young girl' (Szlater was in her second year of teaching), Bowron then talked over the situation with Inspector Stewart, got him to agree to visit the school, and hoped that he 'can assist in a solution.' Meanwhile, the residents agreed to a ratepayers' meeting to discuss the problem.[31]

For each teacher she talked to, Bowron filled out a form recording information on the teachers' name and school, as well as on living conditions and other pertinent information, all of which varied greatly. Often little more than a comment was made as to whether the living accommodations or social life were satisfactory. Phrases such as, 'This is a heavy school,' 'This is not an easy place,' 'This is a hard place for a young teacher,' appear repeatedly in Bowron's reports. Some reports, however, were more detailed, no doubt bespeaking a particularly difficult school or community. Typical was her report for Bainbridge, north of Port Alberni, in January 1929: 'The living accommodation is not good. Mrs. Sterling was living in one of the Company's houses. The mill having closed down the place is desolate ... This is a lonely place for a teacher ... 7 children – 4 of one family – 3 of another – and all have to walk over 2 miles. All young ... I consider this is rather a hard situation for a teacher.'[32]

Many of her reports spoke of 'quarrels with locals' (Beaver River), 'locals obstinate' (Chilco), 'troubles with parents' (Heriot Bay), 'factions' among parents (Lily Lake), and 'parents not liking the teacher' (Three Valley).[33] In all cases Bowron tried her best to smooth things over by actually confronting the troublesome parents or by offering advice to the often distraught teacher as to how she might best resolve the problem she faced. In some cases the situation was considered so difficult that Bowron simply designated the school 'a man's school' in hopes that female teachers, especially young inexperienced ones, not be hired there in future. In July 1929 she wrote the superintendent of education enclosing a list of rural schools 'best served by a) male teachers and b) male teachers or married women.' In her 1932 report she added to these categories a list of schools headed 'c) *not* for inexperienced women teachers.' Railway towns like Field and Begbie, mining towns like Duthie Mines, Lorne Mine, and Coal Creek, and logging camps like Roy and Jackson Bay were definitely 'best served' by men.[34]

Another phrase commonly found in Lottie Bowron's reports was the term 'a lonely school.' As a gregarious woman herself, she was clearly concerned that her female charges should have access to some sort of social life. Unfortunately, many of these communities offered little or no social life at all, a point Bowron frequently noted. The rural teaching force was overwhelmingly single and female. In 1925, for example, out of 903 rural and assisted school teachers, 79 per cent were female, 91 per cent of the females unmarried, and their average age was 23.6 years. By 1930 the proportion of women teachers rose to 83.5 per cent and those who were single climbed to 92.5 per cent.[35] Yet the notion that the rural areas were too rugged and wild for the delicate sensibilities of the young female permeated teacher correspondence with the educational authorities in Victoria well before Bowron's appointment.

In the 1920s many rural school locations became designated by inspectors and others, including teachers themselves, as 'a man's school.' In her answer to a questionnaire from the Teachers' Bureau,[36] Mrs K.E. Easton of the Fort St John School warned in 1923 that this was a 'pioneer settlement,' and she would 'not advice [sic] a lady especially a young one to come here ... Zero ladies here.' Janet A. Mill, who taught near Pender Harbour, cautioned: 'At Donley's Landing no place for young Lady Teacher living alone – no society, etc. ... The situation here I would say is not very good – There is no water at school – no toilet accomodation [sic] for teacher. It is only suitable for a male who likes catering for himself. Rowing and fishing can be had as a pastime.' George S. Quigley who taught in Glencoe seven miles from Soda Creek wrote that the school was 'suitable for married couple or male. Must be prepared to supply own bed and table linen, crockery and cutlery. Water difficult to obtain during winter. Snow and ice good substitutes.' In the far north at Telegraph Creek on the Stikine River with an average winter white population of twelve, Clare Tervo found life 'rather lonely socially.' Despite the 'beautiful scenery' and 'healthful climate' this 'typical frontier town' to her mind deserved 'a man's school.' Similarly, the teacher at Pender Harbour, then a female, had 'no woman neighbours, practically no social life at present.' As late as 1932 Lottie Bowron found Pender Harbour still 'a difficult community to live in.' Yet some communities were far more isolated than Pender Harbour. Dog Creek, for example, sixty miles south of Williams Lake in Cariboo ranching country, was so inaccessible that Pansy Price was not able to get out at Christmas or Easter for holidays. 'The trip is too cold and too long at these times ... 10 months is the full term here.' So Lottie Bowron's observations in the late twenties and early thirties about the prevalence of 'lonely schools' and the lack of social life was not news to Department of Education officials in Victoria. Some locations were so difficult, however, that 'even a man might find it hard,' – Bowron's description of Hulatt, a few miles east of Vanderhoof, a 'hard bootlegging district.'[37] In large part Lottie Bowron was trying to combat the effects of isolation on her female charges.

Occasionally a community could actually prove dangerous for young female teachers. A case foreshadowing that of Mabel Jones in the horror surrounding it was the murder of Loretta Chisholm, a twenty-one-year-old teacher at Port Essington near Prince Rupert. One Sunday morning in May 1926 she left her boarding house for her customary walk before church. She never returned. Her body was found the following day in the bush near a walking path, her chest and the back of her head crushed, jaw and nose broken, and moss forced down her throat probably to stifle her screams. The autopsy revealed that she suffocated to death. A local Indian was indicted, then later acquitted on appeal for lack of evidence. The jury declared that, 'the deceased came to her death as a result of foul play on the part of some person or persons unknown.' The Prince Rupert *Daily News* commented on the hazards of the locality. 'All kinds of characters' gathered in the village during the fishing season but despite warnings about this sort of people, Miss Chisholm persisted in taking her solitary Sunday walks.[38]

Some situations female teachers experienced were more bothersome than dangerous. On Mayne Island Irene Hawes, only eighteen and fresh out of normal school, found the advances of a seventeen-year-old male grade 7 student more than disconcerting. A report recounts how the student 'took one look at the attractive young schoolmarm and decided to lay siege to her, since she was the finest looking maiden he had ever seen. At recess he proceeded to make his intentions known, and the little lady had to beat a strategic retreat.' Mildred McQuillan, who taught at Orange Valley west of Vanderhoof in 1927, reported that the closest she came to a romantic evening was at a monthly dance where she danced with the only man in the hall who attracted her, but was reluctant to become intimate with him for fear of the rumours that she would start in the community. At Hays in the Peace River District a problem arose in 1932 over the teacher entertaining a man in her house. 'The Secretary, I believe, was on the point of asking for a visit from me so I was very glad I arrived when I did,' wrote Bowron. She ended her report with the following advice: 'Miss Teeple's case is one which assists me in coming to the conclusion I came to last year, that no girl – young girl – just out from Normal, should go to the Peace River country, unless she has relatives there, nor is it wisdom for a teacher to stay in the community for her summer holidays.' At Alexander Manson School in the remote Ootsa Lake ranching settlement, a teacher's dismissal was pending on account of the company she kept. Bowron reported: 'Miss Beechy is ... engaged to a man whom the community does not care about, and this man spends far too much time in Miss Beechy's house, having his meals there, etc., and this, with some school problems, has caused the trouble. I called on ... one of the trustees who informed me that the Board was going to dismiss her ... and I believe [it is] willing to give her an opportunity to resign.' Miss Beechy did not return to the school the following year.[39]

Although documentary evidence of amorous adventures is slim, the fact that the teacher was usually young and unmarried presented problems. She had to be careful in her selection of friends. Indiscreet fraternization in an isolated area, as we have seen, could lead to alienation from the community and, in the extreme, physical harm. The teacher, therefore, had to choose her acquaintances and community politics carefully if she were to survive unscathed.[40] An empty social and love life may have embittered her. Often in the remote communities, eligible males were so few that the teacher became eager to leave the area for one with a larger marriage market. Lexie McLeod left Lower Nicola to 'grab a husband' in Vancouver, while Mildred McQuillan married shortly after leaving Orange Valley in December 1927. Margaret Lanyon, who taught in Black Canyon near Ashcroft from 1926 to 1928, felt 'stuck' in the community and eventually left for a less isolated school at Dewdney even though she took a pay cut. Lottie Bowron seemed particularly sensitive to this problem. When she visited Lewis Island near Prince Rupert in June 1929 she found that 'there was not one man on the island' as they had gone away fishing. At Elk Prairie nine miles from Natal she noted that there were simply no young people for a teacher to associate with.[41]

Living arrangements were very important for rural teachers since where and how they lived intimately affected both their work and their private lives. In rural British Columbia public and private lives were much more integrated than is the case today. Problems with boarding arrangements and the lack of facilities for 'baching' were often very stressful for the unmarried teacher and were a perennial problem for most teachers. 'Baching' held numerous difficulties, especially for young, inexperienced female teachers living away from home for the first time. On Thetis Island, the teacher complained that 'nobody will board the teacher. I have just been turned out of my shack and have got another till the end of June.' Five years later in 1928 the new teacher complained: 'One must "bach." Nearest home to school 1 1/2 miles. Can rent for winter but not during summer months. Very hard to find a house at any time.' By the same token, Bowron found the prospect of one of her 'girls' living in a hotel to be no real solution to the accommodation problem. Too often there was a beer parlour just down the hall. Sometimes the teacher was the only woman residing in the hotel, for in many cases, as at Field, it was run chiefly for railway men.[42]

The alternative of boarding – 59 per cent of teachers reporting in the Teachers' Bureau Records in 1928 boarded – presented different problems, especially for the new teacher who often found herself greeted at the train station or steamship dock by at least two trustees, each of whom wanted to offer her board. Her cash income, translated into boarding costs, was prized, especially in cash-poor areas. Typical of the competition was the story told of the Cawston teacher (south Okanagan) who was expected to arrive by the Great Northern Railway from Princeton. Arrangements had been made for her to board at a certain home, but the other family that wanted her went to Hedley by car, took her off the train, and drove her to their home where she stayed. At Stuart River thirty miles from Vanderhoof Bowron noted that 'There is a great deal of jealousy and quarreling over where the teacher boards. This spirit is carried on by the parents towards the teacher, and some of the pupils carry this attitude into class with them, making this a very difficult and unpleasant district to be in.'[43] Few schools boards had teacherages and boarding with parents or trustees only contributed to the 'gossipy' nature of many communities. In such situations, rural teachers had little or no privacy.

Unfortunately, as Bowron discovered, many teachers did not find their initial boarding place to their liking. For those who moved, problems stemming from the original family quite often ensued. According to one teacher in Grant Mine near Wellington on Vancouver Island, 'matters are not very harmonious in the district, one of the main causes being because she [the teacher] changed her boarding place.' In Flagstone in the West Kootenays the teacher (Miss Elwood) 'lost heart and says she will not teach again' following 'a rather trying time no doubt the fact of Miss Elwood leaving their home [playing] a big part.' In still another community, Lakeshaw on Shawnigan Lake, the teacher felt that the family she had previously lived with had 'endeavoured to make things unpleasant for her [and that the father] was trying to get rid of her.'[44]

Whether the teacher bached, boarded, or lived in a hotel, Bowron had another concern. This was the distance the teacher had to travel in order to reach the school. Some teachers had to walk as far as three and a half miles to school, a particularly hard grind in the winter. Even a shorter trek could prove difficult over some terrain. One teacher struggled half a mile through the woods twice each day over a very steep rough trail with a log as a makeshift bridge across a stream. Yet another teacher, an older woman with twenty-seven years teaching experience, had to 'climb down a steep bank to the Kootenay River, cross in a small boat and climb up the other side.'[45] Some teachers, of course, were more fortunate in that they lived within easy reach to the school and a few even had teacherages on the school property.

Another challenge facing many teachers was instructing children of various ethnic backgrounds.[46] Lottie Bowron was especially conscious of the teaching problems faced in ethnically diverse classrooms. A typical comment was her dismay over the situation she found in Mission Creek in 1929: 'this room has 7 nationalities in 42 pupils and is too heavy for any but an experienced teacher and even this is too heavy for one.' In Cultus Lake she found the district not just a lonely place but a difficult one too: 'the children [were], all but three, Czecho-Slovakians.' At Vesuvius on Salt Spring Island she recorded the presence of 'Whites, Japanese, Negroes and one or two halfbreeds.' Students' lack of fluency in English could make a teacher's task that much more difficult. In Ucluelet on the west coast of Vancouver Island she noted 'of 37 pupils 26 ... are Japanese, [and] this, of course, makes the work of the teachers very strenuous.' In Ucluelet East eighteen of nineteen pupils were Japanese, and a high percentage was to be found in Tofino as well. Some ethnic groups, such as Finns and Ukrainians, were distinguished by their radical political leanings. At Greenslide, just south of Revelstoke, Bowron appended a note to her official report: 'I was told that after school the children went to a community hall to be taught their own language – Ukrainian, music, etc. Other people say this is propaganda and communistic teachings.'[47]

Topping the list of 'difficult' ethnic groups were the Doukhobors of the West Kootenays. Not only was attendance irregular – sometimes girls did not attend at all – but the teacher's safety was occasionally at risk. Schools were ideal targets for arsonists protesting, among other

things, government interference with Doukhobor private lives, in particular its insistence that Doukhobor children attend public schools. Police
patrols increased with the number of incidents so that by 1931 the
schools in Brilliant, Carson, Fruitove, Glade, and Winlaw were all
patrolled at night by either the police or a guard. Not one to exaggerate,
Bowron stated that one teacher in Brilliant 'had become a little nervous'
after threats to the school had been made and after 'someone had tried
to break into her residence.' Similarly, in regard to teachers in Fruitove
she counselled, 'there is no doubt that the experience of a bomb having
been placed under the building rather unnerved them, nor is it at all
to be wondered at.' Bowron even recounted her own run-in with a
Doukhobor parent at Brilliant. 'While visiting the teacher in her rooms
before school opened,' she reported, 'a nude fanatic woman came to see
me, her excuse being that some children were fighting and she wanted
me to tell them not to fight.' Bowron refused to see her.[48]

It is not surprising that facing such events teachers would become
distraught. More surprising is how well the teachers stood up to this
kind of stress and harassment. Bowron noted that most teachers
reacted very well and, as best they could, seemed to take these matters
in their stride. Writing about one stalwart soul she remarked, 'this
teacher had rather a trying time recently when an attempt was made
to burn her school ... These things are very unsettling and while the
teachers say little about it, one feels that at times they have their
unhappy moments, but are very plucky.'[49]

Lottie Bowron could do little to stop what she termed 'fanatics' in
these communities, but she did recommend that teachers in Doukhobor
communities have 'special considerations.' Although she did not give
further details as to what these considerations might be, she did provide
suggestions to individual teachers which she hoped would put them
more at ease. In Fruitove she recommended that 'if big lamps were
placed at either end of the school and lighted during the night a sense
of protection might be afforded [the teacher].' In Glade, whose school
was across the river 'where only Doukhobors live' and the only ferry
was run by Doukhobors, Bowron recommended that 'a telephone be
placed in the school.'[50] Finally, her very support of the teachers and
her praise of their courage must have reassured them, if only in a small
way.

Bowron's support for her teachers, or her 'girls' as she called them,
became legendary. As she reassured one troubled teacher, 'I am here
to help if you need me.'[51] When problems did occur she could be counted

on to investigate the matter promptly. When the wife of the secretary of the school board in Devereaux, north of the head of Knight Inlet, was giving the teacher 'an unhappy time,' Bowron approached the secretary and 'asked him to do his best to see that the persecution cease.' Concerning another parent at Lee in the Cariboo, Bowron visited the teacher, two of the trustees, and 'nearly all the people in the community.' Having found that these people supported the teacher and 'that when discord arose in this district it emanated from the Brown Family,' Bowron spoke to the offending man and his children. Although she found it 'rather difficult to get to the bottom of anything he was supposed to have said,' he did admit that he had no actual complaints against the teacher. Furthermore, Bowron left him with the warning that the 'persecution of the teacher must cease or a way would be found to have it cease.' Despite her no-nonsense manner, problems in other communities were more difficult, if not impossible, to resolve. In Coleman Creek near Port Alberni, for example, the secretary informed Bowron that 'while he had nothing against the present teacher, he was not in agreement with married women teaching.' Still less hopeful was the situation in another community (said to be a quarrelsome one) about which she wrote, 'the people here are always threatening to get rid of the teacher – any teacher.'[52] Much teacher/parent, teacher/trustee trouble seems to have derived from the fact that parents expected to exert control over the teacher and she often resisted these efforts. Teachers not from the community – the majority – were 'outsiders,' and common sense tells us that a reasonable length of stay in the community was a prerequisite for such teachers to win the trust and respect of the community. And yet teacher transiency was very high in rural British Columbia.[53]

Bowron took her work seriously and was pleased to note in her second annual report that 'it is seldom indeed that I leave a teacher without an expression of appreciation for the visit and again and again I am told that the knowledge of such an appointment gives them a sense of security.'[54] Certainly, she went beyond her official duties in extending aid to many teachers. In addition to her visits, she frequently wrote teachers giving advice, moral support, and occasionally a message from home. She even visited teachers' families, offering them reassurances about their daughter's situation. The teachers reciprocated with news of their district in addition to any concerns they might have and spoke warmly and openly to her. In response to one letter in which a teacher was having a hard time fitting in, Bowron replied: 'Just remember this, someday you will be the "other teacher." I find in the course of my visits that so often it is the previous teacher, so I am told, who was either splendid, or poor, or good at this or that, or pretty or plain or something. So don't let that worry you in any way. You, I am sure, are doing good work where you are and trying to find your place as you think a teacher should. Can you do more?'[55] In addition to letters of this kind, Bowron performed many other small acts of kindness. Knowing how scarce resources were, for example, she sent a pretty poster to several schools. In her files of letters one can find thank-you notes from children to whom she sent valentines in Sinclair Mills east of Prince George.

Periodically Bowron addressed students at both Victoria and Vancouver normal schools. Forever concerned with teachers' well-being, she remarked in 1930 that the visit to the normal schools not only served to introduce the welfare officer to the students but also afforded 'a splendid opportunity of placing before [them] some of the problems likely to arise in the social and living conditions which they may encounter, and, as well an excellent chance to give some practical advice which may prove of service later on.'[56] Such advice about remote school situations was sorely needed. Many normal school students, aside from those from rural areas, had little idea about what rural teaching in the province was really like. For the student teachers enrolled in Vancouver Normal School, practice teaching in a one-room school was restricted to one week if at all. Even then, practice teaching schools were located in such communities as Burnaby, Richmond, Coquitlam, North Vancouver, Delta, and Surrey which, though sometimes 'rural' in their surroundings, were hardly isolated enough for the teacher to experience the conditions of rural teaching.[57] Practice teaching at the Victoria Normal School was similarly conducted within easy reach of Victoria in school districts unused to rural community impoverishment, settler transiency, and disruptive local politics. To try to acquaint its students with rural school problems, each normal school set up a rural 'demonstration' school within its main building, but the setting was inherently artificial. A teacher recalls that at the Victoria Normal School she 'learned to correlate, that is, overlap timetables,' a procedure that stood the beginning rural teacher in good stead.[58] But this was a far cry from practice in the isolation of a Quick, Rolla, Horsefly, Usk, Big Creek, Ootsa Lake, Chu Chua, or Yahk.

IV

In late February 1934, Lottie Bowron was unceremoniously dismissed by the new Liberal minister of education, George M. Weir. Arriving back in Victoria on 9 March from an extensive trip to the Peace River country, Bowron recorded in her diary how 'the first letter I opened was saying the Rural Teachers' Welfare Officer was to be done away with – a nice greeting after five years of hard work – where is justice I wonder?' The next day she had 'a straight talk' with superintendent of education S.J. Willis who claimed the dismissal was a cabinet decision and offered 'no complaint of any sort against my work.' The next week she called on Premier Duff Pattullo 'who flew in[to] a petulant state, begged me to go – would see me after session [of the Legislature]. Said it [her post] was a political job [,] always thought so and would have attacked earlier if it not for me.' Bowron scribbled in the margin 'a very strange interview.' The next day she tried to see Weir, but he 'can't or won't see me until Tuesday,' she confided to her diary. 'It seems like a fight for justice,' she wrote, and added in typical fashion 'must not forget the teachers ... I'm going down if I have to, with flags flying.' Finally on 20 March, Bowron had an interview with Weir. 'I found him quite "listenable." I felt as though he were learning something about the post – something he didn't know.'[59] Significantly, there is no record that Bowron's case was raised in the House, nor did any of the male inspectorate come to her defence, publicly at any rate. Perhaps they too saw hers as a political appointment or preferred to keep the bureaucracy uniformly male. In any case, as employees of the state the inspectors would not be likely to criticize publicly a decision of the minister of education.

Bowron's letter of dismissal had specified that her duties were to end on 1 April 1934, at which time she would be granted leave-of-absence without pay until 20 November, 'when you will be retired from the service of the Department on pension.' Despite her pressing pleas in person and by letter to Weir to be allowed to 'carry on in my position to the end of June,' he remained adamant about his earlier decision to abolish the post, although he did eventually agree to pay her salary until the end of the school year.[60] By the end of March Bowron was thoroughly discouraged. 'I feel as though I am almost a culprit,' she confessed. 'Someday the worth of this past five years will come out.' Her depression deepened; by the end of April she lamented in her diary, 'what's there to write about – only self.'[61] From the first of June till the beginning of August she wrote nothing in her diary, where she had formerly filled each day's space with news of the day's activities, both personal and professional.

Bowron's dismissal, more accurately a forced retirement, raises a number of questions. Clearly there was a continued need for the service she was performing and there is every evidence that she was carrying out her duties in an exemplary fashion. Perhaps the new Liberal government of Duff Pattullo reasoned that it could not afford the post during the Depression. That she was not replaced lends credence to this hypothesis. On the other hand, nowhere in the correspondence between Bowron and the government officials or in her diary entries is economic restraint suggested as the reason. She may have been fired because hers was a patronage appointment of the previous Conservative administration or because of her earlier close association with Premier McBride. She and others suspected political reasons were responsible for her dismissal.[62] In offering to take up her case with Dr Weir, the Anglican bishop of the Cariboo, Walter Adams, observed: 'You might not be continued, for whatever your associations were or were not, your appointment 5 years ago would be suspect.' Still he personally found it 'extremely difficult to believe that the new party [could] be guilty of such stupidity to economise on a piece of supervision that hard facts had proven to be necessary.' Bowron seems to have been forewarned about her possible dismissal, as hard on the heels of the Liberal election triumph she recounted in her journal how on meeting family friend Bishop Adams in Nelson in January 1934 he had 'said to let him know if I had heard anything about my work ceasing.'[63]

Retired at age fifty-four, Bowron lived on for another thirty years, returning each summer to Barkerville where she became a vocal supporter of the government restoration of the historic gold rush community. While remaining an active club woman and church-goer, she lived out her days as a resident of the Strathcona Hotel in downtown Victoria, having friends to tea and attending luncheons and dinners with her many friends and relatives in the provincial capital.[64]

What are we to make of Lottie Bowron's brief term of office? Her efforts had little long-term effect on the state of rural schooling in the province. This should not surprise us since her duties as both she and Hinchliffe understood them were meant to be pastoral not reformist in nature. Her annual reports to the Department were short and perfunctory, carrying few general recommendations for change. It was rather at the level of the individual school and teacher that Bowron made the greatest impact. Her chief concern was to aid her 'girls,' to make their lives a little easier and more bearable in their often remote locations. To that end she was willing to confront difficult board members and obstreperous parents on behalf of her charges. She continually urged authorities in Victoria to designate certain schools men's schools to be avoided by female teachers. But hiring teachers remained a local responsibility and female teachers still presented themselves as candidates for jobs in rural schools.

Throughout her tenure Bowron seemed to have very cordial relations with the school inspectors – all male – who functioned in the same regions. I found no evidence of animosity toward her nor any sense that she was seen to be infringing upon their territory. On the contrary, the inspectors often drove her around on school visits and frequently cooperated with her in trying to solve teacher problems. Their respective tasks were quite distinct. The inspectors' job was to pass judgment and offer recommendations on teacher pedagogy, teaching materials, the state of school buildings and grounds, and any desirable structural changes to the rural school system. Bowron was to minister to the needs of the female rural school teacher, to offer comfort and solace, and to ameliorate, if possible, the living and working conditions her charges experienced. She was a counsellor rather than an inspector, and if her correspondence to and from teachers is any indication, she was extremely successful in tending to her 'girls' social and psychological needs. Teachers' letters still on file sing her praises, and in many ways she seems to have acted as a surrogate mother, especially to the younger female teachers. There is clear evidence of the merits of same-sex support systems, for these teachers often turned to Bowron for help rather than to the all-male inspectorate.[65] On the other hand, there is little evidence of the existence of female networks between the teacher and the women in the community. My sources, of course, may have served to prejudice this conclusion, but the female teacher may have represented escape from the community and a life most women in it could not have. She was a challenge to their own choices and an alternative model to their daughters. Most people deemed it easier for a male teacher to find company among married and unmarried men alike – to 'go native' – but for female teachers, friendship with married women may have been problematic.

Bowron's experience as a well-known club woman in Victoria before her appointment undoubtedly stood her in good stead as she went about her visitation duties. Previous experience as a teacher was not so important to her work as the resilience, fortitude, and concern for others she had learned as a club woman. Personal autonomy was a characteristic Bowron displayed throughout her life, and she encouraged her teachers to cultivate the same attitude to theirs. By the same token her approach to problem-solving was highly individualistic. She advocated no collective approaches to resolving teachers' work problems. To do so would not have been in keeping with the club woman's credo not to challenge existing socio-economic structures or women's cultural subordination in that area.[66] Lottie Bowron had struggled on an individual level, ministering as best she could, and often with great success, to her many charges. Her motto might well have been, as she told one of them, 'I am ready to be of assistance when I can.'[67]

NOTES

A longer version of this article, entitled ' "I Am Here to Help You if You Need Me": British Columbia's Rural Teachers' Welfare Officer, 1928–1934,' has appeared in the *Journal of Canadian Studies*, 25, 2 (summer 1990). Reprinted with permission.

The author wishes to thank Julie White for sharing with him her study of Lottie Bowron which she completed as a term assignment while a student in the Faculty of Education at the University of Victoria, March 1987; also Paul Stortz, who carried out research at the Provincial Archives of British Columbia as part of a Challenge '87 grant in the summer of that year. Jean Barman, Bill Bruneau, Richard Mackie, Joy Parr, Patricia Roy, Harry Smaller, Neil Sutherland, and Wendy Mitchinson read earlier versions of the article and offered helpful suggestions for improvement. Research for the article was aided by two Humanities and Social Sciences grants awarded through the University of British Columbia Research Grants Committee.

1 Provincial Archives of British Columbia (PABC), Attorney General's records, Inquest no. 351, p 6, report of coroner's inquest; p 4, autopsy report by Dr G.W. Bissett, 16 Nov. 1928
2 PABC, Department of Education Newspaper Clippings, Vancouver *Province*, 21 Nov. 1928; see also coroner's inquest and the testimony of Chris Gibson, president of the Cowichan Lake Logging Company, p 12
3 Inquest 16 Nov. 1928, pp 1, 36. Temporary insanity was a common cover-up for suicide.
4 Dept. of Education Newspaper Clippings, editorial 'Our Rural Schools,'

Vancouver *Province*, Nov. 1928; see also *ibid.*, 'Protect Young Girl Teachers'

5 PABC, Dept. of Education, School Inspectors' Reports, Nixon Creek, 24 Oct., 18 Jan. 1928; Dept. of Education, *Annual Report of the Public Schools*, 1927, p M31

6 Rural status implied a school that was neither urban nor consolidated, and as a result was without the benefit of centralized municipal administration or finance. Still, the rural school on the average was more prosperous than the assisted school which was so impoverished that the teacher's salary and a grant for school equipment and supplies were underwritten entirely by the provincial government. Provision of the schoolroom or building was the responsibility of the parents and other interested persons.

7 *Annual Report*, 1929, p R10

8 Dept. of Education, School Inspectors' Reports, Reports of Rural Teachers' Welfare Officer (hereafter Bowron Reports), 1928–9. Each school report has been filed alphabetically by school year. Bowron's post was referred to by different names, but the designation 'Rural Teachers' Welfare Officer (Women)' was commonly found in correspondence from the superintendent of education, on her business card, and in the way in which she signed her letters. Other titles used in the department's annual reports were Rural Female Teachers' Welfare Officer and Welfare Officer of Rural Female Teachers.

9 The Bowron Lakes in the Cariboo are named after her family. For her attendance at All Hallows School, see student list compiled in Nov. 1939 by Heber Greene, Anglican Archives, Vancouver. For a description of the school, see Jean Barman, 'Separate and Unequal: Indian and White Girls at All Hallows School, 1884–1920,' in Barman *et al.*, *Indian Education in Canada*, I, *The Legacy* (Vancouver: UBC Press 1986), 110–31. Annie Wright School was a popular destination for BC girls from well-to-do families. One of its most distinguished graduates was Mary McCarthy, author of *How I Grew* (San Diego 1987) and *Memories of a Catholic Girlhood* (New York 1957).

10 She was gazetted on 18 March 1904. Bowron to J. Hinchliffe, 30 Jan. 1930. PABC, Add. mss. 347 (McBride/Bowron Papers), vol. 2, file 2/28. McBride died in London on 6 Aug. 1917. Re denial of work, see W.H. MacInnes (Civil Service Commissioner) to Bowron, 7 Feb. 1919.

11 Victoria *Times*, 17 Jan. 1921

12 McBride/Bowron Papers, vol. 2 (2/27). Palmer to Bowron, 17 Dec. 1928; Mrs J.A. Wilson to Bowron, 2 Aug. 1929

13 PABC, Bowron Reports, Lily Lake, 18 Sept. 1931; Dept. of Education correspondence, A.H. Gower, Prince George, to S.J. Willis, 22 April 1929

14 McBride/Bowron Papers, vol. 2 (2/27). Ethel Wilson, Fort Fraser, to Bowron, 15 May 1929. Wilson compliments Bowron for 'heartening up' the teacher in question.

15 *Census of Canada*, 1931, vol. 1, p 296. In 1929 the average weekly industrial wage stood at $29.20. Margaret A. Ormsby, *British Columbia: A History* (Toronto: Macmillan 1964), 441

16 Teaching as respectable employment for women had been accepted from at least the mid-nineteenth century. See Bruce Curtis, *Building the Educational State: Canada West 1836–1871* (Lewes: Falmer Press 1988), 255.

17 Marriage and children was for the time every 'true' woman's ambition. See Veronica Strong-Boag, *The New Day Recalled: Lives of Girls and Women in English Canada, 1919–1939* (Toronto: Copp Clark Pitman 1988), *passim*; also Alison Prentice *et al.*, *Canadian Women: A History* (Toronto: Harcourt Brace Jovanovich 1988), Part 3.

18 Marta Danylewycz, Beth Light, and Alison Prentice, 'The Evolution of the Sexual Division of Labour in Teaching: A Nineteenth-Century Ontario and Quebec Case Study,' *Histoire sociale/Social History*, XVI, no. 31 (May 1983), 82. For a fascinating account of teacher behaviour in the United States, see Barbara Finkelstein, *Governing the Young: Teacher Behavior in Popular Primary Schools in 19th Century United States* (New York: Falmer Press 1989).

19 Letter from Edna May Embury to Paul Stortz, West Vancouver, 11 March 1988

20 Ivan J. Saunders, 'A Survey of British Columbia School Architecture to 1930,' *Parks Canada Research Bulletin*, no. 225 (Nov. 1984)

21 For an extended discussion of the rural school problem in British Columbia in the 1920's, see J. Donald Wilson and Paul J. Stortz, 'May the Lord Have Mercy on You': The Rural School Problem in British Columbia in the 1920's,' *B.C. Studies*, no. 79 (autumn 1988), 24–58; for a case study of the Bulkley and Nechako Valleys, see P.J. Stortz, 'The Rural School Problem in British Columbia in the 1920's,' MA thesis, UBC 1988, chaps. 3–4; and for the Okanagan Valley, see Penelope S. Stephenson, 'Rural Schooling in the Okanagan in the 1920's,' MA thesis, UBC, forthcoming.

22 For confirmation about the importance of localism in the lives of British Columbians, see Cole Harris, 'Reflections on the Surface of the Pond,'

B.C. Studies, no. 49 (spring 1981), 86–93. Similarly a political scientist concludes that 'geographically based parochialism' made local rather than provincial concerns pre-eminent until after the Second World War. R. Jeremy Wilson, 'The Impact of Communications Developments in British Columbia Electoral Patterns, 1903–1975,' *Canadian Journal of Political Science*, 13 (Sept. 1980), 512, 534

23 Thomas Fleming, ' "Our Boys in the Field": School Inspectors, Superintendents, and the Changing Character of School Leadership in British Columbia,' in N.M. Sheehan, J.D. Wilson, and D.C. Jones, eds., *Schools in the West: Essays in Canadian Educational History* (Calgary: Detselig 1986), 285–303

24 L.W. Downey and A.E. Wright, 'The Statutory Bases of the B.C. Educational System: A Report of an Analysis' (Vancouver: University of British Columbia 1977), 9

25 For a discussion of similar factors at work in eastern Ontario in the late nineteenth century, see Chad Gaffield, *Language, Schooling and Cultural Conflict: The Origins of the French-Language Controversy in Ontario* (Kingston and Montreal: McGill-Queen's University Press 1987), *passim*.

26 For a detailed discussion of attendance problems in the Bulkley and Nechako Valleys, see Stortz, 'The Rural School Problem,' chap. 4.

27 See David C. Jones, 'Creating Rural-Minded Teachers: The British Columbia Experience,' in D.C. Jones, N.M. Sheehan, and R.M. Stamp, eds., *Shaping the Schools of the Canadian West* (Calgary: Detselig 1979), chap. 10.

28 For example, Bowron Reports, Houston, 11 Feb. 1930

29 PABC, Add. mss. 44, Lottie Bowron's *Daily Journal, 1931*, 18 Feb.–13 Mar. For a first hand account of life in the Peace River Block at this time, see W.L. Morton, ed., *God's Galloping Girl: The Peace River Diaries of Monica Storrs, 1929–1931* (Vancouver: UBC Press 1979). The block was restored to British Columbia by the federal government in an agreement signed on 20 February 1930. For a description of this, see Dorothea Calverly, 'Peace River Block,' in Lillian York, ed., *Lure of the South Peace: Tales of the Early Pioneers to 1945* (Fort St John, Dawson Creek: Alaska Highway Daily News and Peace River Block News 1981), 7–8.

30 Bowron, *Daily Journal, 1931*, 7 April–2 May

31 Bowron Reports, Nicomen Island, 3 May 1929; Bowron, *Daily Journal, 1931*, 29 March; Bowron Reports, Gabriola South, 31 March 1931

32 Bowron Reports, Bainbridge, 1928–29, Jan. 1929

33 *Ibid.*, Jan.–April 1929

34 The implication here is that men were better able to cope with the problems presented in communities like these. I am not suggesting that Bowron was right in her contention, but only that this was certainly her perception. In a study of Ontario teachers in the late nineteenth century, Harry Smaller found that it was not necessarily true that 'men were better.' H.J. Smaller, 'Teachers' Protective Associations, Professionalism and the "State" in Nineteenth Century Ontario,' Ph.D. thesis, University of Toronto, 1988

35 J.H. Putman and G.M. Weir, *Survey of the School System* (Victoria: King's Printer 1925), 177–9, and *Annual Reports*, statistical tables

36 The Teachers' Bureau Records are officially known as *School District Information Forms for the Teachers' Bureau*, Dept. of Education. They exist for only two years 1923 and 1928, and are located at the PABC, GR 461, organized alphabetically by school and year. Hereafter known as *TBR*.

37 *TBR*, Glencoe, 1923; Telegraph Creek, 1928; Pender Harbour, 1923 and 1928; Bowron Reports, Pender Harbour, 20 May 1932; *TBR*, Dog Creek, 1928; Bowron Reports, Hulatt, 1928–9. About this time a thoughtful inspector advised a male teetotalling teacher at Hulatt to take more account of the community he was in: 'You had better learn to drink a little or you just can't communicate with these people. This is a very heavy drinking country. I'm not suggesting you drink like they do, but if you're a complete teetaller, I don't think you'll get along with them at all.' Quoted in Joan Adams and Becky Thomas, *Floating Schools and Frozen Inkwells* (Madeira Park: Harbour Publishing 1985), 79

38 The case was never solved. For a full description of the murder and legal proceedings, see Prince Rupert *Daily News*, 27 May–16 June 1926 and 22–5 Nov. 1926, and for the appeal, New Westminster *Columbian*, 7 April 1927. The official inquest report is unavailable. Interestingly, when Lottie Bowron visited Port Essington in September 1931, she mentioned in her diary how a local trustee insisted upon relating the 'tragedy of poor Miss Chisholm.' PABC, Add. mss. 44, Lottie Bowron's *Daily Journal, 1931*, Sept. 30

39 Jesse Brown, ed., *Mayne Island Fall Fair* (Mayne Island: Agricultural Society and Fall Fair 1971), 35–6. PABC, Mildred E. McQuillan Diary, 1927. McQuillan's well-written diary reveals her attitudes towards her work and the community she served. She specifies the trials she faced as a young teacher in a remote school – experiences no doubt common

to countless other rural school teachers in the 1920s. Bowron Reports, Hays, Oct. 1931, Alexander Manson, Sept. 1931

40 The importance of keeping up appearances as well as facing up to sexual harassment and lack of respect from suspicious parents, ratepayers, and niggardly trustees is underlined in Robert Patterson's account of Prairie rural teachers at the same time. See his 'Voices from the Past: The Personal and Professional Struggle of Rural School Teachers,' in Sheehan *et al.*, *Schools in the West*, chap. 6.

41 Lawrie (McLeod) interview, 1986; 'McQuillan: Backwoods Teacher,' Victoria *Times-Colonist*, 31 Aug. 1981, p 35. Interview with Mrs Margaret Manning (née Lanyon), retired school teacher, Vancouver, 12 April 1987. Bowron Reports, Lewis Island, 22 June 1929; Elk Prairie, 16 June 1932

42 *TBR*, Shutty Bench, 1928; Hunter Island, 1923; Thetis Island, 1923, 1928; Aleza Lake, 15 Feb. 1930; Brookmere, 5 April 1930; Field, 31 Jan. 1931

43 Kathleen S. Dewdney, 'Christopher Tickell,' *Okanagan Historical Society Report*, vol. 39 (1976), 84; *TBR*, Stuart River, 1928

44 Bowron Reports, Grant Mine, 12 June 1931; Flagstone, 14 June 1932; Lakeshaw, 28 Oct. 1931

45 *Ibid.*, Surge Narrows, 1 Nov. 1929; Champion Creek, 14 Jan. 1932

46 For a discussion of rural teachers' perceptions of children of ethnic minorities, see J. Donald Wilson, 'The Visions of Ordinary Partici- pants: Teachers' Views of Rural Schooling in British Columbia in the 1920's,' in Patricia E. Roy, ed., *A History of British Columbia: Selected Readings* (Toronto: Copp Clark Pitman 1989), 239–55.

47 Bowron Reports, Mission Creek, 31 May 1929; Cultus Lake, 14 May 1931; Vesuvius, 9 Dec. 1931; Ucluelet, 15 March 1930; Ucluelet East, 15 March 1930; Tofino, 16 March 1930; Greenslide, 29 Jan. 1931

48 Mary Ashworth, 'The Doukhobors,' in her *The Forces Which Shaped Them* (Vancouver: New Star Books 1979), chap. 4; Bowron Reports, Brilliant, 20 Jan. 1931; Fruitove, 22 Jan. 1931; Brilliant, 9 June 1930

49 Bowron Reports, Brilliant, 13 Jan. 1931

50 *Ibid.*, Glade, 21 Jan. 1931; Fruitove, 22 Jan. 1931

51 McBride/Bowron Papers, vol. 2 (2/27). Bowron to Miss L. McCall, Bed- nesti, 6 Feb. 1932

52 Bowron Reports, Devereaux, 16 March 1932; Lee, 1 Nov. 1930; Coleman Creek, 21 March 1932; Begbie, 13 April 1929. Normally, in those days, female teachers left teaching when they married. This practice was more strictly enforced in urban than rural areas. Exceptions occurred

where trustees were desperate to secure a teacher, a teacher married a local man, or a married woman was forced into paid employment for a variety of reasons.

53 For details, see Wilson and Stortz, ' "May the Lord Have Mercy on You." '

54 'Report of Rural Teachers' Welfare Officer (Women's), 1929–30,' in *Reports on Public Instruction* (Victoria: King's Printer 1930)

55 McBride/Bowron Papers, vol. 2 (2/27). Bowron to L. McCall, Bednesti, 6 Feb. 1932

56 'Report of Rural Teachers' Welfare Officer (Women's), 1929–30'

57 For example, Bowron reported encountering normal students on practicum at Glen (Coquitlam), Boundary Bay (Delta) and Surrey Centre. Bowron Reports, 23, 24, and 20 Jan. 1930

58 Sylvia McKay [1929, Victoria Normal School], Normal School Project, University of Victoria, interviewer, Judy Windle, tape recording 78-Y-27

59 Bowron, *Daily Journal, 1934*, 9, 10, 15, 16, 17, 20 March

60 McBride/Bowron Papers, vol. 2 (2/27). S.J. Willis to Bowron, 28 Feb.; Bowron to Weir, 31 March; Weir to Bowron, 9 April 1934

61 Bowron, *Daily Journal, 1934*, 26 March, 30 April

62 *Ibid.*, 1 April 1934. Patronage was certainly a central feature of government at this time in British Columbia. See Robert A. Campbell, 'Liquor and Liberals: Patronage and Government Control in British Columbia, 1920–1928,' *B.C. Studies*, no. 77 (spring 1988), 30–53.

63 McBride/Bowron Papers, vol. 2 (2/27). Walter Cariboo to Bowron, 17 March 1934; Bowron, *Daily Journal, 1934*, 18 Jan.

64 PABC, vertical file. Victoria *Times*, 9 Aug. 1960, p 19; *Colonist*, 2 Feb. 1962, p 5; *Colonist*, 5 Feb. 1964, p 5; *Times*, 24 Feb. 1964, p 13. Bowron's entire estate at death amounted to $2,575. Probate documents, 1 April 1964. Provincial court registry, Victoria

65 For the same time period, Veronica Strong-Boag speaks to the importance for many single women of same-sex relationships: see *The New Day Recalled*, 104–6, 218.

66 Gillian Weiss, ' "As Women and as Citizens": Clubwomen in Vancouver, 1910–1928,' Ph.D. thesis, University of British Columbia, 1983

67 McBride/Bowron Papers, vol. 2 (2/27). Bowron to F.L. Richards, Bridge Lake, 14 April 1932

WOMEN TEACHING IN HIGHER EDUCATION

Here Was Fellowship:
A Social Portrait of Academic Women at Wellesley College, 1895–1920

Patricia A. Palmieri

In 1929 historian Willystine Goodsell noted the meager professional opportunities available to academic women. Only in the women's colleges did women professors of all ranks considerably outnumber the men. Goodsell concluded, 'In the realm of higher education this is their one happy hunting ground and they make good use of it.'[1] One such golden arena was the academic community of Wellesley College 1895–1920. Wellesley was the only women's college which from its founding in 1875 was committed to women presidents and a totally female professoriate. In the Progressive era this professoriate was a stellar cast: it included Katharine Coman, historian; Mary Calkins, philosopher; Vida Dutton Scudder, literary critic and social radical; Margaret Ferguson, botanist; Sarah Frances Whiting, physicist; Emily Greene Balch, economist; and Katharine Lee Bates, author of *America the Beautiful*. To outside observers this group had created a female Harvard, a 'bubbling cauldron that seethed,' a 'hotbed of radicalism.'[2] To their students the noble faculty provided a rich world which stirred them. To the next generation of faculty women the 'old crowd' were completely dedicated 'war horses.'[3] To each other, they were kindred spirits, diverse, but united in the 'bonds of Wellesley.'[4]

Today such outstanding academic women are relatively unknown. It is not solely the passage of time, however, that has distanced these women from us; historians have not considered them worthy of study. Traditional scholarship in the history of academe has tended to focus on presidents, not academic faculty. Moreover, there has been an implicit presumption that only one model of the academic exists – that of the male professional. Even in the recent renaissance in women's educational history, historians have tended to dismiss women scholars *a priori*. Thus Sheila Rothman in *Women's Proper Sphere* concludes that women's colleges were dens of domesticity where female virtue and morality 'intruded' on women's intellectual life. According to Rothman, the women's colleges did not hire women renowned for their intellectual achievement, but rather ones representative of 'female grace and virtue.' She asserts that 'they rarely employed teachers of scholarly stature.' In her ground-breaking *Collegiate Women*, Roberta Frankfort, depicts the culture of Wellesley (1885–1910) as one of 'subdued familial grace,' epitomized by Alice Freeman (Wellesley's president from 1881 to 1887). For Frankfort, the faculty of Wellesley play almost no role at all in creating the culture of the college.[5] But to so dismiss the faculty is to misread fundamentally the history of the Wellesley College community in the Progressive era. Indeed, the academic women of Wellesley shaped this major liberal arts college and were responsible for its 'golden age.'[6] In this essay, using both qualitative and quantitative techniques I will sketch a social portrait of the fifty-three women who attained the rank of senior or associate professor at Wellesley College by 1910.[7]

This collective portrait highlights the fact that the women attracted to academe shared a core set of experiences and attributes derived from their sex, class, family relationships, geographic origins, education and social ideals. Such women were comfortable in what they termed their 'Wellesley world'; they fashioned their professional and private lives around the college and each other.[8] They form not merely a collection of disparate individuals, but a discernible social group, who created at Wellesley a cohesive intellectual and social community. That community is as central to my portrait as any of the individual faculty members: it illuminates the history of academe as it was writ by women scholars, outside the research universities so commonly thought to be the only citadels of genuine intellectual creativity.

In this essay I am not particularly concerned with Wellesley's institutional history. However, it is useful to know something of that history for it provides the backdrop to the emergence of the faculty community under consideration. Wellesley's founders Henry and Pauline Durant were bent on establishing more than a women's college. Typical late-nineteenth-century evangelical communitarians, they wanted Wellesley to be a model community which would serve as an exemplar to the nation of the possibilities of individual and societal transformation through the regeneration of women. Wellesley served the alienated

Durants as a sanctuary and a home; it became, for them as well as for early faculty students, a romantic refuge, a 'little world under one roof.'⁹

Wellesley's most radical feature was its dedication to the principle of education of women by women scholars. Wellesley was to be a 'woman's university,' equivalent to Harvard, presided over and staffed entirely by women. This bold experiment captured the imagination of the public. One newspaper noted: 'The President, professors and students are all women; only two men belong to the establishment: the chief cook and the chief baker.' Another hailed Wellesley as an institution which 'confirmed the century's progress.'¹⁰

While Henry Durant lived, however, his patriarchal style and evangelical zeal prevented the attainment of his radical ideal of an academic community controlled by women. For example, several of the first group of women faculty appointed by Durant voiced their dissatisfaction with his strict behavioral code, which they saw as a vestige of the seminary model. Durant forced the resignations of five faculty women in 1876 but replaced them with other college-educated women. With Durant's death in 1881 and the elevation of Alice Freeman to the presidency, the gap between the real and the ideal narrowed. Her appointment created the basis for a genuine female intellectual community.

To students and faculty the twenty-nine-year-old Freeman epitomized the 'new' college woman. Freeman's charismatic personality and exceptional organizational talents allowed her to rally the Wellesley community from within and to elevate Wellesley to a respected place within the ranks of liberal arts colleges. Freeman resigned to marry Harvard philosopher George Herbert Palmer in 1887, but until her death in 1902, she remained Wellesley's most powerful trustee, controlling the college from behind the scenes. She personally selected as Wellesley's next three presidents women who could be trusted to execute her master-plan for the college. By 1899, Freeman had orchestrated a purge against several old-line faculty women, hiring in their stead junior scholars who could teach a new elective curriculum. Further, she wooed and won a hesitant Caroline Hazard as Wellesley's fifth president. Wellesley sorely needed the wealth and social connections that Hazard brought to the presidency. Her gentility and concern for social reform harmonized well with the spirit of social service which characterized the newly hired faculty. Ill-at-ease with the role of president, Hazard left much of the internal administration to the women professors. Using as their power base the Academic Council formed by Alice Freeman, these strong-minded women 'reared the college from its struggling babyhood to glorious womanhood.'[11]

By 1910, fifty-three women had been on the faculty for more than five years and had reached the rank of senior or associate professor. They constitute the faculty group under consideration. Table 1 lists them with their principal academic department.

What characteristics distinguish this group of academic women? They are strikingly homogeneous in terms of social and geographic origins, upbringing, and socio-cultural worldview. Nearly 50 per cent were born in New England, with 22 per cent from the Midwest and another 20 per cent from the Mid-Atlantic region. Four women were born in Europe; there was only one Southerner. Over half (52 per cent) of the group was born in the decade 1855 to 1865, with another 30 per cent born 1865 to 1875. One hundred per cent were single.[12]

Almost all of these women were children of professional, middle-class families. Their fathers were cultivated men – ministers, lawyers, doctors, college presidents and teachers. These men were also committed to abolitionism, temperance and prison reform. They passed on to their daughters their respect for learning, their zeal for social reform, and their preference for service over financial success. Several of the fathers abandoned careers in business or law for more fulfilling service oriented vocations.[13] They were, to use William James's term, 'tender-minded' in their cultural sensitivity and in their ability to form close bonds with their daughters. Almost all took an avid interest in their daughters' education. For example, when Katharine Coman's father saw that she was making little progress in her seminary, he directed her to tell the principal to give her more work. The principal refused because he thought the female mind incapable of comprehending more difficult material. Mr Coman thereupon transferred Katharine to a public high school, scorning the dire predictions of what would happen to his daughter's manners and morals in a co-educational environment.[14]

To a remarkable degree, the academic women of Wellesley grew up with such special sponsorship and familial support. Lida Kendrick, who became a professor of Biblical History, complained in 1881 as a Wellesley freshman of her ill-preparation for college. Her father responded that he regarded her depression as 'nothing more than a temporary blue spell.' He reminded her that she was eminently qualified to distinguish herself and that she should dismiss all doubts from

TABLE 1

Edith Rose Abbot	Art
Emily Greene Balch	Economics
Katharine Lee Bates	English
Malvina Bennett	Elocution
Charlotte Almira Bragg	Chemistry
Caroline Breyfogal	Latin
Alice Van Vechten Brown	Art History
Ellen Burrell	Mathematics
Mary Whiton Calkins	Psychology and Philosophy
Ellor Carlisle	Pedagogy
Mary Alice Case	Philosophy
Eva Chandler	Mathematics
Angie Chapin	Greek
Katharine Coman	History; Economics
Grace Cooley	Botany
Clara Eaton Cummings	Botany
Grace Davis	Physics
Katharine May Edwards	Latin
Margaret Ferguson	Botany
Elizabeth Fisher	Geology
Caroline Rebecca Fletcher	Latin
Eleanor Gamble	Psychology
Susan Maria Hallowell	Botany
Sophie Hart	English
Adeline Hawes	Latin
Ellen Hayes	Mathematics
Marion Hubbard	Zoology
Margaret Hastings Jackson	Italian
Sophie Jewett	English
Elizabeth Kendall	History
Eliza Kendrick	Biblical History
Adelaide Locke	Biblical History
Laura Emma Lockwood	English
Anna McKeag	Pedagogy
Helen Abbott Merrill	Mathematics
Edna Virginia Moffett	History
Annie Sybil Montague	Greek
Margarethe Muller	German
Julia Orvia	History
Ellen Fitz Pendleton	Mathematics
Frances Perry	English
Ethel Puffer	Philosophy
Charlotte Fitch Roberts	Chemistry
Vida Dutton Scudder	English
Martha Hale Shackford	English
Margaret Pollock Sherwood	English

TABLE 1 – continued

Caroline Rebecca Thompson	Zoology
Roxanne Vivian	Mathematics
Alice Waite	English
Alice Walton	Greek; Archaeology
Sarah Frances Whiting	Physics
Mary Alice Willcox	Zoology
Natalie Wipplinger	German

her mind and think of her family who 'hoped that she would dream good things and awake with new vigor for the battle.'[15]

Similarly, Emily Greene Balch's father counseled her against joining him in his law practice because to do so would not provide sufficient opportunity for her talents. He encouraged her instead to be a pioneer and to continue her social science research and her reform activity.[16]

Such fathers often acted not as marriage brokers but as career brokers for their daughters, arranging for them to take special graduate programs and even securing their daughters' professional placement. While Mary Calkins was traveling in Europe after her Smith graduation, her father Wolcott Calkins arranged for Mary to have an interview with Wellesley's president, Alice Freeman. Mary Calkins subsequently joined the faculty. Later, when Mary sought a Ph.D. in psychology from Harvard, which did not admit women, Wolcott petitioned the Harvard Corporation to admit his daughter as a special visitor. Mary Calkins went on to study with William James and Josiah Royce.[17]

Mothers also were ambitious for their daughters. A considerable number of the faculty recalled that their mothers sponsored or even arranged for their higher educations. The mothers of faculty women, many of whom had themselves attended seminaries, 'bewailed the fact that they couldn't go to college' and thus were eager that their daughters embrace the new opportunity.[18] Mothers endorsed as well their daughters' spirited activism. Repeatedly, in reminiscences and autobiographies, the academic women of Wellesley proudly proclaimed that their mothers had not expected them to be passive, submissive, dutiful daughters. Rather, as Ellen Hayes, professor of mathematics, noted: 'Mother never rebuked me for spatterings or stains ... she let me live.' Economics professor Emily Greene Balch echoed this sentiment: 'My mother did not spoil us with tonic. A tumble was not met with sympathy, but with Jump and take another dear.'[19]

Often described as remarkable by their daughters, several mothers had achieved distinction in their own lives and communities. Many mothers had been teachers in seminaries. Often mothers collaborated with their daughters on books or in reform activity. Mother-daughter relationships in this group are characterized by their close, often life-long companionship. Indeed, one of the distinctive features of the Wellesley academic community was its mother-daughter colony. Seven faculty women lived with their mothers. Partially these living accommodations were the result of a demographic pattern in which wives survived their husbands and were then cared for by their daughters. But mothers could substantially further their daughters' careers by providing social and psychological support.[20]

Entire families took pride in and sacrificed for high-achieving daughters. Katharine Lee Bates, the 'gifted and youngest daughter,' was encouraged to go to Wellesley despite familial financial reverses which forced her brother Arthur to find work. Bates's sister Jennie subordinated her own life, caring for their mother and serving as Katharine's secretary and typist. Likewise, when as a senior at Bryn Mawr Emily Balch felt guilty about accepting a fellowship for graduate study in Europe, her sister Annie scoffed at her 'bad New England conscience.' She reassured Emily that she and another sister Betsy would manage the Balch home. She rejoiced in Emily's success and suggested that 'bells should be rung' to extol Emily's honor.[21]

Wellesley had a colony of such supportive sisters. About one-quarter of the academic women in this study had sisters who lived at Wellesley or worked nearby. Some faculty women had their sisters appointed to the faculty. More commonly, sisters administered faculty homes and served as social companions. Thus, the academic women of Wellesley routinely escaped the demands of domesticity; such duties fell to their sisters.

In short, the Wellesley faculty were exempt from what Jane Addams called the 'family claim.'[22] Nor were they expected to be emblems of conspicuous consumption. Rather, they were emblems of another kind – of their middle-class families' desire to purge superfluity, sponsor reform and enhance their status through their daughters' higher education and careers. These women illustrate that what Burton Bledstein calls the 'culture of professionalism' of post-Civil War America was not limited to men; it affected as well the life cycles and careers of women.[23]

Notwithstanding their relative freedom from the social norms of 'true womanhood,' almost all the faculty expressed frustration with the limitations placed on their energies by those social expectations.[24] Repeatedly the academic women reveal that they had been mischievous, even rebellious children. Many felt keenly the contradiction between their privileged family positions and society's demands for their submissiveness. In a sense, many experienced a revolution of rising expectations; their desire to do everything that boys did often tried the patience of even their liberal parents. Quite a few emulated independent, spinster aunts who provided models for – and encouraged – their rebelliousness.[25]

This rebelliousness took many forms. It can be seen, for example, in their attitudes towards religion. Several of the women abandoned the stern, Calvinistic religion of their families, choosing instead more liberal faiths, tolerant of their equal participation and intellectual contribution. Women became Quakers, joined the Companions of the Holy Cross, practiced private faiths, and even became atheists. But it should also be stressed that a late-nineteenth century evangelical, religious impulse underlay the philosophical idealism and civic humanism which characterized the faculty. Many were active proponents of the social gospel.[26]

This cohort of women, reared in rural environs, venerated nature. Their private letters, autobiographies and reminiscences are filled with fond memories of having grown up in close harmony with nature. The faculty found the unspoiled physical environment of Wellesley College, with its three hundred acres of fields and lake, perfectly in tune with their sentiments. The beauty of the Wellesley campus brought them not only aesthetic pleasure, but symbolized as well the struggle of romantic idealism against commercialism and urbanization. Thus, in 1899, a plan to crowd buildings around College Hall, the center of academic life at Wellesley, provoked the faculty's vehement objection. As Ellen Burrell noted, the 'natural loveliness of Wellesley should not be sacrificed' for it was a 'part of the higher values for which the college exists.' Conscious of living in a beautiful environment, the Wellesley faculty reveled in their secular retreat.[27]

Nature as therapeutic was another common theme which resounded in the group's world-view. The entire group moved between their Wellesley world (already a splendid setting) to other escapes in Maine, Massachusetts, and New Hampshire, where they built and gathered in summer compounds.[28]

These women's fondness for nature also appears to have been part of their rebellion against the prevailing societal norms which prescribed

domesticity and passivity for women. Every woman on whom information is available passionately loved being physically out-of-doors. They
were never so happy as when they were mountain climbing, hiking and
bicycling. Sometimes such passion led to humorous extremes, as when
English professor Sophie Jewett 'took her typewriter up into a tree,
having had a loft, complete with table and chairs built into a huge
maple'![29]

These apostles of the strenuous life denounced the excessive con-
finement to which women were subject and lamented its cost in loss of
vigor. In their lives as well as in their educational philosophy they
upheld the image of the pioneer, the New Woman. Individually and
collectively, the academic women of Wellesley fashioned a modern identity for women, though one based paradoxically on premodern virtues
and values. Their ideology emphasized equally women's physical
and intellectual capabilities – strengths which had been sapped by
second-class citizenship and especially by the denial of access to
higher education.

Extensive education was, of course, another common characteristic
of this group. Ninety per cent had Bachelors degrees, 35 per cent
Masters degrees, and 40 per cent held Ph.D.s. In addition to formal
degrees, over 80 per cent studied summers or during leaves both in this
country and in Europe; many did so repeatedly. Education was lifelong.
Mary Case, for example, wrote an essay on Hegel that earned her a
Masters degree in philosophy at the age of 86. Many of the faculty were
highly talented in areas outside of their academic specialty; quite a few
painted, wrote poetry, or were inventors. Some took up second and
even third careers over the course of their lifetimes.[30]

The foregoing are some of the shared characteristics of the women
who made up the senior faculty at Wellesley College 1895–1920. They
give us some clues as to what motivated these women to enter academe.
For some, the choice of the profession was inherent in family culture:
the intellectual life was sanctioned and indeed sanctified. Women like
Margaret Sherwood, Mary Calkins, Mary Alice Willcox, and Alice Van
Vechten Brown, came from scholastic families where brothers and
sisters became college professors. For others, an offer to teach at Wellesley came at a propitious moment, rescuing them from their post-gradu-
ate drift. After her graduation from Smith, Vida Scudder felt like a
'lady in waiting,' waiting not for her destined mate but for her 'destined
cause.' Upon being hired at Wellesley, Carla Wenckebach similarly
informed her family that she had made a 'superb catch: not a widower,

nor a bachelor, but something infinitely superior' – useful, intellectual work.[31]

Another motivation was disillusionment with secondary school teaching. These women were dominant, assertive and highly achievement-oriented. Yet since secondary school teaching had been the most common vocation for women in New England since the 1830s, many of the women had originally chosen or had been channeled into such teaching. But with the opening of the women's colleges, new and more challenging posts became available. Thus Ellen Burrell, after teaching for five years in a seminary, resolved to be a 'big frog in a big puddle,' and joined the Wellesley faculty.[32]

The opportunity for distinction and innovation attracted many of the faculty women to academe. Women who had been the natural leaders of their siblings and their peers sought an adult role where they could again be in the lead. Ellen Hayes captured this motivation when she spoke of college teachers as 'trailblazers.'[33] Those faculty women who found it difficult to justify personal ambition, did feel justified in leading the movement for women's higher education. To these women the reform of women's higher education was a revolution which signalled the millenium; one termed the movement the 'Second Reformation.'[34] To be a part of the academic profession when the women's colleges first opened was romantic, and women college teachers, conscious that they were the vanguard, felt 'flushed with the feeling of power and privilege.'[35]

Recruitment by friends, former mentors and family members also brought many women into the Wellesley community. For example, professor of psychology Mary Calkins was instrumental in having her childhood chum Sophie Jewett appointed in English. In addition, by 1910 there were thirteen Wellesley alumnae on the faculty (30 per cent). Several of these formed mentor-disciple relationships termed 'Wellesley marriages,' in which pairs of women lived together and entwined their lives around the college.[36]

Given these motivations and recruitment patterns, Wellesley was very much like an extended family. Its members, with shared backgrounds and tastes, shared visions of life and work, and often shared bonds of family or prior friendship, could hardly but produce an extraordinary community. In this milieu, no one was isolated, no one forgotten. In contrast to today, when occupational and private selves rarely meet, the academic women of Wellesley conjoined public and private spheres. Individual patterns of association overlapped: one's friends were also friends and colleagues to each other. Networks which provided both social camaraderie and intellectual stimulation were characteristic of Wellesley community. It is difficult if not impossible to dissect this community, for any attempt to do so is in some ways artificial. In this short article it is not possible to convey the full range and depth of this community, but I will sketch some of its contours, quality and flavor.

The Wellesley faculty were not merely professional associates but astoundingly good friends. They formed a world whose symbols were respect for learning, love of nature, devotion to social activism, a fondness for wit and humor, frequent emotional exchanges, and loyalty to Wellesley and to each other. In 1890, when one can discern the beginnings of this group, they were young and at the height of their energies. For example, members of the English department ranged in age from 26 to 31. They had a vivacity and energy that made them 'brimful of life.'[37] Their students remembered confusing them with brilliant seniors and that they were 'more like playmates than professors.'[38] They perceived themselves to be a colony. When someone entered, there was joyful exhilaration; whenever someone died the group mourned together and consoled themselves that their departed friend had 'joined their advance guard on the other side.'[39] With a mean tenure of thirty-two years and with fifteen academic women staying at Wellesley over forty years, theirs was a rich river of memories and shared experiences.

Faculty homes, where women lived together, were centers for social and academic occasions. It was common for women who saw each other during the day – between teaching assignments, at departmental meetings and in the faculty parlor for tea – to drift together in the evenings for fun and conversation. One young instructor recounted her reactions to these nightly roundtables at the home of Katharine Lee Bates, where she lodged for a year: 'Miss Jewett lived with us and Miss Balch who lived down the street had dinner with us every night. And if you ever sat at a table night after night with Miss Jewett who was a poet, Miss Bates, who was a poet and a joker, and Miss Balch ... well ... that was a wonderful year.'[40]

Professionally, collaboration was standard: books were co-authored; lectures and courses conceived in concert; social and political causes sponsored jointly. For example, when Katharine Lee Bates took a young Vida Scudder under her wing in 1887, she introduced her not only to the ways of the English department but also to economics professor, Katharine Coman, who shared Scudder's concern for social reform. Coman and Scudder together formed Denison House, a social settlement in Boston. They were joined in this endeavor by Emily Greene Balch whom Coman had recruited.[41]

The social concerns of the faculty sometimes found expression in literary endeavors. Margaret Sherwood fictionalized in 1899 the group's debate over whether to accept tainted money from John D. Rockefeller in a novel, *Henry Worthington, Idealist*. The Rockefeller monies issue, which divided the community, illustrates not only the idealism of the faculty but also its tolerance for divergent opinion. Conflict was contained by the crosscutting ties of friendship and by loyalty to the group life.[42]

Such loyalty spilled over into concern for the health and welfare of comrades. Thus when Katharine Lee Bates and Katharine Coman were in Spain on a research trip, Emily Greene Balch wrote them frequently. The correspondence is revealing, for it depicts not only Balch's shared interest in her friends' professional work, but her sisterly and motherly attention. In answer to one of Balch's solicitous notes and gifts Coman wrote: 'Dear Emily: Heartfelt thanks are due for the hot water bottle which arrived in good condition and is being cherished for the exigencies of the journey we are about to undertake.'[43] Similarly, the entire community expressed concern for Elizabeth Kendall, who took frequent research trips to China and other remote parts. A slew of letters, birthday greetings and Christmas cards followed Kendall wherever she journeyed; the chain of friendship ceased only with her death in 1952.

Networks at Wellesley reveal not only shared professional and social lives; they were built as well from deeply emotional bonds. Single academic women expected and derived all the psycho-social satisfaction of a family from their female friendships. How to treat such relationships is currently at issue among historians of women. Lillian Faderman, in her recent *Surpassing the Love of Men*, has demonstrated that romantic love between women was common in the nineteenth century. Faderman concludes that such relationships were often not primarily defined by genital contact but were nonetheless sensual, serious engagements, not to be dismissed as sentimental nonsense. Blanche Cook believes that historically 'women who love women, who choose women to nurture and support and to create a living environment in which to work creatively and independently' should be acknowledged as lesbians. Faderman contends that the contemporary term lesbian cannot appropriately be applied to the experience of women in the late nineteenth century. Her discussion of 'Boston Marriages' – friendships between independent career women who were involved in social and cultural betterment – provides an excellent context within which to understand 'Wellesley Marriages.' At Wellesley, the academic women spent the main part of their lives with other women. We cannot say with certainty what sexual connotations these relationships conveyed. We do know that these relationships were deeply intellectual; they fostered verbal and physical expressions of love. Many women who had complained of being shy, isolated individuals before coming to Wellesley became more self-assured and less withdrawn. Frivolity, intimacy and emotional interdependency often developed between senior and associate professors. Lifelong relationships of deep significance to women's careers and personal identities were common at Wellesley.[44]

A few examples should suffice to convey the quality of these relationships. Vida Scudder and Florence Converse were a couple devoted to each other but not to the exclusion of a wider network of friends. They met as teacher and student at Wellesley and became lifelong companions. Besides teaching together, they were also both socialists who labored in the Denison House Settlement. Each wrote books dedicated to the other, and often their fiction draws on their relationship. An aged Scudder wrote that despite being increasingly feeble, she was 'content to stay in my prison of time and space on Florence's account.' When Scudder died, she left their home and the bulk of her money to Converse.[45]

Similarly Katharine Lee Bates and Katharine Coman lived, traveled, and collaborated together. In letters to mutual friends they fondly detailed their numerous walks and conversations and praised each other's accomplishments. Bates nursed Coman throughout her terminal illness. Coman's will left all of her personal possessions to Bates. Bates then moved into Coman's room and thereafter did all her writing there, including *Yellow Clover*, a volume of poetry dedicated to the memory of her lifelong intimate. Publication of these poems inspired the entire Wellesley friendship network (and even Jane Addams) to send Bates notes of appreciation for having captured 'a woman's love for a woman,' and the 'new type of friendship between women.'[46]

Bates's intimacy with Coman did not prevent her from having other deep relationships. The most notable of these was with President Caroline Hazard. The Bates-Hazard friendship is typical of female friendships at Wellesley: it endured for over twenty-five years, fusing private and public roles and giving each mutual support from youth to old age.[47]

As pioneers in their fields at a time when college educated women felt special and united, these women were anxious to encourage, to assist and to learn from one another. Academic women looked to each other for the definition of the professional woman, and for the skills necessary for conducting a professional life. They exchanged bibliographies and syllabi freely. More importantly, women served as mentors and role models to each other. A young, shy, and insecure Vida Scudder reported that she had gained confidence from her association with her senior colleagues. Such associations casually mixed shop talk with gossip sessions, walks, teas and luncheons.[48]

Florence Converse wrote in her 1939 history of Wellesley College that the 'intellectual fellowship among the older women in the community is of a peculiarly stimulating quality.'[49] And indeed, Wellesley fostered many distinguished achievers. The science departments had sixteen members; fourteen are listed in James M. Cattell's *American Men of Science*. A review of five compendia (*American Men of Science, Notable American Women, Dictionary of American Biography, Who Was Who in America* and *Woman in the 20th Century*) found that 50 per cent of the 53 women in this essay were cited at least once. More than 20 per cent were cited two or more times. It is worth noting that no faculty member had achieved prominence prior to Wellesley, and most who achieved distinction in their scholarly fields also were carrying heavy teaching loads. Far from embracing an ethos of domesticity, Wellesley professors pioneered in laboratory and seminar methods, field research, and courses in the new social sciences. Faculty noted with pride their innovations, citing their advocacy of methods and courses current at such places as Harvard or the University of Michigan, or only later adopted by such universities.[50]

The community at Wellesley was also a hothouse of reform. Social activism was pervasive among the faculty. Of the 53 women in this study, 39 (74 per cent) were active in at least one of the following broad areas of reform: women's education and health reform; suffrage; social reform (temperance, consumer leagues, settlements, socialism, pacifism and opposition to tainted monies); and religious activism. Twenty-three women (44 per cent) were active in two or more reform categories. Given these figures it is not surprising that Wellesley was one of the colleges branded by Vice-President Calvin Coolidge in 1921 as a 'hotbed of radicalism.'[51] This contravenes the prevailing scholarly consensus that the Wellesley faculty were proponents of 'subdued familial grace.'[52]

Of course there were costs associated with the creation and maintenance of such a community. Women so deeply involved in so many social reform movements did not always form a united front. Again and again, a recurring question strained friendship ties: when should commitment to social activism yield to institutional loyalty? For example, Katharine Lee Bates, Vida Scudder's mentor, close friend and department head, was appalled when Scudder gave a speech endorsing the Lawrence Strike of 1912. She asked for Scudder's resignation, then quickly rescinded the request. Yet Bates worried lest socialist propaganda intrude upon Scudder's classes and forbade her to teach her famous course on Social Ideals in English Literature that year. Many years later, Bates did not recommend Scudder to succeed her as head of the English Department.[53]

The case of Emily Greene Balch, who was terminated by the college for her pacifism in the First World War, caused the most serious division within this community. Many colleagues disagreed with Balch's politics yet rallied to defend her right to espouse an unpopular cause. They addressed repeated petitions to the trustees to keep Balch at Wellesley. Partially because Balch herself was reluctant to make an issue of her firing, these protests were unavailing. Balch's dismissal severely strained friendships within the community, but not irrevocably. After her activism for international peace drew to a close, Balch chose to retire at Wellesley.[54]

Other tensions beset this faculty community. Wellesley's finances were often precarious, teaching loads were heavy. Women in science often complained that they could only conduct original research at odd moments between teaching and committee work. They envied the 'prima donnas' in belles lettres, but the professors in the humanities also felt constrained by too many students and too heavy a teaching load. In 1919 Vida Scudder rejoiced that retiring Katharine Lee Bates could now listen to her own music, which had been somewhat smothered by the 'drone of student recitations.'[55]

The pressure of teaching caused many women to shelve pet projects, putting them off until retirement. German professor Margarethe Muller decided to retire in 1908, before she became eligible for a Carnegie Foundation pension, in order to 'do a piece of creative work which I have wanted to do for more than fifteen years.' She forfeited the pension yet never completed her manuscript.[56]

Commitment to Wellesley and the desire to remain within the community also at times conflicted with the opportunity for other kinds of professional advancement. An offer of employment from a publishing house attracted poet Katharine Lee Bates. The Wellesley community pressured her not to defect. Personal ties, especially with her companion Katharine Coman, were 'love anchors' keeping Bates at Wellesley. She rejected the offer but confided to her diary that she was a 'reluctant captive.'[57]

To be fair to those who turned down invitations to teach at other institutions, however, it must be said that Wellesley often did offer the better professional opportunity. Mary Calkins, a senior philosopher who was elected president of the American Psychological Association and the American Philosophy Society, rejected an offer from Columbia University because she wanted to remain close to her family and friends at Wellesley and because she feared that she would be trapped teaching elementary laboratory psychology at male-dominated Columbia.[58]

These potent, strong-minded women, who ran their departments in dictatorial fashion, affected not only the style of the college's administration but the career ambitions of junior faculty in the 1920s. In self-conscious recognition of their enormous power they jokingly referred to each other as 'benevolent despots' and 'little Bismarcks.'[59] The situation of younger instructors, locked out of power by these 'absolutely dedicated war horses,' was 'pretty grim.'[60] They were too intimidated to speak at Academic Council and had no vote. A revolt by junior faculty in 1920 was crushed by their senior counterparts. It was not until the late 1940s, when most in the charmed circle had either retired or died, that young faculty found a voice. Even then these junior women stood in awe of their 'exceptional' elders. They envied their dedication and admired their intellectual vitality. The younger generation also admitted that although the old guard kept them impotent in departmental affairs and council, they did allow them full freedom in their classrooms.

Perhaps the most remarkable quality of the Wellesley community was its endurance. Despite the inevitable clash of temperaments, such factors as career commitment, respect for each other, and tender memories bound these women to each other and to Wellesley. When in 1927 professor emeritus Vida Scudder spoke on teaching at Wellesley, she noted that 'cooperation in group life was its highest privilege.' Notwithstanding obstacles and 'weary moments' when they questioned whether their fellowship was a sham, Scudder emphasized that 'At our best we know that it is a triumphant reality. We meet the challenge of our privilege with gayety and courage, and with a sense of the dramatic fascination there is in our task of living together. And through accelerations and retards, through concessions and slow innovations, we do move on.'[61]

Indeed until the end of their lives this extraordinary group remained loyal and committed to each other. The constant stream of life which flowed among them removed in their old age any final sense of isolation, despair or remorse. They looked back on lives which had been fun and which were blessed with the quest for truth, adventure, and friendships. The group, whose mean age at death was 76 years, remained quite healthy, active in social causes, and involved in their work and the college. At the age of eighty-one Margaret Sherwood wrote a novel; at eighty-six, Mary Case wrote a scholarly article on Hegel; Emily Greene Balch wrote essays well into her eighties.

Together the academic women of Wellesley had spent their youths and adulthoods, together they embraced old age and even death. As Margaret Sherwood wrote to her friend Elizabeth Kendall: 'The road seems long as one draws nearer to the end, long and a bit lonely. It is good to have footsteps chiming with one's own, and to know that a friend in whom one has a deep and abiding trust is on the same track, moving toward the same goal.'[62] And echoing these sentiments an aged Vida Scudder wrote to an old student: 'I am sorry for your long winter of illness. It is hard for me to think of you and Florence and my other 'girls' as elderly women, but time marches on. Miss Balch told me last evening that she woke up a night or two ago, laughing incredulously, because she was an old woman! We agreed that age was really just a joke.'[63]

Of course these women were not spared the toll of time. They grew infirm. Rebels till the end, they yearned to be the vanguard still. Emily Balch epitomized this striving when she lamented that at times 'old age was duller than ditch-water.'[64] Yet old age never diminished the spirit of this community. In 1953, over sixty years after the formation of this group, Martha Hale Shackford wrote to a former student: 'Just a word of greeting and good wishes from us (Margaret Sherwood), and, on my part, to tell you that a few weeks ago Miss Sherwood was able to make a call upon Miss Scudder who you know is exceedingly lame and also deaf. Florence Converse was there too. I wish you could have seen the meeting – with our friends sitting on the sofa very much themselves in spite of time.'[65]

These women share one final quality. As old women, they were prone to embellish the memory of their role as pioneers. Faculty autobiographies and reminiscences contain a near-mythic account of their struggles, one which understates the enormous sponsorship and ease with which this select elite navigated the uncharted waters of women's roles in academe. Once again they sought to distinguish themselves, this time from younger generations of college educated women; they thus upheld their collective identity.

Here indeed was fellowship! Women born and reared in a similar tradition, who wove their lives around a similar set of educational and socio-cultural ideals and who remained at the same institution for a lifetime found the meaning of life not simply in professional experiences or achievements but as well in the inexhaustible human treasury of which they were a part. These academic women did not shift their life-courses away from the communal mentality as did many male professionals; nor did they singlemindedly adhere to scientific rationalism, specialization, social science objectivity, or hierarchical associations in which vertical mobility took precedence over sisterhood.[66] Of course this constancy was not the product of choice alone. Many of these academic women were the 'uninvited' – locked out of the research universities, excluded from the professional patronage system of male academics. For example, Harvard refused to grant Mary Calkins a Ph.D., although the entire Harvard philosophy department petitioned that she be awarded the degree. The Museum of Comparative Zoology at Harvard denied Mary Alice Willcox a place because 'we have one room with three windows and a man for each window.' Women chafed in private against this discrimination, but most did not publicly protest, especially as they grew older.[67]

Despite having accomplished so much, many of these women could have done more. Partially this is the result of their relative insulation from the larger academic community. Historian of science Margaret Rossiter has observed that these women, unlike men, were not going to be invited to the major research universities. For them, Wellesley was the pinnacle of their careers.[68] Lacking mobility, many remained satisfied with a few stellar articles or just one good discovery. Many compensated for stalled careers with trips or homes. Despite their class, family backgrounds and a supportive community, as women these academics were susceptible to breakdowns and conflicts over achievement. Several took pains to dismiss or minimize their accomplishments. Vida Scudder, for example, was a prolific writer, ardent social radical and charismatic teacher, who berated herself for 'scattering her energies.'[69] She judged herself a failure by the male norm of achieving professional eminence in a single narrow field. Praise for her individual achievement made Scudder uncomfortable; instead she drew attention to her work in groups. Many others shied away from public recognition, and even refused to list their publications for college and national biographies.[70]

It should be clear that the Wellesley faculty do not fit what Robert McCaughey terms the 'Harvard model' of the modern academic professional – the cosmopolitan who felt no personal attachment to his institution, valuing academic mobility over loyalty. Neither did they tread the predominant path of late nineteenth-century academics outlined by Mary Furner in *Advocacy and Objectivity*: the Wellesley academic women never abdicated advocacy nor relinquished reform as a crucial component of the scholar's role. The Wellesley group of academics defined themselves intellectually and socially in a local, particularistic, face-to-face community rather than a bureaucratic, professional society. In short, their achievements and their legacy defy the prevailing paradigms used to explain the late nineteenth-century culture of academe. Their experience demands that we seek new ways of seeing the richly pluralistic history of the academic profession in the United States and that we devote more scholarship to academic subcultures.[71]

And what of the unique community they created? Hugh Hawkins has highlighted the tragedy of academic life at Johns Hopkins where an unbreachable gulf existed between isolated, specialized researchers. Men there found it extremely difficult to get to know fellow faculty members. A senior professor lamented: 'We only get glimpses of what is going forward in the minds and hearts of our colleagues. We are like trains moving on parallel tracks. We catch sight of some face, some form that appeals to us, and it is gone.'[72] How different from Wellesley where the academic women wrought a world which touched every woman in every aspect of her life, and gave each a sense of belonging to an all-purposive, all-embracing whole. Virtually without exception, historians have seen the research university as an advance over the sterile, old-time, liberal arts college.[73] This view understates the costs of the research university, while at the same time it belittles the benefits of at least some liberal arts colleges. To assess accurately the relative benefits and costs of each educational institution, we need to accord more value to community. For women, the liberal arts college provided a rich and professionally pivotal milieu at a time when the research university denied them careers. At Wellesley, the faculty flourished in what they called their 'Adamless Eden.'[74] Their community cannot be recreated, nor, perhaps, should it. However, like all Edens, it compels us still.

NOTES

This article is from the *History of Education Quarterly*, 23, 2 (summer 1983), 195-214. Reprinted with permission.

I wish to thank the following people for helping me to refine the ideas presented in this article: George H. Ropes; Barbara Sicherman; Joseph Featherstone; Charles Strickland and an anonymous reviewer from the *History of Education Quarterly*.

1 Willystine Goodsell, 'The Educational Opportunity of American Women – Theoretical and Actual,' *The American Academy of Political and Social Science,* 143 (May 1929), 12

2 Diary of Horace Scudder, 23 Feb. 1891, Box 6, Horace Scudder Papers, Houghton Library, Harvard University, Cambridge, Mass. Calvin Coolidge, 'Enemies of the Republic: Are the Reds Stalking Our College Women?' *The Delineator* (June 1921), 67

3 Transcribed oral interview with Lucy Wilson, p 15, 1H/1975, Centennial Historian, Wellesley College Archives (hereinafter cited as WCA)

4 Ellen Burrell to Mildred H. McAfee, 16 Nov. 1938. 3L. Math Department Folder, WCA

5 Sheila Rothman, *Woman's Proper Place: A History of Changing Ideals and Practices, 1870 to the Present* (New York 1978), 39; Roberta Frankfort, *Collegiate Women, Domesticity and Career in Turn-of-the-Century America* (New York 1977), 64

6 Jeannette Marks, *Life and Letters of Mary Emma Woolley* (Washington, DC 1955), 47

7 This social portrait studied every woman faculty member at Wellesley who satisfied two criteria: tenure of at least five years on the Wellesley faculty between 1900 and 1910 and attainment of the rank of associate professor. I imposed these conditions because I was interested primarily in the senior faculty and because records are fuller for them. Selection by these criteria yielded a total of fifty-three women; the two men who met the criteria were excluded. The ten-year duration (1900–1910) seemed to satisfy the need both for a manageable study and for one which would produce a valid picture of a faculty group over time. However, it should be noted that the group mean for service to the college is thirty-two years and this many women were still teaching at Wellesley in the 1920s and 1930s. The quantitative study was processed with the Statistical Package for the Social Sciences (SPSS). I am indebted to George H. Ropes for his assistance in quantifying data.

8 Caroline Hazard speaks of a 'Wellesley world' in 'Tribute to Katharine

Lee Bates,' *Wellesley Alumnae Magazine*, 12, no. 3 (June 1929), 15 (hereinafter cited as *WAM*).

9 Mary Barnett Burke, 'The Growth of the College,' *WAM* (Feb. 1950), 179

10 'A Woman's College,' *Boston Daily Advertiser*, 28 Oct. 1875; Henry A. Tilley, 'Wellesley College for Women,' *Washington Chronicles*, 14 Nov. 1875. 1H Histories, WCA

11 Katharine Lee Bates, 'The Purposeful Women Who Have Reared the College from Struggling Babyhood to Glorious Womanhood, and the Men Who Have Aided Them,' *Boston Evening Transcript*, 16 May 1925. For a more detailed discussion of the Alice Freeman presidency and the years of transition which followed, see Patricia A. Palmieri, 'In Adamless Eden: A Social Portrait of the Academic Community at Wellesley College, 1875–1920,' diss. Harvard University Graduate School of Education, June 1981, esp. chaps. 2 and 3.

12 Statistics computed from data taken from Faculty Biographical Files, WCA; also U.S. Federal Census of 1880

13 Examples of such fathers include Walter Willcox, Thomas Sherwood, Levi Coman

14 Katharine Coman, ed., *Memories of Martha Seymour Coman* (Boston, n.p., 1913), 46

15 Dr Kendrick to Lida Kendrick, 15 Sept. 1881. Elizabeth Kendrick Unprocessed Papers, WCA

16 Francis V. Balch to Emily Greene Balch, 8 March 1896, Folder 89, Box 52, Emily Greene Balch Papers, Swarthmore College Peace Collection (hereinafter SCPC)

17 Laurel Furumoto, 'Mary Whiton Calkins (1863–1930): Fourteenth President of the American Psychological Association,' *Journal of the History of Behavioral Sciences*, 15 (1979), 346–56

18 Jean Dietz, 'Wellesley's Miss Mary Linked Dreams to Real Life,' *Boston Sunday Globe*, 17 June 1962

19 Ellen Hayes as quoted in Louise Brown, *Ellen Hayes: Trail Blazer* (n.p., 1932), 20. Emily Greene Balch as quoted in Mercedes Randall, *Improper Bostonian* (New York 1964), 44

20 The seven faculty women who lived with their mothers are Vida Dutton Scudder, Elizabeth Kendall, Katharine Lee Bates, Katharine Coman, Adelaide Locke, Mary Calkins, Margaret Jackson.

21 Dorothy Burgess, *Dream and Deed: The Story of Katharine Lee Bates* (Norman, Oklahoma 1952), 30–5. Anne Balch to Emily Balch [n.d., probably 1899], Folder 505, Box 63, Balch Papers, SCPC.

22 Jane Addams, 'The Subjective Necessity of Social Settlements,' in Christopher Lasch, ed., *The Social Thought of Jane Addams* (New York 1965), 151–74

23 Burton J. Bledstein, *The Culture of Professionalism* (New York 1976)

24 According to historian Barbara Welter, the mid-Victorian 'true woman' was supposed to cultivate piety, purity, domesticity and submissiveness. Welter, 'The Cult of True Womanhood,' *American Quarterly*, 18 (1966), 151–74

25 Women who were influenced by independent aunts include Emily Greene Balch, Vida Dutton Scudder, Ellen Burrell.

26 Examples of faculty religious attitudes are contained in Margaret Sherwood to Marion Westcott, 17 April 1937, Sherwood Faculty Biographical File, wca; also see 'Gracious Ladies' (newspaper clipping) n.p., n.d., *ibid.*; Vida Dutton Scudder, *On Journey*, 43, 37–390, 416.

27 als. Ellen Burrell to Louise McCoy North, 4 June 1899, wca

28 For information on one such compound, see Anna Jane McKeag, 'Mary Frazier Smith,' *Wellesley Magazine*, 18, no. 1 (Oct. 1933), 6–9

29 Katharine Lee Bates, 'Sophie Jewett: The Passing of a Real Poet,' [untitled newspaper clipping, n.d.], Jewett Faculty Biographical File, wca

30 Emily Greene Balch wrote essays, painted and wrote poetry well into her late 80s; at the age of 50 professor of Latin Katharine May Edwards began another career dating Corinthian coins.

31 Scudder, *On Journey*, 94. Carla Wenckebach as quoted in Margarethe Muller, *Carla Wenckebach, Pioneer* (Boston 1908), 213

32 Ellen Burrell as quoted in Helen Merrill, 'The History of the Department of Mathematics,' p 51. 3L. Mathematics Department Folder, wca

33 Ellen Hayes, *The Sycamore Trail* (Wellesley, Mass. 1929)

34 Louise Manning Hodgkins, 'Wellesley College,' *New England Magazine* (Nov. 1892), 380

35 Florence Converse as quoted in Jessie Bernard, *Academic Women* (New York 1964), 31

36 Dorothy Weeks, a student of this faculty group who returned to live at Wellesley, noted that pairs of faculty women were termed 'Wellesley Marriages.' Personal interview with Dorothy Weeks, 5 Feb. 1978

37 Mary Haskell, 'Professor Wenckebach's Relation to Her Students,' *Wellesley Magazine* (Feb. 1903), 160

38 'Tribute to Miss Kendall,' [Typescript], p 4. Kendall Faculty Biographical File, wca

39 Marion Pelton Guild to Birdie Ball Morrison, 6 Dec. 1930. 6C. Box 2, Class of 1880, WCA

40 Transcribed oral interview with Geraldine Gordon, p 15, WCA

41 Scudder, *On Journey*, 109–10

42 Margaret Sherwood, *Henry Worthington, Idealist* (New York 1899); a fuller discussion of the Rockefeller 'tainted monies' issue is given in 'In Adamless Eden,' chap. 6.

43 Katharine Coman to Emily Greene Balch, 28 Feb. 1914. Coman Unprocessed Papers, WCA

44 Lillian Faderman, *Surpassing the Love of Men: Romantic Friendship and Love between Women from the Renaissance to the Present* (New York 1981), Introduction, pp 190–230; Blanche Wiesen Cook, 'Female Support Networks and Political Activism: Lillian Wald, Crystal Eastman, Emma Goldman,' *Chrysalis*, 3 (1977), 43–61. Also see Carroll Smith-Rosenberg, 'The Female World of Love and Ritual,' *Signs*, 1, no. 1 (autumn 1975), 1–29.

45 ALS. Vida Scudder to Louise Manning Hodgkins, 29 May 1928, WCA

46 Caroline Hazard praised Bates' *Yellow Clover* in a letter to Bates, 25 April 1922, WCA; Vida Scudder to Bates, April 1922, WCA. Jane Addams to Bates, 9 May 1922. Jane Addams Unprocessed Letters, WCA

47 There is extensive correspondence between Caroline Hazard and Katharine Lee Bates in both the Bates and Hazard Papers, WCA.

48 Scudder, *On Journey*, 107–9

49 Florence Converse, *Wellesley College: A Chronicle of the Years 1875–1938* (Cambridge, Mass. 1939), 98

50 The fourteen women scientists listed in Cattell's *American Men of Science* (the first five editions: 1906, 1910, 1921, 1927, 1933) are Calkins, Psychology and Philosophy; Case, Philosophy; Cummings, Botany; Ferguson, Botany; Fisher, Geology; Gamble, Psychology; Hallowell, Botany; Hayes, Astronomy; Hubbard, Zoology; Puffer, Philosophy; Roberts, Chemistry; Thompson, Zoology; Whiting, Physics; Willcox, Zoology. These dictionaries of notable Americans are among the best reference guides to the biographies of academic women. They are by no means exhaustive. Each employs subjective criteria to determine what constitutes achievement. For a discussion of the kinds of women scientists included in James M. Cattell, ed., *American Men of Science*, see Margaret Rossiter, 'Women Scientists in America Before 1920,' *American Scientist* (May-June 1974), 312–33.

51 Calvin Coolidge, 'Enemies of the Republic'

52 Roberta Frankfort, *Collegiate Women*, 64

53 Scudder, *On Journey*, 189–90

54 A full discussion of the Balch case is contained in the epilogue, 'Eden's End,' in 'In Adamless Eden.' See also the extensive correspondence in the Emily Greene Balch papers, SCPC.

55 ALS. Vida Scudder to Katharine Lee Bates, 6 Aug. 1919, WCA

56 ALS. Margarethe Muller to Caroline Hazard, autumn 1908, WCA

57 Katharine Lee Bates to Katharine Coman, 28 Feb. 1891. 3P. Katharine Lee Bates Papers, WCA. Diary of Katharine Lee Bates, 5 March 1896. Box 3, Katharine Lee Bates Papers, WCA

58 Laurel Furumoto, 'Are There Sex Differences in Qualities of Mind? Mary Whiton Calkins versus Harvard University. A 37-year Debate,' pp 42–3, WCA

59 Vida Scudder discusses Katharine Lee Bates' depotism in *On Journey*, 123, and Scudder, 'Katharine Lee Bates, Professor of English Literature,' *WAM*, Supplement, 13, 5 (June 1929), 5

60 Transcribed oral interview with Lucy Wilson, p 15, WCA

61 Vida Dutton Scudder, 'The Privileges of a College Teacher,' *WAM* (Aug. 1929), 327

62 Margaret Sherwood to Elizabeth Kendall, 2 Dec. 1945. Kendall Unprocessed Papers, WCA

63 Vida Dutton Scudder to Jeannette Marks, 9 July 1939, Scudder Papers, WCA

64 Emily Greene Balch as quoted in Mercedes Randall, *Improper Bostonian*, 443

65 Martha Hale Shackford to Jeannette Marks, 27 May 1953. Shackford Papers, WCA

66 For a general discussion of the increasing bureaucratization characteristic of American culture 1870–1920, see Robert Wiebe, *The Search For Order: 1877–1920* (New York 1967); in the various professions this shift manifests itself as a loss of respect for the amateur and the glorification of the highly credentialed professional. See Bledstein, *The Culture of Professionalism*; Mary J. Furner, *Advocacy and Objectivity: A Crisis in the Professionalization of American Social Science 1865–1905* (Lexington, Kentucky 1975).

67 Mary Alice Willcox to Marian Hubbard, 2 Dec. 1927. Willcox Faculty Biographical File, WCA

68 Margaret W. Rossiter, 'Women's Colleges: The Entering Wedge,' in *Women Scientists in America: Struggles and Strategies to 1940* (Baltimore: Johns Hopkins University Press 1982)

69 Vida Dutton Scudder, *On Journey*, 175

70 See, for example, Mary Alice Willcox to Miss Whiting, 27 March 1948. Willcox Faculty Biographical File, WCA; ALS. Louise Manning Hodgkins to Martha Hale Shackford, 12 Nov. 1924, WCA; Emily Greene Balch ['I am no princess ... ']. Folder 604, Box 66, Balch Papers, SCPC

71 Robert A. McCaughey, 'The Transformation of American Academic Life: Harvard University 1821–1892,' *Perspectives in American History*, 8 (1974), 229–32, Mary J. Furner, *Advocacy and Objectivity*

72 Hugh Hawkins, *Pioneer: A History of the Johns Hopkins University, 1874–1889* (New York 1960), 237

73 James McLachlan reviews and criticizes standard historical accounts of the 'old-time' liberal arts college in 'The American College in the Nineteenth Century: Toward a Reappraisal,' *Teachers College Record*, 80 (Dec. 1978), 287–306.

74 When President Caroline Hazard retired in 1910, rumors spread that she was to be replaced by a man. Alumnae and faculty cried out, 'What and spoil our "Adamless Eden"?' 'Man to Rule Wellesley? No! Say Graduates,' *Evening Newspaper*, Minneapolis, Minnesota [n.d., probably 1910]. Hazard Scrapbook, 1909–10, WCA

Scholarly Passion:
Two Persons Who Caught It
Alison Prentice

*This paper is dedicated to the memory of Marta Danylewycz, who was
a passionate scholar, a committed teacher, and a much-loved friend.*

Academic women are increasingly aware of two facts. One is the fact
of our collectively tenuous position in the world of higher education, a
position that, in spite of the contemporary women's movement, has in
many respects improved only very slowly.[1] A second is the fact of a long
history of struggle, by our scholarly-minded foremothers, to gain even
the relatively feeble foothold that we together enjoy as women instructors in contemporary institutions of higher learning. The tale differs
in different national and cultural contexts. But, whatever the context,
the status of university or college 'professor' is not one that has been
conferred easily or always sits comfortably on women.

The contemporary situation of academic women in Canada is beginning to be examined. Some of us are starting to analyze our own
working lives as scholarly women, and more general studies of collective
career paths also proceed apace.[2] A fascinating Quebec film has even
probed beneath the surface in a disturbingly intimate portrayal of
university women – and men – in a variety of roles, from professor to
chargée de cours, graduate student, and academic wife.[3] But we
know little about the scholarly women who preceded us. So far, our
explorations into the history of women's access to academic life in
Canada have focussed almost exclusively on the history of women's
admission to colleges and universities, the development of institutions
of higher learning for women, and women's experience as students in
these institutions.[4] Apart from Judith Fingard's eye-opening examination of women faculty at Dalhousie in the first half of the twentieth

century,[5] we have few historical studies that deal extensively with the Canadian woman scholar or the women who have taught in Canadian universities.[6]

The subject is made complex by problems of definition. How are we to define either the 'scholarly life' or 'institutions of higher learning' in the disparate and rapidly changing educational milieux that have existed over the years in Canada? Perhaps questions of definition – and the position of the woman scholar as well – are particularly difficult in a country whose academic institutions have existed somewhat uneasily on the margins of several overlapping political, economic, and intellectual empires. One answer to the dilemma posed by definition, and the one that I have chosen for this preliminary study, is the biographical answer.[7] By looking closely at the lives of individual women who pursued what *they* defined as important roles in the world of higher learning, we can begin to illuminate the themes that might inform more complex examinations of the place of women in Canadian scholarly life.

Two Ontario women appear to fit the bill. The first, Mary Electa Adams, was a well-known 'lady principal' associated with a number of important academies and colleges for women in the nineteenth century. The second, Mossie May Kirkwood, was an early twentieth-century teacher of English and dean of women at the University of Toronto.[8] By examining these women's lives, I hope to show how the aspirations and teaching careers of two very different scholarly women evolved. The life histories of women like Kirkwood and Adams, I argue, illuminate not just the history of Canadian women's education, but must be taken into account in any more general history of higher education in Canada.

II

The quest of Mary Electa Adams for a role in higher education must be understood in several contexts. One was the context of developing educational opportunities for nineteenth-century women, but in a country where neither the patterns that worked in the United States or in Great Britain were fully viable. Another was the context of higher education in nineteenth-century English Canada. Students of early and mid-nineteenth-century formal schooling are aware of just how blurred were the borders between different categories of institutional education before the late 1800s. For most of the century, the boundaries that existed were determined more by social class than by the ages of the students or even the levels of the studies offered. Common schools were for young people pursuing basic learning, while grammar schools, academies, and 'select' schools offered the same and more to young men and women who were better off and, in some cases, had aspirations to stay in school longer or do more advanced work. To begin with, universities were strictly for young men preparing to enter the learned professions. A complex set of interacting forces altered this situation, producing the three-tiered, largely coeducational, and public educational systems that only gradually emerged during the course of the nineteenth century. Among these forces were a developing commercial and nascent industrial economy that altered work, paid employment, and marriage patterns for most people, male and female alike; the growth of the professions and of the sciences; denominational and institutional competition, coupled with a mood of Christian reformism; and the interests of a state that was also a colony.

If these were the larger forces, a particular one that affected the life of Mary Electa Adams was women's growing quest for useful and remunerative employment, as household economies changed, and as both men and women delayed marriage or embraced the single state permanently. The quest was supported by a women's movement that focussed, in the second half of the nineteenth century, on improving educational opportunities for girls in the light of these trends.

It was in the midst of such forces that men and women like Adams created the women's select schools, seminaries, academies, and convent schools that, until recently, have remained so firmly on the margins of most mainstream Canadian educational history.[9] Why have they been on the margins? The answer is that such institutions fell between the cracks. They did not really seem to belong to the story of the rise of public school systems; nor, it was thought, did they belong to the history of higher education, since they were for women, were eventually relegated to oblivion, or, if they somehow survived, to the status of private 'secondary' schools. Only universities in this scheme of things emerged as public and as sufficiently advanced to qualify as institutions of higher learning. The result was that the Canadian women's academies and colleges of the nineteenth century belonged to no one's past. This is a not uncommon discovery in women's history where we often find that women and their institutions don't fit the categories and frameworks that historians have established as important. The point, we have learned, is to stop challenging the women and their works and to start challenging the categories. It is the latter that are unsatisfactory.[10]

Mary Electa herself has perhaps seemed a somewhat unsatisfactory subject for intensive historical investigation. The founder of no permanent academy or college, she was a woman whose teaching career took her to no less than one American and six different Canadian educational institutions, only two of which have survived to the present day. The records of her life are few. She was a diarist, but all but one of the volumes of her diary appear to have been lost. Apart from this one volume, the best source for Adams' life remains an article published in 1949 by another fascinating but little-known woman scholar, Elsie Pomeroy. Pomeroy's account is particularly important because she had then in her possession, and was able to draw upon, a more complete body of personal materials than can presently be located.[11]

From Pomeroy's brief study we learn that Adams was born to Loyalist parents in Lower Canada in 1823 and came with her family to Upper Canada two years later. She and her two brothers and two sisters were taught at home by their parents. In 1840, at the age of seventeen, Adams went to Montpelier Academy in Vermont, a school that her mother had attended, and there she was admitted to the study of the classics and advanced mathematics. She returned to Canada a year later and finished her formal studies at the Cobourg Ladies' Seminary. Duly graduated as a 'Mistress of Liberal Arts,' Adams did not leave the institutional setting but settled in as a member of the staff, eventually moving with the school's conductors, Mr and Mrs Hurlburt, to Toronto, where she taught at their new Adelaide Academy.

That Adams enjoyed from the beginning of her teaching career a connection to the early movement for higher education for women there can be no doubt. For one thing, the Hurlburts had been associated with the Methodist and coeducational Upper Canada Academy in Cobourg, the short-lived forerunner of Victoria College; Professor Hurlburt had continued on the staff for a brief period after the academy had been turned into a college for boys only.[12] One could also dwell on the choice of the word 'seminary' for the Hurlburts' first attempt at an independent institution for young women. The American historian Helen Lefkowitz Horowitz argues that in this period the term 'connoted a certain seriousness' and the possibility of professional goals which, in the case of women, meant training for careers in teaching.[13] Finally, Pomeroy tells us that Adams continued her 'advanced studies' while teaching for the Hurlburts, already hoping that she might eventually assist in 'breaking down the barriers which prohibited women from taking university training.'[14] Whether or not she would have put it in exactly those words, Adams certainly appears to have gravitated to girls' schools that, at the very least, had ambitions. Her path in this regard was not without major interruptions, however. By the late 1840s she had already been made principal of an academy for girls in Picton, but within a very short time she retired from the position, possibly frustrated that this school could not meet the goals she had in mind for it, but also because she was ill. A vacation in Michigan soon brought a new challenge and Adams was appointed 'Preceptress of the Female Department' at Albion Seminary, a large and relatively well-established American institution where – again using Pomeroy's words – some students achieved a measure of 'university training.' In 1854, however, Adams was drawn back to British North America to undertake a similar job in the women's department of Mount Allison Academy, in Sackville, New Brunswick. There she was joined by her sister Augusta and is credited with establishing, in three short years, a programme that favoured the academic over the ornamental.[15]

Thus far, Adams' path as a ladies' academy mistress was a more or less continuous one. The death of her father altered the pattern, however, and for the next four years our wandering scholar was occupied at home with her widowed mother and Augusta. Adams was in her late thirties when, in 1861, she became the lady principal of the Wesleyan Female College in Hamilton, a school where, once more, her sister Augusta Adams also found employment. At this point, Mary Electa Adams' interest in higher education for women prompted exploratory visits to several women's colleges in Britain, which were made during the summer of 1862. Yet, once again, when their mother died in 1868, both Mary Electa and Augusta Adams resigned their positions. There followed another four-year interlude which the sisters devoted to family life and travel in Europe.

The early 1870s found Mary Electa Adams back in Cobourg, living with Augusta and with three nephews of whom they were evidently now in charge. The Adams sisters' aim was to superintend the education of their nephews and prepare them for Victoria College. But 1872 also saw them embarking on the major educational enterprise of their lives: the opening of a new school of their own. Brookhurst Academy was, according to Mary Electa Adams, intended first to be 'a *home*'; secondly to offer a college course 'with graduation in the university for those

who wish it'; and, thirdly, to offer 'superior advantages for those pursuing Fine Arts and Modern Languages.'[16] The extant volume of Adams'
diary starts soon after the decision to open Brookhurst had been taken
in 1872, and thus allows us to catch a glimpse of the Brookhurst years
and gain some insight into its principal's image of herself as a scholar
and a teacher.

The diary begins, not with Brookhurst's founding, but with texts
copied from journals and books, revealing the diarist's interests, if not
her thoughts or feelings. The interests were wide. One passage concerns
Ruskin's views on the impossibility of altering the 'mental rank' one is
born with; another quotes Hawthorne on the relationship between free
thought and tolerance, and the separation of church and state in the
ancient world. Later there is a passage, evidently copied from *Westminster Magazine*, on the political disabilities of women, and another, from
Dublin University Magazine, on the character of Englishmen. From an
unnamed source there are rhapsodic descriptions of Sappho's poetry
and a lament that most of it has been lost, followed by comments
on the intellectual and social equality with men that the women of
Lesbos enjoyed.[17]

The Brookhurst years must have been busy and were possibly particularly happy ones. There are no further entries in the diary from the
spring or summer of 1872 to September 1879, when the visit of the
Princess Louise and the Marquis of Lorne to the academy was recorded
by a clipping and an appreciative comment. Thereafter, the diary
changes character. Adams went on to use its remaining pages chiefly
for reflections on her age and its fatigues (she was now in her middle
fifties), on the difficult decision to close Brookhurst, and on the anxie-
ties precipitated by her first years at the Ontario Ladies' College at
Whitby, her last academy principalship.

An important impression that emerges from Adams' diary is that its
principal wanted Brookhurst to be small and that, wherever she was,
she valued close relationships with her students. Yet she clearly also
had ambitions for the young women who studied with her that went
beyond the usual goal of 'ladylike cultivation.' The formation of 'character,' as well as 'polish,' were among Brookhurst's aims. But there were
academic ambitions too. Brookhurst tried to be 'more advanced in its
curriculum' than most Canadian ladies' colleges and, as Adams put it,
its conductors very much hoped that their academy would grow 'into
university characteristics, with university privileges.'[18]

There is a sense in which Mary Electa Adams belonged to the first of three periods in nineteenth-century education for women in the United States that Patricia Palmieri has put forward. The 'romantic' period, which Palmieri dates from 1820 to 1860, was the era of Troy Female and Mount Holyoke Seminaries with their great emphasis on religious formation and the training of Christian mothers and teachers.[19] Yet the romantic aura surrounding the concept of what Palmieri and others have called 'republican motherhood' was absent, or was at least extremely muted, in Adams. She clearly saw herself as a mentor and moral guide to her students; but, just as clearly, she was no republican. One feels, too, that strictly academic or scholarly goals attracted her interest as much as character training. The former may have grown in importance because Adams' working life extended across the second period identified by Palmieri, the reformist era which she dates from 1860 to 1890. In the United States, these decades saw the founding of women's colleges like Wellesley, Smith, and Vassar, and the development of a new model for the higher education of women. Such colleges aimed to give their charges as prestigious and demanding a schooling as young men received at a Harvard or a Yale. 'Respectable spinsterhood,' moreover, joined republican motherhood as an ideal for educated women.[20] Physical settings too were different as the single large building typical of the seminary gave way to a variety of more complex arrangements designed to house larger numbers of students and faculty on campus.[21] We have no evidence that Adams entered the increasingly polarized and acrimonious debate on women's ability to cope with higher education that characterized this period in both Canada and the United States, but it is obvious on which side she stood. She wanted a 'solid' education for her young ladies as well as one that encompassed religious principles. The emphasis would be on modern languages and the arts but neighbouring Victoria College, having 'laid open all its privileges' to Brookhurst, was in a position to supply the other components of the complete university course.[22]

The difficulty was that these arrangements did not come cheaply and the competition for students was fierce. 'Our scheme seemed feasible & it has prospered. But lo! Whitby and a great house, & rich men ... put forth a mighty effort to house a great school. Oshawa with a sort of manual labour arrangement gathers up ... many who want education cheap. Brantford picks up the Presbyterian element & Ottawa is omnivorous & all these spring into existence within a year of our commencement.'[23] Clearly, the Adams sisters' intention was to create an educational institution that was academically on a higher level than these rival schools. They may have seen Brookhurst as similar to the American women's colleges that were also emerging at this time, but the proximity to Victoria suggests another model. Certainly by the late 1870s when the academy's future as an independent institution seemed seriously in doubt, discussion of a scheme 'to affiliate with Victoria' was increasingly on its founder's minds. Indeed, at this point the diary implies that this may have been what the Adams sisters had wanted from the beginning. The idea was also, Mary Electa Adams believed, a novel one for Canada. 'If it can be carried out,' she confided to her diary, 'it will be the first in Canada & we should like to have a hand in it.'[24]

Later remarks in fact indicate clearly that Adams took her model from England, rather than from the United States. By May of 1880 she was talking about 'our plan of a "university class" for ladies, of Resident matriculants under protection' and describing the arrangement she wanted as 'something like Girton.' The idea's time had not quite come, however. According to the diary, the faculty of Victoria approved, but opposition had appeared among people who had power. The decision was therefore made to give up Brookhurst. 'It causes me no little feeling,' Adams reported when the closing papers were finally signed. As patronage for 'university purposes' seemed just around the corner, she wondered if she and Augusta should not have held out just a little longer.[25]

The partnership with Augusta, an alliance that makes Mary Electa Adams such a typical nineteenth-century woman educator,[26] may well have been a factor in the decision to close Brookhurst. Augusta, always frail, was feeling unwell. In addition, the nephews for whom the sisters had been responsible were now educated and moving away from Cobourg. Indeed a strong note of ambivalence about her role and responsibilities emerges in the diary when these matters are discussed. An 'establishment,' Mary Electa wrote, 'is exacting & confining.' 'We are in straits at the cross-purposes that affect us ... We have fulfilled our engagement here – all our nephews will be away ... Augusta is not well & needs some change. We could break up if we wished but find a sentimental clinging to what we have struggled for, for nine years ...'[27]

The decision to abandon Brookhurst, then, was not solely a financial or political one. Family needs and the wish to travel had drawn Mary Electa Adams away from her academy life more than once; there was clearly a strong element of this in the breaking up of the academy in the spring of 1880. Only Augusta and the nephews went on their travels, however. Mary Electa, after much soul-searching, reluctantly accepted yet another new principalship, this time at the Ontario Ladies' College, in Whitby. Her ambivalent feelings about her career were now extreme. Like Catharine Beecher, one of Adams' goals had always been to create an intimate home in the schools she inhabited. She was not fond of wandering, she confessed to her diary. And from the beginning, she found the 'palatial buildings' of the Ontario Ladies' College a somewhat overpowering environment for a home.[28]

Far more alienating than the physical setting for this last stage of her career was Adams' uneasy relationship with the Rev. J.J. Hare, a clergyman who appears to have been listed in the college circular not only as the titular head of the college, but also as the supervisor of its lady principal. One of Adams' first acts on her arrival at the college was to insist that subsequent circulars be amended, for she had never intended to accept a subordinate position. The removal of the offending words did not make the partnership a comfortable one, however, and Hare remained a thorn in Adams' side. He interfered, but refused to take responsibility, leaving most of the onerous daily work to Adams, along with the blame if anything went wrong – at the same time taking credit for whatever went well. The contests with Hare, and there were many, were painful for another reason. As Adams wrote in her diary after their first confrontation, 'self-assertion is hateful to me.'[29]

The early years at Ontario Ladies' College were thus not altogether happy ones. Adams was pleased to know that families sent daughters to the school because she was there, but regretted more than once the lost opportunity to be involved in the 'university class' for women which Victoria was clearly in the process of establishing. 'When the end comes,' she wrote during one of her lowest moments, 'I often fear that life will seem a great failure to me.'[30] Mired in endless detail in the running of the school, and always at cross-purposes with Hare, she felt that the Ontario Ladies' College was managed with 'hopeless irregularity.'[31]

Yet if disappointment and frustration plagued Adams in the early 1880s, she believed that she was not alone. Few people achieved 'the particular things ... that they aimed at,' she noted in the journal.[32] And she was not without solace. The diary ends in 1883, but there was already talk of leaving and going to stay with Augusta who, with one of the nephews, had taken up cattle ranching in the Northwest. Helena Coleman, a niece who became the music mistress at the college, was an important companion of the 1880s. And Adams had the satisfaction of seeing Arthur Coleman, a nephew that she had educated, follow his stint as an art instructor at Victoria and Brookhurst with studies in Germany, and the winning of a permanent professorship at Victoria in Natural History and Geology. Things may also have improved for Adams at the Ontario Ladies' College. According to Pomeroy, it was not until 1892 that she finally retired and made her move to the Northwest to be with Augusta.[33]

And what of her goal to create a class for women at Victoria College? The exact situation for women at Victoria at this time is not easy to decipher, but a few women do seem to have been admitted, from some point in the middle 1870s. The first of these was in fact a Brookhurst student, who was awarded an MEL or Mistress of English Literature by the college. It is also true that Victoria faculty members lectured at Brookhurst in the late 1870s – one of them, the instructor in fine arts, Arthur Coleman. In the 1880s more women students were admitted, and by the time the college affiliated with the University of Toronto in 1889, and its move to Toronto in 1892, women's presence was an established fact.[34] In addition, in the mid-1880s long-distance affiliation arrangements had been made between Victoria and a number of Ontario's Methodist women's colleges, affirming the university status of the work that some students did in these institutions and thus the status and credentials of their teachers.[35] But the Ontario Ladies' College, it would appear, was not among them. As she had predicted, women would gain 'university privileges' in her time, but Mary Electa Adams was excluded from playing a significant continuing role in this triumph.

III

Was it properly a triumph? This brings us to a consideration of a woman who aspired to the scholarly life in early twentieth-century Ontario, Mossie May Waddington Kirkwood. Waddington Kirkwood's necessary setting was the coeducational university, rather than a college or colleges created solely for women, for the period of reform that had produced such institutions in the United States did not do so in Canada. Distinguished private and public secondary schools provided employment for academically-inclined women but, in Ontario especially, women's colleges with higher aspirations appear eventually to have either given up their university affiliations and curricula or fallen by the wayside altogether by the first decades of the twentieth century. The preferred Canadian approach seems to have been to found women's classes or departments within the men's universities. The models were perhaps to be found in Great Britain; but the women's departments in Canadian universities typically had far less autonomy than the women's colleges of an Oxford or a Cambridge. Moreover, they initially engaged very few women instructors.[36]

Mossie May Waddington Kirkwood was one of a very small group of Canadian women who nevertheless achieved university teaching positions early in the twentieth century. Born in the last decade of the nineteenth century, she attended St Clement's School and the University of Toronto's Anglican Trinity College, receiving her BA from the latter in 1911. In a recorded interview in which she reminisced about her life and subsequent career at the university,[37] Kirkwood recalled that she had been encouraged to study for an advanced degree by a professor of English, but that Philosophy had been at first her chosen area. Professor Brett, the philosopher with whom she worked, was 'surprised' but not unwilling to take her on. Kirkwood's MA is dated 1913; she completed her Ph.D. in 1919.

The flavour of the times is conveyed by the elderly Kirkwood's memory of her graduate instruction which, she recalled, amounted to visiting Professor Brett weekly at his home. Sent away from her first oral defence to learn more about Hegel, she finally produced a satisfactory dissertation on the development of British thought in the nineteenth century, with special reference to German influences, a work that was published the same year that she received the doctoral degree.[38] While she was doing her MA and starting her doctorate, Mossie May Waddington taught for at least some of the time at St Clement's. But the year after she completed her master's, staff shortages arising from the war produced a unique opportunity for the young graduate to instruct at the university level. Trinity College offered to employ her to teach 'Divinity Greek' and, later on, English as well.

Waddington evidently taught for the college during most of the war but, as it drew to a close, recognized that there was little likelihood that her post at Trinity could continue. Without waiting to be released, she tackled the subject head on with her employers. Discovering that, indeed, her job would end with the war, Waddington wasted no time in landing another one, this time at the university's non-denominational University College, with English Professor William John Alexander. Looking back on this second opportunity, Kirkwood remembered Alexander as a 'wise and experienced man' who was 'very interesting' on the subject of women teaching at University College. He told her that it was 'perfectly correct to have women on the staff, particularly in the field of literature.' In literature, at least, he (and clearly she) believed the woman instructor to be somehow 'normal.'[39]

The years following Waddington's move to University College must have been busy ones. The doctoral thesis was completed and defended and the book published. Presiding over a women's residence from 1919, in 1922 Waddington was officially made University College's dean of women. And in 1923, ten years after the granting of her master's degree, she married Trinity Professor William Kirkwood. The latter event presented a major dilemma for it was apparent that most people, including the new Mrs Kirkwood, thought she should now resign her deanship.[40] But, according to her reminiscences, when the college council met to consider her replacement, its members could not agree on any of the recommended candidates and, after lengthy deliberations, finally asked the newly married Kirkwood if she could carry on. The incumbent dean not only agreed to do so but gained a new assistant as part of the bargain and, for the next six years, Mossie May Kirkwood continued as both dean of women at University College and a college instructor of English. She also became the mother of three children.

Kirkwood's career at the University of Toronto was a lengthy one, continuing well beyond the Second World War, but it was not without changes and adjustments. At University College, she joined with others to fight for better women's residences and won. She also tried to stamp them with her own idea of what a women's residence ought to be. As she described it later, this was a small community of students, led by an older scholar or don, who was there to inspire and encourage, not just to monitor the social lives of the young. The presence of the older scholar was crucial for, in Kirkwood's view, the intellectual spark could not exist in a social void. 'Scholarly passion,' as Kirkwood put it, 'is caught by persons from persons.' Her own mentors, she recalled, had been Professors Brett and Alexander, as well as her husband. As these men had inspired her own efforts, so she hoped that all university students would remember some person or persons who impressed them as being 'shot through with the love of truth.' Clearly, the context for this discussion implied, it would be helpful for women students to have at least some mentors who were also women.[41]

In September of 1929, Mossie May Kirkwood resigned as dean of women at University College, ostensibly 'to devote all her time to her work in English.'[42] This was the reason she gave publicly, but a further reason emerges in the reminiscences. A woman in the dean's office,

Kirkwood recalled, now objected strongly to the continued employment of a married woman in the post. Afraid that the issue would split the college, the dean felt it better to bow out of her administrative role and leave it to someone who was single. Since this was soon after the birth of her third child, family reasons may also have played a part, but Kirkwood's withdrawal from university administration was shortlived. In 1936, on the retirement of Mabel Cartwright as Trinity College's dean of women and principal of St Hilda's, Kirkwood took up these positions at her old college.

As she had at University College, Kirkwood quickly became involved in a successful drive for better residential accommodation for Trinity women. That accomplished, she once again settled into her dual roles as teacher and administrator. The latter she took as seriously as the former, acting in her public capacity as model, rulemaker, and restraining influence, but also providing private counselling, encouragement, or even intervention on a student's behalf, if these seemed called for.

Mossie May Kirkwood's daughter has portrayed her mother as a woman who 'sought broader intellectual and professional opportunities for women, equal chance and reward in employment,' but at the same time emphasized 'the importance of marriage and family life' for both society's good and women's happiness.[43] That there might be conflict between these two goals was muted perhaps, but not denied. The university was a hotbed not only of antagonisms and jealousies, Kirkwood believed, but of even more serious contradictory influences on individuals. She later identified these as the 'warring' influences of 'academic effort' and 'sexual activity.'[44] Indeed, so concerned was she about this conflict and the general position of women in society by the late 1930s, that Kirkwood began to speak about them in public. Earlier talks to women's groups outside the university had focussed on literary subjects, and particularly on women writers.[45] Now she began to focus on questions like the purposes of education for women, women's right to paid employment, and the nature of the university experience for women.

In a small book entitled *For College Women – and Men*, Kirkwood outlined her beliefs about scholarship and teaching. The best teachers at university were at the same time passionate students, she argued. But they must not be expected to starve. The university depended on the power and intellectual vitality of its academics. Using the male pronoun, she went on to describe the scholar's need to live reasonably, to travel, and to have access to 'original sources' for his research.[46] Did Kirkwood mean to exclude women from this discussion of 'university teachers and scientific workers'? Unfortunately, the language is obscure. But the agenda for students of either sex, whatever the sex of the instructor, was clear. The goal of university study for both women and men was to find out what life was for, and then to live it with passion and purpose.[47]

Kirkwood saw three possible and overlapping futures for girls approaching the end of school. They would be mothers and would need to understand 'the needs of human beings.' They would be students and, as such, should throw themselves 'into the passionate search for a little more light and knowledge.' Finally, they would be workers. As workers, they ought to devote themselves to understanding 'the relation between [their] occupation[s] and the whole interests of society.'[48] Importantly, women had a need and a right to work. 'To suggest that merely to be a woman is enough, unless the relationships of wifehood and motherhood make enough demands on the woman's powers for her to use her energies and give herself fully, is a mistaken idea.'[49] Kirkwood cited a Toronto YWCA study of 1505 employed women, showing that fully 17 per cent of these women were supporting individuals who were totally dependent; 42 per cent contributed their earnings to their households; and 25 per cent contributed to the support of dependents in other households. A United States Department of Labor survey of 751 employed single women showed that 33 per cent supported their mothers; of 490 married women, 14 per cent supported dependent husbands. Kirkwood deplored the 'back to the kitchen' or 'back to the home' movements at that time being promoted in fascist Germany and Italy; indeed she deplored them anywhere they were to be found and denounced the idea that all girls should study domestic science. She stated, moreover, her belief in women's right to equal pay for equal work. 'In admitting that feminism has gone to violent lengths at times and degenerated into the "me too" position, it is not necessary to go back on the essential truth of the feminist case. Women must eat to live.'[50]

Mossie May Kirkwood was unwilling, perhaps, to carry the case to absolute equality for women in the workplace. Women as childbearers were different from men. They must work to eat, but should not be distracted by 'the sight of worldly prizes' or the challenge to prove that they were 'as good as men in their avocations.' Women, in fact, had other goals: to use their special insights to fight against the destruction of life, and to fight against war. 'Life and better life' were women's work.[51]

In a published speech that she entitled 'Women of the Machine Age,' Kirkwood took a slightly different approach to the right to work. Women's need to work was not just material. Money, she argued, meant power but it was not just the power to satisfy the needs of the body. It was also the power to satisfy the needs of the spirit. Women who did not wish to trade dependence on a father for dependence on a husband now had the opportunity to seek, in a profession, 'a life of purpose and accomplishment.' Women's need for and right to *meaningful* employment and to power over their own lives had to be recognized and accepted.[52]

What did this mean for women in university teaching? As far as can be ascertained, Kirkwood did not tackle the subject of the academic woman directly. She had managed to gain entry into work that she loved, and to some extent recognized her good fortune in not having had to struggle for the privilege. Not only had several professors encouraged her, she had also had an uncle (only a decade or so older than herself) who was a professor at the university. His presence there surely assisted her progress. She was also able to remain at home and to support her studies with her teaching.

Yet when asked to describe the position of women in university teaching in her time, the elderly Kirkwood had little to say. She recognized that she was probably paid less than comparable men. She also recognized that women were, by and large, excluded from most university teaching and administrative jobs. Household Science, of course, employed only women. In languages, she recalled, there were also women candidates. 'But when you say were they discriminated against, they just weren't appointed, that's all. It was thought that they should teach in the secondary schools. For one thing, most [women] didn't have the money to do graduate work.'[53] Kirkwood also admitted that there was outright opposition to the employment of women scholars at the university, particularly in the case of married women, and especially following the First World War. Not all male university professors or administrators were hostile and she herself had not been 'turned off.' But some women had been, she agreed, because of the prejudice of powerful men against them.[54]

IV

In a recent book which they entitle *Unequal Colleagues*, Penina Migdal Glazer and Miriam Slater have analyzed the strategies adopted by American women who pioneered in the professions at the turn of the century. They focus on four: separatism, superperformance, subordination, and innovation.[55] Some of the new professional women were able to make their way because of the protection of entirely separate women's institutions like the women's colleges; others did the work of three to gain a place in their profession. Still others found they could only survive by accepting subordinate positions or, alternately, by creating new and innovative roles for themselves. Mary Electa Adams chose separate institutions for most of her working life. But at the Ontario Ladies' College and, indeed, in her other principalships, she was to some extent in a subordinate position. This, in part, was the meaning of the term '*lady* principal' with its implication that there might also lurk somewhere a male governing presence – as indeed was the case at the Ontario Ladies' College. Adams' innovative attempt to take charge in her own Brookhurst Academy and, later, to forge a partnership between Brookhurst and Victoria College might have altered this status, but came too early in the history of higher education in Ontario to work to her own permanent advantage. Mossie May Kirkwood relied, at various times, on all four of the strategies outlined by Glazer and Slater. Although they were neither as separate or as independent as either the American or the British women's colleges, the women's residences that Kirkwood helped to create at the University of Toronto did provide some measure of autonomy and, at the very least, a separate space for the dean of women. Certainly, Kirkwood worked hard, combining the roles of dean, English instructor, faculty wife, and mother. At the same time it is also clear that, in the larger university, she accepted a subordinate position – both to individual men and to men's expressed interests. On the other hand, Kirkwood boldly found new jobs and created important roles for herself in the women's deanships. In the end, she managed to hang on to a position in the university, if not the same position, for some forty-odd years.

Far more successful in her quest for the scholarly life than Mary Electa Adams, Kirkwood was the inheritor of the former's struggles. When told that she had been lucky, she replied with great emphasis that she had also been good. Assured in her ability as a teacher, she had had no qualms about pursuing her goal to continue in university teaching once she had been given a taste of it. But Kirkwood's circumstances had also been very favourable: a start at Trinity because of the First World War, a supportive network of male relatives and mentors, and financial and domestic support both before and after her marriage and the birth of the children.[56]

What late nineteenth- and early twentieth-century academic women were unable to do, Glazer and Slater suggest, was to reproduce themselves.[57] Their immediate tasks were too many and their resources too few. It took all of Mary Electa Adams' energy to get women involved in higher education; after 1880, she was forced to abandon both her own institutional creation and the possibility of sharing in the provision of higher learning for women at Victoria College. Kirkwood's achievements were considerable: her own admission to university teaching, the creation of better residences for women, and the publication of her books.[58] She was also determined that the undergraduates over whom she presided would have female as well as male mentors – women who could transmit to them the intellectual passion that makes a life of scholarship possible. But if there were women who 'caught' the 'scholarly passion' from academic women like herself, the numbers who were able to translate their passion into university jobs remained low. The proportion of full-time university faculty who were women in Canada reached a peak of 19 per cent in 1931, but then began to drop and has remained below that figure ever since.[59]

Why did Kirkwood's vision fail to produce an expanding new generation of women scholars and teachers in Canadian universities? Part of the answer is in the relative powerlessness of women like herself. Even Kirkwood seemed to accept the idea that women should be steered into secondary school teaching in the interwar years and the fact that few had the money to go to graduate school. University teachers of this era typically came from a privileged network of men, often men who had the opportunity to go to Europe to study, like Adams' nephew, Arthur Coleman, or who migrated to Canada from the British Isles or continental Europe in the first place. Although Kirkwood had managed to get into this charmed circle, her own position was so tenuous that she had little if any power to promote the admission of other women. And for the generation immediately after hers, we must also take into account the changed character of the university. As Patricia Graham and others have noted for the United States, larger, more 'professional,' and bureaucratic institutions of higher learning were less welcoming and easy environments for women than they were for career-minded and wife-supported men.[60]

A major source of both Adams' and Kirkwood's weakness was a growing mood of hostility towards women in scholarly life, a feeling that Palmieri argues intensified after 1890.[61] For Adams, the hostility was principally encountered in the opposition of Methodist clergymen like J.J. Hare or the 'powerful men' who opposed her plans to take charge of the women entering Victoria College in 1880. There is also a very faint suggestion, if not of outright conflict, at least of a differing agenda from that of her sister Augusta who perhaps preferred retirement to pressing the claims of Brookhurst. For Kirkwood, the conflict was also often muted. But there is absolutely no doubt that she faced significant opposition, not just from men returning from war, but also from at least one woman who felt that married women had fewer rights than the unmarried to certain paid roles in the university. As women who loved women – and men – Kirkwood and Adams (perhaps especially Adams) were also women who could only carry direct conflict so far. Adams admitted to her diary that self-assertion was 'hateful' to her; Kirkwood was perhaps bolder in some circumstances, but often shifted the territory of the battle rather than engage in open conflict with the forces opposed to her.

v

The physicist David Bohm has suggested that, in the experimental sciences, if one gets down to individual cases things become not simpler, but more complex.[62] The lives of Mary Electa Adams and Mossie May Kirkwood reveal the same truth. If we attempt to pinpoint the variables that affected their academic careers, we begin to recognize a very complex as well as a rather contemporary scenario. Certainly the fact of gender was the crucial factor that limited what these women did. Privileged class backgrounds, on the other hand, meant opportunities that were denied to most women – and to many men. Three other factors, however, were also important. One was age: perhaps a younger woman might have succeeded where Adams failed, to secure a permanent alliance between Brookhurst and Victoria. A second, certainly, was marital status: witness the problems Kirkwood encountered in 1923 and again in 1929. Finally, there was something that the married and the single could share, as Adams' and Kirkwood's careers both proved: extended family responsibilities beyond those typically undertaken by comparable men.

Another important variable was Canada's colonial situation. Caught between several models of higher education for women that emanated from the United States and Great Britain, Canadian women who were in a different economic, demographic, and political environment from either, seemed to be struggling for a Canadian compromise – one that the country could afford, as well as one that suited women's needs. How tempting the models of a Vassar or a Girton must have been – yet how remote, evidently, in a colonial state existing under the shadow of two competing powers whose resources were so much greater than Canada's.

Adams and Kirkwood, other women like them, and the men who supported them, got women into men's universities and showed that women could live on the margins of men's scholarly world. Yet however effectively they operated in these special environments, neither was able to make women fully equal partners in Canadian scholarly life, as it was defined then or now. Surely, then, we have to call into question the definitions. What was or is the scholarly life? Does one have to be a member of a university faculty to participate? Finally, is not the exclusion of senior or scholarly women from universities, or their marginality or invisibility in institutions of higher learning, a central fact in the history of higher education?[63] These questions are currently the subjects of intense concern and investigation by scholars whose practice is in the area of women's studies or who identify themselves as feminists. The third question will certainly be answered in the affirmative. We are only beginning to investigate the social construction of masculinity and the relationships between the sciences, the professions, and men's education and educational work. But it is already obvious that an institution that has been predominantly male and that, until recently, has been run almost entirely by men alone, cannot be understood in isolation from the central fact of women's marginality to its functioning, or subordination within its governing structures. Nor can the university be understood apart from the fact of women's roles educating and/or sustaining scholarly men, as their mothers and wives, or even as their aunts – witness the case of the Adams sisters and their nephew, Professor Arthur Coleman.[64]

The problem that we continue to face is the one that Adams could barely contemplate and that Kirkwood and her generation did not manage to solve: the reproduction of the next generation of women scholars and their integration as equal partners in Canadian institutions of higher learning. Following the schema of Glazer and Slater, it's clear that an innovative separatist strategy has been enormously productive for our generation. We have relied to a significant extent on the havens that we have created in women's and feminist studies. The question is whether, from the strength and knowledge gained in these studies, we feminist women – and men – can now achieve the equal partnership between scholarly women and men that seems so obviously necessary and desirable.

The gifts we have to offer are several. Among others, there is the central gift of feminist scholarship itself – which we believe has the power to revolutionize all scholarship, as well as to question the academic structures that contain it. Like both Mary Electa Adams and Mossie May Kirkwood, many of us remain ambivalent and even uncomfortable in our relationship to institutions of higher learning. But scholars we insist on being nevertheless – and, furthermore, scholars who are paid for their work. For, as Mossie May Kirkwood pointed out, women must eat to live. Finally, we also insist on the right to hand on to a new generation of women – and men – our gift of a feminist vision. For we know, as did Kirkwood, that 'scholarly passion is caught by persons from persons.'

NOTES

This article is from *Historical Studies in Education/Revue d'histoire de l'éducation*, 1, 1 (spring 1989), 7–27. Reprinted with permission.

I wish to thank Paul Axelrod, Jo LaPierre, Alison Mackinnon, Pavla Miller, Johanne Pelletier, Jim Prentice, Marjorie Theobald, Sylvia Van Kirk, and Ailsa Zainu'ddin for careful readings of 'Loving Our Enemies: Women and the Scholarly Life,' the Canadian History of Education Association paper of which this article is the revised version. Their insights and suggestions did much to clarify my thinking, as well as many factual details, and I am grateful for their help.

1 A variety of sources show how slowly the percentage of full-time Canadian university faculty who are women has grown over the decades. See, for example, Jill McCalla Vickers and June Adam, *But Can You Type? Canadian Universities and the Status of Women* (Ottawa: Canadian Association of University Teachers 1977), and Anne Innis Dagg

and Patricia J. Thompson, *MisEducation: Women & Canadian Univer-sities* (Toronto: OISE Press 1988), 65–6. Similarly slow growth, but higher proportions, are shown for the United States in Barbara Miller Solomon, *In the Company of Educated Women* (New Haven: Yale Univer-sity Press 1985), 133.

2 See, for example, some of the informally published papers from the Popular Feminism Lecture Series, Centre for Women's Studies in Educa-tion, Ontario Institute for Studies in Education, 1985–8. A detailed examination of individual women (and men) faculty who have been involved in women's and feminist studies is currently under way: Mar-grit Eichler *et al.*, *A Profile of Canadian Women's Studies/Feminist Professors*; and the Canadian Historical Association has recently under-taken to follow up an earlier survey of women in the historical profes-sion in Canada with a new study, to be conducted by Linda Kealey, Memorial University.

3 Denis Arcand, *The Decline of the American Empire*

4 Recent studies dealing with women at English Canadian universities include Margaret Gillett, *We Walked Very Warily: A History of Women at McGill* (Montreal: Eden Press 1981); John G. Reid, 'The Education of Women at Mount Allison, 1854–1914,' *Acadiensis* 12 (spring 1983); and Lynne Marks and Chad Gaffield, 'Women at Queen's University, 1895–1905: A Little Sphere All Their Own?' *Ontario History*, LXXVIII, 4 (Dec. 1986). See also the useful survey by Donna Yavorsky Ronish, 'Sweet Girl Graduates: The Admission of Women to English-Speaking Universities in Canada in the Nineteenth Century,' Ph.D. diss., Univer-sity of Montreal, 1985, and the papers dealing with women in Paul Axelrod and John G. Reid, eds., *Youth, University, and Canadian Soci-ety: Essays in the Social History of Higher Education* (Kingston and Montreal: McGill-Queen's University Press 1989). For recent work on women at francophone/Quebec universities, see the useful survey by Nadia Fahmy-Eid, Micheline Dumont, and Ruby Heap, 'Rapport spécial sur le Québec,' *CHEA Bulletin d'ACHE*, v (May 1988).

5 Judith Fingard, 'Gender and Inequality at Dalhousie: Faculty Women before 1950,' *Dalhousie Review*, 64 (1984–5).

6 Two collections of autobiographical sketches by women graduates who, in some cases, went into university teaching also illuminate the field. Margaret Gillett and Kay Sibbald, eds., *A Fair Shake: Autobiographical Essays by McGill Women* (Montreal: Eden Press 1984), and Joy Parr, *Still Running ...* (Kingston: Queen's University Alumnae Association 1987). See also Margaret Gillett, 'The Lonely Heart: Maude E. Abbott,

1869–1940,' in Geraldine Jonçich Clifford, ed., *Lone Voyagers: Academic Women in Co-Educational Institutions* (New York: Feminist Press, 1989). Abbott and the geologist, Alice Wilson, are also the subjects of essays in Mary Quayle Innis, ed., *The Clear Spirit: Twenty Canadian Women and Their Times* (Toronto: University of Toronto Press for the Canadian Federation of University Women 1966).

7 For insightful discussions of the biographical approach, its strengths and weaknesses, see Susan Mann Trofimenkoff, 'Feminist Biography,' *Atlantis* (spring 1985), and Geraldine Jonçich Clifford, 'The Life Story: Biographic Study,' in John Hardin Best, ed., *Historical Inquiry in Education: A Research Agenda* (Washington: American Educational Research Association 1983).

8 My search for information on these two women has, over the years, captured the interest of several OISE students. I am indebted to the enthusiasm, detective work, and research skills of Glenys Huws, Nancy Kiefer, Marie Hammond, Johanna Selles-Roney, Johanne Pelletier, and Jo LaPierre, who helped to track down – or nail down – much of the documentation for this paper.

9 I am looking back here to the two major Canadian texts: Charles E. Phillips, *The Development of Education in Canada* (Toronto: W.J. Gage 1957), and J. Donald Wilson, R.M. Stamp, and L.-P. Audet, eds., *Canadian Education: A History* (Scarborough, Ontario: Prentice-Hall 1970), as well as to early 'revisionist' educational history exemplified, for example, by Michael B. Katz and Paul H. Mattingly, eds., *Education and Social Change: Themes from Ontario's Past* (New York: New York University Press 1975). Note, however, Ian E. Davey's 'Trends in Female School Attendance in Mid-Nineteenth Century Ontario,' *Histoire sociale/Social History*, VIII (Nov. 1975), which takes up, among other topics, the social character of two mid-nineteenth-century ladies' academies and the class backgrounds of their students.

10 In the field of higher education, Marjorie Theobald has begun the task in innovative studies of ladies' school in nineteenth-century Australia. See her '"Mere Accomplishments"? Melbourne's Early Ladies' Schools Reconsidered,' reprinted in this volume, and 'Scottish Schoolmistresses in Colonial Australia,' *CHEA Bulletin d'ACHE*, v (Oct. 1988), among other papers. For brief discussions of early Ontario academies for women, see Susan E. Houston and Alison Prentice, *Schooling and Scholars in Nineteenth-Century Ontario* (Toronto: University of Toronto Press 1988), esp. chaps. 2, 3, and 10.

11 Elsie Pomeroy, 'Mary Electa Adams: A Pioneer Educator,' *Ontario*

History, XLI, 3 (1949). There is clear evidence both in the one diary remaining and in Pomeroy's account that there were other diaries, although the historian did not identify them in footnotes. The diary and a volume of essays and poems were donated to the archives of Mount Allison University by Pomeroy in the 1950s. I am indebted to Cheryl Ennals of the university archives for creating a microfilm of the diary and allowing me to borrow it. Mary Electa Adams Diary, 1872 and 1879–83, Mount Allison University Archives, Elsie Pomeroy Papers, 5001/11.

12 Marion V. Royce, 'Landmarks in the Victorian Education of Young Ladies under Methodist Church Auspices,' *Atlantis*, 31 (fall 1977)

13 H.L. Horowitz, *Alma Mater: Design and Experience in the Women's Colleges from their Nineteenth-Century Beginnings to the 1930s* (Boston: Beacon Press 1984), 11

14 Pomeroy, 'Mary Electa Adams,' 108

15 Reid, 'The Education of Women at Mount Allison,' 3–10

16 Pomeroy, 'Mary Electa Adams,' 112–13

17 Adams Diary, June (probably) 1872, pp 32–7

18 *Ibid.*, 1 Jan. 1880, p 45

19 Patricia A. Palmieri, 'From Republican Motherhood to Race Suicide: Arguments on the Higher Education of Women in the United States, 1820–1920,' in *Educating Men and Women Together: Co-education in a Changing World*, ed. Carol Lasser (Urbana: University of Illinois Press 1987), 51–3

20 *Ibid.*, 53–6

21 In *Alma Mater*, Helen Lefkowitz Horowitz explores the various arrangements that were developed and the social ideologies behind them.

22 Adams Diary, 1 Jan. 1880, pp 44–50

23 Adams Diary, 1 Jan. 1880, pp 46–7. The 'great house' and 'great school' in Whitby must have referred to the Ontario Ladies' College.

24 *Ibid.*, 22 March 1880, p 63

25 *Ibid.*, 23 May 1880, p 64

26 For a discussion of the importance of sisterly relationships to nineteenth-century women generally, see Carol Lasser, '"Let Us Be Sisters Forever": The Sororal Model of Nineteenth-Century Female Friendships,' *Signs: Journal of Women in Culture and Society*, 14, 1 (autumn 1988). Marjorie Theobald refers to sisters among the various family teams that ran nineteenth-century academies. See her '"Mere Accomplishments"?' and 'Scottish Schoolmistresses'; also Houston and Prentice, *Schooling and Scholars*, chaps. 2 and 3.

27 Adams Diary, 22 March 1880, pp 62–3

28 *Ibid.*, 5 Aug. 1880, p. 81. On Beecher and her quest for a home, see Kathryn Kish Sklar, *Catharine Beecher: A Study in Domesticity* (New Haven: Yale University Press 1973).

29 Adams Diary, 5 Aug. 1880, p 84

30 *Ibid.*, 4 Oct. 1880, pp 94–5

31 *Ibid.*, 24 Oct. 1880, pp 104–5 and Nov. 1880, p 113

32 *Ibid.*, 9 April 1882, p 206

33 Pomeroy, 'Mary Electa Adams,' 116

34 The process of gradually admitting women is described in Anne Rochon Ford, *A Path Not Strewn with Roses: One Hundred Years of Women at the University of Toronto, 1884–1984* (Toronto: University of Toronto Press 1985), 25–7. Ford does not include the Brookhurst student in her account, or the role of Adams in pressing for the admission of women, however. This information comes from Pomeroy, who relies on Nathanael Burwash in addition to the private papers she had in her possession. Burwash, *The History of Victoria College* (Toronto 1927), esp. 257. See, in addition, Ronish, 'Sweet Girl Graduates,' 56–61, in which Adams' role is acknowledged, and women students who attended Victoria in the 1870s and 1880s are briefly described.

35 Pomeroy, 'Mary Electa Adams,' note, 114

36 Two twentieth-century Catholic institutions for women may have been, at least for a time, exceptions to this rule. Mount Saint Vincent, an academy for girls in Halifax, became a women's college (associated with Dalhousie for degree-granting purposes) in 1915. The Collège Marguerite Bourgeoys, founded in 1908, may also have enjoyed a slightly larger degree of independence than the women's departments that were physically located inside the English-Canadian coeducational universities.

37 University of Toronto Archives, B74–020, Mossie May Kirkwood Interview, 1973. Recorded by Elizabeth Wilson (tape and transcript)

38 M.M. Waddington, *The Development of British Thought from 1820 to 1890* (Toronto: J.M. Dent & Sons 1919)

39 University of Toronto Archives, B74–020, Mossie May Kirkwood Interview, 1973, transcript, p 14

40 In a memoir about her mother's career, Kirkwood's daughter, Naomi Kirkwood Kuhn, describes the opposition to Kirkwood's continued employment after her marriage as 'considerable.' Kuhn, 'Two St. Hildians – Mother and Daughter,' in *Sanctum Hildam Canimus: A Collection of Reminiscences*, ed. Barbara Sutton (Toronto: St Hilda's College 1988), 4

41 Kirkwood interview, p 38

42 University of Toronto Archives, Department of Graduate Records, A73–0026/488 (41), Waddington, Mossie May. Clippings. *Varsity*, 27 Sept. 1929

43 Kuhn, 'Two St. Hildians,' 4

44 Kirkwood interview, pp 47–8 and 56

45 UTA, A 73–0026/488 (41), Waddington, Mossie May. Clippings. *World*, 9/12/20; *Mail*, 1/17/23

46 Mossie May Kirkwood, *For College Women – and Men* (1938), 11 and 18

47 *Ibid.*, 25

48 *Ibid.*, Appendix I, 'The Education of Girls,' June 1937, p 64

49 *Ibid.*, Appendix II, 'Women's Right to Work,' Nov. 1937, p 67

50 *Ibid.*, 70–1, 75–7

51 *Ibid.*, 78–81

52 Archives of Ontario, Pamphlet Collection, No. 26, 'Women of the Machine Age' (Social Service Council of Canada, No. 7, The Machine Age Series, 1935), pp 8–9

53 Kirkwood interview, pp 25–6

54 *Ibid.*, pp 29–31

55 *Unequal Colleagues: The Entrance of Women into the Professions, 1890–1940* (New Brunswick, N.J.: Rutgers University Press 1987), 14

56 In a study of several cohorts of graduates from a Swedish normal school for women, Inga Elgqvist-Saltzman and her colleagues have found that the interwar generation of women teachers may have managed marriage and child-rearing more easily than subsequent generations. For the interwar group, domestic help was both more readily available and a more acceptable option. In addition, Elgqvist-Saltzman suggests, the psychological pressures of mothering were perhaps not so severe for that generation. See 'Life Patterns and Cultural Encounters of the Women Teachers at Rostad,' paper presented to the 10th Session of the International Standing Conference for the History of Education, Joensuu, Finland, July 1988.

57 Glazer and Slater, *Unequal Colleagues*, esp. 231–5

58 In addition to her thesis and the small volumes of the 1930s, she published a book on the philosopher Santayana after her retirement as dean of women: *Santayana: Saint of the Imagination* (Toronto: University of Toronto Press 1961).

59 Dagg and Thompson, *MisEducation*, table 7–1, p 65

60 Patricia A. Graham, 'Expansion and Exclusion: A History of Women in American Higher Education,' *Signs*, 3 (summer 1978). Graham is

concerned with changes in the character of institutions of higher learning in the 1930s and beyond. See Rosalind Rosenberg, *Beyond Separate Spheres: Intellectual Roots of Modern Feminism* (New Haven: Yale University Press 1982), on women faculty who taught in large American universities of the early twentieth century, and a section of Alison Mackinnon's documentary study, *The New Women: Adelaide's Early Women Graduates* (Adelaide: Wakefield Press 1986), for the same period in South Australia. For analysis of an environment that nurtured women's scholarly careers at the turn of the century, see Patricia A. Palmieri, 'Here Was Fellowship: A Social Portrait of Academic Women at Wellesley College, 1895–1920,' reprinted in this volume; and Glazer and Slater, *Unequal Colleagues*, chap. 2.

61 Palmieri, 'From Republican Motherhood to Race Suicide,' 56–63
62 David Bohm, 'The Relationship of Mind and Matter,' Public Lecture, Toronto, 11 Oct. 1988
63 I add the term 'senior women' here to cover wives, women administrators and support staff, lab technicians, cleaning staff, mature students – indeed all adult women who play vital roles although they have little official visibility or power in the university.
64 It would be interesting to trace the career of the Adams' niece, the music mistress Helena Coleman, after her retirement from the Ontario Ladies' College. On the subject of academic wives, a group not yet studied in the Canadian context, see Shirley Ardener, 'Incorporation and Exclusion: Oxford Academics' Wives,' and Lidia Sciama, 'Ambivalance and Dedication: Academic Wives in Cambridge University, 1870–1970,' in Hilary Callan and Shirley Ardener, eds., *The Incorporated Wife* (London: Croom Helm 1984). For a negative assessment of the situation of American wives who have been the scholar-partners of their university-employed husbands, see Marilyn Hoder-Salmon, 'Collecting Scholars' Wives,' *Feminist Studies*, 4, 3 (Oct. 1978).

Selected Bibliography

Susan Gelman

Abbott, John. 'Accomplishing "A Man's Task": Rural Women Teachers,
  Male Culture, and the School Inspectorate in Turn-of-the-Century
  Ontario.' *Ontario History*, 78, 4 (Dec. 1986)
Albisetti, James C. *Schooling German Girls and Women: Secondary and
  Higher Education in the Nineteenth Century*. Princeton, N.J.: Princeton
  University Press 1988
Allmendinger, David F. Jr. 'Mount Holyoke Students Encounter the Need
  for Life-Planning, 1837–1850.' *History of Education Quarterly*, 19, 1
  (spring 1979)
Amies, Marion. 'The Career of a Colonial Schoolmistress.' In *Melbourne
  Studies in Education, 1984*, ed. Imelda Palmer. Melbourne: Melbourne
  University Press 1984
Amies, Marion, and Ailsa G. Thomson Zainu'ddin. *Australian Women and
  Education: Gladly Would They Learn and Gladly Teach, A Survey of
  Historical Resources and Research*. Melbourne: Faculty of Education,
  Monash University 1988
Antler, Joyce. 'Feminism as Life Process: The Life and Career of Lucy
  Sprague Mitchell.' *Feminist Studies*, 7, 1 (spring 1981)
– *Lucy Sprague Mitchell: The Making of a Modern Woman*. New Haven:
  Yale University Press 1987
– 'The Educational Biography of Lucy Sprague Mitchell: A Case Study in
  the History of Women's Higher Education.' In *Women and Higher Educa-
  tion in American History*, ed. John Mack Faragher and Florence Howe.
  New York: W.W. Norton 1988
Apple, Michael W. *Teachers and Texts: A Political Economy of Class and
  Gender Relations in Education*. New York: Routledge and Kegan
  Paul 1986

Arbus, Judith. 'Grateful to Be Working: Women Teachers during the Great Depression.' In *Feminism and Education: A Canadian Perspective*, ed. Mary O'Brien *et al*. Toronto: Centre for Women's Studies in Education, Ontario Institute for Studies in Education 1990

Arnez, Nancy L. 'Selected Black Female Superintendents of Public School Systems.' *Journal of Negro Education*, 51, 3 (summer 1982)

Barman, Jean. 'Birds of Passage or Early Professionals?: Teachers in Late Nineteenth-Century British Columbia.' *Historical Studies in Education/ Revue d'histoire de l'éducation*, 2, 1 (spring 1990)

Beatty, Barbara. '"The Kind of Knowledge of Most Worth to Young Women": Post-Secondary Vocational Training for Teaching and Motherhood at the Wheelock School, 1888–1914.' *History of Higher Education Annual*, 6 (1986)

Bergen, Barry H. 'Only a Schoolmaster: Gender, Class, and the Effort to Professionalize Elementary Teaching in England, 1870–1910.' *History of Education Quarterly*, 22, 1 (spring 1983); reprinted in *Schoolwork: Approaches to the Labour Process of Teaching*, ed. Jenny Ozga. Milton Keynes: Open University Press 1988

Berkeley, Kathleen C. '"The Ladies Want to Bring about Reform in the Public Schools": Public Education and Women's Rights in the Post-Civil War South.' *History of Education Quarterly*, 24, 1 (spring 1984)

Bernard, Jessie. *Academic Women*. University Park: Pennsylvania State University Press 1964

Bernard, Richard M., and Maris A. Vinovskis. 'The Female School Teacher in Ante-Bellum Massachusetts.' *Journal of Social History*, 10, 3 (March 1977)

Biddington, Judith. 'The Weekes Family.' In *Not So Eminent Victorians*, ed. R.J.W. Selleck and Martin Sullivan. Melbourne: Melbourne University Press 1984

Black, L. 'Attitudes towards the Female Victorian Elementary School Teacher – Some Empirical Evidence from Wiltshire.' *History of Education Society Bulletin*, 25 (spring 1980)

Braster, J.F.A. 'The Feminization of Teaching: A European Perspective.' In *The Social Role and Evolution of the Teaching Profession in Historical Context*, vol. 5, ed. Simo Seppo. Faculty of Education, University of Joensuu, Finland 1988

Brehmer, Ilse. 'Women as Educators in German-Speaking Europe: The Middle Ages to Today.' In *Women Educators: Employees of Schools in Western*

Countries, ed. Patricia A. Schmuck. Albany: State University of New York Press 1987

Burstyn, Joan N. 'Catharine Beecher and the Education of American Women.' *New England Quarterly*, 47, 3 (Sept. 1974)

– 'Sources of Influence: Women as Teachers of Girls.' In *The Education of Girls and Women*, ed. June Purvis. Leicester: History of Education Society 1985

– 'Historical Perspectives on Women in Educational Leadership.' In *Women and Educational Leadership*, ed. Sari Knopp Biklen and Marilyn B. Brannigan. Lexington, Mass.: Lexington Books 1980

Bystydzienski, Jill. 'Women's Participation in Teachers' Unions in England and the United States.' In *Women Educators: Employees of Schools in Western Countries*, ed. Schmuck. Albany: State University of New York Press 1987

Capen, E.P. 'Zilpah Grant and the Art of Teaching, 1829.' *New England Quarterly*, 20, 3 (Sept. 1947)

Carter, Susan B. 'Academic Women Revisited: An Empirical Study of Changing Patterns in Women's Employment as College and University Faculty 1890–1963.' *Journal of Social History*, 14, 4 (summer 1981)

– 'Incentives and Rewards to Teaching.' In *American Teachers: Histories of a Profession at Work*, ed. Donald E. Warren. New York: Macmillan 1989

– 'Occupational Segregation, Teachers' Wages, and American Economic Growth.' *Journal of Economic History*, 46, 2 (June 1986)

Clarke, E. *The Employment of Female Teachers in Queensland State Schools, 1860–1982*. Brisbane: Department of Education 1983

Clifford, Geraldine Jonçich. '"Lady Teachers" and Politics in the United States, 1850–1930.' In *Teachers: The Culture and Politics of Work*, ed. Martin Lawn and Gerald Grace. London: Falmer Press 1987

– 'Women's Liberation and Women's Professions: Reconsidering the Past, Present, and Future.' In *Women and Higher Education in American History*, ed. Faragher and Howe. New York: W.W. Norton 1988

– 'Man/Woman/Teacher: Gender, Family, and Career in American Educational History.' In *American Teachers: Histories of a Profession at Work*, ed. Warren. New York: Macmillan 1989

Clifford, Geraldine Jonçich, ed. *Lone Voyagers: Academic Women in Coeducational Institutions, 1870–1937*. New York: Feminist Press at the City University of New York 1989

Collier-Thomas, Betty. 'The Impact of Black Women in Education: An Historical Overview.' *Journal of Negro Education*, 51, 3 (summer 1982)

Collins, Cherry. 'Regaining the Past for the Present: The Legacy of the Chicago Teachers' Federation.' *History of Education Review*, 13, 2 (1984)

Concepta, Sister Maria. *The Making of a Sister-Teacher*. Notre Dame: University of Notre Dame Press 1965

Connell, W.F. 'Innovative Headmistress D.J. Ross.' In *Pioneers of Australian Education: Studies of the Development of Education in Australia, 1900–1950*, vol. 3, ed. C. Turney. Sydney: Sydney University Press 1983

Copelman, Dina M. '"A New Comradeship between Men and Women": Family, Marriage and London's Women Teachers, 1870–1914.' In *Labour and Love: Women's Experience of Home and Family, 1850–1940*, ed. Jane Lewis. Oxford: Basil Blackwell 1986

Corr, Helen. 'The Sexual Division of Labour in the Scottish Teaching Profession, 1872–1914.' In *Scottish Culture and Scottish Education, 1800–1980*, ed. Walter M. Humes and Hamish M. Paterson. Edinburgh: John Donald Publishers 1983

Curtis, Bruce. *Building the Educational State, Canada West, 1836–1871*. London: Falmer Press 1988

Danylewycz, Marta, and Alison Prentice. 'Lessons from the Past: The Experience of Women Teachers in Quebec and Ontario.' In *World Yearbook of Education 1984; Women and Education*, ed. Sandra Acker *et al*. London: Kogan Page 1984

– 'Teachers, Gender, and Bureaucratizing School Systems in Nineteenth Century Montreal and Toronto.' *History of Education Quarterly*, 24, 1 (spring 1984)

– 'Revising the History of Teachers: A Canadian Perspective.' *Interchange*, 17, 2 (summer 1986)

Danylewycz, Marta, Beth Light, and Alison Prentice. 'The Evolution of the Sexual Division of Labour in Teaching: A Nineteenth Century Ontario and Quebec Case Study.' *Histoire sociale/Social History*, 16, 3 (May 1983); reprinted in *Women and Education, a Canadian Perspective*, ed. Jane S. Gaskell and Arlene Tiger McLaren. Calgary: Detselig Enterprises 1987

Depaepe, Marc. 'The Feminization of Primary School Teaching in Belgium.' In *The Social Role and Evolution of the Teaching Profession in Historical Context*, vol. 5, ed. Seppo. Faculty of Education, University of Joensuu, Finland 1988

Doherty, Robert E. 'Tempest on the Hudson: The Struggle for "Equal Pay for Equal Work" in the New York City Public Schools, 1907–1911.' *History of Education Quarterly*, 19, 4 (winter 1979)

Dow, Gwyneth, and Lesley Scholes. 'Christina Montgomery.' In *Not So*

Eminent Victorians, ed. Selleck and Sullivan. Melbourne: Melbourne University Press 1984

Drummond, Ann. 'Gender, Profession, and Principals: The Teachers of Quebec Protestant Academies, 1875–1900.' *Historical Studies in Education/ Revue d'histoire de l'éducation*, 2, 1 (spring 1990)

Dyhouse, Carol. 'Miss Buss and Miss Beale: Gender and Authority in the History of Education.' In *Lessons for Life: The Schooling of Girls and Women, 1850–1950*, ed. Felicity Hunt. Oxford: Basil Blackwell 1987

Ellsworth, Edward W. *Liberators of the Female Mind: The Shirreff Sisters, Educational Reform and the Women's Movement*. Westport, Conn.: Greenwood Press 1979

Elsbree, Willard S. *The American Teacher: Evolution of a Profession in a Democracy*. New York: American Book Company 1939

Fahmy-Eid, Nadia, and Micheline Dumont, ed. *Maîtresses de maison, maîtresses d'école: Femmes, famille et éducation dans l'histoire du Québec*. Montreal: Boréal Express 1983

Fingard, Judith. 'Gender and Inequality at Dalhousie: Faculty Women before 1950.' *Dalhousie Review*, 64, 4 (winter 1984–5)

Finkelstein, Barbara J. 'Schooling and Schoolteachers: Selected Bibliography of Autobiographies in the Nineteenth Century.' *History of Education Quarterly*, 14, 2 (summer 1974)

– *Governing the Young: Teachers' Behavior in Popular Primary Schools in Nineteenth-Century United States*. New York: Falmer Press 1989

Fitts, Deborah. 'Una and the Lion: The Feminization of District School Teaching and Its Effects on the Roles of Students and Teachers in Nineteenth-Century Massachusetts.' In *Regulated Children/Liberated Children: Education in Psychohistorical Perspective*, ed. Barbara Finkelstein. New York: Psychohistory Press 1979

Fletcher, Sheila. '"The Educational Service of the Race": The High Calling of the Gym Mistress in the First Half of the Twentieth Century.' In *The Education of Girls and Women*, ed. Purvis. Leicester: History of Education Society 1985

Florin, Christina. 'Who Should Sit in the Teacher's Chair?' In *The Social Role and Evolution of the Teaching Profession in Historical Context*, vol. 5, ed. Seppo. Faculty of Education, University of Joensuu, Finland 1988

Floud, Jean, and W. Scott. 'Recruitment to Teaching in England and Wales.' In *Education, Economy and Society: A Reader in the Sociology of Education*, ed. A.H. Halsey *et al*. New York: Free Press of Glencoe 1961

Fraser, James W. 'Agents of Democracy: Urban Elementary School Teachers and the Conditions of Learning.' In *American Teachers: Histories of a Profession at Work*, ed. Warren. New York: Macmillan 1989

French, Doris. *High Button Bootstraps: Federation of Women Teachers' Associations of Ontario: 1918–1968*. Toronto: Ryerson Press 1968

Gelman, Susan. 'The "Feminization" of the High Schools?: Women Secondary School Teachers in Toronto, 1871–1930.' *Historical Studies in Education/Revue d'histoire de l'éducation*, 2, 1 (spring 1990)

Glenday, Nonita, and Mary Price. *Reluctant Revolutionaries: A Century of Head Mistresses, 1874–1974*. London: Pitman Publishing 1974

Goodsell, Willystine, ed. *Pioneers of Women's Education in the U.S.: Emma Willard, Catharine Beecher, Mary Lyon*. New York: McGraw-Hill 1931

Gordon, Peter. 'Katharine Bathurst: A Controversial Woman Inspector.' *History of Education*, 17, 3 (Sept. 1988)

Gorelick, Sherry. 'Class Relations and the Development of the Teaching Profession.' In *Class and Social Development: A New Theory of the Middle Class*, ed. Dale L. Johnson. Beverly Hills: Sage Publications 1982

Graham, Elizabeth. 'Schoolmarms and Early Teaching in Ontario.' In *Women at Work, Ontario, 1850–1930*, ed. Janice Acton et al. Toronto: Canadian Women's Educational Press 1974

Graham, Patricia Albjerg. 'Expansion and Exclusion: A History of Women in American Higher Education.' *Signs*, 3, 4 (summer 1978)

Green, Elizabeth Alden. *Mary Lyon and Mount Holyoke: Opening the Gates*. Hanover, N.H.: University Press of New England 1979

Gribskov, Margaret. 'Feminism and the Woman School Administrator.' In *Women and Educational Leadership*, ed. Biklen and Brannigan. Lexington, Mass.: Lexington Books 1980

– 'Adelaide Pollock and the Founding of the NCAWE.' In *Women Educators: Employees of Schools in Western Countries*, ed. Schmuck. Albany: State University of New York Press 1987

Grumet, Madeleine. *Bitter Milk: Women and Teaching*. Amherst: University of Massachusetts Press, 1988

– 'Pedagogy for Patriarchy: The Feminization of Teaching.' *Interchange*, 12, 2–3 (1981)

Hakaste, Saara. 'Male and Female Teachers Working Together in the Secondary Schools of Finland from the 1780s to 1860s.' In *The Social Role and Evolution of the Teaching Profession*, vol. 5, ed. Seppo. Faculty of Education, University of Joensuu, Finland 1988

Hancock, Harold B. 'Mary Ann Shadd: Negro Editor, Educator, and Lawyer.' *Delaware History*, 15 (April 1973)

Harley, Sharon. 'Beyond the Classroom: The Organizational Lives of Black Female Educators in the District of Columbia, 1890–1930.' *Journal of Negro Education*, 51, 3 (summer 1982)

Harveson, Mae Elizabeth. *Catharine Esther Beecher: Pioneer Educator*. Philadelphia: Science Press Printing 1932; reprint, New York: Arno Press and the New York *Times* 1969

Hendricx, Carmel. 'Social and Political Attitudes of Women Teachers in Queensland State Primary Schools, 1875–1911.' *Refractory Girl* (spring 1973)

Herbst, Jurgen. *And Sadly Teach: Teacher Education and Professionalizatiron in American Culture*. Madison: University of Wisconsin Press 1989

Hilden, Adda. 'Female Pedagogy Evolved While Training Young Danish Women for the Teaching Profession in the Mid-Nineteenth Century.' In *The Social Role and Evolution of the Teaching Profession in Historical Context*, vol. 5, ed. Seppo. Faculty of Education, University of Joensuu, Finland 1988

Hoffman, Nancy. *Women's 'True' Profession: Voices from the History of Teaching*. Old Westbury, N.Y.: Feminist Press and McGraw-Hill 1981

Holmes, Madelyn. 'The Pioneers: Female Public School Teachers in Salem, Mass., 1830s to 1850s.' *Essex Institute Historical Collections* (fall 1986)

Horn, Pamela. 'The Problems of a Village Headmistress in the 1880s.' *History of Education Society Bulletin*, 26 (autumn 1980)

Houston, Susan E., and Alison Prentice. *Schooling and Scholars in Nineteenth-Century Ontario*. Toronto: University of Toronto Press 1988

Hyams, B.K. 'The Battle of the Sexes in Teachers' Organizations: A South Australian Episode, 1937–1950.' *ANZHES Journal*, 3, 2 (1974); reprinted in *Australian Teachers: From Colonial Schoolmasters to Militant Professionals*, ed. A.D. Spaull. Melbourne: Macmillan 1977

Issel, William H. 'Teachers and Educational Reform during the Progressive Era: A Case Study of the Pittsburgh Teachers' Association.' *History of Education Quarterly*, 7, 2 (summer 1967)

Jacks, O. 'The Employment Patterns of a Selected Group of Female Teachers, 1948–1967.' *West Australian Teachers' Journal*, 59, 10 (Nov. 1969)

Jensen, Joan M. 'Not Only Ours But Others: The Quaker Teaching Daughters of the Mid-Atlantic, 1790–1850.' *History of Education Quarterly*, 14, 1 (spring 1984)

Johnston, Harriett, Jessie P. Semple and A.A. Gray. *The Story of The Women Teachers' Association of Toronto*. Toronto: Thomas Nelson and Sons [1932?]

Jones, Helen. 'The Acceptable Crusader: Lillian de Lissa and Pre-School Education in South Australia.' In *Melbourne Studies in Education, 1975*, ed. S. Murray-Smith. Melbourne: Melbourne University Press 1975

Jones, Jacqueline. *Soldiers of Light and Love: Northern Teachers and Georgia Blacks, 1865–1873*. Chapel Hill: University of North Carolina Press 1980

– 'Women Who Were More Than Men: Sex and Status in Freedmen's Teaching.' *History of Education Quarterly*, 19, 1 (spring 1979)

Kamm, Josephine. *How Different from Us: A Biography of Miss Buss and Miss Beale*. London: Bodley Head 1958

Kaufman, Polly Welts. 'A Wider Field of Usefulness: Pioneer Women Teachers in the West, 1848–1854.' *Journal of the West*, 21, 2 (April 1982)

– *Women Teachers on the Frontier*. New Haven: Yale University Press 1984

Kennedy, Sally. 'Useful and Expendable: Women Teachers in Western Australia in the 1920s and 1930s.' *Labour History*, 44 (May 1983)

Kojder, Apolonja Maria. 'The Saskatchewan Women Teachers' Association.' *Saskatchewan History*, 30, 2 (spring 1977); reprinted in *Shaping the Schools of the Canadian West*, ed. David C. Jones *et al*. Calgary: Detselig Enterprises 1977

– 'In Union There Is Strength: The Saskatoon Women Teachers' Association.' *Canadian Woman Studies/Les cahiers de la femme*, 7, 3 (fall 1986)

Kramer, Rita. *Maria Montessori: A Bibliography*. New York: G.P. Putnam's Sons, 1976; reprint ed, Chicago: University of Chicago Press 1983

Kyle, Noeline. 'Women's "Natural Mission" But Man's Real Domain: The Masculinization of the State Elementary Teaching Service in New South Wales.' In *Battlers and Bluestockings: Women's Place in Australian Education*, ed. Miriam Henry and Sandra Taylor. Canberra: Australian College of Education 1989

– *Her Natural Destiny: Education of Women in New South Wales*. Kensington: New South Wales University Press 1986

Labarree, David F. 'Career Ladders and the Early Public High School Teacher: A Study of Inequality and Opportunity.' In *American Teachers: Histories of a Profession at Work*, ed. Warren. New York: Macmillan 1989

Lamont, Katharine. *The Canadian Association of Headmistresses: A History (1931–1972)*. Montreal: 1972

Laskin, Susan, Beth Light and Alison Prentice. 'Studying the History of an Occupation: Quantitative Sources on Canadian Teachers in the Nineteenth Century.' *Archivaria*, 14 (summer 1982)

Lawn, Martin. 'What Is the Teacher's Job?: Work and Welfare in Elementary

Teaching, 1940–1945.' In *Teachers: The Culture and Politics of Work*, ed.
Lawn and Grace. London: Falmer Press 1987
– *Servants of the State: The Contested Control of Teaching 1900–1930*.
London: Falmer Press 1987
Leinster-Mackay, D.P. 'Dame Schools: A Need for Review.' *British Journal
of Educational Studies*, 24, 1 (Feb. 1976)
Littlewood, Margaret. 'Makers of Men: The Anti-Feminist Backlash of the
National Association of Schoolmasters in the 1920s and 30s.' *Trouble and
Strife*, 5 (1985)
– 'The "Wise Married Woman" and the Teaching Unions.' In *Women Teach-
ers: Issues and Experiences*, ed. H. De Lyon and F. Migniuolo. Milton
Keynes: Open University Press 1989
Lortie, Dan C. *Schoolteacher: A Sociological Study*. Chicago: University of
Chicago Press 1975
Lutz, Alma. *Emma Willard: Pioneer Educator of American Women*. Boston:
Beacon Press 1964; reprint ed., Westport, Conn.: Greenwood Press
1983
Lyons, John E. 'Ten Forgotten Years: The Saskatchewan Teachers' Federa-
tion and the Legacy of the Depression.' In *Schools in the West: Essays
in Canadian Educational History*, ed. Nancy M. Sheehan *et al.* Calgary:
Detselig Enterprises 1986
– 'For St. George and Canada: The Fellowship of the Maple Leaf and Educa-
tion on the Prairies.' In *An Imperfect Past: Education and Society in
Canadian History*, ed. J. Donald Wilson. Vancouver: Faculty of Education,
University of British Columbia 1984
Mackinnon, Alison. 'A New Point of Departure.' *History of Education
Review*, 13, 2 (1984)
– 'Women's Education: Linking History and Theory.' *History of Education
Review*, 13, 2 (1984)
– *One Foot on the Ladder: Origins and Outcomes of Girls' Secondary School-
ing in South Australia*. St. Lucia, Australia: University of Queensland
Press 1984
Margadant, Jo Burr. *Madame le Professeur: Women Educators in the Third
Republic*. Princeton: Princeton University Press 1990
Melder, Keith E. 'Women's High Calling: The Teaching Profession in
America, 1830–1860.' *American Studies*, 13, 2 (fall 1972)
Meyers, Peter V. 'From Conflict to Cooperation: Men and Women Teachers
in the Belle Epoque.' In *The Making of Frenchmen: Current Directions
in the History of Education in France, 1679–1979*, ed. Donald N. Baker

and Patrick J. Harrigan. Waterloo, Ont.: Historical Reflections Press 1980

Moch, Leslie Page. 'Government Policy and Women's Experience: The Case of Teachers in France.' *Feminist Studies*, 14, 2 (summer 1988)

Moeller, Kirsten. 'Danish Female Teachers and Equal Pay, 1898–1922.' In *Women Educators: Employees of Schools in Western Countries*, ed. Schmuck. Albany: State University of New York Press 1987

Monaghan, E. Jennifer. 'Literacy Instruction and Gender in Colonial New England.' *American Quarterly*, 40, 1 (March 1988)

– 'Noted and Unnoted School Dames: Women as Reading Teachers in Colonial New England.' Conference Papers for the 11th Session of the International Standing Conference for the History of Education, Oslo, Norway, 1989

Morain, Thomas. 'The Departure of Males from the Teaching Profession in Nineteenth Century Iowa.' *Civil War History*, 26, 2 (June 1980)

Nelson, Margaret K. 'Vermont Female School Teachers in the Nineteenth Century.' *Vermont History*, 49, 1 (winter 1977)

– 'From the One-Room Schoolhouse to the Graded School, Teaching in Vermont, 1910–1950.' *Frontiers*, 7, 1 (1983)

– 'The Threat of Sexual Harassment: Rural Vermont School Teachers, 1915–1950.' *Educational Foundations*, 2, 2 (summer 1985)

Oates, Mary J. 'The Professional Preparation of Parochial School Teachers, 1870–1940.' *Historical Journal of Massachusetts*, 12 (Jan. 1984)

Oram, Alison M. 'Serving Two Masters?: The Introduction of a Marriage Bar in Teaching in the 1920s.' In *The Sexual Dynamics of History: Men's Power, Women's Resistance*. The London Feminist History Group. London: Pluto Press 1983

– '"Sexual Antagonism" in the Teaching Profession: The Equal Pay Issue, 1914–1929.' *History of Education Review*, 14, 2 (1985)

– '"Sex Antagonism" in the Teaching Profession: Equal Pay and the Marriage Bar, 1910–39.' In *Gender and the Politics of Schooling*, ed. Madeleine Arnot and Gaby Weiner. London: Hutchinson in association with the Open University Press 1987

– '"Embittered, Sexless or Homosexual": Attacks on Spinster Teachers, 1918–1939.' In *Current Issues in Women's History*, ed. Arina Angerman *et al*. London: Routledge Chapman and Hall 1989

– 'Inequalities in the Teaching Profession: The Effect on Teachers and Pupils, 1910–39.' In *Lessons for Life: The Schooling of Girls and Women, 1850–1950*, ed. Hunt. Oxford: Basil Blackwell 1987

– 'A Master Should Not Serve under a Mistress: Women and Men Teachers,

1900–1970.' In *Teachers, Gender and Careers*, ed. Acker. New York: Falmer Press 1989

Owen, P. '"Who Would Be Free, Herself Must Strike the Blow": The National Union of Women Teachers, Equal Pay, and Women within the Teaching Profession.' *History of Education*, 17, 1 (March 1988)

Palmieri, Patricia A. 'Patterns of Achievement of Single Academic Women at Wellesley College, 1880–1920.' *Frontiers*, 5, 1 (spring 1980)

Partington, Geoffrey. *Women Teachers in the Twentieth Century in England and Wales*. Windsor, England: NFER Publishing 1976

Patterson, Robert S. 'Voices from the Past: The Personal and Professional Struggle of Rural School Teachers.' In *Schools in the West: Essays in Canadian Educational History*, ed. Sheehan et al. Calgary: Detselig Enterprises 1986

Pedersen, Joyce Senders. 'Some Victorian Headmistresses: A Conservative Tradition of Social Reform.' *Victorian Studies*, 24, 4 (summer 1981)

– *The Reform of Girls' Secondary and Higher Education in Victorian England: A Study of Elites and Educational Change*. New York: Garland 1987

Pedersen, Sharon. 'Married Women and the Right to Teach in St. Louis, 1941–1948.' *Missouri History Review*, 81, 2 (Jan. 1987)

Perkins, Linda M. 'The Black Female American Missionary Association Teacher in the South, 1861–70.' In *Black Americans in North Carolina and the South*, ed. Jeffrey J. Crow and Flora J. Hatley. Chapel Hill: University of North Carolina Press 1984

– 'The History of Blacks in Teaching: Growth and Decline within the Profession.' In *American Teachers: Histories of a Profession at Work*, ed. Warren. New York: Macmillan 1989

Petersen, R.C. 'The Montessorians – M.M. Simpson and L. de Lissa.' In *Pioneers of Australian Education*, vol. 3, ed. Turney. Sydney: Sydney University Press 1983

Peterson, M. Jeanne. 'The Victorian Governess: Status Incongruence in Family and Society.' In *Suffer and Be Still: Women in the Victorian Age*, ed. Martha Vicinus. Bloomington: Indiana University Press 1973

Peterson, Susan. '"Holy Women" and Housekeepers: Women Teachers on South Dakota Reservations, 1885–1910.' *South Dakota History*, 13 (fall 1983)

Pierotti, A.M. *The Story of the National Union of Women Teachers*. London: National Union of Women Teachers 1963

Poelzer, Irene. *Saskatchewan Women Teachers, 1905–1920: Their Contributions*. Saskatoon, Sask.: Lindenblatt & Hamonic 1990

Pomeroy, Elsie. 'Mary Electa Adams: A Pioneer Educator.' *Ontario History*,
41 (1949)
Possing, Birgitte. 'Purity, Discipline and Ambition: Female Teachers' Didac-
tics of History and Gender in 19th Century Denmark.' In *The Social Role
and Evolution of the Teaching Profession in Historical Context*, vol. 5, ed.
Seppo. Faculty of Education, University of Joensuu, Finland 1988
Prentice, Alison. 'The Feminization of Teaching British North America and
Canada, 1845–1875.' *Histoire sociale/Social History*, 8, 15 (May 1975);
reprinted in *The Neglected Majority: Essays in Canadian Women's His-
tory*, ed. Susan Mann Trofimenkoff and Alison Prentice. Toronto: McClel-
land and Stewart 1977
– 'From Household to School House: The Emergence of the Teacher as a
Servant of the State.' *Material History Bulletin*, 20 (fall 1984)
– 'Themes in the Early History of the Women Teachers' Association of
Toronto.' In *Women's Paid and Unpaid Work: Historical and Contempo-
rary Perspectives*, ed. Paula Bourne. Toronto: New Hogtown Press 1985
– 'Women (and Men) at Normal School: Training Teachers in Mid-19th
Century Canada.' In *The Social Role and Evolution of the Teaching
Profession*, vol. 5, ed. Seppo. Faculty of Education, University of Joensuu,
Finland 1988
– '"Like Friendly Atoms in Chemistry"?: Women and Men at Normal School
in Mid-Nineteenth Century Toronto.' In *Old Ontario: Essays in Honour
of J.M.S. Careless*, ed. David Keane and Colin Read. Toronto: Dundurn
Press 1990
– 'Multiple Realities: The History of Women Teachers in Canada.' In *Femi-
nism and Education: A Canadian Perspective*, ed. O'Brien. Toronto:
Centre for Women's Studies in Education, Ontario Institute for Studies
in Education 1990
Preston, Jo Anne. 'Female Aspiration and Male Ideology: School-Teaching
in Nineteenth-Century New England.' In *Current Issues in Women's History*, ed. Angerman *et al*. London: Routledge Chapman and Hall 1989
Purvis, June. 'Women and Teaching in the Nineteenth Century.' In *Education and the State: Politics Patriarchy and Practice*, vol. 2, ed. Roger Dale
et al. Lewes, England: Falmer Press in association with the Open University Press 1981
Quantz, Richard A. 'The Complex Visions of Female Teachers and the Failure
of Unionization in the 1930s: An Oral History.' *History of Education
Quarterly*, 25, 4 (winter 1985)
Reid, G.A. 'The Victorian High School Teachers' Association, 1912–1926.'

In *Melbourne Studies in Education, 1971,* ed. R.J.W. Selleck. Victoria:
Melbourne University Press 1971

Reynolds, Cecilia. 'Limited Liberation: A Policy on Married Women Teachers.' In *Women Educators: Employees of Schools in Western Countries,* ed.
Schmuck. Albany: State University of New York Press 1987; reprinted as
'Too Limiting a Liberation: Discourse and Actuality in the Case of Married Women Teachers.' In *Feminism and Education: A Canadian Perspective,* ed. O'Brien *et al.* Toronto: Centre for Women's Studies in Education,
Ontario Institute for Studies in Education 1990

- 'Hegemony and Hierarchy: Becoming a Teacher in Toronto, 1930–1980.'
  Historical Studies in Education/Revue d'histoire de l'éducation, 2, 1
  (spring 1990)

Richardson, John G., and Brenda Wooden Hatcher. 'The Feminization of
Public School Teaching, 1870–1920.' *Work and Occupations,* 10, 1 (Feb.
1983)

Rinehart, Alice Duffy. *Mortals in the Immortal Profession: An Oral History
of Teaching.* New York: Irvington Publishers 1983

Rosenberg, Rosalind. 'The Academic Prism: The New View of American
Women.' In *Women of America: A History,* ed. Carol Ruth Berkin and
Mary Beth Norton. Boston: Houghton Mifflin 1979

- *Beyond Separate Spheres: Intellectual Roots of Modern Feminism.* New
  Haven: Yale University Press 1982

Rossiter, Margaret W. *Women Scientists in America: Struggles and Strategies to 1940.* Baltimore: Johns Hopkins University Press 1982

Rury, John L. 'Gender, Salaries, and Career: American Teachers,
1900–1910.' *Issues in Education,* 4 (1986)

- 'Who Became Teachers?: The Social Characteristics of Teachers in American History.' In *American Teachers: Histories of a Profession at Work,*
  ed. Warren. New York: Macmillan 1989

Scharf, Lois. *To Work and to Wed: Female Employment, Feminism, and
the Great Depression.* Westport, Conn.: Greenwood Press 1980

Scott, Anne Firor. 'The Ever Widening Circle: The Diffusion of Feminist
Values from the Troy Female Seminary 1822–1872.' *History of Education
Quarterly,* 19, 1 (spring 1979); reprinted in *Making the Invisible Woman
Visible,* ed. Anne Firor Scott. Urbana: University of Illinois Press 1984

- 'Almira Lincoln Phelps: The Self-Made Woman in the Nineteenth Cen-
  tury.' *Maryland Historical Magazine,* 75, 3 (Sept. 1980); reprinted in
  Making the Invisible Woman Visible, ed. Scott. Urbana: University of
  Illinois Press 1984

Seddon, Terri. 'Teachers' Work: Past and Present.' In *Teachers' Careers in Australia*, ed. P. McKenzie and R. McLean. Melbourne: ACER 1989

Sicherman, Barbara. 'College and Careers: Historical Perspectives on the Lives and Work Patterns of Women College Graduates.' In *Women and Higher Education in American History*, ed. Faragher and Howe, New York: W.W. Norton 1988

Sklar, Kathryn Kish. *Catharine Beecher: A Study in American Domesticity*. New Haven: Yale University Press 1973

Small, Sandra E. 'The Yankee Schoolmarm in Freedmen's Schools: An Analysis of Attitudes.' *Journal of Southern History*, 45, 3 (Aug. 1979)

Spaull, A.D. 'Equal Pay for Women Teachers and the New South Wales Teachers' Federation.' *ANZHES Journal*, 4, 1 (1975); reprinted in *Australian Teachers: From Colonial Schoolmasters to Militant Professionals*, ed. Spaull. Melbourne: Macmillan 1977

– 'The Origins and Formation of the Victorian Secondary Teachers' Association, 1948–1954.' In *Melbourne Studies in Education, 1975*, ed. Murray-Smith. Victoria: Melbourne University Press 1975

– *Australian Education in the Second World War*. St. Lucia: University of Queensland Press, 1982

Spaull, A.D., and M.G. Sullivan. *A History of the Queensland Teachers Union*. Sydney: Allen and Unwin 1989

Staton, Pat, and Beth Light. *Speak with Their Own Voices: A Documentary History of the Federation of Women Teachers' Associations of Ontario and the Women Elementary Public School Teachers of Ontario*. Toronto: Federation of Women Teachers' Associations of Ontario 1987

Strober, Myra H., and Audri Gordon Lanford. 'The Feminization of Public School Teaching: A Cross-sectional Analysis, 1850–1880.' *Signs*, 11, 2 (winter 1986)

Strober, Myra H., and David Tyack. 'Why Do Women Teach and Men Manage?: A Report on Research on Schools.' *Signs*, 5, 3 (spring 1980)

Strober, Myra H., and Laura Best. 'The Female/Male Salary Differential in Public Schools: Some Lessons from San Francisco, 1879.' *Economic Inquiry*, 17, 2 (April 1979)

Sugg, Redding S. Jr. *Motherteacher: The Feminization of American Education*. Charlottesville: University Press of Virginia 1978

Sullivan, M.G., and Andrew D. Spaull. 'Teachers' Work in Queensland, 1880–1930.' In *Family, School and State in Australian History*, ed. Marjorie R. Theobald and R.J.W. Selleck. Sydney: Allen and Unwin 1990

Swint, Henry Lee. *The Northern Teacher in the South, 1862–1870*. Nashville,

Tenn.: Vanderbilt University Press 1941; reprint ed., New York: Octagon Books 1967

Sysiharju, Anna-Liisa. 'Women School Employees in Finland.' In *Women Educators: Employees of Schools in Western Countries*, ed. Schmuck. Albany: State University of New York Press 1987

Szreter, R. 'Concerns of Women Teachers as Reflected in *The Journal of the Women's Education Union*, 1873–1881.' In *The Social Role and Evolution of the Teaching Profession in Historical Context*, vol. 5, ed. Seppo. Faculty of Education, University of Joensuu, Finland 1988

Teachers' Federation of Victoria. *Oral History of Women in Teachers' Unions*. Melbourne: Teachers' Federation of Victoria 1987

Theobald, Marjorie R. 'Women Teachers' Quest for Salary Justice in Victoria's Registered Schools, 1915–1946.' In *Melbourne Studies in Education, 1983*, ed. Imelda Palmer. Victoria: Melbourne University Press 1983

– 'Agnes Jane Grant.' In *Not So Eminent Victorians*, ed. Selleck and Sullivan. Melbourne: Melbourne University Press 1984

– 'Julie Vieusseux: The Lady Principal and Her School.' In *Double Time: Women in Victoria – 150 Years*, ed. M. Lake and F. Kelly. Ringwood, Victoria: Penguin Books 1985

– 'Scottish Schoolmistresses in Colonial Australia.' *Canadian History of Education Association Bulletin*, 5, 3 (Oct. 1988)

– 'Women's Labour, the Family and the State: The Case of Women Teaching in an Elementary Schooling System in Australia, 1850–1880.' In *Family, School and State in Australian History*, ed. Theobald and Selleck. Sydney: Allen and Unwin 1990

Thomas, J.B. 'University College, Bristol: Pioneering Teacher Training for Women.' *History of Education*, 17, 1 (March 1988)

Thomlinson, Leila. 'Oxford University and the Training of Teachers (1892–1921).' *British Journal of Educational Studies*, 16, 3 (Oct. 1968)

Tyack, David B., and Myra H. Strober. 'Jobs and Gender: A History of the Structuring of Educational Employment by Sex.' In *Educational Policy and Management: Sex Differentials*, ed. Schmuck *et al.* New York: Academic Press 1981

Underwood, Kathleen. 'The Pace of Their Own Lives: Teacher Training and the Life Course of Western Women.' *Pacific Historical Review*, 55, 4 (Nov. 1986)

Urban, Wayne J. 'Teacher Organizations in New York City, 1905–1920.' In *Educating an Urban People: The New York City Experience*, ed. Diane Ravitch and Ronald K. Goodenow. New York: Teachers College Press 1981

– *Why Teachers Organized*. Detroit: Wayne State University Press 1982

- 'New Directions in the Historical Study of Teacher Unionism.' *Historical Studies in Education/Revue d'histoire de l'éducation*, 2, 1 (spring 1990)
Van Essen, Mineke. 'Female Teachers in the Netherlands, 1827–58.' In *Women Educators: Employees of Schools in Western Countries*, ed. Schmuck. Albany: State University of New York Press 1987
Vaughan-Robertson, Courtney Ann. 'Sometimes Independent but Never Equal – Women Teachers, 1900–1950: The Oklahoma Example.' *Pacific Historical Review*, 53, 1 (Feb. 1984)
- 'Having a Purpose in Life: Western Women Teachers in the Twentieth Century.' *Great Plains Quarterly*, 5, 2 (spring 1985)
Vicinus, Martha. '"One Life to Stand beside Me": Emotional Conflicts in First Generation College Women in England.' *Feminist Studies*, 8, 3 (fall 1982)
- *Independent Women: Work and Community for Single Women, 1850–1920*. Chicago: University of Chicago Press 1985
Victorian Secondary Teachers' Association. *Women in the VSTA*. Melbourne: Victorian Secondary Teachers' Association 1987
Walker, Eva K. *The Story of the Women Teachers' Association of Toronto, vol. 2, 1931–1963*. Toronto: Copp Clark 1963
Ward, L.O. 'H.A.L. Fisher and the Teachers.' *British Journal of Educational Studies*, 22, 2 (June 1974)
Wells, Anna Mary. *Miss Marks and Miss Woolley*. Boston: Houghton Mifflin 1978
Widdowson, Frances. *Going Up into the Next Class: Women and Elementary Teacher Training, 1840–1919*. London: Hutchinson 1983
- '"Educating Teacher": Women and Elementary Teaching in London, 1900–1914.' In *Our Work, Our Lives, Our Words: Women's History and Women's Work*, ed. Leonore Davidoff and Belinda Westover. Basingstoke: Macmillan Education 1986
Williamson, Noeline. 'The Employment of Female Teachers in the Small Bush Schools of New South Wales 1880–1890: A Case of Stay Bushed or Stay Home.' *Labour History*, 43 (Nov. 1982)
- 'The Feminization of Teaching in New South Wales: A Historical Perspective.' *Australian Journal of Education*, 27, 1 (1983)
Wilson, J. Donald. 'Visions of Ordinary Participants.' In *A History of British Columbia: Collected Readings*. ed. Patricia E. Roy. Toronto: Copp Clark Pitman 1989
Wilson, J. Donald, and Paul J. Stortz, '"May the Lord Have Mercy on You": The Rural School Problem in British Columbia in the 1920s.' *B.C. Studies*, 79 (autumn 1988)

Woody, Thomas. *A History of Women's Education in the United States*. 2 vols. New York: Science Press 1929

Zainu'ddin, Ailsa G. Thomson. 'The Corr Family.' In *Not So Eminent Victorians*, ed. Selleck and Sullivan. Melbourne: Melbourne University Press 1984